Ted Grant
The Permanent Revolutionary

The Man, His Life and Ideas
(9 July 1913 – 20 July 2006)

Alan Woods

Wellred Publications, London

Ted Grant: The Permanent Revolutionary
by Alan Woods

First published by Wellred 2013 © Alan Woods

UK distribution:
Wellred Books
PO Box 50525
London E14 6WG
United Kingdom
Tel: +44 (0) 207 515 7675
contact@socialist.net

US distribution:
Wellred, PO Box 18302, Minneapolis, MN 55418
sales@wellredusa.com

Wellred on-line bookshop sales: www.wellredbooks.net

Printed by Lightning Source, England
Layout by Niklas Albin Svensson

British Library Cataloguing in Publication Data
A catalogue record for this book is available from the British Library

ISBN – 978 1 900 007 47 4

If you would like to contact the author about the content of this book, you can do so using the address editor@marxist.com

Cover design by Hamid Alizadeh and Filip Staes

Contents

Prologue and Acknowledgements	6
The Early Years	10
New Horizons	25
The War Years	45
In Defence of Trotskyism	74
The Times That Try Men's Souls	107
The Tide Begins to Turn	144
The Tide Turns	163
The Militant Tendency	177
How Militant Was Destroyed	189
A New Beginning	226
Memories of Ted	244
Index of names	280

To the memory of Jimmy Deane and Pat Wall

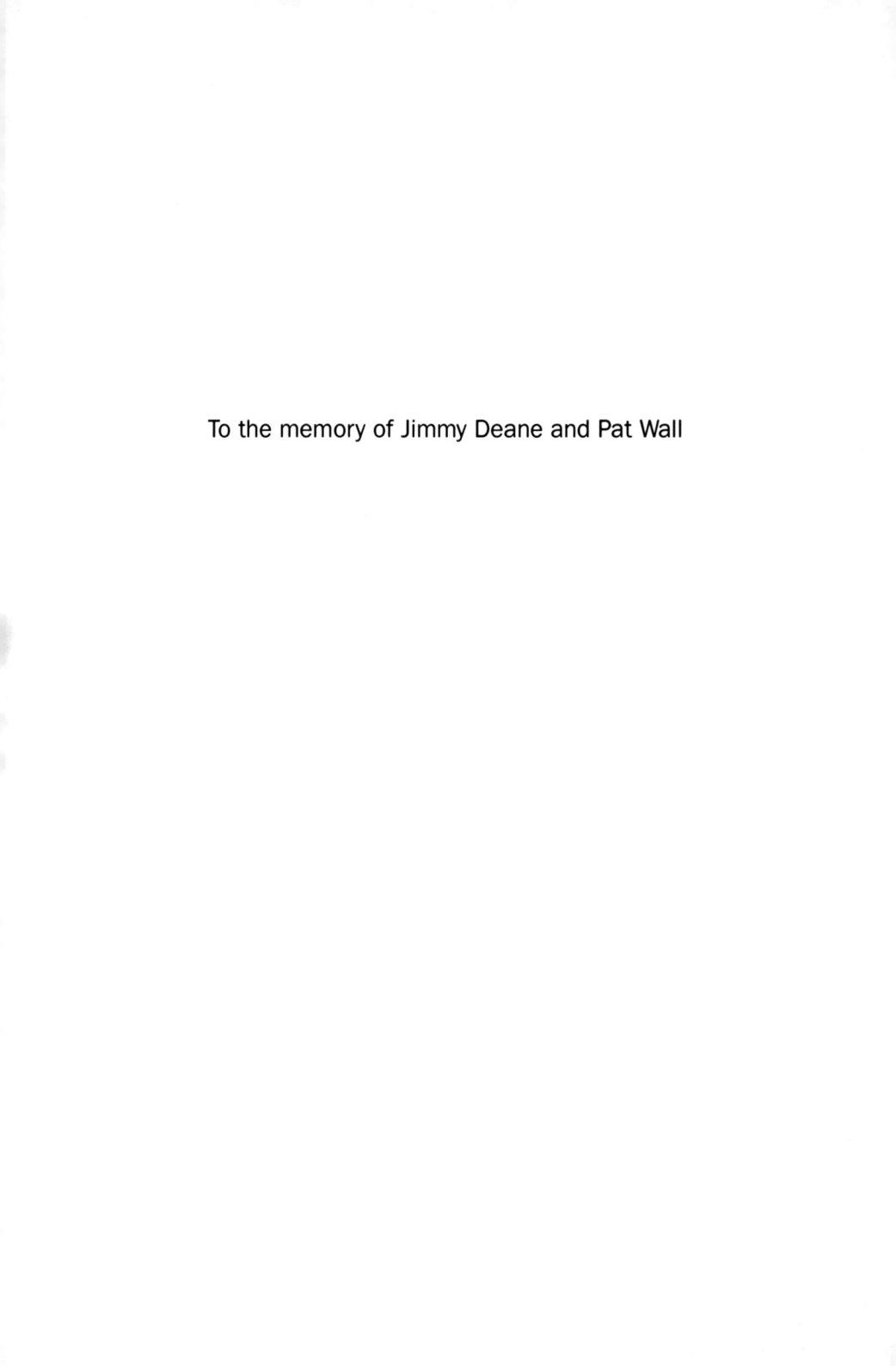

Prologue and Acknowledgements

To write a biography of Ted Grant is a daunting task. Although many people knew Ted and worked with him, very few ever got really close to him. In the course of a long and fruitful life, Ted played many roles. But he was actually rather a private person in some respects. He very rarely talked about his past and was reluctant to answer questions about it. His overriding concern was politics and he gave little importance to such matters.

I knew and worked closely with Ted Grant for all my adult life. Ted was the greatest influence over my political life and thought, and I believe I was the closest person to him. Before he died, Ted made Ana Muñoz and I his executors and gave us the rights to his writings. Ted's elder sister Rae once told me: "You know my brother better than I do." When she was alive, I had many conversations with Rae which provided a lot of biographical information. Sadly, Rae is no longer alive to receive my thanks, but I would like this book to serve as a tribute to her for all she did to give Ted moral (and material) support and encouragement in the most difficult moments of his life.

In the years I collaborated with Ted—almost half a century—I had many conversations with him and can remember many of the things he told me about himself. I have attempted to put these things together as completely as I can. However, these memoirs are necessarily incomplete. To gain a deeper insight I recommend the reader study Ted's book *The History of British Trotskyism* and, in particular, his collected works, two volumes of which have already appeared, with a third in preparation.

This book is therefore the work of many people. That was inevitable because of the difficulty in assembling the material for the biography of a very remarkable man. Extremely valuable background material was provided by Rob Sewell, who has done more research on Ted's life than anybody else and is extremely knowledgeable about the subject. Among other things, he interviewed Ted's sister Rae, Millie Lee, who had come over from South Africa with Ralph Lee in 1937, as well as others who were close to Ted. This book has drawn extensively on his researches.

Another valuable source was the Ted Grant archive, which contain valuable unpublished interviews and correspondence. When Ted finally moved from the flat in Islington where he had lived for many years, a large number of letters were discovered in drawers. These were of all kinds: some personal—letters from members of his family—and some political, including many from his lifelong comrade and friend Jimmy Deane.

They all shed a fascinating light on Ted's life, ideas and relationships. None of them, as far as I know, have ever been published before. I have decided to include the most interesting ones in their entirety. Although I am conscious of the fact that this may sometimes interrupt the flow of the narrative, this inconvenience is more than justified by their intrinsic interest.

Unfortunately, there are not so many letters written by Ted Grant himself. Probably many have been lost or destroyed. But I suspect there is also another reason. Ted was not the world's most diligent letter writer. This can be seen by the repeated requests from Jimmy Deane and Ted's relatives for letters, and also the fact that most of Ted's letters that have survived commence with apologies for long silences.

The main reason for this, I believe, was not laziness or absent-mindedness, or even the pressures of work. There was another reason. Ted Grant was a perfectionist. Whereas others would be content just to write a few lines, Ted would wish to write a long political statement. This was time-consuming, and so the task of replying to a letter would be postponed from one day or week, or month, or year, to the next.

Many of the handwritten letters were often written in diabolical handwriting. I wish to thank Ana Muñoz for her patient and determined work in deciphering and typing out these old letters, to provide me with invaluable source material.

A lot of work on this correspondence was done by Francesco Merli, whose painstaking research into the Ted Grant archives in preparation for his *Collected Writings*, has uncovered valuable material that has never been published before. Among other things he discovered a handwritten letter from Ralph Lee to Ted dated 1948, which casts new light on what happened to him. Thanks also to Alun Morgan for his researches into Jimmy Deane's archive at Warwick University and Jock Haston's archive at Hull.

Even more recent investigations by Roy Grant (no relation) has shown that even when Ted spoke about his past, he was playing his cards close to his chest and being a little coy about his ancestry. The information provided by several ancestral websites made by surviving members of his family, shows that Ted had many more relatives than he ever let on. The data they collected, augmented by new findings made by Roy, has revealed far more about Ted's relatives than he ever told us.

My thanks also are due to Fred Weston, Francesco Merli, Harry Whittaker and John Peterson for proofreading and making useful suggestions. Many thanks also to Niklas Albin Svensson and Ainhoa Murguiondo for their work on the layout and other technical matters, to Hamid Alizadeh for organizing the production and layout, and to Filip Staes, Ajmal Waqif and Mark Rahman for the cover design.

We have accumulated a number of pictures over the years and we are indebted to the following people for their help: Phil Lloyd, Rae Blank, Millie Haston, Ann Ward, Adrian Jones, Alex Grant, Terry McPartlan, Lal Khan and Ana Muñoz.

For obvious reasons it was impossible to mention all the many comrades who worked with him over the years in Britain and internationally. To all those who remained loyal to Ted to the end I express my warmest gratitude, for they are in the final analysis the real protagonists of this book.

An unbroken thread

As soon as it became known that I was working on this book, comrades began to send me anecdotes about Ted. However, I have resisted the temptation to reproduce a long series of personal anecdotes, which would be easy to do, as Ted was rather eccentric, and even rejoiced in his eccentricities. But to give undue weight to this aspect would be to perpetrate a great injustice to the memory of a man who was, before all else, a very serious political figure.

In the Introduction to his *Lectures on the Philosophy of History* Hegel wrote scathingly about the kind of superficial biographies that seek to exploit the personal foibles and weaknesses of great men and reduce history to the level of gossip:

> "No man is a hero to his *valet-de-chambre*," is a well-known proverb; I have added—and Goethe repeated it ten years later—"but not because the former is no hero, but because the latter is a valet." He takes off the hero's boots, assists him to bed, knows that he prefers champagne, etc. Historical personages waited upon in historical literature by such psychological valets, come poorly off; they are brought down by these their attendants to a level with—or rather a few degrees below the level of—the morality of such exquisite discerners of spirits. (Hegel, *Lectures on the Philosophy of History*, § 34)

Although there are many personal memories of friends and comrades, those who only remember Ted Grant in terms of anecdotes miss the whole point of his life and work. However, I am conscious of the fact that a biography is not a history book and in addition to the historical data and political theory it must deal with the man. I have therefore included some anecdotes in the last section, but only insofar as they cast light on Ted's character and life.

Ted always spoke of the unbroken thread that connects our Tendency to the ideas and traditions of Marxism, which we can trace through the RCP and the WIL, right back to the International Left Opposition. He told me that before the Second World War, there was an old comrade in our ranks who had been a member of the First, Second, Third and Fourth Internationals.

I never met that man, of course. But in the course of my life I have met several splendid comrades who had been members of the RCP. Their firm grasp of Marxist theory and unshakable belief in socialism and the revolutionary mission of the proletariat always struck me as something especially admirable. Sadly, most are no longer with us. One of the few surviving members of that remarkable generation is that redoubtable veteran, comrade Bill Landles in Tyneside.

Ted Grant was and still remains the personification of the unbroken thread that links the present generation with the rich tradition that stretches back through the Left Opposition to the Bolshevik Party of Lenin and Trotsky, and before that to Marx and Engels. However, today, one hundred years after his birth, Ted Grant is not just a symbol. He always played a most active and leading role in the movement, where he not only defended the ideas of Marxism, but developed and enriched them in a profound and creative manner. His writings provide us with a rich treasury of ideas and cast light on the burning questions of our epoch.

The impact of his ideas and work went far beyond the narrow confines of small left groupings. When Ted Grant died almost seven years ago, obituaries were published in all the main bourgeois papers in Britain, including *The Guardian*, *The Times*, *The Financial Times*, *The Daily Telegraph* and *The Independent*. This fact alone demonstrates beyond the shadow of a doubt that this man, whether you agreed or disagreed with him, made an indelible mark on British politics.

In writing this book I am, at least in part, paying a debt to the man who taught me everything I know about Marxism and whose ideas I continue to defend—ideas that have withstood the test of time and provide a solid basis on which the new generation can build. On the occasion of the one hundredth anniversary of his birth, I offer my recollections of this great man as a modest contribution to the understanding of the new generation, the people whom Ted always prized the most.

Ted, who had an irrepressible sense of humour, did not spare his opponents in private conversation. However, at bottom, even his jokes and little comments usually had a political basis. He lived and breathed politics, that is to say, Marxist, revolutionary politics, which always was foremost in his mind, even in the unlikeliest contexts.

It is that political aspect that I have concentrated on, for the simple reason that Ted Grant was a political animal. More than anybody else, one can say of Ted Grant: ideas were the man, and the man was his ideas. By this, I do not mean he was indifferent to other things, to literature, science and the lives of people. On the contrary, Ted, like old Engels, was a marvellous human being. His motto might well have been the famous quotation by the Roman writer Terence: "*Homo sum, humani nihil a me alienum puto*"—"I am a human being. I consider nothing that is human alien to me".

London, March 2013

Chapter 1

The Early Years

The childhood shows the man, as morning shows the day. (John Milton)

Family background

Although he lived most of his life in Britain, Ted Grant was South African by birth, and never quite lost his native accent. He did not talk a lot about his past life and his family, but sometimes one learned snippets of information about his formative years. Although numerous relevant records could be accessed, it was unfortunate that no family historian had specifically focused on Ted's siblings or his parents, though there were a number descended from his uncles, aunts and cousins.

None of these descendants appear to have coupled Isaac Blank to his adopted name of Ted Grant. Their family trees simply states Isaac was born in Johannesburg and subsequently disappeared from the records. Probably out of ignorance, they misguidedly wrote off Isaac Blank as someone of little consequence. How wrong they were!

Until now, Ted Grant was always thought to have had no family to speak of, but Lauren Naama Goldberg's researches into her own ancestry includes the Johannesburg Blanks and provides a staggering list of family names and supporting data.[1]

Regrettably, Lauren's sources are presented with few birth years, so it has been difficult to structure all the information she has accumulated into a format showing the relatives in any order of seniority. Ted's father Max, possibly the most senior of his own siblings, is at the top of the list.

Max Blank came originally from Lithuania. The records show that he was born in Tauragė, an industrial city and the capital of Tauragė County (not to be confused with the Ukrainian city of Taganrog, where Chekhov was born). It is also known by its German name Tauroggen. It is situated on the Jūra River, close to the border with the Kaliningrad Oblast, and not far from the Baltic Sea coast.

When Max Blank was born, Lithuania was part of tsarist Russia, which Lenin described as the prison house of nations. And no national group was so oppressed as the Jews. Lithuania was part of what was known as the Pale of Settlement—that part of the Russian Empire in which Jews were allowed permanent residency, and beyond which it was generally prohibited, except

---

[1] http://www.judelmanfamily.com/familytree/gft0000383.html

for a limited number of categories. Lithuania was therefore historically home to a large and influential Jewish community.

The Lithuanian Jewish community was almost entirely wiped out by the Nazi Holocaust. The family tree in fact shows that one of Ted's aunts died in the Holocaust at the hands of the Nazis, together with her husband Hirsch Herman Srago and their five children, Israel, Sonya, Moshe Lev, Rasha Raya and Yachel Samuel (all first cousins of Ted). Other more distant relatives, such as Abraham Reubon Goldin, a second cousin of Ted's, also died in the Holocaust. But in the period under consideration, those horrors were the music of a nightmarish future.

It was natural that the most vigorous and progressive elements in the Jewish community should join the revolutionary struggle against tsarist oppression. By the end of the 19th century, there was a strong Jewish workers' movement in Lithuania, organized by the Bund, the General Jewish Labour Bund in Russia and Poland, which was founded in Vilnius, the capital, on October 7, 1897. The Bund's objective was to unite all Jewish workers in the Russian Empire into a united socialist party.

Needless to say, not everybody was so convinced of the prospects of socialist revolution in tsarist Russia. Other, no less energetic but less politically inclined people, who felt the need to escape the constant oppression and discrimination, found another way out: that of emigration. The end of the 19th century and the early years of the 20th century saw a massive wave of Jewish emigration from the Russian Empire.

Among those fleeing persecution in search of a better life was Max Blank. His birth date is not known, but it would have been around 1869. We do know that his father was called Israel Blank and his mother Rosalia Shereshevsky. He left Lithuania sometime towards the end of the 19th century, and we find him in Paris in 1900-01, but he may have arrived earlier.

Max's wife, Adelle Margolis, was born in France on Christmas Day 1885. I imagine that, like her daughter, Rachael (Rae), she always kept up an elegant appearance. The family lived in Le Marais, which is in the centre of Paris, to the west of Place de la Bastille; it was and still is the hub of the Jewish community in the French capital. The family were involved in the fur trade. Max and Adelle met in Paris through Ted's grandmother and married in 1901. She was much younger than her husband. Although she spoke English fluently, she retained her strong French accent throughout her life.

At the time of their marriage, Adelle was only 16 years of age, and Max 32. One guesses that he must have had considerable charm and swept this young girl off her feet. What her parents thought of this man from a far-off land with dubious career prospects and a strong Russian accent, is not known. There is a photograph of Adelle together with Max taken about 1901 in Paris, which was given to us by Rae. It is a wedding photograph, and they have the appearance of a prosperous Jewish middle class couple. He is smartly dressed in a suit, with a flower in his buttonhole.

Why did they decide to leave Paris? Maybe Max was already looking for more promising outlets for a man of enterprise. But there may have been other reasons too. Having left Lithuania, to escape the stifling anti-Semitic atmosphere that existed there, Max first moved to Paris, where he lived in the Jewish quarter. This was at the time of the Dreyfus affair. Captain Alfred Dreyfus, a young French Jewish army officer had been sentenced in 1894 to life imprisonment after being falsely accused of passing French military secrets to the German Embassy in Paris. In spite of later evidence that proved his innocence, there was a cover up on the part of high-ranking French officers. The celebrated open letter by Émile Zola which appeared in a Paris newspaper in January 1898 under the title "J'accuse", caused a public outcry and a mass campaign in favour of Dreyfus. This eventually led to Dreyfus being declared innocent in 1906.

The Dreyfus case provoked a serious crisis that shook the French establishment to its very foundations, but revealed a widespread anti-Semitism in France and this may have been one of the reasons why Max was very soon to leave for South Africa, together with his wife, mother-in-law and newly born child Rose (born in January 1902). Their second child, Israel, was born on South African soil in 1903. The choice of South Africa was probably driven by some connection with people they knew who had emigrated there and Max saw it as a land of promise. He must have been a very energetic and enterprising man—a bit too enterprising, as things turned out.

There had been Jewish people in South Africa from the 16th century, when the first Dutch settlers started to build Cape Town. By the end of the 19th century, their numbers had grown. In the Boer War, when the Afrikaners fought the British, there were Jewish fighters on both sides, although it seems most fought on the side of the British.

In fact, Lithuanians dominate the Jewish community in South Africa to an extent seen in no other country, even present-day Lithuania. Ted's family tree reveals that other, more distant relatives also ended up emigrating to South Africa. Among South Africans of Lithuanian-Jewish descent were figures like the late communist Joe Slovo and veteran anti-apartheid activist Helen Suzman (also from Germiston). The presence of Joe Slovo in this list is no accident. This Lithuanian Jewish community on the Rand had links with Russian revolutionary movements going back to the 1880s, and the South African Communist Party had a strong base there. This fact played a decisive role in Ted's early political development.

South Africa

Ted's father does not appear to have had any overtly political affiliations. Like many educated Jews at that time, he probably held vaguely liberal views. But he had come to South Africa to secure the future of his family, not to overthrow the existing order. He got on with his work and he managed very well. He was engaged in the mineral business. That was a very lucrative trade in South Africa and the family was comfortably well off. They had two sons, Israel (Isy) named after his grandfather and Isaac, ten years younger than his brother, and three daughters, Rose (the eldest, born in January 1902), Rachael (born in 1912) and Zena, the youngest.

Isaac Blank, the future Ted Grant, was born on the 9th of July, 1913, in a large house in Spilsbury Street, Germiston, just outside Johannesburg. The town had been established in the early days of the gold rush when two prospectors, John Jack and August Simmer, struck gold on the farm of Elandsfontein. Both men made fortunes and the town sprung up next to the mine in the early days of the gold rush. Germiston today is South Africa's sixth largest city, with 70 percent of the western world's gold passing through its gold refinery. It also boasts South Africa's biggest railway junction and the busiest civil airport, Rand Airport.

Johannesburg itself had grown out of the newly discovered neighbouring goldfields in the 1880s, which attracted enterprising people from many countries like a magnet. In 1921, the world's largest gold refinery, known as the Rand Refinery, was established in Germiston. After that, Germiston experienced phenomenal growth and development. The growth of industry and mining turned it into a boom town. Naturally, all this wealth was based on the exploitation

THE EARLY YEARS | 13

Wedding photograph of Max Blank and Adelle Margolis, Ted's parents

of the black working class that lived and worked in appalling conditions. But for the whites it was an opportunity to rise, and with a bit of luck, get rich.

Isaac Blank was born into a reasonably well off family. He seems to have lived a fairly happy childhood, free from the want and grinding poverty that was the lot of the black children who surrounded him. Unusually for someone born and bred in that country, Ted was allergic to the sun. But he assured me that it was not always the case. He told me: "When I was young I used to go to the river and stay there all day, swimming and lying around in the sun and would come home as black as charcoal." But he said the sun later caused a skin irritation. Therefore, he always kept out of the sun and urged us all to follow his example, though without much success.

These scant memories, these faint glimmerings from a long gone past, do not speak of an unhappy childhood. They speak of sun and laughter. The present was carefree and the future looked bright. But there were dark clouds on the horizon and the family later fell on hard times.

Max had a problem: he was too fond of gambling, and as time went on, this became an obsession. In my experience, compulsive gamblers are very often charming people, with a carefree and completely irresponsible outlook on life. When I think of Max Blank I see Mr. Micawber, the colourful character in Dickens' novel *David Copperfield*, who gave the famous advice: "Annual income twenty pounds, annual expenditure nineteen and six, result happiness. Annual income twenty pounds, annual expenditure twenty pounds ought and six, result misery."

Micawber was always "confidently expecting that something will turn up", though nothing ever did. This character, as is well known, was a portrait of Charles Dickens' father, who ended up in the Marshalsea prison for debtors in Bermondsey. Similarly, Max Blank's obsession with gambling ended in ruin. Max, who still retained a soft Russian accent, took to heavy gambling on the horses every Saturday, while little money went to Adelle for the upkeep of the children. "His mineral water factory went bust, as he was far too busy with the horses", stated Rae years later. He had soon spent all the money they had and was deep in debt. The result, as old Micawber predicted, was misery.

Tolstoy's book *Anna Karenina* begins with the words: "Happy families are all alike; every unhappy family is unhappy in its own way." That was true of the Blank household. It is easy to imagine the consequences of Max's gambling. There would have been endless rows about money, tears, pleadings, promises to reform that were immediately broken, and in the end, an inevitable divorce. After a long and apparently happy marriage, this must have been a painful experience for all concerned.

Relations between Max and Adelle, and Max and his children became strained to breaking point. Rae recalled the time when she, Rose and her father were riding to his farm in a horse-drawn carriage. She noticed that the reigns had chafed the horse and it was bleeding. She demanded her father stop the carriage, and chastised him for his cruelty. After her protests, he eventually brought the carriage to a halt, and Rae, who was utterly distraught, ran into a nearby field, sobbing.

She never had anything to do with her father after that episode.

It is perhaps significant that the only memory Rae had of her father was of a man who was cruel to a horse. It is often said that daughters are more attached to their fathers whereas sons are closer to their mothers, yet she had no memories of warm affection, embraces or kisses, only of senseless brutality. However, there is absolutely nothing else to suggest that Max Blank was a cruel man. How can we explain this apparent paradox? The memory is highly selective and can play tricks. It is also a very effective filter. With the passing of the years, some memories fade, while others become more vivid. This process of selection is not accidental.

The father of Stalin was written out of history by his official biographers. The fading of that particular memory was certainly no accident. There is ample evidence from people who knew the family to indicate that the drunken shoemaker had a vicious streak and subjected his son to savage beatings. But nobody, including Rae, ever suggested that Max was cruel to his wife or children, except in one thing: that by his irresponsible behaviour he wrecked the marriage and the family. For an adolescent girl, that would have been unforgivable and deeply hurtful.

Who knows what really happened on the day that remained so vividly in her memory all her life? The marriage was disintegrating, and probably also the character of her father. When an irresponsible person is forced to come face to face with reality, everything falls to pieces. On that day evidently Max was either taking out his anger and frustration on a poor animal, or else simply too absorbed in his own problems to worry about anything. Rae's sense of shock was not only a reaction to the suffering of the horse. In effect, she was saying to her father: "How could you be so cruel to me, to my mother, to all of us?"

Her estranged feelings towards him even went as far as refusing to attend his funeral, but she was persuaded to go reluctantly by her mother-in-law. In a similar way, Rose also took a dislike to him. It was a troubled relationship that overshadowed the whole family.

At this point the colourful but ruinous Max Blank disappears from the narrative. I have no idea what became of him. To what extent did his father influence Isaac's character? Ted was certainly not a racing addict, but he was very fond of a little "flutter" on the horses, and a frequent visitor to the betting shop. In any case, Ted rarely spoke about him. But he talked affectionately about his mother: "She was a very gentle woman who was very lenient on me—a bit too lenient," Ted recalled wistfully.

Eventually, Adelle remarried and had another daughter, Anita (known to the family as Nita). When they grew up, Nita left South Africa for a new life in California, while Rae moved to Paris and got married. Only Isy, Rose and Zena remained in Johannesburg. It was Isy who took over the family store with the help of Rose, who died of a heart attack in 1968. Poor Adelle had a tragic end, as we shall see.

We do not know what effect this family crisis had on young Isaac, but it is perhaps significant that he stayed with his father for a six-month period after the divorce, after which he went to live permanently with his mother. This suggests there may have been a tussle over the custody of the children. At any rate, such events can leave deep scars on young minds. Rae was certainly bitterly critical of her father. It may be that this family turmoil had the effect of making the young Isaac think more critically about life in general. But this is only a hypothesis.

The family now found itself in straitened circumstances. But Ted's mother must have been a very strong and determined woman. In order to earn a living, she had established and ran a small general-store-come-grocery shop in Johannesburg, where the children also helped out from time to time. In the meantime, Ted was sent off to boarding school and his sisters to the convent to continue their education.

Ted was a bright pupil, as were the girls, and he had a sharp and inquisitive mind. Ted told me that he had rejected religion at a very young age. He related a conversation he had with a teacher at school who was explaining the first *Book of Genesis*, quoting the famous opening verse of the *Bible*: "In the beginning God created the heavens and the earth." Isaac asked him: "And who created God?" His interlocutor was at a loss for an answer. This persuaded the youngster that perhaps the Bible did not have the answer at all. He began to look elsewhere for explanations. This search after the truth took him straight to Marxism.

In his youth Ted could speak Afrikaans, the language of the Afrikaaners, which was originally a dialect of Dutch. He had unfortunately forgotten how to speak it, but sometimes when we had meetings in Holland and Belgium he could understand the odd word or phrase of Dutch. But other things he did remember. He could sing the Italian Red Flag, *Bandiera Rossa*, in Zulu. Often at socials he would also sing in Xhosa *Nkosi Sikeleli Afrika* (Lord Bless Africa), the beautiful and haunting song of the African Liberation Movement, parts of which have now been integrated into the National Anthem of South Africa:

Nkosi Sikeleli Africa
Malup hakanyiswu phando lwayo
Yiswa imithanda zo yethu
Nkosi Sikelela.

All this shows that South Africa was always present in the depths of his mind. When he visited me in Spain for the first congress of the newly established Spanish section of the Committee for a Workers' International in 1976, he said the peaches reminded him of his childhood and he looked quite wistful. He told me more than once that he would have liked to go back, just once before he died. But he never did.

This is the sum total of all I managed to glean from Ted about his childhood in South Africa. When he ceased to be Isaac Blank and became Ted Grant, he became a thoroughbred Englishman. And yet deep down I believe he retained a special affection for the land where he was born. How much of South Africa remained in his consciousness it is hard to say. But that a small piece of it remained lodged in his heart to the end, I am quite sure.

The early years

As a young boy in South Africa, Ted became a Marxist and joined the Communist Party. I asked him how he became interested in Marxism. He told me that he was first aroused to political life by the treatment of the black servants: "You have no idea how badly the black workers were treated," he said. "They were called 'kaffirs'." He described how the poor blacks lived in shacks without basic amenities and lived mainly on corn on the cob, or as they say in South Africa, mealies (which he pronounced millies).

An interesting insight into Ted's thinking on this subject was a conversation I once had with him about the Boer War. I pointed out to him that Trotsky had supported the Boers against the British. To this he replied simply: "That is because he did not know how they treated the blacks. It was really a kind of slavery," he continued. "In reality the blacks were enslaved to the whites collectively. You cannot imagine anything worse than that. The whites would even address an old black man as 'Boy'." (He pronounced this word imitating a strong Afrikaans accent which he invested with a kind of menacing snarl).

The memory of these first stirrings of political awareness stayed with Ted for the rest of his life. He had a deeply ingrained sense of injustice and a burning hatred of all kinds of discrimination and oppression. He felt a powerful identity with oppressed people of all kinds. This was an important part of his psychological make-up. For some Marxists, the fight against oppression is only an abstract idea, but for Ted Grant it was deeply felt with every fibre of his being. It was this that

Zena and Rae, Ted's sisters

made him embrace the revolutionary cause, heart and soul. But to determine what concrete form these first, vague, embryonic feelings of revolt would take required a catalyst.

This took human form in another remarkable man, Ralph Lee. Ted's acquaintance with Ralph Lee was the result of a fortunate accident. Lee had been a veteran member of the South African Communist Party (CPSA), which he is said to have joined at the time of the 1922 Rand Revolt. But by the time Ted joined, the international Communist movement was in a ferment of change. These were the years when the Stalinist bureaucracy was consolidating its hold on power in the USSR.

A group of militants in the South African Communist Party opposed Stalinism and moved towards Trotskyism (Bolshevism-Leninism). Lee had come into contact with the movement by chance, when he picked up material from the American Trotskyists, the Communist League of America, led by James Cannon, in a bookshop in Johannesburg, including Trotsky's *Critique of the Draft Programme of the Comintern.*

Together with Murray Gow Purdy, Lee formed a small Trotskyist group that attempted to do work in and around the CPSA in Johannesburg and the Rand. Their main contacts were with the sizeable Lithuanian Jewish community in which the CPSA had deep roots. This was the community from which Lee himself came; his name is an Anglicisation of what was originally Raphael Levy. A Jewish Workers' Club set up under Stalinist influence in 1931 was a major base of Communist activity.

In the early 1930s, Ted's family decided to move from Germiston to Klerk Street in Johannesburg, near the family grocery store. The large house was owned by Ted's uncle George, who had made money from mining, and who also shared the house with them. Being short of money after the breakup of her marriage, Ted's mother was obliged to take in lodgers. In one of those strange coincidences in which history is so rich, one of those lodgers happened to be a friend of the family, Ralph Lee. They all stayed in this large house, including uncle George and Ted's grandmother, who never managed to learn English, and spoke only her native French. The three lodgers slept in separate rooms in the courtyard adjacent to the main building.

As a good Communist, Ralph was always on the lookout for potential contacts, and engaged in discussions with the two boys living next door. The neighbours were of Scottish descent, Ted remembered. But while Ralph had a certain influence over them, he failed to recruit them to the cause. Through regular discussions, he managed to win over Ted's younger sister Zena to Marxism, but he failed with Rae. "The house was always full of people", remembers Rae. "There were all of us, with our friends, then Ralph and Ted with their acquaintances, and the lodgers. Frequently, we all sat around a huge dining table, and were fed by my mother. French stew seemed to be the favourite dish, I recall."

The new lodger also took a keen interest in young Isaac (as he was still called then), and played an enormous role in Ted's early political development. The young lad was curious about politics and they discussed political questions and literature endlessly. At the age of 14, Isaac's eyes were opened to a whole new world of ideas through the writings of Bernard Shaw, HG Wells, Maxim Gorky, Jack London, and later, Marx, Engels and Lenin. Ted told me he had started to read *Capital* when he was 14. This marked the beginning of a lifelong passion for Marxist theory. By the time he was 15, Isaac was a confirmed Marxist. Under Lee's influence he joined the CPSA.

After Ted finished boarding school at age 15, he left school and got a job in a shipping company chasing up invoices, which gave him plenty of time to read. "My early vivid recollections of Ted", remarked Rae, "was him dashing about on his bike." She believed this must have been a large part of his job.

Still only in his early twenties, Ralph Lee was also closely associated with another young Trotskyist, Murray Gow Purdy, who in turn had been a pupil of the very first South African Trotskyist, Frank Glass—a founding member of the Communist Party of South Africa (CPSA). Glass and his wife, Fanny Klennerman, had established a left-wing bookshop in Von Brandis Street, in downtown Johannesburg, called Vanguard Booksellers, and it was here that they picked up their first copy of the American *Militant*. Frank Glass was eventually expelled from the CPSA.

Ralph Lee knew Glass from his days in the CPSA and used to send Isaac to buy copies of *The Militant*, the newspaper of the American Trotskyists, from Vanguard Booksellers. Soon, the young enthusiast was buying his own copy from the shop. Many years later, in an interview, Glass recalled a young schoolboy, presumably Ted, religiously coming to his shop to buy copies of the Trotskyist paper. Like many others, Glass left South Africa for greater opportunities elsewhere. He ended up in China in 1930 where he played a pivotal role among the Chinese Trotskyists, and later in the United States. Ted later paid tribute to the important role played by James Cannon and the American Trotskyists in spreading Trotsky's ideas during this period, despite the serious disagreements he later had with Cannon.

Eventually, Ralph's political activities began to worry Ted's mother, who was concerned that these revolutionary views would get her children into deep trouble. Lee, being out of work, also failed to pay the rent, and ended up owing Ted's mother a great deal of money. This added to her growing resentment against him. Eventually, Ralph moved out of the lodgings and

THE EARLY YEARS | 19

Ralph Lee

Ralph and Millie in Johannesburg, 1936

Millie Kahn (bottom left) on one of her trips

befriended a young left-wing girl called Millie Kahn. Before she died, Rob Sewell interviewed her, and I quote below from his unpublished notes of this interview.

Like so many of the Jewish community in Johannesburg who had escaped from the pogroms in Eastern Europe, Millie came from a political family. Her mother was a close friend of Fanny Klennerman, who had been expelled from the CP for Trotskyist sympathies. Fanny succeeded in winning Millie over in support of the Russian Revolution and Trotsky. While Millie ended up becoming a Trotskyist, her sister joined the Stalinist CPSA. They never spoke to each other after that.

Millie came across Ralph Lee, who was several years older, in the Marxist discussion groups that he had organised in Johannesburg. After that their personal relationship blossomed. "He swept me off my feet", said Millie 70 years later. She remembered Ralph as a very tall, thin, handsome man. This can be seen from the few existing pictures of him. He was certainly a colourful and charismatic figure. While in the Communist Party, he had been involved in cat-burglaries and other such revolutionary adventures on behalf of the movement. Millie brought in an income to keep them both by working for her mother's millinery business, while Ralph concentrated full-time on the revolutionary struggle.

"He was an avid reader. He used to sleep all day and read all night. He never worked", remarked Millie with a chuckle. "He never wanted to." They moved around a lot, forced from one place to another, but then settled—at least for a while—in a place, more of a shack, next to the Laundry Workers' Union headquarters in Johannesburg. (Rob Sewell, *Interview with Millie Kahn*, January 19, 2002, unpublished, Ted Grant Archive).

Millie was a very adventurous and independent-minded woman, and in her youth, despite being warned by her parents, took boat trips alone, "hopping" from one place to another along the Cape coast. There is a photo of Millie in 1929 on such a trip. Millie and Ralph's revolutionary friendship soon resulted in them living together and then getting married. Ted acted as best man at the marriage ceremony, so this must have been sometime in 1933, a year before he left for England.

Ted came to the decision to leave home for political reasons, and moved in with Ralph some time in 1932. He did this without informing the family. He simply left one morning. The family had no idea where he had gone. Even many years later, his sister Rae was under the impression he had gone straight to England, but in fact he had stayed in Johannesburg for two years before going to London in the autumn of 1934. As you could expect, his mother was utterly distraught when Isaac left home. But he thought this was for the best. His mind was made up. He would dedicate his life to the revolutionary movement.

The black working class

Very early on Ted saw the enormous revolutionary potential of the black proletariat. This stayed with him for the rest of his life. I remember in the 1980s with what tremendous enthusiasm he greeted the heroic movement of the black South African workers organised in the COSATU trade unions fighting against the monstrous Apartheid regime. However, Ted had a very realistic view of the black workers and the working class in general. He never had the kind of superstitious awe that was characteristic of middle class white intellectuals, who often begin with an abstract and idealised view of the workers, only to desert the movement and return to their own class as soon as they get tired of it. How often have we seen this phenomenon—and not only in South Africa!

Ted did not approach the working class in an idealistic or sentimental way. He described how on weekends they would go to places called *shabeens* and drink the potent liquor known as *skokeeean*, and often end in drunken brawls. Ted recalled that it was a common tactic used in fights in the *shabeens* for someone to shout out "No kicking!" while lashing out with his boots. He used this as a graphic and amusing analogy to those on the Left who, while acting in a very aggressive way to their political opponents, are very thin-skinned whenever anybody criticises them.

He saw the black workers not as poor oppressed people who needed a helping hand from the white middle class, but as comrades in a common struggle. He was a true internationalist, completely devoid of any hint of patronising condescension. His indignation was directed against the system that generated exploitation and oppression in all its forms. He stood, not for petty reforms of an inherently unjust system, but for its revolutionary overthrow. To that end, he sought to help the black workers to get organized, starting with the most basic unit of proletarian organization: the trade union.

Apart from Isaac, Ralph Lee's group consisted of Purdy, Millie Kahn, Raymond Lake, John Saperstein, Max Basch, Ted's sister Zena Blank, and not much more. It was just a handful of people, but they had big ideas. In April 1934, they constituted themselves as the Bolshevik-Leninist League of South Africa. They drew up a policy statement and sent an open letter criticising the Stalinist line of the CPSA. In other words, they threw down the gauntlet to the leadership. This led to their immediate expulsion.

To conduct revolutionary work under such conditions must have taken some guts. They had to face not only the opposition of the state but also the hooligan tactics of the Stalinists, who did not hesitate to use violence against the "Trotsky-fascists", breaking up meetings, beating people up and so on. The League attempted to establish contact with the International Communist League. They worked mainly in the Johannesburg area, although they also established contacts in other urban centres. They established links with another newly founded Trotskyist group in Cape Town. Both groups were to shortly fuse into one single Trotskyist organisation, called the Workers' Party of South Africa.

In June 1934, Purdy had become Organising Secretary of a revived African Laundry Workers' Union. In an attempt to build a base amongst the black working class, the group turned its whole attention to this work. This was the first practical initiative aimed at recovering the field of black trade union work, which the Stalinists had first wrecked and then abandoned.

The work in Johannesburg was not confined to the organising of trade unions. There were branch meetings, classes, open air public meetings, and so on. Under the most difficult conditions, and in complete isolation, they managed to pull together an initial nucleus. The small but determined group attempted to organize the black workers and played an important role in the garment workers' strike.

With the turn to this trade union work, Ralph and Millie had moved into a shack next to the union headquarters, and began to raise funds for the union. "We lived next to the union offices", Millie recalled. "Sure, it was damned uncomfortable, but what did we care? They used to hold the union meetings in our back yard. We tried to raise money in various ways. I remember

The committee of the African Laundry Workers' Union, with Murray Gow Purdy (middle) Johannesburg, 1934

we collected bottles, cut off the tops, and then painted them. Ralph was pretty good at art. But otherwise it was a dud financially." (Rob Sewell, *Interview with Millie Kahn*)

Within a matter of months, and after a successful recruiting drive, a strike took place towards the end of August, which resulted in the union winning recognition at a number of firms. Millie recalls bravely marching with the black strikers through the centre of Johannesburg. "I was on my own as the other comrades were away, I believe, and I got quite a lot of abuse and taunts from people shouting from the buildings. But we remained defiant." (*Ibid.*)

Ian Hunter described the circumstances of the strike:

> The new union soon faced a severe test, a test, moreover, precipitated at a time when Lee was away visiting contacts in Durban. Negotiations to establish union recognition, overtime and weekly pay ran into an impasse. On 28 August a confrontation took place at the Reliance, one of the largest laundries. The employers presented an ultimatum, accept their terms, or leave. The 90 black union members walked out. The next day they returned with Purdy, which resulted in the union giving its own ultimatum to all three of the largest plants, the Reliance, the New York and the International. The expiry date passed, and on 6 September a further 90 members at the other two establishments left work. A strike procession the next day led to Purdy's arrest on a charge of inciting disorder, a ploy frequently employed by the authorities against political and industrial challenges. Millie Kahn [Millie Lee], as she then was, has described how she walked with the black laundry workers through a gauntlet of abuse from white women. The corrugated iron dwelling which was home to Lee and Kahn became the strike headquarters.
>
> Tactical problems abounded. Any strike action by natives faced the threat of action by the authorities on any number of pretexts. Purdy attempted to minimise the opportunities for intervention by making great play of "peaceful tactics", and refraining from the use of pickets. He was criticised by the Communists on both accounts for not being sufficiently aggressive. Even the one processional rally which was held had nevertheless led to confrontation with the authorities. On the other hand, the Communist Party was to some degree more conciliatory than might have been expected. Despite criticising

Purdy's leadership, the CP publicly offered support and assistance. The IKAKA Labour Defence even contributed to Purdy's bail. Nevertheless, the Stalinists were kept at arms' length, their motives being rightly questioned, and the only organisational help sought was from the Trades and Labour Council (the South African TUC), which involved fewer strings.

On 6 September the *Johannesburg Star* reported an apparent breakthrough, with all three main plants conceding union recognition, and two offering in addition the 2/6d pay rise necessary to translate monthly pay to a four weekly cycle. Would that things had been so simple! In reality the concession of union recognition was only tacit and not formal. Formal recognition was still demanded, yet barely 50 per cent of the New York and International workers were supporting the Reliance. Worse still, no help was forthcoming from the Rand Steam plant, and Leonardo's were bought off. Meanwhile, replacements were beginning to be found even for the skilled ironers. Seventy-three of the Reliance strikers now found themselves arrested for criminal breach of contract. Prosecutions were started at the other plants as well. The focus of attention now shifted to what had suddenly become a test case for master and servant legislation.

One of the strikers, Oscar Maboa, who had been at the centre of the altercation which had led to the initial walkout, was taken as a test case on 20 September. He was acquitted, but only on the grounds that certain of the manager's comments could have been construed as dismissal. Acquitted of the charge of illegal strike, the 73 thus found themselves sacked. This was a pyrrhic victory with a vengeance. Almost all of the strikers at all three firms had already had their jobs taken by replacements. The Stalinist organ Umsebenzi was not slow to lay this all at Purdy's feet. (Ian Hunter, *Raff Lee and the Pioneer Trotskyists of Johannesburg, Revolutionary History*, Volume 4, no. 4)

A dedicated revolutionary, Millie brought her considerable organisational abilities and skills to bear in these interventions. It was these abilities that were later put to enormous use in the building of the Trotskyist movement in Britain. She provided the consistent organisational drive in the leadership that was to last until the breakup of the Revolutionary Communist Party in mid 1949.

In spite of the outcome and repression, this strike nevertheless represented a historic struggle and a landmark in the history of the black South African working class. If nothing else, the struggle of the Laundry Workers' Union left behind an important tradition of struggle and organisation.

Workers' Party of South Africa

The group had some success in setting up new branches, particularly in Alexandra Township (a black township on the northern tip of Johannesburg), but in general, the objective conditions for revolutionary work in South Africa were extremely difficult. The recruiting of members was a painfully slow and laborious business. The difficulties gave rise to frustrations that were reflected in internal problems in the group. The outlook was far from promising.

The members of the group were beginning to reevaluate their work and perspectives, drawing far-reaching conclusions. With world war looming, they decided that their energies would be better employed in Europe. Not long after the laundry workers' strike, two of the younger members of the group, Max Basch and Isaac Blank, decided to make the break. Given the Commonwealth connections that provided easy access and no language barrier, Britain was the obvious place to go. Britain was also one of the key countries of world imperialism and had a correspondingly strong working class, where energetic young comrades could sink deep roots.

They left Johannesburg for Cape Town, where they stayed with the Cape Trotskyists whilst waiting for a convenient ship to Europe. It was here that the man who became known as Ted Grant made his first-ever public speech, a report of the events of the laundry strike, at an open air street meeting organized by the Cape Town Lenin Club outside the Castle Street Post Office. "I didn't speak too well", recalled Ted much later, with a laugh. It was his last political act on South African soil and the beginning of a new stage in his life. Soon afterwards he and his comrade Max Basch would set sail for Europe, leaving South Africa behind forever.

Those who remained behind faced enormous problems. The difficulties are alluded to in the correspondence of the time. "The caretaker in the tenement where Mil and I live", wrote Ralph Lee to Paul Koston, an American Trotskyist who helped head the organisation in Cape Town, "has objected to the 'Kaffirs' who visit our room. We have been déclassé for a long time with our neighbours, the usual riff-raff of billiard room rats, odd jobs gentlemen, canvassers, taxi drivers and trollops that inhabit 'buildings'. So now we pack up and move again." (*Lee to Koston*, 12 April 1935).

To add to the difficulties there were conflicts inside the organization. Purdy was an adventurer and somewhat unstable. He clashed repeatedly with Lee. On 12 April, 1935, Lee wrote to Koston, then the secretary of the WPSA: "Our personal relations are now strained to the utmost. The way he glowers openly at me during branch meetings is ludicrous, and we can hardly exchange a civil word, let alone discuss any questions."

These debilitating internal conflicts added to the difficulties of a small isolated group. On 17 May, Lee wrote again to Koston:

> I feel quite despondent at this moment about the immediate prospects of the International and the Workers' Party of South Africa (…). Our immediate pressing task is to discover links with the masses of workers.

Finally, on 9 June, 1935, Lee wrote to Koston in despairing terms: "party affairs are in a hell of a mess here."

Eventually, Purdy was expelled and the group reorganised on a healthier basis. Purdy later went to India, where he advocated a line that placed heavy emphasis on the question of caste, rather than class, as the main issue—a line that Ted completely rejected. In the end, Ralph and Millie, together with a small group of comrades, decided to follow the others to London.

CHAPTER TWO

NEW HORIZONS

If we have chosen the position in life in which we can most of all work for mankind, no burdens can bow us down, because they are sacrifices for the benefit of all; then we shall experience no petty, limited, selfish joy, but our happiness will belong to millions, our deeds will live on quietly but perpetually at work; and over our ashes will be shed the hot tears of noble people. (Marx, *Letter to His Father*, 1837)

With Leon Sedov in Paris

Thomas Paine once wrote: "The world is my country, all mankind are my brethren, and to do good is my religion". That same revolutionary internationalist outlook is echoed in one of those stirring old Italian anarchist songs:

Nostra patria è il mondo intero
nostra legge è la libertà
ed un pensiero
ribelle in cor ci sta.

Our fatherland is the whole world,
Our law is Freedom
And a rebel thought
Is in our heart.

You have to admire the revolutionary spirit of the old anarchists. That same spirit beat in the hearts of these young comrades and the same rebellious thought was embedded in the depths of their soul, although unlike the anarchists they were guided by the scientific principles of Marxism. They were prepared to leave behind their homes, their friends and families, mothers, fathers, brothers, and sisters, and travel to the other end of the world to fight for the cause of socialism. And this decision they took with a light heart, unhesitatingly, cheerfully and with no regrets.

In the autumn of 1934, Max and Isaac clambered up the gangplank of a German-owned passenger-cargo ship. In view of Hitler's recent accession to power, the comrades in Cape Town thought this was a bit risky at the time, but these fears turned out to be baseless. The journey proved to be uneventful but painfully slow, taking about six weeks to reach Europe. As the ship steamed lethargically along the coast of West Africa, the only relief from boredom were the occasional stopovers at numerous ports where the ship took on cargo and new passengers.

There was one such stop-off at Lagos that stood out in Ted's memory. They had disembarked for a coffee, following the other passengers in search of a decent café. They ended up in a small coffee place where a most unpleasant surprise awaited their fellow white South Africans. The latter, being used to "whites only" places, were horrified when blacks sat down next to them, probably quite deliberately. Speechless with impotent rage they were reduced to muttering: "bloody kaffirs!" But they could not do a thing about it. "Oh, we had some great laughs then!" recalled Ted.

During the long sea journey, as the ship gradually left the warm southern seas to enter colder and more turbulent waters, the young revolutionaries discussed excitedly till the early hours of the morning the prospects of revolutionary work in Europe. They decided that it would be advisable to change their names, mainly to avoid any negative consequences that their political activities might cause for relatives in South Africa. Max Basch changed his name to Sid Frost. It seems that the name of Ted Grant was "lifted" from one of the ship's crew, in a similar way that Trotsky took the name of one of his tsarist jailers. I imagine Able Seaman Grant would have been a bit surprised to know his name had become famous.

Eventually the ship reached the shores of France. After an eight-hour night train journey they arrived in Paris. Paris! That enchanted city of pleasure: the Eiffel Tower, the Louvre, the magical River Seine with its ancient bridges, its waters reflecting the majestic cathedral of Notre Dame, the Avenue des Champs-Élysées with its cinemas, cafés, luxury specialty shops and neatly clipped horse-chestnut trees, the lively cafés of Montmartre, the exotic night life... All that could attract a couple of adventurous young men who had never been outside South Africa was there for the taking. But that side of Paris interested them very little, if at all. They had come to Paris for far more important reasons.

Trotsky, their hero, was living in France at this time, and they were obviously keen to meet him. But they were immediately doomed to disappointment. The political situation in the country was highly unstable. Trotsky had written:

> The situation is revolutionary, as revolutionary as it can be, granted the non-revolutionary policies of the working-class parties. More exactly, the situation is pre-revolutionary. In order to bring the situation to its full maturity, there must be an immediate, vigorous, unremitting mobilization of the masses, under the slogan of the conquest of power in the name of socialism. This is the only way through which the pre-revolutionary situation will be changed into a revolutionary situation. (Trotsky, *Whither France?* 1934)

Under these conditions Trotsky's presence in France became a very controversial issue. Only a few months earlier, in February 1934, the fascists had attempted to bring down the government. Both the Stalinists and the fascists were waging a furious campaign against Trotsky, who was completely isolated in the mountain village of Domesne, near Grenoble. Given the tight security surrounding his household, it was out of the question for two unknown young comrades from South Africa to visit him.

Before they left South Africa they had been given instructions on how to make contact with the French comrades. They were to walk along a famous boulevard (probably Boulevard du Montparnasse) and wait opposite a certain café. For about an hour they waited on the street with growing impatience. They were becoming anxious (was this the right café?) when finally their contact showed up. They were to meet Trotsky's eldest son Leon Sedov and his partner Jeanne Martin, Erwin Wolff (who was subsequently murdered by the GPU in Spain), Pierre Frank, Erwin Bauer and Raymond Molinier.

Paris was now the centre of the International Left Opposition, the place where the celebrated *Bulletin of the Opposition* was produced by Leon Sedov. Ted and Sid stayed there about a fortnight before departing for England. They had a long discussion with Leon Sedov, mainly about the situation in France. Trotsky had suggested that the Trotskyists should enter the Socialist Party (the SFIO). This was known as "the French turn"; although in reality, Trotsky had already proposed something similar for Britain. Molinier, Frank and the others were against entry and later Trotsky broke with them. This was to become a common feature among the so-called Trotskyists, and not only in France.

Leon Sedov was pleased to hear that they were going to Britain. Ted had the impression that he wasn't very happy with the way things were progressing in Britain and in particular with the leadership of the group, who had only recently commenced work within the Independent Labour Party. His later experience showed him why. "He was a good guy", recalled Ted, referring to Leon Sedov. "He asked us whether our group was composed of workers, and when we said it was he was delighted."

This little anecdote is highly significant. In the early days the Left Opposition was plagued with crises and splits, mainly reflecting the unsatisfactory class composition of the organization. The truth is that many of those who came over to the Opposition did not do so because they were convinced Bolshevik-Leninists, but as a reaction against the excesses of Stalinism. Some were demoralised elements, others were tired and worn out, and many were politically disoriented. There were ultra-lefts, anarchists, syndicalists, Bordighists and other deviations.

All these problems were present in a concentrated form in the French Trotskyists. They were mainly petty-bourgeois types. Trotsky was well aware of this problem. "The Old Man had a lot of trouble with them," Ted said, referring to Trotsky. That fact is well expressed in Trotsky's book *The Crisis in the French Section*. This covers the period 1935-36, and therefore, what is written there would apply to the time when Ted met Leon Sedov. Most revealing of all is the transcript of an interview Trotsky gave to Fred Zeller, who was then a leading French Left Young Socialist.

When Fred Zeller reproached Trotsky with the bad conduct of his followers in France, he did not attempt to defend them: "You know, he said, there isn't much choice. You have to work with the material you have on hand. That is not always convenient." (Trotsky, "On Organizational Problems", November 1935, in *The Crisis in the French Section*, p. 67)

Trotsky insisted that the French Trotskyists must work in the Socialist Party, in great measure as an antidote to the bad social composition of the French group. In general, many of those "revolutionaries" who object in principle to work in the Labour Movement are only expressing the inability of the petty-bourgeois sectarians to approach the proletariat and its organizations. Like Lenin, Trotsky had a very clear and realistic attitude to the mass organizations of the class, and knew how to creatively develop transitional slogans that really corresponded to the concrete conditions. By contrast, the sectarians regard slogans and tactics as a kind of Categorical Imperative, abstractions outside of space and time. Molinier and Frank were expelled within a year, on Trotsky's insistence, after breaking with the French group.

Another person they met was a man who called himself Etienne. He was working closely with Leon Sedov on the *Bulletin of the Opposition*. "I did not like the look of Etienne," Ted recalled. "There was something about him I did not trust." Ted's instinct proved to be correct. The man he knew as Etienne turned out to be an agent of Stalin's GPU whose real name was Mark Zborowski.

Following orders from the GPU, Zborowski had infiltrated the Left Opposition and worked his way into a position at the top of its apparatus. Through his work in publishing the *Bulletin of the Opposition*, he gained access to secret information that he passed on to Moscow. As a result, the contents of the Bulletin were placed on Stalin's desk every morning, sometimes before the magazine had even been printed. This gangster later played a key role in the murder of Leon Sedov, which was a serious blow to the Left Opposition.

In London

In December, Ted and Sid crossed the Channel, arriving in a cold and foggy England. They had exchanged the clear blue skies of South Africa for the glowering grey of rainy London. But Ted very quickly adapted to his adopted country and soon became very English indeed. In fact, he was the most English man I have ever known.

The England he found was a country in crisis. True, it had not yet reached the critical point that was reached with Mussolini in Italy or Hitler in Germany. Nor was it about to erupt into a civil war as Spain was on the point of doing. The former workshop of the world had built up a layer of fat, and the Empire gave it a degree of protection against the worst effects of the world crisis of capitalism and prevented an immediate collapse.

All over Europe the brown tide of fascism was advancing. Hitler was consolidating his tyrannical rule. In Austria, the armed workers of Vienna had taken to the streets and were put down. In France, the fascists of the *Croix de Feu* staged violent demonstrations aimed at overthrowing the Radical government. The Stalinists, still under the influence of the Third Period frenzy, had joined with the fascists in an attempt to oust the "Radical Fascist" Daladier. In October, the workers of Asturias in Spain staged an insurrection to prevent the clerical-fascist CEDA of Gil Robles from entering the government.

On April 8, 1935 in the Welsh spa town of Llandrindod Wells, the Conservative leader Stanley Baldwin addressed the National Council of Evangelical Free Churches. In his speech he defended the government's *White Paper* on defence, and urged an increase in the size of the Air Force. Giving voice to that smug sense of superiority that characterised the British ruling class at that time, he said that when he looks at what is happening in Europe. "I sometimes feel that I am living in a madhouse."

Commenting on Baldwin's speech, Trotsky wrote:

> Baldwin thinks that Europe is a lunatic asylum; England is the only country that has kept her reason: she still has the King, the Commons, the Lords... England has avoided revolution, tyranny, and persecution. As a matter of fact, Baldwin understands exactly nothing about what is taking place before his very eyes. There is a much greater distance between Baldwin and Lenin, as intellectual types, than between the Celtic druids and Baldwin. England is nothing but the last ward of the European madhouse, and quite possibly it will prove to be the ward for particularly violent cases. (*The Labour Party and Britain's Decline*, in Trotsky, *Writings on Britain*, vol. 3, p. 30)

In fact, the world crisis was already hitting Britain hard. There was mass unemployment and hunger marches. The Labour Party had won two elections and formed two governments. The second was a government of crisis. Ramsay MacDonald was Prime Minister in the 1929-31 Labour government. When he was unable to gain support for cuts in unemployment benefit in 1931, he broke away from Labour to form a National Government with the Tories and Liberals.

In 1932, the Independent Labour Party (the ILP), split away from the Labour Party and moved sharply left in the direction of centrism (that is, moving towards a revolutionary phraseology without fully breaking with reformist practice). Trotsky urged the small number of followers he had in Britain to enter the ILP, but with the customary prejudices of sectarianism that infected the Trotskyist movement from the beginning, they wasted time and threw away an opportunity, which the Stalinists were not slow to seize.

At the other extreme of the political spectrum, Mosley's fascist movement, the British Union of Fascists, closely modelled on the Italian and German versions, was beginning to raise its ugly head. Oswald Mosley was an upper class adventurer who entered British politics as a Tory, switched to Labour, then split to form the New Party, which he transformed into the British Union of Fascists in 1932. Moseley's Blackshirts had achieved some modest electoral success in the East End of London in the 1937 London Council Election, but their activities provoked strong opposition in the working class. They were also organizing provocative marches through poor Jewish areas in the East End.

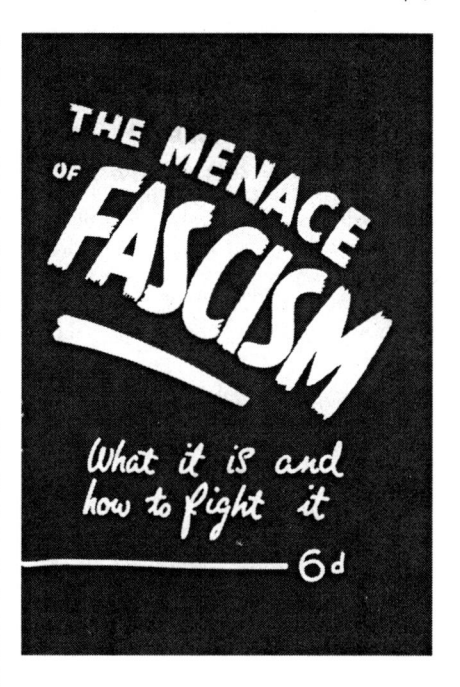

The victory of Hitler had sent shock waves through the British Labour Movement. Ted said:

> At the TUC Conference there was uproar. The delegates were demanding to know how was it possible for the mighty German labour movement to be smashed without even calling a general strike. Walter Citrine (later Lord Citrine) said: "Comrades! If our German brothers had fought it would have meant civil war. The streets would have been running with blood". In the event there was terrible bloodshed. Millions perished in the concentration camps, and Hitler's victory paved the way for the Second World War in which 55 million people lost their lives.

Ted and the other comrades threw themselves into the growing anti-fascist movement. They were advocating Trotsky's policy of the united front of workers' organizations against fascism. That culminated in the celebrated Battle of Cable Street on Sunday, October 4, 1936, when 100,000 workers mobilised to stop the Blackshirts from staging a march in the East End. There is a photograph of Ted on a barricade in Long Lane, Bermondsey, in South London, taken in 1937, which was reproduced in the 1948 edition of his pamphlet *The Menace of Fascism*, published by the Revolutionary Communist Party. This activity enabled the comrades to make contact with the rank and file of the Communist Parry and especially the Young Communist League, which became a fruitful ground for recruitment.

While Ted was still getting on his feet in London, he received a lacerating personal blow. Tragic news came from South Africa. His mother, who suffered from gallstones, had gone for an operation to remove them. It was a routine operation and should have been straightforward, but her usual doctor was unavailable and she was operated on by a stand-in surgeon. Unbeknown to them, the man had a drinking problem. When Ted's sister Rae visited her mother in hospital she noticed that blood was seeping through the blankets. During the operation, he had severed a major artery and her life was draining away. She bled to death a few days later.

Rae explained how the family agonised over who would contact Ted and how they could break the news of the tragedy. Eventually, it was Rae herself who contacted her brother. It must have been a completely shattering experience. Ted loved his mother deeply and yet he had left her without saying goodbye. He was tortured by regrets and feelings of guilt, but what could he do? Separated by thousands of miles and with no money, he was in no position to return to South Africa. To make matters worse, the family believed the surgeon was drunk at the time of the operation. They contemplated taking legal action. "But what was the point?" said Ted bitterly. "Nothing could bring our mother back."

"Bloomsbury bohemians"

The entire history of the international Marxist movement provides ample proof of the demoralizing effects of exile on revolutionaries. Marx and Engels broke off all relations with the German exile groups in London after the defeat of the revolutions of 1848-49, preferring to consolidate their links with the British Chartists and trade unionists. Lenin and Trotsky frequently criticised the poisonous atmosphere in exile circles that sink into a sordid swamp of gossip, character assassination and petty intrigues.

In this case, however, the situation was very different. The young South Africans who had recently arrived in London were not the shattered and demoralized flotsam and jetsam of a defeated revolution, but fresh and enthusiastic revolutionaries, eager to plunge into the work. They had taken a conscious decision to leave their homeland, not under any external compulsion, but in search of broader and more fruitful avenues for revolutionary work.

By contrast, the "native" Trotskyist groups in Britain had all the typical features of exiles. They were in fact exiles in their own land. Although geographically they were based in Britain, they might as well have been on the planet Mars. The first Trotskyist groups in Britain were, like the French, dominated by petty-bourgeois elements, organically incapable of breaking out of the small circle mentality and finding a road to the working class. They were sick with the disease of sectarianism, which has plagued the movement from its inception and which Trotsky criticized many times:

> Though he may swear by Marxism in every sentence, the sectarian is the direct negation of dialectical materialism, which takes experience as its point of departure and always returns to it. A sectarian does not understand the dialectical interaction between a finished program and a living (that is to say, imperfect and unfinished) mass struggle. The sectarian's method of thinking is that of a rationalist, a formalist and an enlightener. During a certain stage of development rationalism is progressive, being directed critically against blind beliefs and superstitions (the eighteenth century!) The progressive stage of rationalism is repeated in every great emancipatory movement. But rationalism (abstract propagandism) becomes a reactionary factor the moment it is directed against the dialectic. Sectarianism is hostile to dialectics (not in words but in action) in the sense that it turns its back upon the actual development of the working class.
>
> The sectarian lives in a sphere of ready-made formulas. As a rule, life passes him by without noticing him; but now and then he receives in passing such a fillip as makes him turn 180 degrees around his

axis, and often makes him continue on his straight path, only... in the opposite direction. Discord with reality engenders in the sectarian the need to constantly render his formulas more precise. This goes under the name of "discussion". To a Marxist, discussion is an important but functional instrument in the class struggle. To the sectarian discussion is a goal in itself. However, the more he discusses, the more actual tasks escape him. He is like a man who satisfies his thirst with salt water: the more he drinks, the thirstier he becomes. Hence the constant irritability of the sectarian. Who slipped him the salt? Surely, the "capitulators" of the International Secretariat. The sectarian sees an enemy in everyone who attempts to explain to him that an active participation in the workers' movement demands a constant study of objective conditions, and not haughty bulldozing from the sectarian rostrum. For analysis of reality the sectarian substitutes intrigue, gossip and hysteria.

These remarks from his 1934 article *Centrism, sectarianism and the Fourth International* could have been written with the British Trotskyists in mind.

Tactics are a concrete question. Lenin and Trotsky were always extremely flexible on organizational and tactical questions. At one point (1933), Trotsky even suggested the setting up of an International including centrist parties (the German SAP, Centrist groups in Holland, and even the ILP), together with the International Left Opposition. This initiative did not succeed because the centrist leaders, fearing the ideas of the International Left Opposition, rejected it. But it shows the flexibility Trotsky always displayed on such questions.

Ted described the situation thus:

> There was a small group called *The Red Flag* which was Groves, Wicks, Sara and Dewar. They had been four district members of the Communist Party and were expelled for standing for a United Front against Hitler in Germany. The ILP had split from the Labour Party for the wrong reasons, the wrong method, the wrong policy and at the wrong time, as Trotsky said.
>
> Trotsky said that they should go in to the ILP and Groves, Wicks and the others, being haughty gentlemen, said "no way". Trotsky had an instinct on this question. The ILP was a centrist party, with about a 100,000 members at that time, mostly workers, and Trotsky suggested that they could win big sections of the ILP and perhaps even a majority to Marxism, but they rejected it and it caused a split and only the younger elements went into the ILP. Within two years they had not only not entered the ILP, but they had actually collapsed into the Labour Party. That is what happened to Groves, Wicks and so on, with all their profession of the principle of the revolutionary party and so on that they claim. Anyhow that was their line. (Sam Bornstein, *Interveiw with Ted Grant*)

Thus, only a small group of fifteen or twenty people finally went into the ILP. Unfortunately, they were young people, mostly green and very inexperienced. And they had entered the ILP very late, when it was already losing ground. They were known as the Marxist Group. When they finally arrived in London, Sid Frost and Ted found accommodation in Kings Cross, and began to work closely together in the Marxist Group. They both joined the Holborn branch of the ILP, and carried on revolutionary work within its ranks. Ted delivered a speech on the "Workers' Movements in South Africa" in the spring of the following year.

They produced a whole series of documents, but the ILP was very undemocratic and refused to allow factions, so they had to act in a semi-clandestine fashion, although everybody knew what was happening. They made certain gains, growing to perhaps forty or fifty members after a couple of years. Perhaps their biggest success was winning CLR James, who was a famous cricketer from the West Indies, in 1935.

In October 1935, when Mussolini invaded Abyssinia (now Ethiopia), a controversy broke out inside the ILP. By this time, the Stalinists had dropped their Third Period ultra-leftism and were moving rightwards in the direction of popular frontism. As a result, the Comintern supported the policy of the League of Nations in advocating sanctions against fascist Italy to halt its invasion of Abyssinia. The Labour Party had the same line.

The ILP opposed the League sanctions, and instead advocated a policy of workers' sanctions against Italy. That was a better position, but the ILP leadership spoiled it with muddle headed centrist arguments, as Ted recalled, "[John] McGovern made a speech in which he said he was against both dictators, Haile Selassie and Mussolini. Our position was that as Abyssinia was a colonial country we supported them. There were no differences in our Tendency over that." (*Ibid.*)

Trotsky sharply criticised the ILP leadership for failing to distinguish between a poor oppressed colony and an imperialist nation. He was even more scathing about the ILP's electoral policy. In the General Election of 1935, the ILP was demanding that support be given only to those Labour Party candidates who opposed sanctions. However, this idea was not fully accepted by the leadership of the Marxist group, which had a confused position on this question.

Millions of Labour voters still had illusions in Atlee and Morrison and it was necessary to put them to the test. In practice, the ILP policy amounted to a partial boycott of Parliament. But it is ABC that you do not boycott parliament unless you are in a position to overthrow it. Trotsky wrote, "The ILP's misfortune is that it doesn't have a truly Marxist programme. That too is why its best activities, such as sanctions against British imperialism, are always influenced by pacifist and centrist mixtures". (Trotsky, *In the Middle of the Road, The ILP and the Fourth International*, September 1933).

Ted pointed out that,

> Trotsky had suggested that the ILP should put up a half a dozen candidates, and in all other constituencies they should support Labour candidates, irrespective of whether they were for or against sanctions. Well, there was almost a split [in the Group]. But when Trotsky came down firmly on the side that said we vote for Labour candidates irrespective of whether they were for or against sanctions, the group accepted that position once it was explained (...). (Sam Bornstein, *Interview with Ted Grant*)

However, the British Trotskyists had wasted time and the possibilities for revolutionary work in the ILP were waning rapidly. Trotsky came to the conclusion that there was nothing more to be gained by working in the ILP, which was in steep decline. As the party in opposition, the Labour Party swung sharply to the left and made big gains, while the right-wing split-off led by Ramsay MacDonald was wiped out.

Trotsky saw that there were clearly more favourable opportunities opening up within the Labour Party, especially in the Labour League of Youth. "Since the ILP youth seem to be few and scattered, while the Labour Youth is the mass youth organisation," he wrote, "I would say: Do not only build fractions—seek to enter. The British section will recruit its first cadres from the thirty thousand young workers in the Labour League of Youth." (Leon Trotsky, *Writings, 1935-36*, p. 203).

From then on, Ted helped to develop the Bolshevik-Leninist Group within the Labour Party, which became known publicly as the Militant Group, after the name of its paper.

In the middle of 1937, they were joined by Ralph Lee and a small number of other comrades, recently arrived from South Africa. They were all shocked at the poor state of Trotskyism in Britain, which a despairing Ted described as "your typical Bloomsbury bohemians".

Gerry Healy at Hyde Park corner 1942

Ted Grant

Ajit Roy

The campaign against Lee

The precursor of what then became the main British Trotskyist organisation, the Workers' International League, and later the Revolutionary Communist Party, was known as the Paddington Group, the most active branch of the Militant Group. Although it had just eight members, it was, in reality, the beginnings of genuine Trotskyism in Britain. The Paddington Group was far more audacious than any of its other branches. Despite the smallness of its numbers, the group was very active, selling papers in Hyde Park Corner and propagandising the ideas of Trotsky.

Nowadays, Hyde Park Corner is dominated by religious fanatics and assorted cranks spouting nonsense from the top of a ladder. But in the 1930s, it was a vibrant place of political debate where the Left was well represented, and there were passionate discussions on the burning political issues of the day. Many working class families from the provinces, coming down to London for the day, would visit Hyde Park and stop for a while to listen to the speeches. There was not much money around and it was a free source of entertainment. Ted said they made a lot of contacts like that.

There was one contact, however, that they must have regretted ever meeting. Gerry Healy was a member of a Stalinist gang who went to Hyde Park to pick arguments with, provoke and physically assault Trotskyist speakers. One victim of his provocations was Jock Haston, who was then a member of the Militant Group. In the course of their repeated arguments, in which it seems they even came to blows, Haston succeeded in winning Healy over to Trotskyism. That was in 1937.

But there were problems inside the Militant Group. The energy and resourcefulness of the young South Africans was in direct contradiction to the amateurism and passivity of the leaders of the group. Ted was staying with Haston at the time. He recalled that, out of 800 copies of the *Militant* sold, 500 were sold by the Paddington group. "We were very dynamic," he said, "and the leaders thought that Haston, Lee and myself might take over the leadership."

In common with all the other British Trotskyists, the Harber group had been educated in the narrow spirit of a small circle. Lacking a real political life of their own, such groups live in a state of constant hysteria, in which the rumour mongers and purveyors of gossip are the heroes of the hour. The Militant Group was just such an outfit.

Gossip is a poisonous thing that corrodes the organization and destroys all trust between comrades, but it is the very lifeblood of small groups with an unhealthy class composition that are divorced from the real life of the workers and the labour movement. The most disgusting rumours about Ralph Lee, originating from the South African Stalinists, were being circulated. It was insinuated that Ralph Lee had stolen money from the Laundry Workers' Union during the strike. In fact, the opposite was the case. Ralph and Millie had put a lot of their own money into the union. But to the slanderers and gossipers the truth was what mattered least of all.

The real reason for the campaign against Ralph, as Ted suspected, was because the leaders of the Marxist Group feared the energy and dedication of the South African newcomers, which cruelly exposed their own inertia and amateurism. It was they who put these dirty allegations into circulation. This behaviour poisoned relations between the two groups and inevitably led to a split in December 1937.

The rumours were started by Charlie Van Gelderen. This story was completely false, but it suited the Militant leaders, who used it to turn people against the Paddington Group. In the election for the Executive that took place at one of the monthly meetings of the Militant Group

WORKERS' INTERNATIONAL NEWS

VOL.1 NO.1   1 JANUARY 1938   TWO PENCE

G.P.U. STALKS ABROAD

Open Letter to All Working Class Organisations
by Leon Trotsky

The international working-class movement is being consumed by a frightful disease. The carrier of the contagion is the Comintern or, to speak more exactly, the G.P.U., which uses the apparatus of the Comintern as its legal cover. The events of the last few months in Spain have shown what crimes the unbridled and utterly depraved bureaucracy of Moscow is capable of, supported by its servitors which it recruits from among the declassed dregs of humanity. It is a question neither of " occasional " assassinations nor of " occasional " falsifications. It is a question of a plot against the international working-class movement.

It is obvious that the Moscow trials were possible only under a totalitarian regime in which the G.P.U. dictated not only to the accused but also to the counsel for the prosecution and for the defence. But these judicial falsifications were from the very beginning conceived as the point of departure for a campaign of extermination directed against the opponents of the Moscow clique on the international arena. On the 3rd of March Stalin delivered a speech to the plenum of the Central Committee of the Russian Communist Party in which he proclaimed that " the Fourth International is composed, as regards two-thirds of its membership, of spies and saboteurs." This impudent declaration, typical of Stalin, already clearly shows at what the Cain of the Kremlin was aiming. His schemes, however, were by no means limited to the cadres of the Fourth International. In Spain, the P.O.U.M., which was waging an implacable struggle with the Fourth International, was counted among the " Trotskyites." After the P.O.U.M. came the turn of the Anarcho-Syndicalists and even of the Left wing Socialists. Anyone who protests against the repression of the Anarchists is now counted as a Trotskyist. Falsifications and crimes are multiplying in a hideous progression. Doubtless one can place certain particularly scandalous details to the account of the excessive zeal of isolated agents. But the work as a whole is strictly centralised and is being carried out according to the plan elaborated in the Kremlin.

On 21st April there met at Paris an extraordinary plenum of the Executive Committee of the Comintern at which were present the most trustworthy representatives of the 17 most important sections. The sessions were of a strictly secret character. Only a brief statement to the effect that the attention of the plenum had been concentrated upon the international struggle against Trotskyism found its way into the world Press. The instructions had been sent from Moscow, coming direct from Stalin. Neither the debates nor the decisions were published. It appears from all the information we have received and from the subsequent events that this secret plenum was in fact *a congress of the most responsible international agents of the G.P.U. whose object was to prepare the campaign of false accusations, delations, abductions and assassinations against the adversaries of Stalinism in the working-class movement of the whole world.*

First issue of *Workers' International News*, the theoretical magazine of the WIL

the Paddington comrades were surprised when they didn't get any votes. Since they were by far the most active and successful branch, they were absolutely staggered when they were so heavily defeated. Only later did they discover the cause.

The leaders had gone around spreading the poisonous story about Ralph Lee. If they had really believed it, they should have confronted him with it, but they never did, preferring to repeat this dirty story to the whole group. The only ones who knew nothing about it were the Paddington comrades. They only found out about it by accident, although they could see that something was wrong.

At the next meeting, they raised the question forcibly, demanding another election, but were voted down. There was a gasp. Somebody said the leaders were rotten, but what could they do? Furious at this conduct, Haston walked out, and the others walked out in solidarity with him. The moment they walked out of the door, Harber moved their expulsion.

Expelled from the Militant Group, they began to meet to discuss what was to be done. Ted recalled:

> We met late into the night for many nights. We discussed and discussed, and finally came to the conclusion that it was a waste of time to stay in this petty bourgeois group. The atmosphere had been poisoned and it would be an absolute nightmare. We would eventually get the leadership of the group, but it wouldn't be worth it. So we decided to launch the WIL. We decided then something we have carried out ever since in practise: to turn our backs on the sects. They were a waste of time, mostly rubbish. We would build our movement from workers. (Sam Bornstein, *Interview with Ted Grant*)

The first issue of *Workers' International News* came out in January 1938. They were only a handful, but what they lacked in numbers and resources they made up for with sheer youthful élan and revolutionary enthusiasm. In the early days of 1938, some recruits were won from the ILP Guild of Youth. Others were recruited at Hyde Park. Ted said:

> We had eight members. We were active; we sold in Hyde Park, Piccadilly and Tottenham Court Road. Where there were strikes, we intervened and won people that way, we won workers. We were the only workers' group as you know. We wanted workers; we did not want the rubbish that was in the other groups again.
>
> Most of the other people won weren't in the Labour Party either. We won people from the unions, we won some at Hyde Park, we won some from nothing at all, fresh workers, from strikes and so on. I don't think we won one member from the Labour Party at that time. That was the paradox, but our orientation was correct. (*Ibid.*)

The Moscow Trials

In the summer of 1936, the world was stunned by news of trial of the "Trotsky-Zinoviev Centre". The defendants, who were accused of intending to kill the leaders of the party and government, included leading Old Bolsheviks such as Zinoviev, Kamenev, Smirnov and others. They confessed to the most heinous crimes against the Revolution and the USSR, pouring dirt on their own heads in the process.

Lenin's old comrades were accused of having committed the most grotesque crimes against the Revolution. Usually, they would be accused of being agents of Hitler and the Mikado. In the same way, during the Thermidorian reaction in France, the Jacobins were accused of being agents of England. The man who acted as the accuser of these famous old revolutionaries and comrades of Lenin was State Prosecutor Andei Vyshinsky, the former Menshevik and bitter

Leon Trotsky
THE LESSON OF
SPAIN
The Last Warning!
INTERNATIONAL
3D

opponent of Lenin and the October Revolution. This was the man who described these Old Bolsheviks as, "These mad dogs of capitalism, [who] have tried to tear to pieces the very best of the best people of our Soviet land".

The only "evidence" produced was the confessions of the accused themselves. They confessed to terrorism, wrecking and working for Hitler. Zinoviev, in a lifeless voice, claimed he was the political inspirer of the murder of Kirov. Trotsky, who was effectively under house arrest in Norway, at first, could not understand why they had confessed to such monstrous lies. But it soon became clear that these confessions were extracted under torture, or by blackmail and tricks.

Since the fall of the Soviet Union, the archives of the GPU and the CPSU have become available for inspection. There is not a shred of evidence for the existence of any "Trotsky-Zinoviev Centre", nor for any terrorist acts organised by the Opposition against Stalin. Ever since Khrushchev's infamous secret speech to the CPSU 20th Congress in 1956, everybody knows that it was Stalin who was behind the murder of Kirov in December 1934.

The purpose of this first trial was to prepare the ground for other, more sweeping trials. Stalin's aims were simple: to completely destroy all those who could become a rallying point for the discontent of the masses. They even went as far as arresting and murdering thousands of people who had been totally loyal to Stalin, whose sole crime was their direct link to the experience of the October revolution. The trial of the 17, the so-called "Anti-Soviet Trotskyist Centre" (Radek, Pyatakov, Sokolnikov, etc.) followed in January 1937.

Then there was the secret trial of the army officers (Tukhachevsky, Yakir and others). This decimated the Red Army and had catastrophic consequences when Hitler invaded the Soviet Union. The monstrous witch hunt culminated with the trial of the 21 (Bukharin, Rykov, Rakovsky, etc.). It was dangerous to be friend, neighbour, father or son of any of those arrested. In the concentration camps there were to be found whole families, including the children. Trotsky's own children, grandchildren and relatives all fell victim to Stalin's infernal machine.

The main defendant was not present at the trials. Leon Trotsky, after having been denied the right to asylum by all the countries of Europe, finally found refuge in Mexico, where he was welcomed by its head of state, the progressive anti-imperialist general Lázaro Cardenas. From these distant shores, Trotsky watched as the never-ending chain of horrors unfolded. He described the notorious Moscow Trials as "a unilateral civil war against the Bolshevik Party".

Trotsky took the initiative in setting up the Dewey Commission to investigate all the charges against him. He organised an international protest campaign against the Moscow trials. The British Trotskyists reacted energetically to this appeal. They published articles and turned up at meetings of the YCL and Communist Party to denounce the Moscow trials and put the Stalinists on the spot. They obtained the support of Labour Lefts, notably Sydney Silverman, whose sons Roger and Julian joined our Tendency in the 1960s.

After the Second World War, the RCP, in collaboration with Trotsky's widow, Natalia Sedova, tried to appeal to the Nuremberg Trials for War Crimes. They issued a leaflet that contained photos of all of Lenin's Central Committee, each with a caption "shot", "committed suicide", "disappeared" or "dead". In the centre was a photo of the man who organized the extermination of Lenin's Party with the caption: "Stalin, the executioner, alone remains". As could be expected, the Nuremberg judges paid no attention.

How not to unify

Shortly before the war, the Workers' International League obtained its first printing machine. More accurately, they got hold of an ancient wreck, which Lee, who was very skilful, managed to get to work. They published a theoretical magazine called *Workers' International News* and also a paper called *Youth for Socialism*. They also produced a small pamphlet of Trotsky's article *The Lessons of Spain*, with an introduction that Ted wrote in collaboration with Ralph Lee.

In August 1938, shortly before the Founding Conference of the Fourth International, James P. Cannon of the US Socialist Workers' Party came to London with the aim of uniting the different groups of British Trotskyists in a single organization. Because of their special relationship with Trotsky, the leaders of the SWP thought they had a privileged position in the international Trotskyist movement. This was particularly the case with Cannon, who took it for granted that the British Trotskyists would follow his lead in all things.

Ted recalled their first meeting with Cannon. By then they had thirty members, all workers. When they told Cannon he expressed disbelief. He had been told by the other groups that we had ten or at the most fifteen. So they invited him to a meeting in Haston's house where he could speak to the members. None of the other groups were able to do this, for the simple reason that they had next to no members to whom to speak. Ted estimated that the largest was CLR James' group, which had fourteen or fifteen people. The comrades argued that unity was only possible on the basis of an agreed tactic. The idea that it was possible to cobble together a unified group with two tactics was unprincipled. It wouldn't work. There had to be one tactic, with the minority having the right to win over the majority.

Cannon was unconvinced, but agreed to come to a meeting. He came, at half past seven on the dot. There were ten people there, and Cannon said: "let's start". The comrades replied: "give the others a chance to get here, just another few minutes." By twenty to eight there were twenty people, and at a quarter to eight there were thirty people in the room. They did not reach agreement, but Cannon tried to persuade them to unify with the other groups. They told him that he would unite three groups into ten. He then asked if they would come to the Unity Conference and they agreed to come and put their case.

The members of the WIL were understandably cautious. After their recent experience with the Militant group, they were unsure as to how any meaningful unity could be achieved. But they dutifully went along to the conference, all thirty of them, which was almost a majority. They were, of course, fully in favour of the Fourth International and held Cannon in high esteem, but when they turned up at the Conference they were utterly scandalized at what they saw. The full story can be found in *The History of British Trotskyism*.

Ralph Lee had a biting wit. When he saw what was happening, with doors opening and closing and people going round and round, canvassing and lobbying as the different participants engaged in horse-trading and

Max Shachtman and James P. Cannon

back-room deals, he likened it to a French bedroom farce. The only people who were neither lobbied nor consulted were the members of the WIL.

At bottom, the problem was that it is impossible to unite groups with radically different policies, tactics and orientation. The comrades of the WIL tried to point this out to Cannon, but he was unimpressed. He demanded unity and that was all there was to be said. In the end, the WIL refused to join, arguing that the unification agreement, which allowed those Trotskyists opposed to entry to engage in open work, was bound to fail.

The manoeuvring was so blatant that in the end even CLR James was beginning to have second thoughts. According to Ted, the only way that Cannon could get him to agree to the so-called fusion was to promise him behind the scenes that he would take him to America. Observing these shenanigans, Lee warned Cannon: "You are going to tie their tails together like Kilkenny cats and they will tear each other to bits."

Cannon's reply was entirely in character. He said: "We crush splitters like beetles." Henry Sara, who was in the chair, said to Lee "you can't talk to a guest like that". Ted got up and protested that "even if comrade Trotsky were present, we would have the right to put forward any position we like. That is the democracy within our movement no matter who is here."

On such a basis no viable unification could be arrived at. Ralph Lee's warning was confirmed within one week. Maitland, who was there for the RSP, was repudiated by his own group and they rejected unification. Other splits soon followed. Within six weeks the whole thing was already a shambles. Cannon was not pleased. He was used to getting all his own way. He blamed the WIL for his problems. The resulting resentment he felt towards the "awkward squad" of Lee, Haston and Grant lasted for years and had very negative consequences.

At the Unity Conference, Cannon asked Ted and Jock Haston to go and see him. He asked them if they would send a delegate to the founding conference of the Fourth International and ask for sympathetic affiliation. They answered that they would apply for sympathetic affiliation, although they might not be able to raise the funds. Cannon replied: "Do what you can. If not, send a letter." As they did not have sufficient funds to travel to the conference, they drew up a letter. They discussed it and agreed on a text expressing support for the Fourth International and asking for acceptance as a sympathising section, which was dictated to Millie Lee, the only one who could type.

In 1938, the founding conference of the Fourth International recognised the Revolutionary Socialist League (RSL), which was what emerged from the "unity conference", as the official British section. The French delegate moved that the WIL should be accepted as a sympathetic section. It would almost certainly have been accepted, but for the intervention of Cannon, who took his revenge on the comrades in the most petty and spiteful way.

The letter of the WIL was not read out. Instead, Cannon delivered a diatribe against the WIL for having split, allegedly over mere personal grievances. This was entirely false, as Cannon knew very well. In conclusion, Cannon advocated recognition of the RSL. This proposal was naturally accepted since the delegates had not been given the correct information. On the basis of a whole series of lies, the WIL's request for sympathetic affiliation was rejected.

As a result of these manoeuvres, the WIL was unjustly censured. "All purely national groupings", the official statement read, "all those who reject international organisation, control and discipline, are in their essence reactionary." When Cannon wrote a report for Trotsky about

The office of the Workers' International League, 61 Northdown Street, London

the Fourth International's founding conference, he gave a dishonest and distorted version of his visit to Britain and the fusion conference and gives the following assessment of the WIL:

> The Militant group in the past six months had suffered from an unfortunate split led by Lee which resulted in the creation of another group without any principled grounds for the split (the *Workers' International News*). This could only introduce confusion and demoralization—the more so since both groups work exclusively in the Labour Party. At the same time, the Liverpool branch had withdrawn from the Militant group on opportunistic lines. (…)

> In the London conference, a week later, I had their support [the Edinburgh group] from the start for a general unification. This undoubtedly exerted considerable pressure on the [CLR] James group.

> The political resolution accepted as a basis for unification provided that the *main emphasis* should be placed on work in the Labour Party without making Labour Party membership compulsory upon those comrades who have not been members up till now. This at least provides a definite orientation for the united group. It was the maximum possible. It seems to me that the most important thing, if we could at least get a correct orientation, was to bring all the comrades together and get them in the habit of functioning in one organization which would be firmly affiliated to the Fourth International. We carried on a strong crusade against irresponsible splits and made it clear that the international conference would do away with the possibility of a multiplicity of groups, and recognize only one section in each country. (…)

> The Lee group consists of about thirty, mostly youngsters, who have been deeply poisoned with personal antagonism to the leadership of the Militant group. They attempted to obstruct the unification but were pounded mercilessly at the unification conference, and their ranks were badly shaken. Their attitude was condemned by the international conference.

> Shachtman, during his visit to England, also had a session with this group. His opinion is the same as

mine—that they will have to submit to the international decision and come into the united British section or suffer a split. It is only necessary for the British section to take a firm and resolute stand in regard to this group, and in no case to acknowledge its legitimacy. Unfortunately, this is easier said than done. The English comrades, alas, are gentlemen. They are not accustomed to our "brutal" (i.e. Bolshevik) treatment of groups who play with splits. (James P. Cannon, *Impressions of the Founding Conference*, October 12, 1938, in Joseph Hansen, *James P. Cannon—The Internationalist*, July 1980)

In the last sentence of this tendentious and one-sided report we see the essence of Cannon's brand of "Bolshevism". This was the first example of Cannon's manoeuvres against the British comrades. It was not to be the last. Soon after, Max Shachtman visited London to justify what they had done. Ted recalled that he got a hot reception:

> It was Shachtman who got the backlash of that when he came to speak at a meeting [in London]. We laid into him like hell. At the end he tried to justify it by saying it was just a manoeuvre. He tried to back Cannon, although he was already in disagreement with him (...) and the outline of the split was already there. You have got to give him [credit for] that. All he could say was that it was a manoeuvre. He was aghast, but he repeated that it was a good manoeuvre, it was for the best.
>
> (...) The important thing to remember is that Trotsky never attacked the WIL in the whole of his writings. He was waiting to see what was going to happen. He knew [how] Cannon and those people behaved. He had experience of them, and therefore Trotsky never attacked us. (...) He wrote praising us, praising our getting a press, praising the introduction that Lee and I wrote to the pamphlet *Lessons of Spain*. (Sam Bornstein, *Interview with Ted Grant*)

Ted remembered their joy when they received a letter from Trotsky congratulating them on publishing this pamphlet, in which he emphasized how important it was for a revolutionary organization to have its own printing press, independent of capitalist establishments. Somehow, over the years, this letter went missing and, as far as I know, has never been found, a fact that Ted bitterly regretted. Ted thought that Haston had given all this material to Healy after the RCP and Healy's group fused in 1949.

Everything indicates that Trotsky was following the work of the WIL with interest, and was receiving regular material from them. Although formally outside the International, Ted and the others still continued to regard themselves as part of it. "We saw ourselves as the bastard child of the International", he explained. They were confident that sooner or later they would be recognized as the rightful British section. History proved them right. As we have seen, the "unified" group started to break up as soon as the conference was over.

The WIL, however, continued to make steady progress, even taking chunks out of the RSL. They won over the entire RSL Liverpool and Leeds groups, bringing over the entire Deane family in Liverpool in the process.

In a small group, personal relationships can play a disproportionate role. Millie Lee was a very pretty girl with auburn hair and a bubbly, exuberant character. She was completely dedicated to the cause and had good organizational skills, although she was not a profound thinker. Jock Haston was a handsome seafarer with a strong Scottish accent, enthusiastic, intelligent, articulate and bold. For the second time in her young life, Millie was swept off her feet. Maybe her relationship with Ralph Lee was already on the rocks, but in any case, she left him and went to live with Haston. They stayed together until his death. It must have had a very bad effect on Ralph and may well have played a role in his decision to return to South Africa.

The reasons for this decision are in fact unclear to me. They may have been personal (the breakdown of his marriage), or for health reasons (the British climate was causing him problems), or perhaps he was worn out by the constant attacks made on his person. Probably it was a mixture of all these things. Either way, it was a fateful decision. In 1940, Ralph Lee went back to South Africa.

On returning to South Africa, Lee attempted to resume his revolutionary work. Apparently, before leaving, he had shifted towards Shachtman's position that Russia was not a deformed workers' state, but rather, that it was a new form of society called "bureaucratic collectivism". But he never raised this publicly, and Ted was adamant that he was never a Shachtmanite.

Lee later established the South African WIL, which was engaged in a number of struggles, but conditions were even more difficult than pre-war, and they all ended in defeat. The organization soon collapsed. Already worn out by his bad experience in Britain, Ralph was now mentally and physically exhausted, ill and penniless. Contrary to the poisonous gossip spread by Harber and co., he had spent all his money on the movement and was now completely broke and suffering considerable hardship. All this undermined his health and morale. In the Ted Grant archive there is a handwritten letter to Ted. It bears the signature of Ralph Lee. It is short but deeply moving. I reproduce it in full:

> Dear Ted,
>
> I got your letter sent per that red-haired girl—I have forgotten her name. It was so long ago that I suppose you have forgotten it. I could not work up enough energy at the time to reply. But apologies are, I think, unnecessary between you and me.
>
> I have been corresponding recently with MGP [Murray Gow Purdy]. I want you now, by return of post, to tell me how he stands with you, politically and personally. Answer right away, by air letter.
>
> Tell me also about yourself. Are you getting enough to eat? Are you having any fun?
>
> As for myself, I have been this many and many a year, in Swift's phrase, "like a poisoned rat in a hole, dying of rage." Very sad, is it not?
>
> Best wishes
>
> Ralph[2]

This letter is dated Johannesburg on July 15, 1948. It shows the close personal relationship between the two men, which continued in spite of Ralph's long struggle with depression, the physical separation, and long periods of silence. It also casts a tragic light on Ralph's state of mind. We know nothing of what happened to Ralph Lee afterwards. The official records show that he died in South Africa in 1965. Ted believed he had committed suicide long before then.

---

[2] From the Ted Grant Archive.

> 141 Pritchard St.,
> Johannesburg
> 15 July 1948
>
> Dear Ted,
>
> I got your letter sent per that red-haired girl — I have forgotten her name. It was so long ago that I suppose you have forgotten it. I could not work up enough energy at the time to reply. But apologies are, I think, unnecessary between you and me.
>
> I have been corresponding recently with M.G.P. I want you now, by return of post, to tell me how he stands with you, politically and personally. Answer right away, by Air Letter.
>
> Tell me also about yourself. Are you getting

Ralph Lee's letter to Ted 1948

Chapter Three

The War Years

There is only one way of avoiding the war—that is the overthrow of this society. However, as we are too weak for this task, the war is inevitable. (Trotsky, *Some Questions on American Problems*, 1940)

The murder of Trotsky

As the beat of war drums grew ever-louder in Europe, another bloody drama was being played out in Mexico. Stalin regretted that he had committed the serious error of exiling the leader of the Opposition in 1927. Subsequently, in 1937, he had issued the order for the assassination of Trotsky, and was discontented that it had not yet been carried out. He demanded that the man he most feared should be eliminated without delay.

Pavel Sudoplatov was the man charged by Stalin himself with the murder of Trotsky. In his memoirs, he describes how Stalin saw the Trotskyist movement as a serious danger. He also understood that without Trotsky, the movement would be helpless. At a secret meeting in the Kremlin, Stalin told Sudoplatov and Beria, the boss of the NKVD:

> There are no important political figures in the Trotskyite movement except Trotsky himself. If Trotsky is finished the threat will be eliminated. (Pavel Sudoplatov, *Special Tasks, the Memoirs of an Unwanted Witness—a Soviet Spymaster*, p. 67)

The first attempt, in May 1940, was a bungled affair. An armed gang led by the Mexican painter and Stalinist, David Alfaro Siqueiros, attacked Trotsky's house in Coyoacan in the middle of the night. The bedrooms were sprayed with machine gun bullets, but miraculously nobody was killed. The young Esteban Volkov (Seva) was wounded in the foot. Esteban told me he thought that the gunmen were nervous and did not even put the lights on. They fired into the dark and failed to hit their intended target. "Perhaps they did not want to see the faces of their victims", he said.

After the attack, the guards began to strengthen the perimeter defences. Esteban explained that Trotsky was sceptical about the attempts to "fortify" the house against attack: "The next attack will be completely different", he said, which it was.

On 20 August, 1940, a man dressed in a raincoat entered the Trotsky household in Coyoacán. He was greeted as an old friend by the young guards who ushered him into the room where Leon Trotsky was waiting to correct an article he said he had written.

The man known as Jacson (Ramón Mercader) stood behind the old man as he was reading the manuscript. Silently, from underneath his gabardine, he produced an ice pick. Suddenly, the air was rent by a piercing scream. The guards rushed in—too late! Despite putting up a superhuman struggle, Trotsky had been mortally wounded. His last recorded words were: "I am confident of the victory of the Fourth International. Go forward!"

Many years later Ted Grant remembered the day the news of Trotsky's murder came over the radio, as he lay in bed in a London hospital: "One can't imagine the fury, anger and frustration felt by all the comrades throughout the world. It was the second time they had tried to assassinate him; this time they succeeded".

In 1990, commemorating the 50th anniversary of the assassination, Ted wrote:

> The events of the war at that time were so stupendous that Trotsky's death didn't have the impact it would have had in peacetime. That is why Stalin calculated on murdering Trotsky at that time. He thought it wouldn't be noticed in the general turmoil of the war. But it made an enormous impact on us and made us even more determined to carry on Trotsky's work, as we have done in Britain and internationally in the succeeding years. (...)
>
> Our immediate response was to launch a campaign to expose the Stalinists' crimes. The news of the assassination was presented by J.R. Campbell in the Communist Party's *Daily Worker* of those days in an absolutely scandalous way, as if one of Trotsky's followers had murdered him and Stalin and the bureaucracy had nothing to do with it. We exposed this lie.
>
> At the time I was involved in the Workers' International League, building up the struggle against the imperialist war. We were campaigning for a Labour government to come to power and then, if necessary, wage a revolutionary war against Hitler, after having nationalised the economy.
>
> Without Trotsky we would have been blind. He was in many ways even greater than Lenin, in the theoretical work he did between 1923 and 1940 to deepen and develop the ideas of Marxism and Leninism. His analysis of the events in Spain, particularly the 1931-37 revolution, France, Britain at the time of the general strike, China in 1925-27, and Germany in the struggle against Hitler, armed his followers for the struggles that lay ahead.
>
> Above all; without Trotsky we would not have had an analysis of Stalinism. His criticisms of the Communist International were shown over and over again to be correct in the light of events. (*Militant*, August 17, 1990)

The British comrades were bitterly critical of the American Socialist Workers' Party for not having guarded Trotsky better but didn't say anything publicly. Ted told me the comrades were stunned and heartbroken by the news. "We were furious at the SWP and the guards who were supposed to be protecting the Old Man", he said. "How was it possible for a man dressed in a raincoat in the summer to be left alone with Trotsky?"

The SWP tried to make all kinds of excuses. They said that the Old Man did not like to have a guard present when he was in a political discussion with someone. Ted indignantly brushed this aside: "Comrade Trotsky was a disciplined Bolshevik. If the guards had insisted that they were responsible for his protection and had to be present, he would have accepted it."

Many years later, Gerry Healy, who had for years been a stooge of Cannon and the Americans, accused Joseph Hansen of being an agent of Stalin's GPU. He launched a noisy campaign and invited us to participate. Ted refused. He did not believe the accusation, although he did consider the Americans to be guilty of a grave dereliction of duty.

I discussed this several times with Trotsky's grandson, Esteban Volkov. Although he personally had warm memories of the American guards, he admitted that they lacked any professionalism: "They were not guards at all but only young kids", he said. He gave me one example. Trotsky found that the young American guard Robert Sheldon Harte had left the door open, and sharply rebuked him: "Harte, if the GPU get through that door, you could be killed." His words were prophetic. After the raid on Trotsky's house in May 1940, Harte was kidnapped and murdered. Although Trotsky refused to believe it, he turned out to be a Stalinist agent, who was probably murdered because he had had second thoughts after the attack.

Esteban pointed out that even if Mercader had failed in his attempt, Stalin would have found other means to kill his grandfather: "They could have dropped a bomb on the house or poisoned the water system and killed us all."

But such arguments made little impression on Ted, who replied: "Even if he had been given another year to write, just think what a contribution he could have made!" Ted considered that the best works of Marx, Engels, Lenin and Trotsky were written towards the end of their lives, because these works were the product of their most mature understanding and experience:

> We felt a burning regret, because perhaps Trotsky's best work was done in the last year of his life. His book, *In Defence of Marxism*, remains correct to this day in its analysis of the Soviet Union and the processes of Stalinism.
>
> He showed that the bureaucracy was not a new class or new formation but an aberration from socialism which could not bring socialism. His marvellous book on Stalin was also written at that time, though it was only published in 1945. Stalin exerted pressure on the governments of the United States, Britain and other countries to prevent the publication of Trotsky's work until after the end of the war. These works gave a sound theoretical foundation to the movement. If he had lived—for another five years, turning out material of that sort, it would have been an enormous plus for the development of the workers' movement.
>
> He would have supported our analysis of these events—that there would be a consolidation of capitalism, in the industrialised countries at least, and a consolidation of Stalinism in Eastern Europe and the Soviet Union for a temporary period, a period which has now passed.
>
> If Trotsky had lived on into the post-war period it would not have made a fundamental difference to the course of events—the victory of Stalinism on the one hand and the revival of capitalism on the other. This was due to the policies of Stalinism and reformism which prevented the carrying through of the revolution, which Trotsky had looked forward to.
>
> In France, Britain, Germany and other countries if the so-called Communist Parties had been revolutionary parties they could have carried through the revolution on the European continent and solved the problems of the working class nationally and internationally once and for all.
>
> But had Trotsky lived on he would have armed the workers better. There would not have been the absolute disasters perpetrated by those who claimed to be supporters of Trotsky but in reality completely distorted his ideas. And there would not have been so many losses from the movement at that time and later if Trotsky had been there to direct and guide it. (*Militant*, August 17, 1990)

The assassination of Trotsky in August 1940 dealt a devastating blow to the young and untested forces of the Fourth International. Stalin certainly knew what he was doing when he murdered Trotsky. When he gave the order for the second attack, Sudoplatov pointed out that this would mean putting in danger the extensive network of Stalinist agents who had infiltrated the Trotskyist movement worldwide. Stalin answered:

> The elimination of Trotsky will mean the total collapse of the entire Trotskyite movement, and we will have no need to spend any money on combating Trotskyites and their attempts to undermine the Comintern or us. (Sudoplatov, Op. Cit., p. 76)

Stalin was not far wrong in his assessment. The leaders of the Fourth International were not up to the level of the tasks posed by history. Deprived of Trotsky's leadership, they made a series

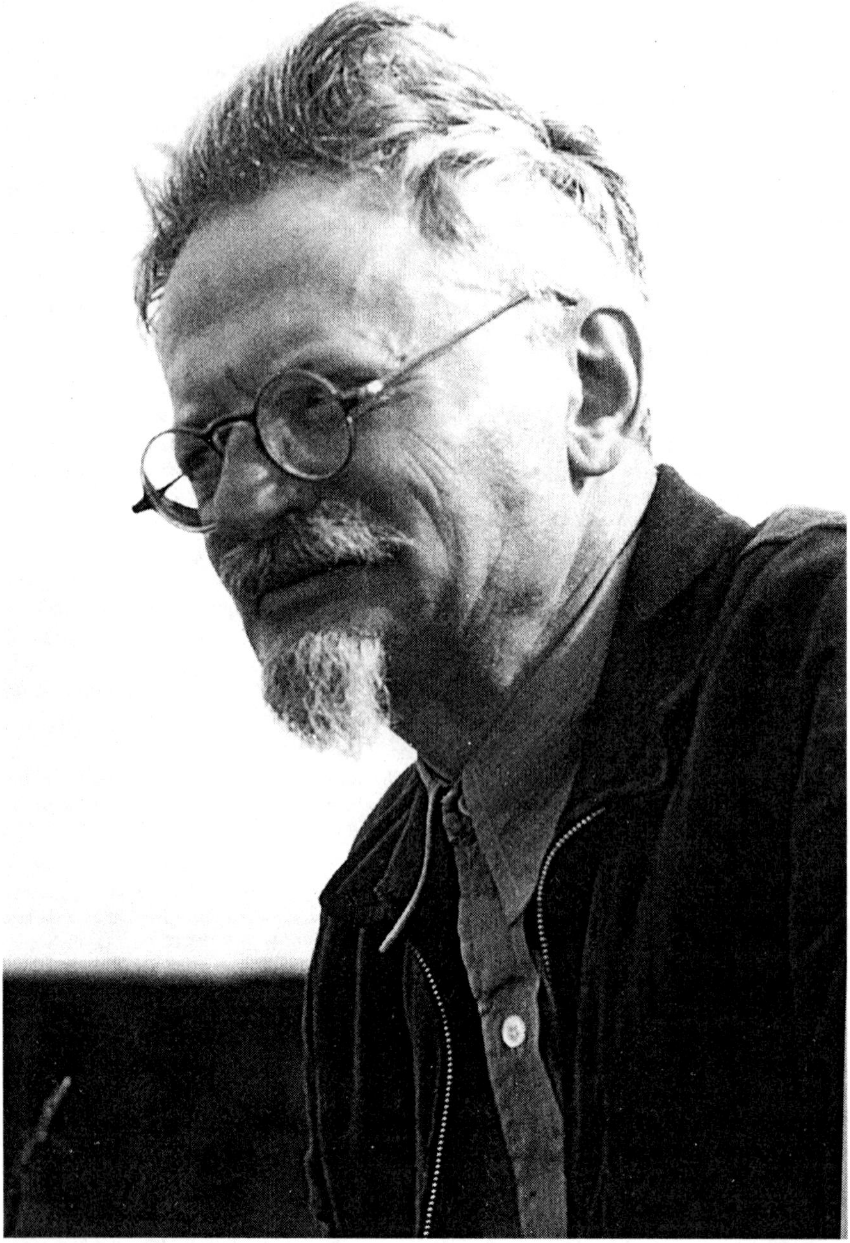

of fundamental mistakes. Only the leadership of the RCP in Britain was able to readjust to the new situation on a world scale after 1945. Ted was profoundly inspired by Trotsky's sacrifice and determination in defending the ideas:

> Even now, when I think back to the assassination of Trotsky it brings tears to my eyes. What enormous sacrifices he made. His family was murdered, his comrades, the old Bolsheviks, were entirely annihilated. There was a victory for Stalinist and reformist reaction. Trotsky went right through all that but it did not stop him from doing the necessary work to prepare the cadres for the development of the movement. It is on the basis of his ideas, extending and deepening them however, that we will go forward to victory. (*Militant*, August 17, 1990)

The outbreak of war

Britain's policy of appeasing Hitler in the 1930s was partly an expression of weakness on the part of Chamberlain and his faction. But it was also an attempt to divert Hitler's attentions towards the East—towards a war with the Soviet Union. Hitler allowed them to entertain this illusion by swallowing first Austria and then Czechoslovakia. But the invasion of Poland, an ally of France, was one step too far. Britain and France declared war. In order to protect his rear flank, Hitler signed a pact with Stalin. This left his hands free to turn west and crush France with one mighty blow.

The outbreak of war changed everything. All the calculations of the imperialist powers were thrown into confusion. The French bourgeoisie had felt supremely confident behind the trenches and concrete bunkers of the Maginot Line, but was astonished to see Hitler's armies brush its defences aside as a man swats a fly.

Ted pointed out that the French ruling class was more afraid of the French workers than of Hitler. With memories of the Paris Commune burned on its consciousness, the cowardly French bourgeois refused to arm the population to resist Hitler. They preferred to kiss the Nazi jackboot and hand Paris over to the tender mercies of the Gestapo rather than face the risk of another Paris Commune.

Britain was now in a dire position. The British army had suffered a crushing defeat and thousands of British soldiers were trapped on the beaches of Dunkirk, where they were at the mercy of the German Stuka fighter-bombers. They were only rescued by the skin of their teeth by an improvised armada of fishing vessels. Since the British are experts in presenting a defeat as a victory, the "Dunkirk Spirit" has ever since been held up as a most glorious moment in our history. In reality it was the most ignominious of defeats.

The threat from the state was recognised by the comrades, who at one stage at the beginning of the war were expecting to be made illegal. In preparation for such an eventuality, they sent Jock Haston to Ireland to investigate the setting up of a radio station to broadcast to Britain. But before that, Gerry Healy left the country, without consulting the group. He was afraid of being called up into the army, and in order to avoid this he went to Ireland. This was entirely contrary to party policy, as he knew full well. Ted commented:

> Healy beat it, and then we decided to send Haston to try and establish a group in Ireland in the event of our being made illegal. (...) Nobody knew what was going to happen and we were raided on the first day of war. In the event of our being made illegal, we intended setting up a radio station in Ireland, and would get material over here by ship and so on. So we first sent Haston over and then we sent Tommy Reilly over and then John Williams in order to establish a group. [I will provide] the details of how Healy was expelled.

> Well, what happened was they were working in the Labour Party and doing very well, and Healy became the business manager of the *Plough and the Stars* which was the paper of the [Irish] Labour Party. Now they were living on a small amount of money that we were able to send at that time. They were a small collective, and Healy said he had [received] no money from the Labour Party. [But] they found out [that he had]. There was a row and he was expelled. But Haston persuaded them to rescind the expulsion and that he [Healy] be sent back to Britain, as Healy was a good organiser. Haston and myself were quite wrong on that question. (...) Every time he was expelled, we always brought him back because he was a good organiser, although that was not sufficient reason to bring him back. (Sam Bornstein, *Interview with Ted Grant*)

The Irish mission was not very successful, and in any case, the WIL was never illegalised. However, while he was in Dublin, Jock Haston entered into contact with members of the IRA and the Irish Labour Party, including Nora Connolly O'Brian, the daughter of the famous Irish Marxist and Labour leader James Connolly, who was shot by the British after the Easter Rising of 1916. Nora was very sympathetic and helped the comrades a lot.

Haston, with his usual flare, won over several members of the IRA to Trotskyism, a fact that did not endear him to the leadership, which was pro-German with right-wing and fascist leanings. The IRA sentenced Jock to death, whereupon he hastily returned to London. This story reminded me of the case of Brendan Behan,[3] who, when he was sentenced to death by the IRA, said: "They have sentenced me in my absence, so they can carry out the sentence in my absence too!"

At home the mood was bordering on desperation. Ted recalled: "I have never seen anything like it. People were really scared. They expected the Germans to invade at any time. There was no enthusiasm for the war, as there had been in 1914. People had already been through that experience and they knew what war was like. But they were prepared to fight in what they believed was a war for democracy against Nazism."

In order to get the support for the war, Churchill and the ruling class were compelled to conceal their real interests and cover themselves in the cloak of "democracy". Before the war they had all been admirers of fascism. Churchill, in particular, spoke highly of Mussolini, and most of his class saw in Hitler a bulwark against Bolshevism.

In publications like *Searchlight* and *Youth for Socialism*, which was later renamed *Socialist Appeal*, Ted wrote article after article exposing the hypocrisy of the British ruling class and laying bare the naked class interests that lay behind the official demagogy about the "struggle to defend democracy". In September 1939, in the *Youth for Socialism* lead article entitled *Down with the War*, he wrote:

> Defence of whose country? Defence of the landlord and the boss!
>
> We defend the country when we have a country to defend. Cut down the profits out of war 100% first. Let the mines, factories, railways and workshops come under the control of the working class. The working class on both sides of the frontier has no interest in the struggle of one or another group

---

[3] Young Brendan Behan had taken part in a failed bombing campaign at the Liverpool docks and was sent down to Borstal jail for youth offenders for three years. In 1942, he returned to Dublin an IRA political hero but developed a serious drinking problem and often landed in jail for being drunk and disorderly. After one such episode he was court-martialled by the IRA for "bringing the movement into disrepute". He was sentenced to death and told to show up for his execution. Apparently he was notified of the sentence in a pub, to which Behan replied, "You tried me in my absence. You can shoot me in my absence". He later became a famous writer.

of vultures fattening on the corpses of the working people. If British capitalists win the war, they are preparing to carve up Germany among their allies and themselves. Already the *Evening News*, formerly an enthusiastic supporter of Hitler, when he was destroying the trade unions and other organisations of the working class, former enthusiastic backer of Mosley and British fascism, has hinted in its leader columns of this intention upon the part of the British ruling class. If Hitler wins he will impose his monstrous tyranny on the whole other sections [sic] of Europe and the colonies, as he has upon the Czech people. British workers and German workers have no reason to slaughter one another. Let us turn upon our real enemies, the German and British capitalist class. (*Youth for Socialism*, vol. 2 no. 1, September, 1939)

Lenin and revolutionary defeatism

To understand Ted Grant's position during the Second World War it is necessary to understand the real essence of Lenin's "revolutionary defeatism" during the First World War. There is perhaps no part of Lenin's writings that has been as distorted, misunderstood and misrepresented as his position on war. In 1914, he said that the defeat of Russia was the lesser evil, and called on the workers to turn the imperialist war into a civil war. Ever since then, there have been people who repeat these words and imagine themselves to be great Leninists, parading their intransigent "Bolshevism" like a little boy with a new pair of shoes.

It is necessary to understand the concrete conditions in which these works were written and who they were aimed at. Endless confusion has arisen from the fact that this has not been grasped by people who have read a few lines of Lenin without understanding Lenin's method. Why did he think it necessary to express himself in such extreme terms?

Ted explained that in 1914, Lenin was not writing for the masses. During the First World War, Lenin was completely isolated. The slogans he advanced at that time were not intended for the masses. *Lenin was writing for the cadres*. If we do not understand this, the most grotesque errors can result. Moreover, the way in which Lenin formulated the question of defeatism left a lot to be desired.

The betrayal of the leaders of the Second International signified the end of the Social Democracy as an instrument for the fight for socialism. It caused tremendous confusion, demoralisation and disorientation in the ranks of the Marxists everywhere, including Russia. Not for the first time, tended to exaggerate a formulation in the heat of a polemic, in order to hammer home a point that had not been grasped by his own supporters.

Lenin himself was at first taken aback by the overwhelming tide of national chauvinism which seemed to sweep all before it. Cut off from Russia, he was also worried by the possibility of vacillations among his own supporters on the question of war and the International. It was necessary to re-establish basic principles. The stakes were very high. What was involved was the fate not just of the Russian, but of the world revolution. For this reason, diplomacy and ambiguity was out of place. Lenin's wife Nadezhda Krupskaya explains:

> Ilych deliberately put the case very strongly in order to make it quite clear what line people were taking. The fight with the defencists was in full swing. The struggle was not an internal Party affair that concerned Russian matters alone. It was an international affair. (Krupskaya, *Reminiscences of Lenin*)

The idea that a military defeat of Tsarism would accelerate the process of revolution in Russia was obviously correct and was confirmed by events. But to go before the masses in Russia with the bald assertion that the revolutionaries were for the victory of the Kaiser would have been suicidal. As a matter of fact, it would have been defencism turned inside out, and would have laid them open to the accusation (used later by the Provisional government) that the Bolsheviks were German agents.

The change of regime from tsarist autocracy to a bourgeois democratic republic after the February Revolution in 1917 did not mean that the war on Russia's side was any less imperialist than before. But when he returned to Russia, Lenin said that he had found, as well as the usual social-chauvinist crowd, a wide layer of honest working class defencists in the soviets who had to learn by experience and argument the reactionary nature of the war. Here is what Lenin wrote in April 1917 in an article entitled: *Honest Defencism reveals itself*:

> Events in Petrograd during the last few days, especially yesterday, illustrate how right we were in speaking of the "honest" defencism of the mass as distinguished from the defencism of the leaders and parties.
>
> The mass of the population is made up of proletarians, semi-proletarians, and poor peasants. They are the vast majority of the nation. These classes are not at all interested in annexations. Imperialist policies, the profits of banking capital, incomes from railways in Persia, lucrative jobs in Galicia and Armenia, putting restraints on the freedom of Finland–all these are things in which these classes are not interested.
>
> But all these things taken together just go to make up what is known in science and the press as imperialist, annexationist, predatory policy. (Lenin, *Collected Works*, Volume 24, pp 204-206)

How Lenin spoke to the masses

With his unerring instinct for the psychology of the masses, Lenin was able to adapt his policy of revolutionary defeatism to changing conditions and present it in a way that ordinary Russian workers, soldiers and peasants could understand. To have merely repeated the old slogans would have been to cut off the Bolsheviks utterly from the working class. A new approach was needed, which reflected the difference between writing and speaking for small groups of party activists, and addressing the broad mass of workers recently awakened to political life.

Let us see how Lenin presented the question of war in 1917. In a speech to the Soviet, which was still overwhelmingly in favour of the Mensheviks and Social Revolutionaries at this stage, Lenin ruthlessly stripped away all the diplomatic verbiage to lay bare the class interests that lie beneath:

> The capitalists continue to plunder the people's property. The imperialist war continues. And yet we are promised reforms, reforms and more reforms, which cannot be accomplished at all under these circumstances, because the war crushes and determines everything.

However, having explained the imperialist nature of the war, Lenin goes on to explain that the Bolsheviks were not preparing to abandon the military fight against German imperialism:

> It is slander to say the revolutionary struggle for peace that has begun from below might lead to a separate peace treaty. The first step we should take if we had power would be to arrest the biggest capitalists and cut all the threads of their intrigues. Without this, all talk about peace without annexations and indemnities is utterly meaningless. Our second step would be to declare to all people over the head of their governments that we regard all capitalists as robbers—Tereshchenko, who is not a bit better than Milyukov, just a little less stupid, the French capitalists, the British capitalists, and all the rest.

Clearly impressed, almost in spite of themselves, the majority decided to give the speaker extra time, and Lenin continued his speech, exposing the imperialist nature of the war, but, again taking into account the "honest defencist" inclinations of his audience, explained revolutionary defeatism in a language which could get an echo from the workers and soldiers. We are not pacifists, he says. We are prepared to fight against the Kaiser, who is also our enemy. But we do not trust the capitalists. Get rid of the ten capitalist ministers! Let the soviet leaders take the power, and we will wage a revolutionary war against German imperialism, while fighting to extend the revolution to Germany and all the other belligerent powers. That is the only way to get peace:

> When we take power into our own hands, we shall curb the capitalists, and then the war will *not be the kind* of war that is being waged now, because the nature of a war is determined by what class wages it, not by what is written on paper. You can write on paper anything you like. But as long as the capitalist class has a majority in the government the war will remain an imperialist war no matter what you write, no matter how eloquent you are, no matter how many near-socialist ministers you have...
>
> The war remains an imperialist war, and however much you may desire peace, however sincere your sympathy for the working people and your desire for peace—I am fully convinced that by and large it must be sincere—you are powerless, because the war can only be ended by taking the revolution further. When the revolution began in Russia, a revolutionary struggle for peace from below also began. (...) And if circumstances then obliged us to wage a revolutionary war—no one knows, and we do not rule out the possibility—we should say: "We are not pacifists, we do not renounce war when the revolutionary class is in power and has actually deprived the capitalists of the opportunity to influence things in any way, to exacerbate the economic dislocation which enables them to make hundreds of millions." (...) The capitalists are in a situation where their only way out is war. When you take over revolutionary power, you will have a revolutionary way of securing peace, namely, by addressing a revolutionary appeal to all nations and explaining your tactics by your own example. (Lenin, *Collected Works, Speech to the First All-Russia Congress of Soviets*, vol. 25 pp. 21-23 and 26-27)

What is most striking here is the complete absence of Lenin's earlier formulations on "revolutionary defeatism". No reference to civil war. No call to the soldiers to turn their bayonets against their officers, and certainly no hint that the defeat of Russia would be the "lesser evil". This change reflects an important shift in Lenin's approach to tactics since February.

The question of defencism versus revolutionary defeatism, which he frequently presented in very black-and-white terms in the previous period, turned out to be not so simple. Of course, fundamentally, Lenin's position on the war had not changed. But the way in which revolutionary defeatism had to be presented was quite different. Here we have the real essence of Leninism, not the lifeless caricature that reduces Lenin's method to that of a priest mindlessly repeating the words of the Catechism without ever thinking about what they are supposed to mean.

The Proletarian Military Policy

> We can't oppose compulsory military training by the bourgeois state just as we can't oppose compulsory education by the bourgeois state. Military training in our eyes is a part of education. (Trotsky, *On Conscription*, 1940)

The most decisive question for revolutionaries is the attitude to war. The outbreak of war posed new problems for the Trotskyist movement. On the question of war, Trotsky had exactly the same dialectical method as Lenin. Before he was murdered in August 1940, he had worked out a transitional programme for the new situation that arose from the war. It had nothing in common with the abstract schemes of the ultra-lefts who presented a caricature of Lenin's policy of revolutionary defeatism.

Like Lenin in 1917, Trotsky set out from the concrete conditions of the American working class in 1940, which were not at all the same as in Russia in 1917. Of course, the imperialist

RCP demonstration, May Day, 1947

character of the war was the same in its essence. But the way in which it was perceived by the workers was different, and this had to be taken into account. As Trotsky explained:

> The present war, as we have stated more than once, is a continuation of the last war. But a continuation does not imply a repetition. As a general rule, a continuation implies a development, a deepening, a sharpening. Our policy, the policy of the revolutionary proletariat towards the second imperialist world war, is a continuation of the policy elaborated during the last imperialist war, primarily under the leadership of Lenin. But a continuation does not imply a repetition. In this case, too, a continuation means a development, a deepening and a sharpening. (Trotsky, *Writings, 1939-40*, p. 411)

Shortly before his death, he gave very concrete advice as to how the Trotskyists should approach tactics in the new conditions:

> If one proceeds only on the basis of the overall characterisation of the epoch, and nothing more, ignoring its concrete stages, one can easily lapse into schematism, sectarianism, or quixotic fantasy. With every serious turn of events we adjust our basic tasks to the changed concrete conditions of the given stage. Herein lies the art of tactics. (Trotsky, *On the Question of Workers' Self-defence*, in *Writings, 1939-40*, p. 103)

He went on to outline the Marxist approach to the war:

> Without in any way wavering from our programme we must speak to the masses in a language they understand. "We Bolsheviks also want to defend democracy, but not the kind that is run by sixty uncrowned kings. First let's sweep our democracy clean of capitalist magnates, then we will defend it to the last drop of blood. Are you, who are not Bolsheviks, really ready to defend this democracy? But you must, at least, be able to the best of your ability to defend it so as not to be a blind instrument in the hands of the Sixty Families and the bourgeois officers devoted to them. The working class must learn military affairs in order to advance the largest possible number of officers from its own ranks."
>
> "We must demand that the state, which tomorrow will ask for the workers' blood, today give the

workers the opportunity to master military technique in the best possible way in order to achieve the military objectives with the minimum expenditure of human lives."

"To accomplish that, a regular army and barracks by themselves are not enough. Workers must have the opportunity to get military training at their factories, plants, and mines at specified times, while being paid by the capitalists. If the workers are destined to give their lives, the bourgeois patriots can at least make a small material sacrifice."

"The state must issue a rifle to every worker capable of bearing arms and set up rifle and artillery ranges for military training purposes in places accessible to the workers."

Our agitation in connection with the war and all our politics connected with the war must be as uncompromising in relation to the pacifists as to the imperialists.

"This war is not our war. The responsibility for it lies squarely on the capitalists. But so long as we are still not strong enough to overthrow them and must fight in the ranks of their army, we are obliged to learn to use arms as well as possible!"

Women workers must also have the right to bear arms. The largest possible number of women workers must have the opportunity, at the capitalists' expense, to receive nurses' training.

Just as every worker, exploited by the capitalists, seeks to learn as well as possible the production techniques, so every proletarian soldier in the imperialist army must learn as well as possible, when the conditions change, to apply it in the interests of the working class.

We are not pacifists. No. We are revolutionaries. And we know what lies ahead for us. (*Ibid.*, pp. 104-5)

However, the Proletarian Military Policy was not accepted by many who called themselves Trotskyists. Mostly they took an ultra-left position that was a complete caricature of what Lenin had written in 1914. Since they never understood Lenin's position, how could they be expected to understand what Trotsky was saying?

We see the same thing repeated time and time again. We saw it on the issue of entrism, which many "Trotskyists" rejected "on principle" before the war. We saw it again on the war question. And we saw it on an even bigger scale after the war, when the leaders of the Fourth showed their complete inability to understand Trotsky's method and eventually abandoned Trotskyism altogether. As Rob Sewell points out:

> When Trotsky raised the proletarian military policy, it provoked widespread opposition within the ranks of the Fourth International. Many leaders, such as those of the Belgian and British (the RSL) sections, deliberately purged any references to this policy. The Belgian group, for example, struck out several paragraphs on this question from the clandestine version of the May 1940 Manifesto. There were also "reservations" held by the French section and even the European Secretariat of the Fourth International. As a consequence, their whole approach, rooted in a false appraisal of the real situation, completely failed to connect with the working class faced with the onslaught of Hitler fascism. Their tactics were stuck in the past and tainted with pacifism. As a result, they were confined to the fringes. Even the American SWP, which had adopted the military policy under Trotsky's pressure, interpreted the policy in a passive fashion, reducing it to mere propaganda divorced from any perspective for workers' power. (Introduction to Ted Grant's *Writings*, Vol. 1, p. 24)

The confusion of the leaders of the Fourth was evident from the conduct of Pierre Frank, who was in exile in Britain at the start of the war. In 1940, he was calling on the British workers to occupy the factories. At that time, with Hitler's troops poised to invade, the workers were voluntarily working long hours in the factories to produce arms to defend the country. This detail showed just how out of touch these "leaders" were from the real world of the working class. This condemned them to isolation and impotence in the face of the war.

The RSL had a completely ultra-left position on the war. Masquerading under the banner of Lenin's revolutionary defeatism, they advanced the idea "the victory of Hitler is the lesser evil." Ted said: "they were very rrrrevolutionary—in the bedroom!" Of course, they would never have dared to say things like that in the factories or union branches. One of them did raise this nonsense in his Labour Party branch—and was surprised when he was expelled!

The mistake of the RSL has been repeated a thousand times since by all the ultra-lefts who imagine that they are great Leninists because they have read a few lines of Lenin that they have not understood. All these people repeat like automata isolated phrases of Lenin and Trotsky, which, torn out of their historical context, become utterly meaningless.

The WIL/RCP in the war

The Workers' International League (WIL), and later, the RCP, developed Trotsky's Proletarian Military Revolutionary Policy and applied it brilliantly to the concrete situation in Britain. Ted told me: "When we first read about Trotsky's Proletarian Military Revolutionary Policy we were very pleased, because we had worked out the same position as the Old Man independently."

It is only fair to point out that initially, even some of the leading comrades in the WIL had doubts about Trotsky's line on the war. But Ted embraced it wholeheartedly. In February 1941, two articles by the EC majority published by the *Socialist Appeal* and the *Workers' International News* sparked an internal debate. Jock Haston, Millie Lee and Sam Levy were on one side, and Ted Grant, Harold Atkinson, Andy Paton and Gerry Healy were on the other. Jimmy Deane also supported Ted's position on the war.[4] Later Ted recalled:

> We had the position of Trotsky and the American SWP. In fact, the Americans actually produced some of the articles from the *Appeal* in their paper. (...) The material we put into the paper at that time (...) was very good. Haston objected. At that time he had an ultra-left position. Like all ultra-lefts, he ended up as an opportunist. (...) Although it is true that Healy was on our side, he tried to turn it into a monstrous, personal, factional thing. But we stopped that: Atkinson, myself and Andy Paton. (Sam Bornstein, *Interview with Ted Grant*)

Full agreement within the WIL was eventually achieved through democratic discussion and the development of events themselves. In the meantime, the Fourth International's official section (RSL) was putting forward a completely incorrect position. In 1943, Ted wrote a brilliant reply to the RSL, where we read the following:

> War is part of the life of society at the present time and our programme of the conquest of power has to be based, not on peace, but on the conditions of universal militarism and war. We may commiserate with the comrades of the RSL on this unfortunate deviation of history. But alas we were too weak to overthrow imperialism and must now pay the price. It was necessary (and, of course, it is still necessary) to educate the cadres of the Fourth International of the nature and meaning of social patriotism and Stalino-chauvinism and its relation towards the war. Who in Britain in the left wing has done this as vigorously as WIL? But we must go further. The *Transitional Programme*, if it has any meaning at all, is a bridge not only from the consciousness of the masses today to the road of the socialist revolution, but also for the isolated revolutionaries to the masses.

> The RSL convinces itself of the superiority of its position over that of Stalinism and reformism. It

---

[4] See Ted Grant's Writings, Vol. 1 for all documents of this dispute.

SOLDIERS HOME AND ABROAD ANSWER BEVIN

WHAT THE SOLDIERS THINK OF ERNEST BEVIN'S REGULATION 1AA AND THE PROPAGANDA OF THE CAPITALISTS THAT THE STRIKERS WERE STABBING THE BOYS IN THE BACK, CAN BE SEEN FROM THE PAPER OF THE 8TH ARMY OF WHICH A FACSIMILE IS REPRODUCED BELOW.

Sergeant Lawson failed to get a resolution passed by the soldiers of the 8th Army condemning strikes in war time.

A further indication of the mood of the workers is uniform can be seen from a petition sent to the Home Secretary signed by 82 soldiers in the R.E.s. The petition reads as follows:

"The undersigned members of the Armed Forces protest to the Home Secretary, Mr. Herbert Morrison, against the arrest of Roy Tearse, Heatum Lee and Ann Keen.

They are detained under the Trade Disputes Act of 1927. This Act was instituted in revenge for the General Strike by the Conservative Government of the time. The Labour Movement has always condemned the Act as hostile to the working class.

Tearse and his comrades are accused of fomenting the strike amongst the apprentices and the coal miners. We do not believe that this is true. That they gave guidance and advice to the miners and apprentices is to their credit, for that is the job of all faithful workers' leaders.

We believe that the real reason that they are under arrest is because they offered the only solution to the coal crisis, i.e., nationalisation. The real and chief culprit in the strikes is the Government, who prefer to leave this basic industry in the hands of a few exploiters. The Government's solution lay in intensifying this exploitation on the one hand, and drafting unwilling apprentices down the pits on the other.

We soldiers are also workers. We do not want to come back to a life where living conditions have been driven down to intolerable levels. We consider the miners' fight as a struggle to maintain these rights. We condemn all talk of the miners (as well as

(Continued on page 2)

SOLDIERS' PETITION SENT TO HOME SECRETARY

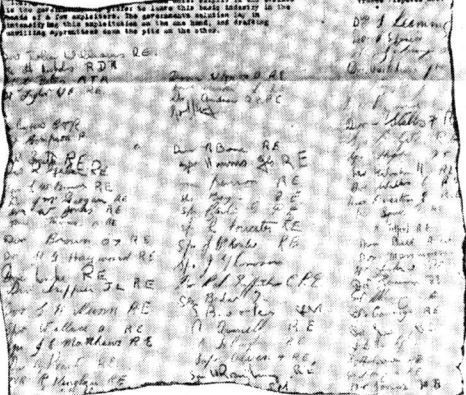

MORE TRAINS FOR MILITARY P[

But this excuse does not hold water, since many other organisations are holding their Conferences as usual.

It is obvious that the leadership of the Labour Party has eagerly seized this pretext as a way out of a situation which even at best would be embarrassing and painful to them.

The opening of the Second Front would give added importance to a Conference of the representatives of the working class to discuss the issues whereby the fate of Europe is being decided. But the leaders are content to leave the fate of the workers in the hands of the capitalist class without giving the rank and file the opportunity to voice its opinions.

The real truth of the matter is that the leadership has seized the opportunity to avoid facing the rank and file delegates at this juncture. Throughout the country, in the unions and

---

EIGHTH ARMY NEWS

EIGHTH ARMY MEN SAY TO WORKERS:

"Right to Strike is Part of the Freedom we Fight for"

THE Welsh coal strike has raised in many minds the question, "Should strikes be allowed in war-time?" Here is the answer of Eighth Army men who have just debated the subject.

"STRIKES ARE HARMFUL TO OUR NATIONAL INTERESTS ABROAD, FOR THEY CREATE THE IMPRESSION OF NATIONAL DISUNITY AND DIVERSION FROM THE MAIN PURPOSE OF OUR WAR EFFORT. THEY MAKE RUSSIA SUSPICIOUS OF OUR SINCERITY AND GIVE GERMANY MATERIAL FOR INJURIOUS PROPAGANDA IN OCCUPIED AND NEUTRAL COUNTRIES."

One of the most telling arguments in a strong indictment of strikes in war time, this statement of Sgt. J. Lincoln FAILED to gain sufficient Eighth Army Signals' support to carry his proposal that strikes in war-time should be declared illegal.

Eight Army News article reproduced in Socialist Appeal, May 1944

comforts itself that it maintains the position of Lenin in the last war. This would be very good... if the RSL had understood the position of Lenin. However, for Trotsky and the inheritors of Bolshevism, we start (even if the RSL correctly interpreted Lenin, which it does not) where the RSL leadership finishes! We approach the problem of war from the angle of the imminence of the next period of the social revolution in Britain as well as other countries. The workers in Britain, as in America, [quoting Trotsky] "do not want to be conquered by Hitler, and to those who say, 'let us have a peace programme' the workers will reply: 'but Hitler does not want a peace programme'. Therefore we say, we will defend the United States [or Britain] with a workers' army with workers' officers, and with a workers' government, etc.".

Those words of the Old Man are saturated through and through with the spirit of revolutionary Marxism, which, while uncompromisingly preserving its opposition towards the bourgeoisie, shows sympathy and understanding for the attitude of the rank and file worker and the problems which are running through his mind. No longer do we stop at the necessity to educate the vanguard as to the nature of the war and the refusal to defend the capitalist fatherland, but we go forward to win the working class for the conquest of power and the defence of the proletarian fatherland. (Ted Grant, *Reply of WIL to the RSL criticism of "Preparing for Power"*, Writings, Vol. 2, pp. 375-6)

Frank Ward (left) in uniform

These words convey very well the essence of Trotsky's proletarian military policy. Marxists do not have one policy for peace, and another, totally different policy for war. Long ago, Clausewitz explained that war is only the continuation of politics by other means. Instead of adopting the impotent attitudes of pacifism, the Marxists must develop a revolutionary proletarian policy in war, which is a continuation of the revolutionary class politics we pursue in "normal" times.

While denouncing the imperialist character of the war, and demanding that the Labour leaders break with the bourgeoisie, it was necessary to explain our programme in language the workers could understand and accept. Instead of opposing conscription, it was necessary to propose transitional demands to the effect that the workers should exercise control over military training, which should be closely linked to the factories and the trade unions, the election of officers, full rights for soldiers, etc.

Following Trotsky's advice, the WIL and then the RCP did outstanding work in the armed forces. In Ted's case, however, military service did not last very long. Having been called up for the Pioneer Corps in 1940, he almost immediately had a traffic accident that resulted in a fractured skull. He was invalided out of the army and spent the rest of the war pursuing revolutionary activity.

The case of Frank Ward was rather more typical of party policy. I knew Frank in Swansea when I was in the Young Socialists, and he explained to me how he succeeded in winning over

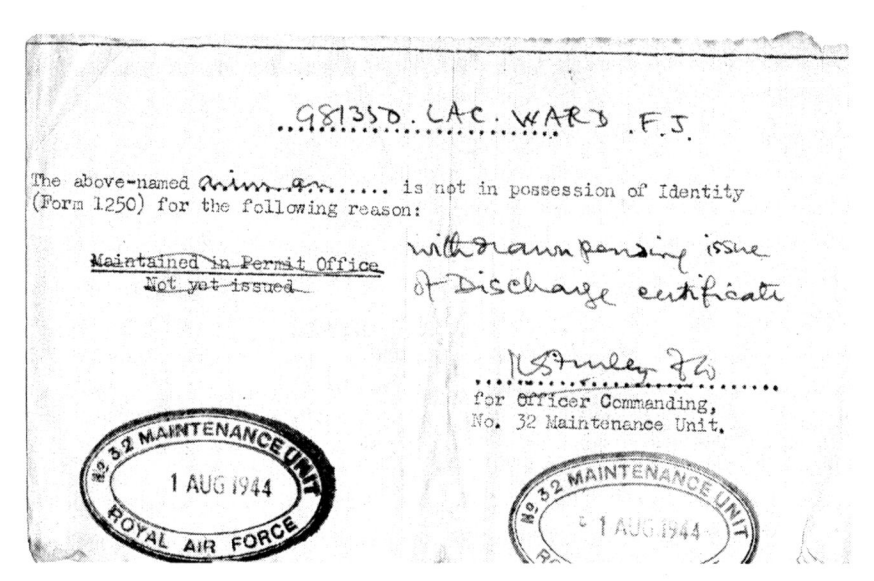

Papers announcing Frank Ward's discharge

all his comrades-in-arms when he was in the air force. So successful was he, that in order to remove him, he was honourably discharged from the RAF, and spent the rest of the war trying to get back in. All issues of *Socialist Appeal* carried letters and articles by soldiers. Andy Paton, a WIL Executive Committee member, wrote regular reports under his pen name Andrew Scott for *Socialist Appeal* while in the army.

In their eagerness to persuade people that this was a "war for democracy", the British ruling class had to make some concessions. One of these was to allow a measure of political debate inside the armed forces. The chairman of the "forces parliament" in Egypt was a Trotskyist elected by the soldiers of the Eighth Army. In February 1944, over 600 attended a session which voted to nationalise the banks, build four million houses, and nationalise land, mines and transport.

"Our Eighth Army"

In his lead-off at the 1943 WIL congress, published in *Workers' International News*, January 1944, Ted said: "The ruling class says it is their Eighth Army, but in fact it is *our* Eighth Army". Ted's passing remark about "our" Eighth Army was intended as a comment on the growing influence of the Trotskyists in the army.

A few months later, in March 1944, the fusion congress of the WIL with what was left of the RSL gave birth to the Revolutionary Communist Party (RCP). Ted and the other leaders of the RCP were shocked and surprised when they found out that these words were torn out of context and inserted for factional reasons by the IS representative (Sam Gordon, known in the party as Stuart) in his report of the RCP founding congress, circulated to all members of the US SWP. The report was presented in such a way as to distort the real proportions of the different groups involved in the fusion, which were an embarrassment to Cannon. It would have revealed to SWP members that the vilified WIL comprised the vast majority of delegates attending the congress. Furthermore, Gordon insinuated that some of the leaders of the unified party were displaying defencist and chauvinistic tendencies, or a "deviation of national colouring", in Stuart's words, echoing the factional accusations thrown at the WIL by the old RSL.

Stuart could not have heard these words at the RCP congress, because Ted Grant's speech had been given at a previous congress of the WIL, several months earlier.

That Stuart was the source of these distortions was not a surprise to the comrades. They had become well acquainted with his methods during the long and frustrating preparation for fusion. Already, Stuart's manoeuvres had elicited a collective protest to the IS on behalf of the WIL leadership in September 1943.[5]

The real question was the following: how was it possible that a completely dishonest report, written by a biased source, was published and distributed by Cannon and the leadership of the SWP, without even checking the contents of the report with the RCP leaders themselves? They could have easily answered Stuart's accusations in detail, and thus, a serious incident could have been avoided. But that was not the method of Cannon and co., as Ted and his comrades were to discover in the future.

A sharp reply to Stuart's "report" by the RCP was issued in January 1945, in the form of an *Open letter to SWP members*. Among other things, Stuart's report stated:

> In defence of the resolution on military policy, a leader of the majority in the new CC made some remarks that called forth astonishment and protest, particularly among those in agreement with the resolution, which is by and large a correct statement of the international policy. Characteristic of these remarks was a reference to Montgomery's Eighth Army as "*our* Eighth Army". The protests only brought reiteration from the speaker with a stronger emphasis than before: he spoke *with pride* of "*our* Eighth Army".

The RCP leaders expressed their sense of outrage:

> To tear a phrase out of its context for the purpose of demonstrating a "deviation", is nothing short of a scandal in the ranks of the Fourth International. And that such stuff should be circulated by the PC [Political Committee] of the SWP without a check is not easy to understand.
>
> This "scene" is supposed to have taken place at the fusion conference. This is false. The incident, distorted above, took place at the WIL conference in 1943, during a discussion not on military policy, but on European and British perspectives. The resolution to which comrade Grant was speaking is published in a pamphlet, *The world revolution and the tasks of the British working class*, drafted by him and accepted as a basic document by the fusion conference.

They continued:

> This speech was edited for publication, and several illustrations of minor mutinies and struggles among the ranks of the forces which led to this statement, were omitted because of government censorship.
>
> The background to this speech can be seen when one takes into consideration that the Tories received 14 seats out of 600 in the elections to the mock Forces' Parliament in Cairo, Labour received the overwhelming votes of the soldiers, Commonwealth[6] next, and then the Stalinists. So great was the

---

5   See, Reply to comrades Cooper and Stuart, in Ted Grant, *Writings*, Vol. 2, pp. 396-412.
6   Commonwealth was founded in July 1942, by the alliance of two left wing groups, the 1941 Committee – a think tank brought together by writers J.B. Priestley and Tom Wintringham – and the neo-Christian Forward March movement led by Liberal MP Richard Acland, along with independents and former Liberals.

radicalisation that the authorities dissolved this "Parliament". A Trotskyist was elected Prime Minister of the Benghazi "Forces' Parliament" which was also disbanded.

Another indication of the radicalisation of the Eighth Army: during the tremendous campaign which accompanied the arrests of our party members for "inciting to strike", the *Eighth Army News* published a full page article under the headline: "The right to strike is one of the freedoms for which we fight".

One would have imagined that the revolutionary content of this speech was clear. (*Open Letter to SWP members*, in Ted Grant, *Writings* Vol. 2, pp. 460-77)

The same "intransigent Leninists" had earlier complained that the WIL was "defencist" because it put forward the transitional demand for deep air-raid shelters in which the workers could find refuge from German bombers. Evidently it was the internationalist duty of the workers of Britain to display a stoic calm while the German workers in uniform rained fraternal bombs on them and their families from on high. A highly original interpretation of proletarian fraternisation!

It is not even worth mentioning the clownish antics of the RSL. It is self-evident that during the war, the WIL was *de facto* the only voice defending the policies of the Fourth International in Britain. The reason for this was that the "official" section, the RSL, proved to be completely incapable of building. Like so many groups that claimed the mantle of Trotsky, they had an entirely abstract conception of Trotsky's ideas and were unable to put them into practice or to find a road to the workers.

The Revolutionary Socialist League was a complete flop. Its ultra-left position on the war condemned it to utter sterility. As a result, it stagnated within the Labour Party, and in the end, the International lost patience with its "British section". By contrast, the growth of the WIL convinced them that the time had come to change their bets. Cannon had to beat a retreat.

However, even now the WIL was not recognised as the official section. Instead, the International Secretariat pressed for a fusion. The only way Ted and his comrades could get into the Fourth was to spend a lot of time and energy in painful negotiations for a principled fusion. This was because of the dominant position the WIL achieved in the British Trotskyist movement and the parallel disintegration of the RSL. This eventually led to a fusion congress which gave birth to the Revolutionary Communist Party, British section of the Fourth International.

(...) The point is the Americans wanted to save face. The RSL was split into three. (...) And what happened is that they insisted we should unify with them, and we unified on our terms. In order to get some sort of face-saver they unified their three groups a week before, and unified with us a week after. (Sam Bornstein, *Interview with Ted Grant*)

Later, Ted recognised that the RSL had been badly treated by Cannon and the leaders of the Fourth, but he also recognized that they were a completely sectarian and petty-bourgeois outfit. "They were real Bohemians," he said, unable to suppress his laughter. "Some of them even went around dressed in cloaks and sandals. That was really something in those days!"

Ted Grant's role

The RCP in its heyday attracted the best kind of proletarian elements, which made up over 90 percent of its ranks. Ted was always very proud of the work done by the WIL and the RCP, of which he often spoke with enthusiasm. During the war and afterwards, he was effectively the political leader of the WIL, and later the RCP. He was political secretary of the WIL and the editor of *Socialist Appeal*. Even after Haston was elected political secretary of the RCP, Ted continued writing most of the important political documents and statements.

Of course, there were other outstanding comrades, especially Jock Haston. Once Lee went back to South Africa, the collaboration between Ted and Haston was the very foundation for the successes and the development of the WIL and the RCP, and it was also one of the main reasons why Ted tried so tenaciously to save Haston later on.

Jock Haston was a brilliant organiser, a dynamic man and a charismatic leader. Ted remembered him as "a very friendly bloke, a good builder of the Tendency. Haston was one of the main builders of the RCP, there is no doubt about that". There were many other talented people: Jimmy Deane, Harold Atkinson, Heaton Lee, Roy Tearse, Millie Lee, Andy Paton and many others. But in the theoretical field, there was only one outstanding figure, and that was Ted Grant.

In the 1980s, Sam Bornstein and Al Richardson wrote a book about British Trotskyism called *War and the International* (published in 1986). This book has serious faults. In particular, the authors systematically play down Ted's leading role, while exaggerating the role of all kinds of secondary and minor figures and groups.

This is no accident. As is usual with people who have left the movement and dedicate themselves to commenting from the sidelines, Bornstein had an axe to grind. It is always the same story. It was the same story in Marx's day, when the forgotten men, the "Men of Exile"—Schapper, Willich, Vogt and so many others—were constantly trying to belittle Marx's role. In this way, the small men try to boost their own petty contributions. But one can never really raise one's own prestige by undermining others. Reading this kind of thing always brings to one's mind the celebrated verses of Jonathan Swift:

> So nat'ralists observe, a flea
> Hath smaller fleas that on him prey;
> And these have smaller fleas to bite 'em.
> And so proceeds Ad infinitum. (Swift, *Poetry, a Rhapsody*.)

In preparing the present book, I read both *War and the International* and also some unpublished material the authors wrote in preparation for it. What is interesting is not what they put in, but what they left out. Among the material that is largely omitted or ignored is the contents of an interview with Ted Grant dated 22 August, 1982. In this interview, Sam Bornstein tried (unsuccessfully) to push Ted into a corner on the question of his role in the leadership of the WIL and RCP. He asked:

> Then who would you say were the theoreticians in the movement? You dealt with all the organisers.
>
> Ted: Well, apart from myself, we didn't have any. That is the truth of the matter. Who did we have?
>
> Sam: I'm not arguing, I only want your point of view.
>
> Ted: Well, we didn't have any. That is the truth of the matter. We had good writers, good speakers, good organisers, and in any case you didn't need so many theoreticians. (Sam Bornstein, *Interview with Ted Grant*)

Bornstein pretended to have a very scientific and objective approach to history. But long experience has taught me to distrust such pretended objectivity. Every author approaches history with some bias or other, and it is far better to declare one's interest in advance, rather than try to hoodwink the reader into accepting a spurious objectivity when what they have before them is a clearly biased account. As Hegel once said, the facts do not select themselves. In reality, Bornstein selected the facts in such a way as to seriously distort the truth, and ignore or belittle Ted's role.

What we have here is a misguided attempt to establish a kind of "historical fair play", whereby each and every individual is posthumously awarded a medal for his or her part in the revolutionary movement, no matter how insignificant that role happened to be. But this in itself represents a most serious distortion of the facts. It is like those old paintings from the period before the science of perspective was introduced into art, in which all objects are depicted as if they were of the same height and dimensions, whether they are one metre away from the observer or twenty kilometres, a castle or a hut, a giant or a baby, a mountain or a molehill, an elephant or a gnat.

When the late Spike Milligan, one of Britain's most noted comedians, wrote his autobiography, he entitled it *Adolph Hitler, My Part in His Downfall*. The second volume was entitled *Monty—My Part in His Victory*. The Monty in the title refers to Field Marshal Bernard Montgomery, who led the British army in the Battle of El Alamein in North Africa. Since Mr Milligan's role was that of a private soldier in the British army, I doubt whether either Hitler or "Monty" had ever heard of him. He laughs while shouting: "I was there too, you know!" But this, of course, was an intentional part of the joke.

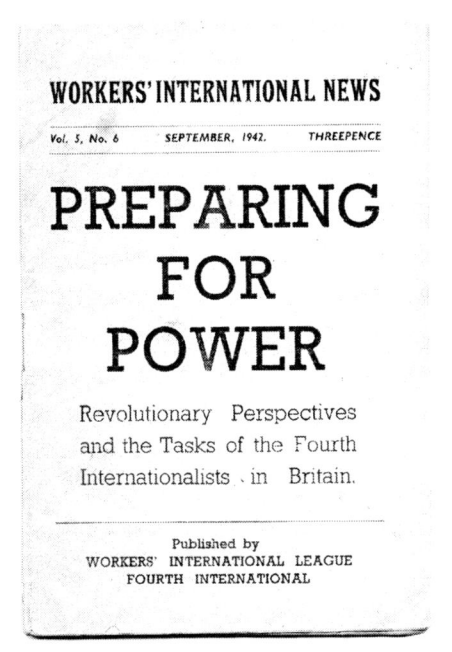

Unfortunately, the same cannot be said of those who, having played a minor or even insignificant role in the prehistory of the Trotskyist movement, are constantly tugging at the shirt sleeves of history, shouting: "I was there too, you know!" Spike Milligan was always ready to laugh at himself and that was part of his charm. But retired Trotskyists all take themselves terribly seriously. Their attempts at "historical objectivity" consist in boosting their own petty role and reducing everyone else to the same Lilliputian level. When Spike Milligan does the same thing it is very funny. When people who have neither a sense of proportion nor of humour follow his example, it is merely ridiculous.

I once had an interesting discussion with Ted about the theoreticians in the Bolshevik Party, he said:

> If we look at the Bolshevik Party, who was there apart from Lenin and Trotsky? Bukharin perhaps. He wrote some interesting books: *Historical Materialism, Imperialism,* and *The ABC of Communism*. They are worth reading. But when you read them, you can see what Lenin was driving at when he wrote in his *Testament* that Bukharin had never properly understood dialectics.

As a political tendency Bukharinism has long since disappeared. Ted pointed out that in the early 1930s, the supporters of the Right Opposition were much stronger than us:

WORKERS' INTERNATIONAL NEWS

Vol. 5, No. 6   SEPTEMBER, 1942.   THREEPENCE

PREPARING FOR POWER

Revolutionary Perspectives and the Tasks of the Fourth Internationalists in Britain.

Published by
WORKERS' INTERNATIONAL LEAGUE
FOURTH INTERNATIONAL

The Bukharinites had a strong base in several countries, including the USA (the Lovestone group) and Germany (the Brandlerites). They were much bigger than us. But where are they today? They have been completely liquidated by history. As for Zinoviev and Kamenev, who reads their books nowadays?

In saying that there were only two great theoreticians in the Bolshevik Party, does that imply that there were no other leading figures in the party? It does not. People have different capabilities, and the revolutionary party would be unthinkable without a whole series of different individuals whose personal qualities enable them to play different roles. Zinoviev was a talented agitator, but the agitator's art, depending as it does on the spoken word, dies with the man. Kamenev was an able propagandist; Sverdlov a brilliant agitator. All of them played an important role, yet none of them can be considered a theoretician. Trotsky made the same point on more than one occasion:

> Moreover, one makes the revolution with relatively few Marxists, even within the party. Here the collective substitutes for what the individual cannot achieve. The individual can hardly master each separate area—it is necessary to have experts who supplement one another. Such experts are often quite passive "Marxists" without being complete Marxists, because they work under the control of genuine Marxists. The whole Bolshevik Party is a marvelous example of this. Under Lenin's and Trotsky's supervision, Bukharin, Molotov, Tomsky, and a hundred others were good Marxists, capable of great accomplishments. As soon as this supervision was gone, even they collapsed disgracefully. This was not because Marxism is a secret science, it is just very difficult to escape the colossal pressures of the bourgeois environment with all its influences. (Trotsky, *Writings*, Supplement 1934-40, pp. 592-3)

In my own case, I have no problem in nailing my colours firmly to the mast. I have always been a follower of Ted Grant, who I regard as the man who defended and developed the ideas of Trotsky after the Old Man was murdered. I do not see anyone else who has any genuine claim to this role, least of all in Britain. That there were many other admirable comrades who made great sacrifices to build the movement there can be no doubt. But Ted was quite justified when he challenged Sam Bornstein to name another theoretician in the leadership of the WIL or RCP.

I note that Bornstein was unable to reply. This silence speaks volumes. Let us speak for him. The undeniable fact is that Ted Grant wrote all the main documents of the WIL and the RCP, and a great many of the editorials and theoretical articles in the journals. The publications of this period, including *Youth for Socialism*, *Workers' International News* and *Socialist Appeal*, contain a wealth of valuable political material that is well worth reading today.

The Stalinists and the war

At the start of the war, blindly following the Moscow Line after the Hitler-Stalin Pact, the British CP was pursuing an ultra-left policy, a caricature of Lenin's policy of revolutionary defeatism, demanding, in effect, peace on Hitler's terms. Ignoring the concrete conditions, they fomented strikes at the slightest pretext, at a time when the British workers were working round-the-clock for the war effort.

However, the abandonment of the policy of popular frontism, and the adoption of an ultra-left policy in the first days of the war did not shake the confidence of the working class Communists, though many middle-class fellow-travellers immediately jumped ship. What really caused dismay in the ranks was the next change of line. When, in the summer of 1941, Hitler cynically broke his pact with Stalin and attacked the Soviet Union, Moscow required a totally different policy.

In their bid to secure the "Second Front" to help the Soviet Union, the CP leaders became the most fervent supporters of Churchill and the government on the shop floor. Overnight, without any explanation, the imperialist war became a "progressive war against fascism". At the drop of a hat, the Party performed a 180 degree somersault, and called a halt to all strikes. Instead, they now demanded the workers step up war production.

The CP had convened an industrial conference to discuss the development of the strike movement, which they hastily transformed into a conference to discuss how to increase productivity! Naturally, this sudden change of line provoked sharp differences in their ranks. This was too much for many Communist workers to swallow. How could such a policy be justified? What did it all mean? The only people who gave explanations were the Trotskyists of the WIL and later the Revolutionary Communist Party.

While consistently calling for the defence of the USSR, the WIL advocated a policy of class independence, calling on the Labour Party to break the coalition with the Tories and Liberals and take power on the basis of a socialist policy of nationalising the banks and monopolies under workers' control and management.

The Stalinists were particularly rabid in their hostility to strikes, denouncing the Trotskyists and worker militants as "agents of Hitler", allegedly betraying "our" soldiers. However, the soldiers did not share this view. A petition signed by 82 soldiers was sent to Labour leader Ernest Bevin in protest against the 1AA regulation that was used to arrest four leading RCP members—Jock Haston, Ann Keen, Heaton Lee and Roy Tearse. Bevin was responsible for the introduction of this anti-strike regulation as Minister of Labour in the wartime government. The petition was in reply to the attack the state waged against the RCP during the apprentices' strike, and was published by the *Eighth Army News,* and republished by the *Socialist Appeal* in May 1944.

Unfortunately for the Stalinists, the mood among sections of the working class was starting to swing towards a rising militancy. All the traditional strongholds the CP had within the working class were affected sooner or later by this mood (especially in the mining areas), and the WIL propaganda began to get an echo among them. Unrest in the coal fields intensified during the summer of 1942. At a time when the Stalinists were acting as the worst strike breakers, the WIL and then the RCP were attracting a layer of militant workers and trade unionists, organised around the Militant Workers' Federation, and led some important strikes. The *Socialist Appeal* was avidly read by militant workers throughout the country, many of whom regarded themselves as communists.

A vociferous campaign was launched by the right-wing Tories through the mouthpiece of the coal owners, the *Daily Telegraph,* and the former pro-Nazi *Daily Mail.* The campaign was joined by the Communist Party of Great Britain. The Stalinists were hysterical. They even called on Herbert Morrison, the Home Minister (and Labour Party member) to suppress the *Socialist Appeal*—which he refused to do. Incidentally, Morrison was responsible in January 1941 for enforcing the 18-months long ban on the *Daily Worker* (the CPGB's main paper), a ban the WIL publicly opposed. During their ultra-left Third Period, the Stalinists had hounded Morrison mercilessly, so it is quite possible that by acting in this way, he was quietly taking revenge on them.

The CP leaders had identified the threat posed by the WIL, and had earlier published a pamphlet called *Clear out Hitler's Agents*, penned by William Wainwright, and mainly aimed at labelling the ILP and the WIL as Hitler's agents. The pamphlet urged workers to treat a Trotskyist "as you would treat an open Nazi" and to "clear them out of every working class organisation and position". But these attempts at slandering the Trotskyists backfired against the Stalinists.

The WIL's reply was a 4-page leaflet called *Factory Workers: Be on your Guard: Clear out Bosses' Agents*. A lead article in the *Socialist Appeal* signed by Ted exposed mercilessly the lies the campaign was based on and ran a witty challenge:

> £10 Reward
>
> To any member of the Communist Party who can prove that the so-called quotations from Trotskyist publication in their pamphlet *Clear Out Hitler's Agents* are not forgeries.
>
> – Or –
>
> To any member of the CP who can show one page of this pamphlet which does not contain a minimum of five lies. (Ted Grant, *New Allies of the Communist Party*, Socialist Appeal, September 1942)

The challenge was also reproduced on leaflets and widely publicised in many work places. Ten pounds was a lot of money in those days. The workers' curiosity was aroused. With their characteristic sense of humour, they besieged the Stalinists, challenging them to collect the £10! Needless to say, they never did.

The apprentices' strike

The most outstanding action of the new-born RCP was its participation in the Tyneside Apprentices' strike in the spring of 1944. This was a very significant event, because it took place during the war, when all the Labour and trade union leaders were opposed to any strike action. Leading members of the Newcastle RCP, most notably Heaton Lee, Jack Rawlings and Ann Keen, intervened in the strike from the word go, and recruited the apprentices' leader, Bill Davy. Roy Tearse, the Party's industrial organizer, got involved and made a big impact on the strike.

The government and the Special Branch were quickly drawn in to take action against these "subversives". They soon raided the RCP headquarters in London and branches, and then arrested Heaton, Ann, Roy, and later Jock Haston, who was the general secretary at that time. They were charged with evading the provisions of the Trades Dispute Acts of 1927, brought in after the defeat of the General Strike of 1926, and in particular with breaking the even harsher anti-strike regulation 1AA introduced by Labour minister Ernest Bevin.

Very quickly, the RCP organized a broad Anti-Labour Laws' Victims Defence Committee, which involved Labour left MPs such as Nye Bevan, Sydney Silverman, S.O. Davies, W. G. Groves, and the main leaders of the Independent Labour Party such as John McGovern, James Maxton, Walter Padley and Fenner Brockway. Ted was also on the committee for the RCP as editor of *Socialist Appeal*. They waged a marvellous campaign, with help from trade unions and Labour Parties, agitating throughout the labour movement. And as we have seen, they also got an echo in the armed forces, with the petition signed by soldiers that was sent to Bevin in protest against the arrest of the "Four".

The leaders of the strike and the RCP were put on trial. Our comrade Bill Landles, then a young apprentice, was called as a defence witness. The comrades received jail sentences of

THE WAR YEARS | 67

The Communist Party launched a vociferous campaign against the Trotskyists, accusing them of being Hitler's agents and calling on workers to treat them as fascists. The two pamphlets on the left are examples of this campaign against the WIL.

clear out Hitler's agents!

An exposure of Trotskyist disruption being organised in Britain

By W. Wainwright

2D

A MEETING

called by the "Socialist Appeal"

To Expose the Attacks of the "Sunday Dispatch" & Communist Party

HOLBORN HALL

Sunday, Dec. 21st, at 6.30

Speakers: E. GRANT, Editorial Board "Socialist Appeal"
S. BIDWELL, Assist. Sec. London D.C., N.U.R.
A. ROY, A.E.U.
RACHEL RYAN, Engineering Shop Steward
G. HEALY in the Chair. QUESTIONS AND DISCUSSION

Auspices: Workers' International League (Fourth International)

Printed and Published by E. Grant, 61 Northdown Street, N.

Hitler's agents exposed!

By JOHN MAHON

THREEPENCE

Factory Workers

BE ON YOUR GUARD

Clear Out the Bosses' Agents!!

UNDER the guise of a struggle against "Trotskyism" the leadership of the so-called "Communist" Party have instructed their members in the factories to launch a campaign of lies and slander against leading shop stewards and prominent trade unionists.

THE object of this campaign is twofold:
1. It seeks to undermine the strong rank and file trade union movement which has been built up in the factories during the last few years.
2. It is the "all clear" signal to reactionary employers to victimise and frame-up active trade unionists.

You must know the Truth

"COMMUNIST" Party Policy today fully supports the handful of profiteers who run this war in their own interests. Those who carry out THAT policy in the factories are doing the bosses' dirty work. They are BOSSES' MEN who must be exposed and cleared out.

WHEN our brothers in the mining industry were on strike for better conditions against the tight-fisted tyranny of the coal-owners it was the "Communist" Party which urged its members to blackleg and scab.

The WIL conducted a counter-offensive against the attacks, explaining that the Stalinists were behaving as agents of the bosses, in an attempt to split the workers.

between six months and a year. They appealed, and with Haston's knowledge of the law, managed to get the verdicts squashed. The party had managed to win not only Bill Davy, but also a group of apprentices. This victory set the scene for the battles ahead.

The successes of the RCP attracted the attention of Britain's intelligence service, MI5, which attempted to infiltrate the party. The seriousness with which the authorities took the work of the organization is shown from the MI5 report, which was made public a few years ago, and published in Ted Grant's *History of British Trotskyism*.

Ted remembers there was one agent, I think he was called Inspector Jones, who applied for membership. He humorously said: "We were suspicious of him from the start: we thought he must be a cop because of the size of his feet." So they played several tricks on him. They gave him a hard probationary period involving paying a lot of money "to prove he was serious". With this money they were able to print Trotsky's *Transitional Programme*.

As a member, Jones showed an unusual interest in acquiring a copy of each and every paper, document and leaflet the Party produced. So as a joke they deliberately "skipped" an issue of the paper by printing the wrong number. The poor man nearly went mad asking everyone where he could get the "missing number". Probably he thought it contained the plans for the insurrection!

Later, the RCP's headquarters was raided by the police. Ted says they had some guns hidden, in case they ever needed them in the future, but the police never found them, which was just as well. When I asked him where they were hidden, he replied: "Up the chimney!" When the comrades were pulled in for questioning, they recognised this same Inspector Jones at the police station, and he (rather naively) asked them to keep quiet about his identity. When they were asked where they got the money from to publish the *Transitional Programme* they said: "Ask Inspector Jones!"

The four arrested: Jock Haston, Ann Keen, Heaton Lee and Roy Tearse

Several years later, Jock Haston took out all the guns which had been stored in his flat after the dissolution of the RCP and put them into a big sack. Not knowing exactly what to do with them, he called Scotland Yard and arranged for them to be quietly handed in at a local police station, no questions asked. Jock Haston recalls:

> Some months later Superintendent Jones (he was by this time a Superintendent) (…) came round to see me with a list of all guns and ammunition that I had turned in, the serial numbers, where they had been manufactured, and all the rest of it, and told me that they knew, that they had had a whisper that we had guns stored away (…). (Al Richardson, *Interview with Jock Haston*, April 30, 1978, unpublished, Ted Grant Archive)

Unfortunately, we don't know the identity of the informer the police apparently had within the RCP.

The Neath by-election

Ted explained why it was necessary to modify our tactics during the war: "Since the Labour Party was largely an electoral machine, its inner life dwindled almost to nothing during the war. The Party branches ceased to meet. Most importantly, the Labour Youth, which had been our main field of work before the war, virtually ceased to exist, as the youth had been conscripted into the armed forces."

This made a change of tactics necessary. At first, the comrades turned to the ILP, where they made some gains. But after 1941, new opportunities presented themselves in the Communist Party. The strike-breaking, class-collaborationist policies of the Party's leadership provoked growing discontent. The WIL and then the RCP therefore paid increased attention to the CPGB.

Throughout the war, the Labour Party agreed to an electoral truce with the Tories. They were all in the wartime coalition, so there were hardly any elections. An exception was the by-election in working-class Neath in 1945. Given the peculiar conditions in this election, the RCP fielded a candidate in this safe Labour seat, as a way of raising the ideas of Marxism and winning new members. South Wales had a revolutionary tradition, especially in the mining areas, which at that time covered most of South Wales. When the Communist International was formed in 1919, the only trade union bodies in Britain to join it were the South Wales miners and the Clydeside Shop Stewards in Scotland.

South Wales has a long tradition of bitter class struggle and its people have long memories. In my own family I remember as a child listening to talk about "the strike" as if it were something that had happened yesterday. But they were talking about the 1926 general strike. After the defeat of the general strike, the miners remained doggedly out for months until they were literally starved back to work. Winston Churchill commented that "the rats have gone back to their holes". That was remembered and bitterly resented.

Even during the war, when Churchill's popularity was at its height, people in the South Wales Valleys would boo when he appeared on the cinema newsreels. It was therefore an excellent place to put forward revolutionary ideas. The Revolutionary Communist Party's candidate was Jock Haston, its general secretary. This was the first time any Trotskyist organisation had stood a candidate in a British Parliamentary election. The RCP had only been established one year earlier, and had not previously had a base in South Wales. Nevertheless, the Neath election was a considerable success for the RCP.

Ted played an active role in the campaign. There is a photograph of him together with Jimmy Deane and Jock Haston outside the campaign headquarters in Neath. Typically, while Jock and Jimmy are smiling at the camera, Ted is not even looking into the lens. He has his face buried in the pages of the *Socialist Appeal*. He was never particularly photogenic, nor was he at all public relations-conscious, but the sub-text here is clear: never mind the personalities; it is our ideas and programme that count.

The RCP stood on the platform of revolutionary internationalism. It proudly declared: "Our candidate will fight on a platform of uncompromising hostility to the imperialist war, for the breaking of the Coalition, for the overthrow of the Churchill Government and for Labour to take power on a Socialist platform". Their main slogan was "Break the Coalition, Labour to Power." Of course, the RCP did not expect to win the seat. That was never a realistic outcome. But it got a significant vote, and more importantly, it got its ideas across to a far wider public than ever before. The ideas of Trotskyism were very well received by the workers at a time when nobody else was putting forward a revolutionary programme.

The Stalinists, who regarded South Wales as one of their strongholds, were beside themselves with rage. They did everything possible to disrupt the RCP's campaign, including fist fights, but without success. The RCP made a big impact with its programme and ideas—not least among sections of the CP workers. The Communist Party offered its full support to the Labour candidate and campaigned against the RCP, using the elegant slogan: "A Vote for Haston is a Vote for Hitler".

The RCP repeatedly challenged the CP to a public debate. At first they refused, but were in the end forced to agree to hold a debate in Neath. They put up Alun Thomas, leader of the Communist Party in West Wales, to speak against Haston. His speech was full of venom. During the meeting, which attracted about 1,500 people, among other priceless pearls proffered by comrade Thomas was the following:

> In Russia they defeated fascism because they shot all the Trotskyists and the Fifth column scum, and if we had our way, these people on this platform would be shot.

As Marx would have said: "Every word a piss-pot, and not an empty one." But despite all the abuse, the RCP's case was beginning to get an echo in the ranks of both the CP and the Labour Party. The local ILP also split over support for Haston and some of them joined the RCP.

The Labour candidate, D. J. Williams, repudiated the Stalinist's support, opposing its policy of a popular front with the Conservatives and Labour after the war. He seems to have been a decent man. Haston remained on good terms with him, and when the RCP fell apart in 1949, Williams helped him to find a job with the National Council of Labour Colleges.

The outcome for the RCP was that it won 1,781 votes, compared to 30,847 for the Labour candidate. Paradoxically, by arousing such great interest, the RCP campaign served to boost the vote for Labour. A highly significant fact, as Ted told me, was that many workers would come up to them after an enthusiastic RCP election meeting and say: "I agree with everything you say. Why are you not running as the candidate of the Labour Party?" The success in Neath caused a lot of problems with the CP.

A few miles away from Neath, along a desolate, wind-swept valley, lies the small mining town of Gwaun-cae-Gurwen, popularly known as G-C-G, or "the Waun". Here the RCP established an active branch, mainly of miners who had come over from the Communist Party.

The War Years | 71

From left to right: Anne Ward, Bill Davy, Sastry, John Lawrence, Heaton Lee, Ted and Jimmy Deane

Jock Haston discussing with comrades outside the Neath election campaign headquarters

The leading spirit was one Johnny Jones "Crown", a self-educated man, like many Welsh workers at that time who took the trouble to raise themselves above the terrible conditions of life to conquer for themselves the world of culture and ideas. Johnny used to write marvellous articles for the *Socialist Appeal*, from which you could get a clear idea of the lives, thoughts and aspirations of working people.

A young miner called Olwyn Hughes joined this group. He never really left it till the moment of his death in 1998. It took some guts to be an active Trotskyist militant in a CP stronghold like that. The Stalinists looked on them as traitors or worse, and on more than one occasion, criticism was not limited to verbal exchanges. Olwyn, who was a member of the RCP in G-C-G at that time, gave me the following example.

One of the RCP members (I don't remember his name) was quite a tough man, although quietly spoken. He and Olwyn were chatting over a pint in the local miners' club, when a particularly fanatical Stalinist came up behind them and began making loud comments about the alleged "Trotsky-fascists".

Olwyn's companion turned round and addressed the provocateur: "Are you talking about me?" The man had scarcely had time to reply in the affirmative, when the fists started to fly. The aggressor ended up on the carpet, whereupon the victor looked challengingly round the room: "Now then. Anyone else got anything to say?" They did not.

Olwyn described to me the impression Ted made on him when, still a young miner, he came to London to meet the leading comrades: "He struck me as a bit of an egg-head [intellectual]", he said, laughing. He described to me how Ted and the other full timers would invite them to a Lyon's Corner House and treat them to a cup of coffee, while giving them a long lecture on the class nature of Eastern Europe and the errors of the theory of state capitalism. But when it was time for lunch, they would go to a café where the young Welshmen would have to put their hands in their pockets to pay! It was a lesson Olwyn never forgot and he would never allow me, a full timer, to pay for a pint of bitter, which was usually in the Miners' Welfare Club. Incidentally, there was a room in the Welfare in which there was a bust of Lenin, again a reference to Amman valley's revolutionary heritage.

Olwyn also gave a description of Harrow Road, the RCP headquarters, which seemed a hive of activity. There were people coming and going all the time. He recalled: "there were a lot of Yanks, many of them sailors, members of the SWP, coming straight off the ships to deliver books and materials and have discussions. There were mattresses on the floor where full-timers and others would sleep."

Years later (I think it was in 1971), when I was a Militant full timer in South Wales, Rob Sewell and I went to sell the paper at a demonstration against the Industrial Relations Bill in Ammanford, not far from G-C-G. That town became known in the area as Little Moscow and the Communist Party was once very strong there. We sold the paper on the demonstration and then went to a public meeting in the Miners' Hall. The main speaker was Trevor James, the regional head of the NUM. He made a very fiery speech, denouncing the Tories in the language of the class struggle, and he finished by saying: "The working class will never succeed until we gain our ultimate objective: workers' state power!" We later found out he had been close to the RCP.

Socialist Appeal, March 1942

CHAPTER FOUR
IN DEFENCE OF TROTSKYISM

Eclectics live by means of episodic thoughts and improvisations that originate under the impact of events. Marxist cadres capable of leading the proletarian revolution are trained only by the continual and successive working out of problems and disputes. (Trotsky, *What Next for the German Revolution?* 1932)
As a dog returns to its vomit, so a fool repeats his folly. (*Proverbs* 26:11)

The USSR and the war

The end of the war confronted the RCP and the Fourth International with an entirely new situation, which had not been foreseen by Trotsky. The outcome of the Second World War was different than that worked out by Trotsky in 1938. The war in Europe resolved itself largely into a war between Stalinist Russia and Nazi Germany. Anglo-American imperialism miscalculated the perspective completely when they bet that that the USSR would be defeated by Germany.

"The war developed on different lines to what even the greatest theoretical geniuses could have expected," Ted said on many occasions. But Trotsky was not the only one in error. The perspectives of Roosevelt, Churchill, Stalin and Hitler were even more mistaken.

Hitler thought he could get a quick and easy victory in Russia. In part he was intoxicated by the speed of his victory in France. But the main factor that convinced him was the wholesale destruction of the cadres of the Red Army in Stalin's purges. This received further confirmation with the poor showing of the Red Army in the Finnish campaign of 1939-40. He overruled the objections of his generals, who thought that Germany could not fight a war on two fronts, by saying: "They do not have good generals".

Trotsky feared that the Soviet Union could be defeated as a result of Stalin's policies. This nearly happened at the start of the war, when millions of Soviet soldiers were encircled, captured and sent to death camps where they perished of starvation and ill-treatment. The blunders of Stalin allowed Hitler's armies to advance right up to the outskirts of Moscow.

This convinced not only Hitler, but also Churchill, that the Soviet Union would be defeated in a matter of weeks. But things turned out very differently. Ted said that in part this was due to the peculiar nature of German fascism. The idea of racial superiority is common to all imperialist nations. Fascism is only the distilled essence of imperialism. But in this case, the distilled essence had a particularly poisonous character.

The demented racist Hitler saw Russia as a land that must be occupied by the German master race. The Soviet people were only sub-human "Untermenschen", inferior Slavs ruled by "Jewish

Bolsheviks". He did not expect them to put up a serious fight. "All we have to do is to kick in the door and the whole rotten edifice will come tumbling down," he said.

The inhuman treatment of the Soviet population, the massacres, pogroms and innumerable atrocities immediately galvanised the population against the invaders, not just the working class but also the bulk of the peasantry. That was an important factor, as Ted pointed out: "Trotsky wrote that for the USSR the biggest danger was not the guns and tanks of the enemy but the cheap commodities they would bring in their baggage. However, Hitler's armies did not bring cheap commodities, but gas chambers." He added: "If instead of the German army, Russia had been invaded by the Americans, things might have turned out differently."

The turning point is often said to have been the Battle of Stalingrad, where about 800,000 German and Axis troops were either killed or captured, including the entire German Sixth Army and its commander-in-chief. That was a shattering blow to Hitler. By comparison, the British victory in the Battle of El Alamein was a puny affair.

However, Ted always said that the Battle of Kursk in July and August 1943 was really the decisive battle of World War Two. "That was the biggest tank battle in history", he said. The Germans had about 3,000 tanks and assault guns, 2,110 aircraft and 435,000 men. It was one of the greatest concentrations of German fighting power ever assembled. But it was not enough.

The Red Army tore the guts out of the Wehrmacht. The Germans suffered irrecuperable losses and were put to flight. In the end, the Soviets defeated the Nazi invaders and advanced into the heart of Europe, in what Ted described as the greatest military advance in all history. "The main reason for the victory of the Soviet Union was the nationalised planned economy", he explained many times. "The Russians were able to dismantle all their industries in the West—1,500 factories—put them on trains and ship them east of the Urals where they were beyond the reach of the Germans. In a matter of months, the Soviet Union was out-producing the Germans in tanks, guns and airplanes."

Alarmed by the swift advance of the Red Army, which was sweeping all before it, Churchill and Roosevelt rushed to open a second front in Europe, after dragging their feet for two years, expecting the Soviet Union to be defeated. "If they had not organized the Normandy landings in 1944, they would have met the Red Army, not in the middle of Germany but on the English Channel", Ted said.

Ted never tired of praising the fighting spirit and military prowess of the Red Army, and the courage of the Soviet workers and peasants who succeeded in defeating the armies of Hitler, despite having all the resources of Europe at their disposal. He always spoke of this with the greatest enthusiasm, as if it were his own personal victory, so fully did he identify himself with the land of October, its people, their victories and their sufferings.

This great victory, despite all the mythology that was subsequently created about Stalin the "Great War Leader", was *in spite of* Stalin and the bureaucracy. They had brought the Soviet Union to the very brink of catastrophe. Just one example will illustrate this. Ted said:

> Tukhachevsky, the hero of the Civil War, was a military genius. He was the first to understand that the Second World War would be fought with tanks and aeroplanes. His theories were actually put into practice by the Germans with their *Blitzkrieg* [lightning war]. By contrast, the British and French strategists were still working on the assumption that the next war would be, like the First World War, based on trench warfare. The bankruptcy of this strategy was immediately exposed in 1940, with the fiasco of the Maginot Line. Yet Stalin replaced Tukhachevsky with men like Budyonny who believed that the Second World War would be fought with cavalry.

Only the superhuman determination of the Soviet workers and soldiers to defend the USSR and the gains of the October Revolution, and the striking superiority of the nationalized planned economy saved the day. Yet, despite all their crimes and blunders, it was Stalin and the bureaucracy who gained most from the victory of the USSR in the war. Far from being undermined by war, the Stalinist bureaucracy emerged enormously strengthened. Their authority and prestige were boosted, and the regime was enabled to survive for decades longer. The historic victory of the Red Army fundamentally changed the balance of forces in Europe and on a world scale.

Moreover, the hold of the Moscow bureaucracy over the Communist Parties of Europe and the world was stronger than ever. And for the Fourth International, the road to the Communist workers was closed. This had very serious consequences for the perspectives of socialist revolution in Europe.

The war was moving inexorably to a close. The workers returned from the battlefields determined never to return to the poverty and mass unemployment of the pre-war period. They were confident and militant—and they were still carrying guns. In the 1945 general election, Labour swept to power with a big majority. Churchill was humiliated. The newly elected Labour MPs, elated by their success, sang the *Red Flag* in the Mother of Parliaments. Alarmed, Churchill demanded the immediate demobilisation of the army. When that was done, he then launched a campaign against Labour for leaving the country disarmed. There was a general ferment in society, but the beneficiaries were the Labour leaders, who were actually delivering on their promise of reforms, not the Fourth International.

Conflicts with the leadership of the International

Ted was always in conflict with the so-called leaders of the Fourth International. His colossal admiration for the Old Man was equalled by his poor opinion of these people, whom he saw as the epigones of Trotsky. Once he said to me: "We thought that at least these people would be manure for the future, but they were not even that." He recalled what Marx had written in *The German Ideology:* "How right was Heine when he said about his imitators: 'I have sown dragon's teeth and harvested fleas'."

Trotsky himself was doubtful about the calibre of the leaders of his own movement. The old generation of Bolshevik cadres had been decimated by Stalin. One by one, they were either murdered or else capitulated to Stalin. Trotsky's old friend and comrade in arms, the outstanding Balkan Marxist, Christian Rakovsky was the last to break under the terrible pressure. This was a terrible blow to Trotsky. After Rakovsky capitulated, he felt completely alone, in the sense that there was nobody he felt he could exchange ideas and discuss problems with.

In his *Diary in Exile,* written in 1935, he wrote:

> Rakovsky was virtually my last contact with the old revolutionary generation. After his capitulation there is nobody left. Even though my correspondence with Rakovsky stopped, for reasons of censorship, at the time of my deportation, nevertheless the image of Rakovsky has remained a symbolic link with my old comrades-in-arms. Now nobody remains. For a long time now I have not been able to satisfy my need to exchange ideas and discuss problems with someone else. I am reduced to carrying on a dialogue with the newspapers, or rather through the newspapers with facts and opinions. (Trotsky, *Diary in Exile*, 1935, p. 53)

Trotsky was under no illusions about the leaders of the Trotskyist movement, as his earlier quoted comments to Fred Zeller clearly show. He placed all his hopes in the new generation that would be forged in the fire of events. But events turned out differently to what he had anticipated.

During the war, the SWP (in the USA) and the WIL/RCP (in Britain) were the main groups able to keep a legal structure. The Opposition in the USSR had been long liquidated; the European sections were unable to keep up regular contact, if any, during the war, and barely survived. The SWP became the main point of reference after Trotsky's death, but the structures of the IS (International Secretariat) of the Fourth were almost nonexistent and depended on the SWP for money.

Cannon, as far as I know was not directly involved in the IS, but of course he was regarded as a political heavyweight. His contacts with Trotsky gave him great authority in the eyes of the sections of the Fourth, which tended to look up to the American comrades for guidance and inspiration.

This was further enhanced by the famous trial of 28 members of the SWP and Teamsters' Union, Local 544, that had begun on October 27, 1941. Eighteen were found guilty of "advocating the desirability of overthrowing the government by force and violence", which resulted in the imprisonment of Cannon and other SWP leaders. The WIL, despite being officially kept outside the International, regularly reproduced material and news from the American SWP.

The emergence of the European Secretariat towards the end of the war then switched the centre of gravity of the Fourth back towards Europe. In February 1944, a European Conference of the Fourth International appointed a new European Secretariat and elected Michel Raptis, a Greek Trotskyist living in France, as the organisational secretary of its European Bureau. He is better known as Michel Pablo.

Among the new European leaders was Pierre Frank. He had played a very bad role before the war in the French section, when he was a member of the faction of the adventurer Raymond Molinier and was expelled. When in 1940, Frank and Molinier tried to get back into the Fourth International they wrote to Trotsky, who was extremely sceptical about allowing them back. "I am ten times more cautious than before. Unfortunately your letter doesn't dissipate my doubts," he wrote on the 1st of July, 1940. This was written less than two months before his death.

It was very unusual for the Old Man to say such a thing about anybody and it showed his complete distrust of Frank. But Trotsky was not present to raise any objections. Despite Trotsky's misgivings, Frank wormed his way back into the International by joining the reunified French section, then becoming a delegate to the 1946 international conference. There he was not only accepted back without any questions asked, but was given a leading position on the IS. Later on, they tried to conceal Frank's past clashes with Trotsky. In his obituary of Frank, Mandel did not even mention them. The same goes for Frank's so-called history of the Fourth (*The Fourth International: The Long March of the Trotskyists*). In this way, the history of the Fourth International has been systematically rewritten and falsified.

Pablo, Frank, Mandel and other leaders had an entirely false perspective, which was shared by Cannon and the SWP. Shortly before his death, I interviewed Ted and asked him what the basis of the disagreements was. He answered as follows:

> There were a whole series of disagreements of a fundamental character. After the death of the Old Man,

the leaders of the Fourth International were completely out of their depth. Mandel, Pablo, Frank, Hansen and the others had a completely ultra-left position. They repeated what Trotsky had said in 1938 without understanding Trotsky's method. As a result they landed in a mess.

The reason for this was their failure to understand that the Second World War developed in a way that was not foreseen by Trotsky in 1938. That could not have been foreseen even by the greatest Marxist. Not only Trotsky, but also Hitler, Churchill, Roosevelt and Stalin had not foreseen what happened. The Second World War in Europe was really a gigantic battle between the Red Army and Hitler, with all the resources of Europe behind him. The victory of the USSR strengthened Stalinism for a whole historical period. At the same time the reformists and Stalinists saved capitalism in Europe.

This provided the basis for a recovery of capitalism that developed later into an enormous economic upswing. This meant that the forces of Trotskyism were in a difficult position, because reformism and Stalinism were strengthened. The illusions in Stalinism were further strengthened by the victory of the Chinese Revolution in 1949, and the overthrow of capitalism in Eastern Europe, albeit in a distorted, bureaucratic way.

On the other hand, the road to the reformist workers was also closed to us. The economic upswing allowed the reformist leaders to carry out far-reaching reforms. The Labour government in Britain was the only Labour government in history that actually carried out its programme. There were enormous illusions among the workers. We were isolated. (*The theoretical origins of the degeneration of the Fourth*, Interview with Ted Grant, October 2004)

The leadership of the British section of the Fourth International (the Revolutionary Communist Party) had already concluded that because of these developments, the perspectives that Trotsky had outlined in 1938 had been falsified by history. It was necessary to work out a new perspective, taking into account all these developments. The British RCP disagreed with the idea that capitalism was heading immediately for a deep slump, and pointed out that an upturn in the economy was already underway. But the so-called leaders of the Fourth were blind to all this.

The British comrades did get a certain echo, but the leaders had the majority. They did not like the RCP because the British leadership thought for themselves and would take no nonsense from them. Ted said: "They could never beat us in a political argument, so they resorted to organizational intrigues and manoeuvres against us. This is death for a revolutionary organization."

Conflicts in the SWP

A ferocious conflict erupted in the American SWP over the policy to be adopted towards the European revolution. It was a struggle between the followers of James Cannon, and a minority led by Felix Morrow, the author of a very good book, *Revolution and Counter-revolution in Spain*. Morrow formed a bloc with Albert Goldman which challenged the Cannon leadership over their perspective for Europe. Morrow explained that rather than dictatorship in Europe, propped up by American bayonets, the bourgeoisie would rest on the Stalinists and reformists to save the situation and introduce a prolonged period of bourgeois democracy.

Under these circumstances, Morrow felt that the revolutionary party would need to stress democratic and transitional demands. While Morrow and Goldman certainly held a more correct appraisal than the SWP leadership, criticising their perspective of immediate slump and war, and tentatively raising the possibility of a counter-revolution in a democratic form, their

Ernest Mandel (left) and Michel Raptis ("Pablo", right)

over-emphasis on democratic demands betrayed a great deal of confusion. As usual with Cannon, the battle was fought with organizational measures and "no holds barred".

Morrow had been removed as editor of the monthly journal *Fourth International* because he refused to allow it to be used as a vehicle for Cannon's views. This factional struggle was carried over into the International Secretariat. Morrow's writings and speeches were circulated in internal bulletins by the WIL/RCP leadership. The RCP had some sympathy with them in contrast with Cannon's false perspectives. Ever since 1943, Ted had raised the possibility that the Stalinists and reformists would be able to divert the revolution into popular front channels. He had foreseen, given the failure of the revolutionary wave, the possibility of a counter-revolution in a democratic form, which is what eventually happened.

However, Ted and Haston did not support all of Morrow's political positions, especially his exaggerated emphasis on democratic demands. They were certainly not involved in a factional sense. They were keeping an open mind to the arguments, while Cannon was demanding support based on blind loyalty. Cannon, however, was convinced that the RCP was actively backing Morrow's faction, and he again manoeuvred against the British leadership. This was untrue, but Cannon judged everyone by his own standards and methods. So for him it was quite natural to set up and back Gerry Healy's faction against the leadership of the British section.

When I asked Ted why they did not support Morrow, who appeared to have a better position than Cannon, he merely shrugged his shoulders and said that they did not agree with either side. He said: "They had a better position than Cannon and Hansen. But they also made some mistakes, so we did not support them. But Cannon accused us of supporting them and of interfering in the internal affairs of the SWP. This was rich coming from Cannon, who had always been interfering in the affairs of the British section!"

To give a flavour of the methods with which Cannon dealt with internal opposition, I quote from a speech made by Cannon in October 1945 about the so-called bloc of Morrow and the RCP. He said:

> You talk about the regime in our party. You have got a bloc partner in England called the leadership of

the RCP. You know what kind of regime they have got? Jock Haston stood up in the last Conference of the RCP and defended Morrow and Goldman against the methods of Cannon...

That is the regime in the RCP who are supporting Goldman and Morrow against our regime, and with whom they have concluded a bloc. And I challenge them to deny it. Talk about unprincipledness. You will deny it and we will prove it because we have the dope on you. You are helping Haston and [Ted] Grant to fight Healy right now. You are sending personal letters to Haston to help them in the fight against Healy—to utilise against Healy. You are in a bloc and you are already ashamed of it openly, but we will expose that bloc and all the rest of it. And we will take the fight on the international field. You go ahead and line up your bloc. We will work with those people who believe in the same principles, the same programme and methods that we do. And we will fight it out and see what happens in the International. (October 7, 1945, from Cannon, *Writings and Speeches, 1945-47*, p. 183)

This speech is sufficient to expose the bullying tone of Cannon and his way of dealing with political opponents. Morrow was eventually expelled from the SWP in 1946 for "unauthorized collaboration" with the Shachtmanites. He eventually moved to the right and drifted out of politics. The same thing happened to Haston later. One might say of them what Lenin was supposed to have said about Paul Levi: "He lost his head. But he had a head to lose."

Their conduct contrasts sharply with Ted's stamina and persistence in defending and developing the position in spite of all difficulties. But the manoeuvres of the leadership of the Fourth against the British leadership went on ceaselessly. This is documented in the strong protest issued by the RCP political bureau against Stuart (Sam Gordon) and Cooper's actions and reports.[7]

Trotsky's prognosis falsified

Behind the superficial questions of prestige, petty ambitions, and rivalry within the leadership of the Fourth International, there were very serious political differences, which soon came to the fore. When Trotsky was assassinated by a Stalinist agent in 1940, the weak forces of the Fourth International were deprived of its leading spirit. The untested leaders of the International proved to be unequal to the tasks posed by history. They buckled under the pressure and abandoned the ideas and methods of the Old Man, but Ted and his comrades in the leadership of the RCP in Britain were the only ones capable of reassessing the situation.

Trotsky's calculation proved correct in the sense that the Second World War was succeeded by a revolutionary wave in Greece, Italy, France and other countries, but the masses remained under the influence of the Communist Parties and, in some cases (Britain, Germany) the Social Democracy. The Stalinists and Social Democrats succeeded in heading off the revolution and saving capitalism. This was the political premise for the post-war economic upswing. The reasons for the post-war economic upswing were explained by Ted Grant in much detail in *Will There be a Slump?* (1960). Here we can only give a brief outline of those reasons.

There were many different factors, such as post-war reconstruction, the discovery of new industries during the war, and to some extent the increased involvement of the state ("state capitalism") through arms expenditure, deficit financing and nationalisation, which, for a temporary period partially mitigated the central contradiction of private ownership of the means of production.

---

[7] See previous chapter. "Reply to comrades Cooper and Stuart" and "Open letter to SWP members", in Ted Grant, *Writings*, Vol. 2.

However, the main factor which acted as a motor-force driving the world economy, was the unprecedented expansion of world trade. *The Financial Times* (December 16, 1993) pointed out: "Over the whole period between 1950 and 1991, the volume of total world exports grew twelve times, while world output grew six times. More startlingly still, the volume of world exports of manufactures rose twenty three times, partly because this is where trade liberalisation was concentrated, while output grew eight times."

These figures clearly show how the rapid expansion of world trade in the post-war period acted as a powerful motor-force which drove the growth in output. This is the secret of the capitalist upswing from 1948 to 1974. It means that, for a whole historical period, capitalism was able *partially* to overcome its other fundamental problem—the contradiction between the narrowness of the national market and the tendency of the means of production to develop on a global scale.

From a Marxist point of view, this was a historically progressive development, which creates the material basis for a socialist society. The strengthening of the working class and the squeezing out of the peasantry in Western Europe, Japan and the United States also changed the class balance of forces within society to the advantage of the proletariat.

The leadership of the Fourth International, on the other hand, understood nothing. Mandel, who was supposed to be an economist, steadfastly denied any possibility that the economy would revive. Later, when the reality was carved on his nose, he was obliged to revise his opinion. He dedicated his PhD dissertation to the theory of "late capitalism", based on the idea of a "third age" of capitalist development—a complete capitulation to Keynesianism.

But in 1946, together with Pablo, Cannon and all the others, he had a perspective of immediate economic slump, of war and revolutions, and Bonapartist dictatorships everywhere. They even held the position that the Second World War had not ended. This was entirely false and ultra-left. Ted predicted a period of bourgeois democracy in Europe, not Bonapartism or fascism, but counter-revolution in a democratic form, and urged the Fourth International to draw the conclusions and act accordingly. But the leaders were deaf to all these arguments and they made every imaginable mistake because of it.

They merely regurgitated the half-digested words of Trotsky from 1938 without the slightest understanding of his method. They were hopelessly out of touch. The Fourth International refused to accept that the revolutionary wave had been defeated for the time being. Instead, they took refuge in false optimism, platitudes, and meaningless generalisations, like those we find in the resolutions of April 1946:

> Under these conditions partial defeats like those in Greece, temporary periods of retreat like those in France and Belgium, do not demoralize the proletariat. On the contrary, in the course of the coming economic struggles, the treacherous character of its leaders is revealed anew by the experiences. The repeated demonstration by the bourgeoisie of its inability to re-establish an economic and political regime of the slightest stability offers the workers new opportunities to go over to ever higher stages of struggle.
>
> On the other hand, the swelling of the ranks of the traditional organizations in Europe, above all the Stalinist parties, reflected the first stage of radicalisation of the masses, and has reached its peak almost everywhere. *The phase of decline is beginning.*[8]

---

[8] "The New Imperialist Peace and the Building of the Parties of the Fourth International", Resolution adopted by the Second International Conference of the Fourth International, Paris, April 1946.

The revolutionary party is above all its ideas, perspectives, methods and traditions. With these completely erroneous perspectives, it is no wonder the Fourth International went into a deep crisis. If they had listened to the British comrades, things would have been different. We would still have had to fight against the stream for a long time, but we would have preserved the cadres, kept the movement together, and prepared for new advances when the situation began to change, as it did change, and is changing now.

The 1946 Conference

In April 1946, delegates from the principal European sections, and a number of others, attended a "Second International Conference". This set about rebuilding the International Secretariat of the Fourth International. Michel Raptis (Pablo) was appointed Secretary and Ernest Germaine, a Belgian intellectual whose real name was Ernest Mandel, began to play a leading role.

Although he was a member of the IEC, Ted was unable to go because he did not have a British passport. But he admitted to me that he was not particularly enthusiastic about going anyway, "because I knew what it would be like". The RCP moved a series of detailed amendments to the Manifesto of the Fourth International, which were written by Ted and defended in Paris by Jock Haston and Jimmy Deane.

When they came back to London they reported that it was a mixture of ultra-leftism and opportunism. They were bitterly disappointed by the leaders of the Fourth—Pablo, Mandel, Pierre Frank and the others. Ted had already clashed with Frank in 1945, when he attended the RCP congress, where he was advocating the setting up of factions on each and every question, no matter how petty. He understood nothing on this or any other question, as Trotsky knew very well.

They could never convince either the leadership or the rank and file of the RCP through a democratic discussion and political argument. So they used a stooge to do the dirty work for them. This was Gerry Healy. He had no ideas of his own, but acted like a complete zombie, carrying out the orders from Paris, and gathering a small clique around him.

Healy was always 101 percent behind the International leadership. In fact, he was the original "Pabloite", completely following Pablo's line. But there is a law that if someone supports you 101 percent today, he will be 101 percent against you tomorrow. And that happened with Healy. Later he broke with Pablo and supported Cannon, until he broke with him too. In the end he fell out with them on every issue. That is how it goes with these people.

It is always a political question in the end. In 1946, the leadership of the Fourth was politically ultra-left (although with these types ultra-leftism is always combined with elements of opportunism). Later they became complete opportunists. This is what happens to people who do not take a dialectical position. These people started by saying that every word of Trotsky was correct, without understanding the Old Man's method.

One of them, Sam Gordon (alias Stuart), was back in Britain in 1947, and the comrades challenged him about what Trotsky had written in 1938, when he said that within ten years "not one stone upon another" would be left of the old Internationals (that is, the Social Democracy and the Stalinists), and the Fourth International would become the decisive force on the planet. He replied: "Don't worry. There is still one year to go." That was the extent of their understanding. Later they performed a 180 degree somersault over our heads and took

Meeting at the 2nd world congress of the Fourth International in Paris (1946). From left to right: Pierre Favre (PCI, France), S. Santen (Sec. RCP Holland), Pierre Frank (PCI), Jock Haston (RCP), Colin de Silva (speaking, LSSP, Ceylon) and Munis (emigré Spanish group)

the opposite position—that Trotsky was completely wrong. They naturally ended up with a completely revisionist position. The result was a complete mess.

Eastern Europe: the Marxist theory of the state

After the war, Ted and the other leaders of the RCP reconsidered the situation in Russia. As a part of the discussion on the class nature of the Soviet Union, they even considered the various theories of bureaucratic collectivism, which had been advanced by people like the American Trotskyist Max Shachtman, as a possible explanation of what was happening in Russia and Eastern Europe.

Shachtman said that the Stalinist bureaucracy was a new class and that Soviet Russia was a new kind of slavery. As a result of careful consideration, in which Ted conscientiously re-read the basic Marxist writings on the state, he came to the conclusion that the theory was wrong and decisively rejected it. Ted came down firmly on the side of Trotsky's analysis of the Soviet Union, as outlined in works like *The Revolution Betrayed* and *In Defence of Marxism*.

He defended the view that the Soviet Union was a deformed workers' state—one in which private property and capitalism had been abolished, yet where the workers did not hold political power. Before (and after) the war, Shachtman argued that the working class must be the owners of the state in the transitional period, but that that was not the case in Stalin's Russia. In a speech he made in 2000, Ted summarized his answer to those arguments. I am quoting from notes I made of that meeting:

> One must be careful before inventing a new theory. First we must try to explain things on the basis of the old theory. Trotsky's theories have stood the test of time. We cannot just invent a new class. It must be given a role in production. Where is it? It does not exist: it is just the old bureaucracy grafted onto a workers' state.
>
> If there is a new slave class, as Shachtman argued, then Marx, Engels, Lenin and Trotsky were all wrong. We would have to invent an entirely new social formation—state capitalism or bureaucratic collectivism—which was entirely unknown to Marx and was not predicted by him. Moreover, this entirely new form of class society, based on a kind of slavery, has the ability to develop the means of production to an unheard-of degree.
>
> If we say that the bureaucracy is a new class, certain things flow from this. This would require us to completely revise Marxism. But that is not necessary. In reality, a workers' state can assume different forms according to the concrete conditions. In the same way, there can be all kinds of aberrations in history: the bourgeois state can be democratic, fascist or Bonapartist. But the essence of capitalism remains the same: the central contradiction of wage labour and capital stays the same (wage slavery).
>
> If there is a new ruling class that never existed before, what is its role historically? Marx referred to slavery, feudalism and capitalism. If there is a new ruling class, there must be a new working class also. There cannot be one without the other. As we explained to Shachtman, there must be a new slave class. But it is the same with the working class.
>
> The Soviet working class was not the same working class as under capitalism. They had a different consciousness because of social ownership of the means of production. The workers looked upon state property as "our property". Even under the rule of the Stalinist bureaucracy that was the case to some extent.

In Britain, the theories of bureaucratic collectivism never got much support. However, Tony Cliff, who came to Britain from Palestine in 1947, put forward the idea that, not only the regimes in Eastern Europe, but also Russia itself were state capitalist. In two long documents in reply to Cliff, Ted demolished the argument that Russia was state capitalist, pointing out that the theory of state capitalism leads to one contradiction after another and ultimately to a break with Marxism:

"If Russia was capitalist in any sense that Marxism would understand, it must have the law of motion of capitalism, that is, booms and slumps," he said. "At first Cliff tried to show that there were booms and slumps in Russia. When he could not find any, he said: 'OK, so there are no slumps in Russia. But there are also no slumps in the West either'." At the time, capitalism was in a period of economic upswing. From this, and using the method of shallow empiricism that was always his trade mark, Cliff concluded that capitalism could avoid slumps by means of what he called the "permanent arms economy". This was a variant of bourgeois Keynesian economics and marked a complete revision of Marxism. As usual, one theoretical error led to another. In all of this there is not a trace of dialectical thinking.

Jimmy Deane wrote to Ted from Liverpool on September 16, 1948. The first part is a lengthy report of Jimmy's stay in Coventry. It shows the bad state of the RCP branch there, with personal conflicts, bitterness towards the leadership, etc. This is already a sign that the difficult objective situation was beginning to affect the morale of the comrades. It was therefore imperative that the leadership provide the necessary theoretical material to rearm the movement. The question of the class nature of the regimes in Russia and Eastern Europe was a fundamental part of this ideological rearmament.

There is an urgent note in this letter that shows the deep concern felt by Jimmy at this time:

> When can we expect the publication of the reply to Cliff? I'm looking forward to it. I think you should introduce plenty of factual material (perhaps in the form of an appendix) proving your thesis on Eastern Europe. If the document is long, so much the better. A full and clear exposition of ideas on these questions is just what both our party and the International need. (*Jimmy Deane to Ted Grant*, September 16, 1948, in the Ted Grant archives)

I am sure that Jimmy's expectations were satisfied to the full. When Ted finally finished his document, it was well worth the wait. In complete contrast to Cliff's superficial empiricism, *The Marxist Theory of the State, Reply to Tony Cliff*, displayed a masterly grasp of the Marxist dialectical method. In my view, this work, and other works of this period, constitute the only really new contribution in the post-war period to Trotsky's theories, on which they are firmly rooted. Ted found the answer in Trotsky's last writings on Poland and Finland. On the other hand, it was necessary to apply Trotsky's dialectical method to the new situations that were opening up in Eastern Europe and China.

In 1940, shortly before he was assassinated, the Old Man had explained that when the Red Army entered Poland and Finland, they would be forced to introduce a nationalised planned system on the lines of Stalinist Russia. Once in power, the Stalinists would lean on the working class to expropriate the landowners and capitalists. We would have to support this as a historically progressive measure. But the working class would soon find itself under a new kind of subjugation and would have to pay for this by a new, political, revolution against the bureaucracy.

Ted explained the precise mechanism by which the Stalinists destroyed the old bourgeois state in Eastern Europe and installed themselves in power without the direct participation of the working class. After 1944-45, the bourgeois fled from Eastern Europe before the irresistible advance of the Red Army. Before the war, in his polemics with Shachtman and Burnham, Trotsky explained in advance what would happen when the bureaucracy entered Poland and the Baltic States. They immediately nationalised the economy. Indirectly, they based themselves on the proletariat. They leaned on the workers to expropriate the capitalists.

Using the analogy with what Trotsky had written about Poland and Finland, Ted argued that the so-called communist countries of Eastern Europe were in fact run on the same lines as the Soviet Union, and he used the term proletarian Bonapartism to describe them (Trotsky had previously used the term soviet or proletarian Bonapartism in his

Max Shachtman in the 1960s

writings). As he later explained in an *Open Letter to the British Section Fourth International*, September-October 1950:

> The collapse of capitalism in Eastern Europe enabled Stalinism as a Bonapartist tendency to manipulate the workers and manoeuvre between the classes—establishing deformed workers' states of a Bonapartist character with more or less mass support. Stalinism in the present peculiar relationship of class forces, basing itself in the last analysis on the proletariat—in the sense of standing for the defence of the new economic form of society—is Bonapartism of a new type manoeuvring between other classes in order to establish a regime on the pattern of Moscow.

Ted and the RCP welcomed these revolutions because they led to the abolition of landlordism and capitalism. Yet it was not enough simply to characterise these states as workers' states without more qualification. It was necessary to explain the concrete conditions in which they arose, which determined their character as deformed workers' states. While defending the nationalised property forms, Ted pointed out that the working class would have to overturn the bureaucratic deformations with a political revolution in the future, replacing the totalitarian bureaucracy with workers' democracy.

The leaders of the Fourth failed to understand these developments. At first, they tried to argue that, while the USSR was a degenerated workers' state, the regimes in Eastern Europe were capitalist. Then, at the time of Tito's split with Stalin, they performed a 180 degree about-face and proclaimed Yugoslavia to be a healthy workers' state. They proclaimed Tito to be an unconscious Trotskyist. He was the first of many such "unconscious Trotskyists".

The Chinese Revolution

The leaders of the Fourth equally had no understanding of what was happening in China. Cannon was predicting that Mao Zedong would capitulate to Chiang Kai-shek. This was at a time when the Chinese Red Army was advancing rapidly, sweeping all before it, and Chiang's army had the biggest rate of desertion of any army in history. Ted said that Shachtman had his followers rolling in the aisles with laughter when he ridiculed the SWP's position on China. Shachtman quipped: "Mao is trying to capitulate to Chiang Kai-shek. The problem is he can't catch up with him!"

It is astonishing that Ted not only predicted the victory of Mao Zedong, but also explained what programme Mao would carry out—before Mao himself put it forward. At a time when Mao was still writing about a long period of capitalism in China, Ted explained that he would have to nationalise the means of production and set up a state in the image of Stalin's Russia. In other words, Mao would come to power and set up a deformed workers' state (proletarian Bonapartism). That was precisely what happened.

Even more astonishing was Ted's prediction that Mao's China would inevitably come into conflict with Stalinist Russia. He made this prediction in the late 1940s in a document called *Reply to David James*, when there was not the slightest indication of any conflict between Moscow and Beijing. It took over a decade for the prediction to come true, in the shape of the Sino-Soviet dispute, but it came true nonetheless.

Later, Ted wrote a long document on China in which he went through the entire history of that country. He made the mistake of sending this document to Pierre Frank in Paris, and never saw it again. Unfortunately, there was no copy and Ted was forever lamenting its loss. Nevertheless, he left plenty of other valuable documents on China, from which his views can be clearly understood. A careful reading of these works is completely indispensable for an understanding not only of the Chinese Revolution, but of the colonial revolution in general.

Every revolution has common features, but also important differences that reflect the peculiarities of national development. In the case of China, Ted showed that for thousands of years, there had been a history of peasant wars, which would eventually overthrow the ruling dynasty. But all that would happen was that the heads of the peasants would fuse with the Mandarin ruling class to form a new dynasty. Social relations would remain untouched and the endless cycle of Chinese history would continue uninterrupted.

Before the war, Trotsky posed the question of what would happen when the Chinese Red Army entered the towns. He tentatively suggested that the same thing would happen, but with a difference. He thought it likely that the leaders of the Red Army would fuse with the bourgeoisie, preparing the way for the development of capitalism in China. But because of the peculiar development of the Second World War, things worked out differently. As with all of Trotsky's pre-war predictions, he would undoubtedly have modified this perspective, had he not been cut down by a Stalinist assassin. Marxist perspectives are conditional by nature, and must be developed and updated on the basis of changing conditions – something the leaders of the Fourth were woefully incapable of doing.

Trotsky's prediction was a very reasonable hypothesis, given the policy of popular frontism that every Stalinist party in the world accepted, including the Chinese. As late as 1949, Mao was still putting forward the idea of a "hundred years of capitalism". He insisted that he would only expropriate "bureaucratic-capital".

In the first stages, Mao did everything to prevent the workers from taking power, and to crush whatever elements of an independent workers' movement had emerged. When the Red Army entered the cities, they called on workers *not* to strike or demonstrate. As in Spain in 1936, Mao did not form a coalition with the bourgeoisie, but with the mere shadow of the bourgeoisie. But whereas in Spain, the shadow was allowed to take on substance, in China it was snuffed out.

Mao's original idea was to form a coalition government with the representatives of the workers, peasants, the intelligentsia, the national bourgeoisie and even progressive landowners. However, there was a slight problem. The bourgeoisie had fled to Formosa (Taiwan) with Chiang Kai-shek. Formally speaking, this was a popular front government. But there was a fundamental difference between this government and the popular front in Spain in 1936. That difference was the People's Liberation Army, the peasant army controlled by the Chinese Stalinists.

Engels explained that the state, in the last analysis, is armed bodies of men. The old bourgeois state had been smashed by the Red Army. Having used the peasant Red Army to smash the old state, Mao balanced Bonapartist-fashion between the bourgeoisie, and the workers and peasants, in order to consolidate the new state and concentrate power into his hands.

In spite of his stated perspective of a prolonged period of capitalist development, having taken power, Mao very soon realised that the rotten and corrupt Chinese bourgeoisie was incapable of playing any progressive role. Thus, leaning on the working class, he proceeded to nationalise the banks and all large-scale industry and to expropriate the landlords and capitalists.

This was not so difficult. As Trotsky remarked, to kill a tiger one needs a shotgun, but to kill a flea, a fingernail is sufficient. Mao created a new state in the image of Moscow—not the democratic workers' state of Lenin and Trotsky, but the monstrously deformed workers' state of Stalin. In his *Reply to David James* (1949) Ted wrote:

> The Marxist method starts with a class analysis of society and any of its phenomena or organs, but it does not end there. It is necessary from there to analyse all the cross-currents and interactions within the given class definition. In dealing with Yugoslavia and China, it is necessary first to have the essentials firmly in mind. Without the existence of Russia as a degenerate workers' state, without the weakening of world imperialism as a result of the war, Eastern Europe would have taken on an entirely different pattern. These events can only be explained on the basis of the survival of Russia with its nationalised property forms; the survival of Stalinism at the helm of a vastly strengthened Russia as the outcome of the war. It is this which led to the extension of the revolution in a deformed, Stalinist shape, to the other countries.

In order to explain the peculiar character of the post-war regimes in Eastern Europe, the Chinese Revolution, and the colonial revolution in general, Ted took as his starting point Trotsky's basic thesis and applied it to the new situation. In *Against the Theory of State Capitalism—Reply to Tony Cliff* (1949), he explains:

> Anyone who compared the Bonapartist counter-revolution with the revolution—at least in its superstructure—would have found as great a difference as between the regime of Lenin and Trotsky in Russia and that of Stalin in later years. To superficial observers the difference between the two regimes was fundamental. In fact, insofar as the superstructure was concerned, the difference was glaring. Napoleon had reintroduced many of the orders, decorations and ranks similar to those of feudalism; he had restored the Church; he even had himself crowned Emperor. Yet despite this counter-revolution, it is clear that it had nothing in common with the old regime. It was counter-revolution on the basis of the new form of property introduced by the revolution itself. Bourgeois forms of property or property relations remained the basis of the economy.

The abolition of landlordism freed China from the burden of semi-feudal relations. The liquidation of private ownership of industry, and the introduction of the state monopoly of foreign trade, gave a powerful impetus to the development of Chinese industry. However, the nationalisation of the means of production is not yet socialism, although it is the prior condition for it.

The movement towards socialism requires the conscious control, guidance and participation of the proletariat. The uncontrolled rule of a privileged elite is not compatible with genuine socialism. It will produce all sorts of new contradictions. Bureaucratic control signifies corruption, nepotism, waste, mismanagement and chaos, which eventually undermine the gains of a nationalised planned economy. The experience of both Russia and China prove this.

Once again, the leaders of the International failed to understand the nature of the processes taking place. They began by characterising Mao's China as capitalist, and then decided it was a healthy workers' state after all. Later they even compared the Cultural Revolution with the Paris Commune. All this confusion shows just how far they had lost their bearings.

Nationalist degeneration

How was it possible for Ted to anticipate these developments even before Mao had come to power? Once again he based himself on what Trotsky had written as early as 1928, in the discussions of the new *Draft Programme of the Communist International*, in which Stalin and his (then) ally Bukharin elaborated the anti-Leninist theory of socialism in one country, advanced for the first time in 1924 by Stalin.

WORKERS' INTERNATIONAL NEWS

Theoretical Organ of Workers' International League
Fourth International

Vol. 5. No. 11   June, 1943.   THREEPENCE

INDEX

THE RISE AND FALL OF THE COMMUNIST INTERNATIONAL   BY TED GRANT
EDITORIAL — THE ROAD IS CLEAR FOR THE FOURTH INTERNATIONAL.
A GRAPHIC HISTORY OF BOLSHEVISM - - - - LEON TROTSKY
CRITICISM OF THE DRAFT PROGRAMME ADOPTED AT THE SIXTH CONGRESS OF THE COMINTERN, 1928 - - - - LEON TROTSKY
LENIN'S LAST LETTER TO THE BOLSHEVIK PARTY — THE SUPPRESSED TESTAMENT.

The Rise and Fall of the Communist International

By TED GRANT

The Third International has been officially buried. In the most undignified and contemptible fashion it would be possible to conceive, it has passed off the stage of history. Hurriedly and without consultation with all the adhering parties, not to speak of the rank and file throughout the world, without any democratic discussion and decision, as the result of the pressure of American imperialism, Stalin has perfidiously abandoned the Comintern.

To understand how it is that this organisation which aroused the terror and hatred of the whole of the capitalist world has come to such an inglorious end at the bidding of capitalism, it is necessary to review briefly the stormy rise and even stormier decline of the International. The decree for its dissolution was merely an acknowledgment of what had long been known to all informed people; that the Comintern as a factor-making for world Socialism was dead and had departed forever from its original aims and purposes. Its demise was predicted and foreseen long in advance.

The Third International grew out of the collapse of capitalism in the last war. The Russian Revolution sent a wave of revolutionary fervour through the ranks of the working class throughout the world. To the war-weary, disillusioned and embittered masses, it came as a message of hope, of inspiration and courage, it showed the way out of the bloody chaos into which capitalism had plunged society. It was born as a direct consequence of the betrayal and breakdown of the Second Inter-

---

A mistake in theory will sooner or later manifest itself in a disaster in practice. This was always understood by Lenin and Trotsky, and Ted always tirelessly repeated the same idea. Trotsky, with amazing foresight, warned the leaders of the international communist movement that if this false theory was accepted by the Comintern, it would be the beginning of a process that would inevitably lead to the national-reformist degeneration of every communist party in the world—whether in or out of power.

At the time, Trotsky's warnings were ignored by the leaders of the communist parties. They considered themselves to be revolutionary internationalists and Leninists. They all stood for

world revolution. How could the Comintern possibly degenerate on national-reformist lines? The very idea seemed simply preposterous!

Those haughty leaders of the communist parties who disdained Trotsky's good advice in 1928 soon found that he was right. Under Stalin, the communist parties were subordinated to the USSR and forced to carry out a policy in the interests of Moscow's foreign policy—that is to say, in the interests of the Soviet bureaucracy.

Having followed every twist and turn dictated by the Moscow bureaucracy, the Communist International was summarily dissolved by Stalin in 1943 without even calling a congress. The history of the Comintern was traced and analysed by Ted in *The Rise and fall of the Communist International* (*Workers' International News*, June 1943).

After the death of Stalin, the communist parties of Western Europe gradually separated themselves from Moscow and became increasingly independent. But this did not mean a return to the old position of Leninist internationalism. To the degree that the CPs became more independent of Moscow, they became more dependent on the pressures of their "own" national bourgeoisie and reformism. Under the guise of "Eurocommunism" they moved over to a position that was indistinguishable from Social Democratic reformism. They adopted in its totality the position of national reformism.

An even worse situation existed in those countries where the Stalinists had come to power. Each national bureaucracy, starting with Yugoslavia, asserted its right to follow its own national "road to socialism". In effect, each national bureaucracy was defending its own narrow national interests against those of the Moscow bureaucracy.

An extreme case of this was the clash of interests between Moscow and Beijing. This clash had nothing to do with principled political differences, as some people imagined. It was simply dictated by the conflicting interests of the rival ruling bureaucracies of Russia and China. It did not serve the interests of the working people of either state.

Lenin would undoubtedly have advocated the formation of a socialist federation of the USSR and China, linking the immense productive potential of both countries. Such a step would have been in the interests of the peoples of both the Soviet Union and China. Instead of this, Ted pointed to the repulsive spectacle of Soviet and Chinese comrades "discussing their differences in the fraternal language of rockets and artillery".

This was a crime against proletarian internationalism and it was the direct result of the Stalinist theory of socialism in one country. It led to the complete degeneration, disintegration and decay of the once powerful world communist movement. Years later Ted commented:

> The Stalinists thought they understood everything. In reality they understood nothing. Today, over half a century later, history has punished the Stalinists for their crimes. In Britain they have been virtually liquidated as a political force. The remnants of the Stalinists have become indistinguishable from the right-wing trade union bureaucracy. But at that time they were still a force to be reckoned with in the British labour movement.

From defeat to rout

About this time, Ted received an unexpected visit, a "blast from the past". Murray Gow Purdy, who had developed extreme ultra-left tendencies, had left South Africa and gone first to Abyssinia, and then on to India, where he established a party called the Trotskyist Mazdoor Party. Muddled politically, Purdy developed an erroneous theory that India's untouchables caste were the proletarian vanguard. He was nevertheless fully involved in the struggle for national independence from Britain, and was sentenced in early 1946 to 10 years imprisonment as a result of a "revolutionary expropriation".

On his early release after Independence in 1947, he was immediately deported. The following year, he attended the Second World Congress of the Fourth International in Paris, and also visited Ted in London for some discussions. As an ultra-left, Purdy was very critical of the RCP's approach, which he considered not revolutionary enough. But disillusioned with Trotskyism, he subsequently dropped out of the movement and disappeared from the political scene, never to be heard of again.

Politically, Ted was in good spirits, but financially he was not so buoyant. His sister Rae helped him by sending him clothes from Paris. There is a letter from Jimmy Deane in Paris on this subject. But the other comrades were not much better off. As is plain from the letter that followed:

Paris. 24 June 1947

Dear Ted,

Another hasty note. I'm at Raoul's place at the moment—he is living in great poverty. It occurred to me that you may agree to give one of your four suits to Raoul. He has hardly a cloth to his back—somewhat like my own present condition.

If you agree, please write your sister asking her to permit me to select a suit (it shall not be the best) for Raoul. Here it is impossible for a professional to find clothes, whereas in England one still has an even chance of cadging—as you well know!

You mentioned that you may give one of the suits to me, well, if you will, you can give it to Raoul instead.

Please write within a few days Ted.

Warmest greetings,

Jim

The letter from Paris is no coincidence. Jimmy had been sent to France for the 1946 Conference and he later lived in Paris for some 18 months. He must have felt very lonely, as the hostility on the part of the International Secretariat towards the British party was increasing. Pablo and Cannon were infuriated at the RCP's resistance to the demand that they immediately enter the Labour Party. This was determined by their false perspective of an imminent economic catastrophe, world war, fascism, the rapid rise of a centrist current in the Labour Party, etc.

Jimmy attempted to counteract the International leadership's backing for the Healy minority in the RCP, and to stop them from splitting the British section. As a result, they spread poisonous rumours against him. This was mainly the work of Cannon's representative, Sam Gordon (Stuart). Isolated and personally disappointed, he nevertheless made some friends, including the Indian representative, Kamlesh Banerjee and other Trotskyists from the Indian sub-continent, and some young members of the French section, the Parti Communiste Internationale. Finally, the financial strain of maintaining a representative in Paris became too much on the cash-strapped RCP. In the autumn of 1947, Jimmy returned to London.

The programmatic documents of the RCP in the 1940s, virtually all of which were written by Ted, show a profound grasp of the new world situation that arose after 1945. They have stood the test of time and can be read with profit by Marxists today. The British RCP

Jock Haston discussing with Sylvia Cozer, administrative secretary of the Fourth International, in Paris 1946

characterised the regimes in Western Europe (France, Belgium, Holland, Italy) as regimes of counter-revolution in a democratic form. By contrast, people like Pablo and Frank harped on about "Bonapartism", the "strong state", the imminent danger of a nuclear war, fascism and so on and so forth. As we have already seen, they even argued that the Second World War had not ended.

Ted used a military analogy to characterise the situation:

> In war, when an army is advancing, good generals are important. But they are a thousand times more important when an army is forced onto the defensive. With good generals the army can retreat in good order, preserving the bulk of its forces, and holding onto key positions, preparing for a new advance when conditions permit. But bad generals will turn a retreat into a rout.

It is hard to imagine worse "generals" than the ones who stood at the head of the Fourth International after Trotsky's death. Pablo, Mandel, Cannon, Hansen, Frank, Maitan and the others made every conceivable mistake and a few more besides. It was of people like this that Ted commented: "Among the cadres of the Fourth International, there are comrades who have not sufficiently understood this lesson. They continue to live on the 'revenue from a few ready-made abstractions' instead of concretising or partially rectifying previous generalisations."

James Cannon was probably the best of them. At least, Ted used to say, he had roots in the workers' movement. He undoubtedly possessed talent, but it was the talent of an agitator and

Jimmy Deane, Sylvia Cozer and Dumar in Paris 1946

an organiser. He was never a theoretician. His writings are all agitational and his understanding of Marxism was quite shallow. The one book that could claim to have a theoretical character was *The Struggle for a Proletarian Party*, and that was, in effect, dictated by Trotsky. Trotsky's reservations about him were clear during the struggle with Shachtman and Burnham before the war. Ted often said that there is nothing more dangerous in revolutionary politics than a person who is theoretically weak, but who imagines him or herself to be a great theoretician. Such people will inevitably resort to organizational manoeuvres in order to compensate for their political shortcomings.

Ted once said: "Trotsky never approved of Cannon's organizational methods". I asked him how he knew this, and he answered: "It was common knowledge. Everybody knew about it at that time." This is confirmed by somebody who was very close to Trotsky at that time, his secretary, Jean van Heijenoort. In his book *With Trotsky in Exile* we read the following:

> I had had my last conversation with Trotsky. We spoke about the situation in the American Trotskyite group, which was undergoing a serious crisis... Trotsky feared that Cannon, with whom he was politically allied, would tend to replace the discussion of political differences with organisational measures, thereby precipitating the expulsion of the minority. "Cannon has to be held back on the organisational plane and pushed forward on the ideological plane", he told me. (Jean van Heijenoort, *With Trotsky in Exile*, p.145-6)

As we have seen, the relations of the British section with Cannon were bad even before the war. Cannon thought the British Trotskyists ought to accept the leadership of the Americans. He was convinced that his personal relations with Trotsky ought to give him a borrowed authority, not understanding that the only authority a genuine revolutionary leader can ask for is a political and a moral authority. He was guided by prestige politics—a very dangerous disease, with results that are invariably fatal.

When Cannon came to Britain before the war to unite the Trotskyist groups prior to the founding Conference of the Fourth International, he expected to be obeyed. But to his chagrin, he found that Ted and his comrades were not prepared to be bullied or pushed into a fusion that they regarded (correctly) as unprincipled.

After the war, the Revolutionary Communist Party was in a much stronger position, after having successfully built up a sizeable force. But by expressing differences with the Americans, they were asking for trouble with the International Secretariat. Relations with the IS had indeed been strained for some time. This was motivated by petty considerations such as Cannon's jealousy of the rising importance of the British section.

I believe that one of the main problems the leaders of the International had with the British comrades from the very start was that they knew they did not have a shred of authority with them. Worse still, the British leaders simply did not take them seriously. People who are obsessed with personal prestige take themselves very seriously indeed. They can put up with attacks and insults, but the one thing they cannot stand is not being taken seriously.

Cannon, Pablo and Healy

Following Trotsky's assassination in 1940, Cannon was effectively in control of the Fourth International. But he lacked Trotsky's moral and political authority. However, he was well-schooled in the gentle art of manoeuvring and used this to further his ends, with disastrous results. It is no accident that Cannon was initially an enthusiastic supporter of Zinoviev and his methods.

The International leadership could not win in a battle of ideas, so they resorted to other methods. With the backing of Sam Gordon (Stuart), Cannon, and then Pablo, Healy was continually manoeuvring against Ted Grant and the other RCP leaders to gain control of the organisation from 1943 onwards.

We have already mentioned how Healy was won over to Trotskyism by Jock Haston when, as part of a group of Stalinists, he tried to disrupt the WIL's activities at Speaker's Corner. After he joined the WIL, Healy's characteristic activism was regarded by Ted and Haston as an important resource. However, he immediately displayed total disregard for discipline (as it was apparent from the Irish episode which was referred to earlier), and was prone to intrigue. As his responsibilities within the WIL increased (including leading responsibilities in the EC), Healy periodically exploded at meetings and openly blackmailed the rest of the leadership by threatening his resignation in order to force through a particular decision. Ted and Jock Haston had to confront Healy several times, but always accepted him back into the organisation, in the hope that he would put his organisational skills at the service of the movement.

In February 1943, things came to a head, and Healy was expelled from the WIL:

The expulsion of Comrade G. Healy from our organisation will no doubt come as a shock to many of our members. The apparent suddenness of the action has made it necessary for the PB [Political Bureau] to explain the background of his expulsion from WIL.

At the conclusion of his industrial report on the second day of the National Central Committee meeting of February 6th and 7th, which was attended by provincial delegates, as well as the officials of the London District Committee, Comrade Healy stated that he was resigning from the organisation and joining the ILP on the following day; his action was not motivated by political differences but his personal inability to continue further work in our organisation with J. Haston, M. Lee and E. Grant.

He then left the meeting and was thereupon unanimously expelled from WIL by the Central Committee.

The same afternoon he discussed the question of entering the ILP with two leading London [ILP] members, who imparted the information to Fenner Brockway.

His action came as a complete surprise to the Central Committee since he had not intimated his intentions in the course of the previous sitting of the CC or in his industrial report. While many of the comrades present witnessed this scene for the first time, the majority of London CC members had witnessed a similar occurrence on numerous occasions since the beginning of 1939. In the first stages of these ultimatums in the form of "resignations" from our organisation, there was no political issue whatsoever bound up with his actions. But in the latter stages it was usually linked up to political issues which were the subject of controversy between the EC, the PB and G. Healy.

The first "resignation" was made to the organisation when *Youth for Socialism* was, for purely technical reasons, changed from a duplicated journal to a printed one at the beginning of 1939. Comrade Healy, who was then the formal publisher of *Youth for Socialism*, took strong objection because the decision had been taken in his absence! Later, in 1939, he again "resigned" on a similar insignificant issue on the same basis of personal pique.

At the end of 1939 when he was in Eire as a member of a delegation of comrades sent there by our centre, as the result of a controversy over secondary tactical issues relating to local activity, he "resigned" from the local and stated that he intended to join the Irish Labour Party to fight our organisation. For this action he was expelled by the Irish Group. After some discussion between the National Organiser and G. Healy, and between the NC and the Irish Group, it was conceded that he be sent back to England without the publicity of denouncing him before the organisation as a whole, and thus make it possible to utilise his energy in the interest of our party in Britain.

In 1940, the first really serious breach came when his "resignation" was linked to a political issue. At that time, Comrade Healy, who was then the representative of the EC in the capacity of National Organiser, was in Scotland. The constitution of the organisation had been redrafted by the EC with the object of bringing the statutes of the organisation into line with its development from a London local into a national organisation. As a representative of the EC, he was responsible for EC policy. Having any differences with the body that elected him, it was his elementary duty to raise such differences with that body, and failing satisfaction, then taking the question up with the membership. Instead of conducting himself as a responsible official and discussing his differences with the EC, he pressed forward a series of amendments to the Constitution through a number of locals with which he had close contact in his capacity as National Organiser. These amendments were of an opportunist character, reducing the Constitution to a federal, instead of a centralised basis. When called upon by the EC to defend his policy, he failed to put up any defence whatsoever, but instead launched a slanderous and personal attack upon two of the leading comrades in the centre and "resigned" from the organisation, because of his inability to work with these comrades.

In the last instance, comrade Healy's industrial report was to have been the subject of criticism and there is no doubt that his action was bound up with that question. Although he was invited to remain in the meeting for the political discussion on the industrial work, he refused to do this, but stated he could not work with the comrades mentioned.

On three other occasions a similar situation arose when the CC was presented with "resignations" arising out of insignificant issues.

During this period the EC made every concession to him, despite these continued disruptive acts. On each occasion, discussions were held with him in which the error of this type of ultimatum was demonstrated. During the whole of this period, the EC refrained from publicly branding these actions for what they were: crass irresponsibility, thereby allowing him to maintain a measure of authority in the organisation, and afford him the possibility of continued activity in the organisation, and afford him the possibility of continued activity in our ranks. This was done because it was believed that his undoubted organisational energy and ability could be harnessed in the interests of our party and that these concessions were to the benefit of both comrade Healy personally as well as of our organisation as a whole. (*Statement of the PB on the expulsion from WIL of G. Healy*, February 15, 1943, in Ted Grant, *Writings*, Vol. 2, p. 347-8)

Healy was then readmitted within the WIL. However, he was filled with resentment. He bore a grudge towards the rest of the leadership of the WIL and immediately started his intrigues all over again, this time joining his forces with Sam Gordon (Stuart) and later with Pablo.

Healy could never succeed in an honest political debate. At no time did he gain the support of more than a quarter of the RCP's members, which by 1947, had already dwindled and numbered a little over 300. However, his constant factional intrigues and dishonest methods rendered a proper political debate within the RCP impossible. And in the context of a difficult objective situation, it spread demoralisation among the membership.

Healy's twists and turns over political questions were positively comical. One of the disagreements with the leadership of the Fourth was over the issue of the Red Army and Eastern Europe. The RCP put forward the slogan for the withdrawal of the Red Army from Eastern Europe.

At a Central Committee meeting in February 1946, Healy voted for an RCP resolution demanding the Red Army's withdrawal. Two months later, pursuing what he took to be the line of the IS, he performed a 180 degree turn and launched a noisy campaign against the "revisionist" policy of the RCP leaders, and what he defined as the "anti-Internationalist leadership of the British Section". Unfortunately for Healy, in June, the International Executive Committee of the FI came out in favour of the withdrawal, a change of line of which he was completely ignorant.

The EC had sent a telegram to Paris asking for clarification of the International's position. The International had reconsidered their earlier position and realised it was untenable. They wrote back saying that they were for the withdrawal of the Red Army. Healy knew nothing about this letter and continued to rant and rave against the RCP's alleged revisionism. When he was asked to attend a meeting of the Political Committee on a different matter, he was shown the letter. Healy looked completely stunned for a moment—then said, "Well, so we got agreement"! So that was it. They got agreement—by letter! The comrades looked at each other in blank disbelief. Such a complete lack of principle was unprecedented in the movement.

Unable to win a majority by democratic means, Healy began to work openly for a split. His group decided to demand that the IEC divide the RCP and allow the minority to enter the Labour Party. That was merely a ruse to blackmail the party, since Healy intended to do it anyway. Standing the truth on its head, they accused Ted and Haston of fomenting "an atmosphere of crisis and ideological terror in the ranks" and hounding "worker critics with expulsions and threats".

In September 1947, despite the RCP's energetic protests against "a disgraceful manoeuvre to get rid of the democratically elected leadership of a section of the Fourth International", the IEC accepted the minority's request, and the next month a special conference of the RCP ratified the International's decision to split the party. It was a mortal blow to the RCP.

As a result, Healy's group broke away from the RCP. In so doing, they were carrying out the policy dictated by FI secretary Michel Pablo, who justified it as a way of winning over "whole sections of the workers in the Labour Party and in the trade unions affiliated with it to revolutionary action".

In vain, the RCP leaders tried to explain to the IS that there were no conditions for conducting successful revolutionary work in the Labour Party at that moment in time. As we explained above, the 1945 Labour government was the only Labour government in history that actually carried out its programme, nationalizing the railways, coal and steel, and introducing a sweeping programme of reforms that led to free education and a free health service—what is now known as the welfare state.

There were thus huge illusions in reformism. How could it be otherwise? Under these conditions, the right wing was in complete control of the Labour Party. The Labour Left was far weaker than it had been before the war. The road to the Labour workers was therefore blocked for Marxism. These were the conditions in which Healy's group began its work inside the Labour Party. They entered the Labour Party, as Ted pointed out, at the wrong time and with the wrong methods.

However, once in, far from fighting for a Marxist programme, they engaged in the deepest of deep entrism. They formed a secret organization known as the "Club", and in effect merged with the left reformists in such a way as to become virtually invisible. The Leninist policy of the united front is summed up in the slogan: march separately and strike together. But the first principle of the united front is: no mixing up of programmes and banners. This is precisely what Healy did, however. Far from winning over Labour workers to revolutionary ideas, as Pablo claimed, Healy was turning Trotskyists into left reformists.

His Socialist Fellowship included left MPs like Fenner Brockway and even Bessie Braddock, and Healy collaborated with them, not on immediate concrete issues, which would have been permissible, but on the basis of a common reformist programme. What we had here was not episodic agreements with the left reformists but *a programmatic bloc*, which was sheer liquidationist opportunism. The paper of Healy's Club, *Socialist Outlook*, was in reality a left reformist paper. They had sacrificed the building of a revolutionary organization for the sake of acquiring an amorphous and fictional "influence" on the Labour Left.

The Healy group attacked the RCP for not supporting this opportunist line. "They [the RCP] opposed the central tactic of the movement around *Socialist Outlook*. At that time, in the Labour Party, the evident task for revolutionaries was to assist the organisation of a Left Wing", stated the Healyites. They declared that their priority was not to build a revolutionary tendency, but rather to "build the Left" around *Socialist Outlook* and later *Tribune*.

Replying to this, the comrades stated: "Quite apart from the incorrectness of the idea of 'organising the Left', the 'tactic' of the *Socialist Outlook* entailed the complete subordination of

Healy and Co. to those 'Lefts' like Bessie Braddock, who was the 'parliamentary correspondent' of this journal, as well as holding shares in it."

Comrade Ted always rejected the idea of "building the Left". In *Problems of Entrism* (1959) he explained:

> Our job in the preparatory period, which still exists, is patiently winning the ones and twos, perhaps of small groups, but certainly not the creation of a mass revolutionary current, which is not possible at the present time. To attempt to shout louder than one's voice merely results in hoarseness and ultimately the loss of voice altogether. We have to establish ourselves as a tendency in the Labour Movement.
>
> Opportunism is only the other side of adventurism. Both rise out of a false assessment of objective circumstances, or of a surrender to the immediate environment. That is why, without a firm theoretical basis and collective control of the movement, it is easy to succumb to one mistake or the other (...).

While the Marxists will participate in the Left, it has never been our task to "build the left". The Left can only be built on the basis of events. Even if we wanted to do so, our forces are far too small. The Left can only be built by the hammer blow of events and not the efforts of a tiny group. Those who have attempted to do so, have inevitably ended up in the swamp of opportunism.

This was not a new question. Every attempt to cuddle up to the Lefts has led to disaster. Even before Healy, Trotsky strongly criticised Pierre Frank and Raymond Molinier (among the leaders of the French Trotskyists) who proposed a bloc, not with reformists, but with a centrist current. Trotsky completely broke with them. He wrote: "When Molinier tried to replace the party programme by 'four slogans' and create a paper on that basis, I was among those who proposed his expulsion." (Trotsky, *In Defence of Marxism*).

How the RCP was destroyed

Like Ted, Jock Haston was completely opposed to this opportunism. But by this time, Haston was demoralized. The party was facing growing difficulties and losing members. Under these conditions, Haston raised the idea of entry into the Labour Party. Ted and Jimmy were not at all convinced. There were many doubts in the ranks of the party. Some (the Open Party faction) were in favour of maintaining the RCP as an open party. Ted agreed that the conditions for entry laid down by Trotsky did not exist, but he argued that, in the given objective conditions, only modest gains could be made regardless, whether inside or outside the Labour Party. On the other hand, he expected that the conditions for entry would mature at some point, and preparatory work could be conducted, and certain gains could be made. But mainly in order to save Haston and maintain the unity of the leadership, Ted and Jimmy assented. That was a big mistake.

The RCP approached the International in Paris, but were told in so many words: don't ask us, speak to our British section in the Labour Party. Negotiations were opened with Healy, who agreed to unity, but only on certain conditions. Allegedly in order to facilitate unification, there was to be no discussion of the disputed questions for the initial period of six months. Meanwhile, all the property, offices, etc., was to be handed over to the "united" leadership—that is, to Healy.

Ted opposed these conditions, but the majority of the leadership disastrously acquiesced and the "unification" was accepted. In July 1949, the RCP formally dissolved itself, and its members joined the Labour Party individually. By the edict of the IS, they were placed under the leadership of Healy, on the absurd grounds that his utterly false political perspectives had been proved correct.

The former members of the RCP majority far outnumbered Healy's 80 or so supporters, and would certainly have deposed him at the Club's 1950 conference, if there had been a minimum of democracy in the group. But there was not. The decision to halt discussion on the disputed issues was a manoeuvre aimed at paralysing the comrades who disagreed with Healy. Once the fusion took place, Healy acted in a dictatorial fashion, expelling people on the most trivial pretexts up and down the country.

Ted recalled: "The atmosphere was really terrible. The theoretical level was abysmally low. It was really ignorant." Haston was shattered. In February 1950, he resigned, unable to stand the poisonous atmosphere any longer. Most of the few assets the RCP had were in the name of Haston, but, according to Ted, by this stage Haston was too demoralized to take legal action, and therefore all the assets of the RCP ended up in Healy's hands. For this reason, Ted always insisted that the property of the organization should never be in the name of one individual, no matter how trustworthy.

Charlie Van Gelderen wrote to Ted on the Haston situation in a letter dated May 8, 1950. In it, Van Gelderen writes about an EC resolution against Jock Haston. Apparently, in spite of Haston having resigned, the EC (that is to say, Healy) was insisting on expelling him, together with his wife Millie. Ted opposed that decision and Van Gelderen seems to agree with him, but decided not to defend that position and to state differences on the procedure—a rather cowardly attitude—but one that was dictated by Van Gelderen's own demoralisation and complete subordination to the leadership of the International. He writes:

> After turning the matter over in my mind over and over again, I have come to the conclusion that this is not an issue which would justify defiance of [the] Club decision—though I am still hoping that the EC will be shifted from their position. If Jock had issued some sort of statement which would have contained some rebuttal of the EC's political charges against him, we could have used that as a basis for a fight against the EC resolution, but he has behaved in a completely irresponsible manner, both before and after his resignation, leaving high and dry those who were closest to him. We just haven't a leg to stand on.
>
> From my point of view, there is another factor, which follows on the views I expressed to you. I have no principled differences with the present leadership, though, of course, there is a possibility that these may develop in the course of the discussion on Eastern Europe, on which I have very definite views. For me, the FI is my only and final political home. If events should be so shaped that I am compelled to sever my connection with it, then it's goodbye to politics for me for a long long time to come. I am certainly not prepared to start any fresh "regroupment". You will agree, I feel sure, that the JH question is not sufficiently important for me to commit political hari-kari at this stage.

The letter is concluded by an amusing remark,

> PS: By the way, as a result of your betting venture, you owe us 6/- less 1/2d so, when you can spare it, this little sum will be most welcome. (*Van Gelderen to Ted Grant*, May 8, 1950, in the Ted Grant archives)

Weakness invites aggression. The refusal to make a stand against the wave of expulsions only encouraged Healy to continue. Millie Kahn (now Haston's wife), Roy Tearse, George Hanson and George Noseda, were all pushed out. At the executive in March 1950, Jimmy Deane argued that the resolution condemning Haston's embrace of reformism should wait until he had produced a written statement, but they passed it anyway. When he subsequently informed

SOCIALIST APPEAL

SPECIAL NUMBER.   JULY, 1949

DECLARATION

ON THE DISSOLUTION OF THE REVOLUTIONARY COMMUNIST PARTY AND THE ENTRY OF ITS MEMBERS INTO THE LABOUR PARTY

Healy of his disagreement with the leadership's approach, he was required "to indicate in writing political support for the EC resolution condemning Haston, without any reservations *immediately.*" (*EC Statement on the Conduct of JD*, May 24, 1950).

That was the last straw for Jimmy. He was expelled from the Club in June 1950 for failure to respond. He wrote to his brother Brian on June 4, 1950: "(…) even the Stalinists don't conduct themselves in this way. The Club is not a Trotskyist movement but a degenerate clique." He wrote a letter to Ted urging him to gather together all those who remained to fight to defend the genuine traditions of Trotskyism, but this plea has an almost despairing tone. It is dated May 6, 1950:

> Dear Ted,
>
> I hope Arthur has passed on to you that masterpiece of slander and evasion from Healy. I should like to have your suggestions. Personally I feel like getting down to quite a lengthy reply in which I would try to show what has really happened to the movement.
>
> What are you doing Ted? What is your perspective? And what are you prepared to do within the present outfit to push a line?
>
> Frankly, I think that we must try to get together the few remaining comrades capable of thought. We should organise a meeting and allocate: a) the production of a political resolution on perspectives for Trotskyism, b) a document critically analysing the work accomplished and demonstrating the lack of perspective, tactic, etc., contained in the Healy resolution of 1949. (What a stupid resolution this is!)
>
> These are both necessary for the pre-conference discussion, presuming that we are still in at the time. (Healy has completely isolated me so far as the life of the Club goes, apart from Liverpool). In fact the Liverpool branch has received nothing from London, not even a reply to its letters, etc.
>
> If you could afford it I would come to London to discuss with you and Harry; but I am finding it more difficult to manage. As much as you dislike writing letters couldn't you drop a line from time to time?
>
> I don't know if you have thought about the question of your own political future. I suppose you have. But don't you think you should work out a path in which you could make some real contribution. I personally feel that you could do a tremendous amount if you would (even at the expense of everything else) concentrate upon writing—we would produce it here, if other sources could not be found… You must do something Ted, you are the only one capable of defending and developing the real programme of our movement.
>
> What position have you taken up on Jock? What do you think we should do? Please write, if not yourself dictate to Arthur—make Arthur work hard as a "secretary" (!) (By the way I'm pleased he's got work.)
>
> Ask Arthur to return H's letter—I must reply to it soon.
>
> Take care of yourself and please write me a long letter *soon*, very soon.
>
> Best wishes to you, Arthur and Harry (is he still in England?)
>
> Jim
>
> PS. How are Jock and Millie, on what basis did Roy Tearse resign? Could you please ask Millie to send me Heaton's [Heaton Lee] address? He's in Birkenhead.

But it was already too late. Healy proceeded to expel all those who refused to break personal contact with Haston. Ted too was expelled, after 22 years membership of the Trotskyist movement. He was also a member of the Executive Committee of the Fourth International, but that made no difference to Healy or his masters in Paris. There is a note of desperation in a letter written by Jimmy Deane to a French comrade and friend, Raoul, on June 25, 1950, not long after his expulsion:

> The situation of the movement in England is terrible. There has been a complete collapse. Jock, Millie [illegible] and the other leading comrades have left the movement. Healy and his supporters have gained complete control of what is left. Only recently I have been expelled because along with Ted Grant I represented a potential political opposition to Healy's role. You know Raoul the most amazing things happen in this small group. People are expelled right and left without any serious reason. Of course I am fighting for my reintegration in the group and have just sent off an appeal to Izzie. Perhaps

c/o Ericsson Telephones Ltd,
Head Post Office,
Craven Arms,
Shropshire.

May 6th 1950.

Dear Ted,

I hope Arthur has passed on to you that master-piece of slander and evasion from Healy. I should like to have your lengthy suggestions. Personally I feel like getting down to quite a reply in which I would try to show what has really happened to the movement.

What are you doing Ted? What is your perspective? and what are you prepared to do within the present outfit to push a line?

Frankly, I think that we must try to get together the few remaining comrades capable of thought. We should organise a meeting and allocate a) the production of a political resolution on perspectives for Trotskyism, b) a document critically analysing the work accomplished and demonstrating the lack of perspective, tactics contained in the Healy resolution of 1949. These are both necessary for the pre-conference discussion, presuming that we are still in at that time. (Healy has completely isolated me so far as the life of the Club goes, apart from L'pool). In fact the Liverpool branch has received nothing from London, not even a reply to its letters, etc.

If I could afford it I would come to London to discuss with you and Harry; but I am finding it more difficult to manage. As much as you dislike writing letters couldn't you drop a line from time to time?

I don't know if you have thought about the question of your own political future. I suppose you have. But don't you think you should work out a path in which you could make some real contribution. I personally feel that you could do a tremendous amount if you would (even at the expense of everything else) concetrate upon writing - we would produce it here, if other sources could not be found.. You must do something Ted, you're the only one capable of defending and developing the real programme of our movement.

What position have you taken up on Jock? What do you think we should do? Please write, if not yourself dictate to Arthur - make Arthur work hard as a secretary(!) (By the way I'm pleased he's got work.)

Jimmy Deane's letter to Ted

G. [Gabriel, i.e. Pablo] knows what is taking place here and supports it, but if he knew or understood the truth, he would be horrified.

The [Healy] grouping here has prevented any political discussion for almost a year. No political discussion has been allowed in the branches, and now on the eve of the pre-conference discussion I have been expelled and others have been threatened with expulsion. Let me repeat the charges are stupid in the extreme. No one can treat them seriously.

There is no public organ of Trotskyism. Healy combines the most ultra revolutionary phrases with the most disgusting opportunism. The paper is nothing but a vehicle through which the most barren and dangerous elements express themselves. Dangerous because, as LT [Trotsky] pointed out, they act as a left-cover for the LP bureaucracy. Instead of exposing these left demagogues it actually supports them. The paper has never attacked the Stalinists.

Things have come to a pretty pass. I see that G. [Pablo] has now come over to the position we proposed on Yugoslavia, etc. The Group here now has no position of its own on anything, but continues nevertheless, to conduct a campaign against the positions held by the ex-RCP (you know of course that we fused with Healy and entered the LP) on Britain, where we have been a hundred per cent correct, on Yugoslavia where, again, we were the only ones in the International to state that this was a workers' state, on European recovery, where we stood bitter hostility because we said there would be recovery—so on and so on.

However we do not feel despondent. Truth comes out in the end. The fact that Joe Hansen, E.R. Frank, G. and others finally arrive at basically the same conclusions as we on Yugoslavia and Eastern Europe is only proof of this. The present period is perhaps a necessary one in the clarification and sorting out of our ideas. That is the task. To prepare patiently and seriously for the future.

Jimmy was far too optimistic about the moral scruples of Pablo and Mandel. Ted's expulsion was ratified at the Third World Congress on the motion of Ernest Mandel who was known by his Party name, Ernest Germaine.

There was an irony to all of this. Healy was notorious in the whole movement as a gangster. An old member of the ILP I once met described him as a "horrible little monster", and that opinion was almost universal. Healy had been expelled from the WIL on several occasions for his bad behaviour. But on each occasion, he would appeal against his expulsion and Ted and Jock would support his acceptance back into the Party, in the hope of making use of his organizational skills. But now that the boot was on the other shoe, Healy showed no such generosity.

Jock Haston was effectively driven out of the movement by Healy. But he was also a victim of the so-called leaders of the Fourth International. Soon after, Haston broke with Trotskyism altogether and moved to the right, although remaining in the Labour movement.

I only met him on one occasion, and that was in the 1970s, many years after he had been separated from the Trotskyist movement. But I had an inkling of how far he had moved. This was a time when the bosses were pushing hard to introduce productivity deals and measured day work in place of piece work, which the workers had managed to turn to their advantage on the basis of strong union organization in the workplaces.

In order to succeed, the bosses needed to involve the unions in what was really a counter-revolution on the shop floor. When I was studying this plan I was given a document published by the education department of the ETU, the electricians' union, which was then under extreme right-wing leadership. When I read the article on measured day work I was surprised at the line of argument, which defended a reactionary position with left-sounding arguments.

The author argued that Lenin was in favour of raising labour productivity and even defended Taylorism in the 1920s. However, he conveniently failed to mention that Lenin was talking about the need to raise labour productivity *in a workers' state*, not under capitalism! He even claimed that measured day work could be a step in the direction of workers' control. The name of the author was—Jock Haston. This is conclusive proof of the old saying: "the devil can quote scripture".

I think it was at a Labour Party Conference when Ted introduced me to Haston. He was visibly aged, and not merely by the passing of the years. Gone was the dashing, handsome, energetic revolutionary of the RCP. In his place stood an aged, broken man, attempting to conceal his apostasy from himself with a thin veneer of cynicism. He was not at all hostile, however, but came across as tired and worn out, a man with nothing left to give, a living phantom.

I have often had occasion to note the same phenomenon in people who have dropped out of the movement, especially when they have previously played a leading role. They seem to lose their bearings, not just in politics but in life. They drift aimlessly, like a rudderless ship, until they sink without trace.

I watched Ted's face as he stood next to his old comrade-in-arms, and noticed an expression I had not seen before, and never saw afterwards. It was a pained expression of deep regret and sadness, as if to say: "Old friend, what have you done? What a terrible waste!" But Ted said nothing except a few pleasantries and they parted without ever communicating anything to each other. After all, what was there to say?

As a postscript to this sorry tale, it seems only fair to add that Gerry Healy got his just deserts in the end. He was exposed by his own comrades as a swindler and a tyrant, and kicked out of his own organization, having been found guilty, among other things, of corruption, abuse of office, and serious sexual offences against female comrades. His name, if it is ever remembered by future generations, will be forever equated with shame and iniquity. So there is some justice left on earth after all.

"They have destroyed the Fourth International"

The destruction of the RCP removed the only serious obstacle in the path of the degeneration of the Fourth International. After that, Pablo, Mandel and Frank felt free to ride roughshod over internal democracy and wipe out all dissent by organizational means. All opposition was ruthlessly crushed. No dissent was allowed. They were only interested in an obedient organization, forgetting what Lenin had once warned Bukharin: "You want obedience? You will get obedient fools".

When Mandel and Frank timidly tried to raise objections to Pablo's line, they were soon brought to heel by the Boss. Behind it were considerations of personal prestige. Pablo is quoted as saying: "What do you wish? As for me, I have my baton as a marshal. I cannot accept being thrown out of the International Secretariat." (Quoted in R.J. Alexander, *International Trotskyism*, p. 381). This winged phrase just about sums up the mentality of such people: generals without an army, puffed up with their own importance and eaten up with the sickness of prestige politics.

The Zinovievist methods of the International leadership were a recipe for new crises and splits. These people could not stay together for long: "Unlucky at fusions and lucky at splits", Ted used to joke. In 1953, the Fourth International duly split in two: the Americans set up a rival outfit to Pablo in Paris. This was really only a split between two rival cliques. But for Gerry Healy, the split between Pablo and Cannon was manna from heaven.

Healy, the former slavish supporter of Pablo, immediately jumped ship and went over to Cannon. The Russian peasants had a saying: "God is in heaven and the tsar is far away." As far as Healy was concerned, it was preferable to have the International leadership in New York rather than in Paris: the further away the better. He now had virtually a free hand in Britain.

The same manoeuvres that had been carried out in Britain were now continued in France. It is no accident that there was fierce opposition to Pablo in France. The IS was based in Paris and the French Trotskyists could see how their "leaders" were carrying on. The leader of Raoul's faction was Marcel Bleibtreu (also known as Pierre Favre). When Pablo raised the idea of "entrism *sui generis*", the majority of the French section (the Parti Communiste Internationaliste, or PCI) had moved into opposition to Pablo, and by 1952, his faction had the majority of the PCI, leaving Pablo in a minority. But being in a minority never prevented Pablo from deciding the political line. He merely suspended the majority! This split the French section in two.

Jimmy Deane, who was especially interested in the French section, looked on, appalled at the reports coming from across the Channel. He wrote an indignant letter to someone called Bob with instructions it be passed urgently to Ted Grant. It is dated Liverpool, July 23, 1952:

Dear Bob,

Thanks for your letter, I'm sorry to be a little late in replying.

I have received a collection of material and a letter from France. There have been some important developments there. It's a long story and, in any case, I haven't yet had an opportunity of "reading" the documents—*some of which we must have translated and distributed*. They are dynamite. We must see that every Healyite receive the news.

For the last 18 months the IS has been seeking to destroy the French majority—you will remember that the anti-Pablo elements gained the majority. For a time even Pierre Frank, [Jacques] Privas and Germaine [Mandel] opposed Pablo (Gabriel) and his manoeuvres. It is clear that Pablo exceeded in using "international discipline", threats of expulsions and sanctions (a repeat experience of Britain), to force the majority to accept the decision of the 8th plenum of the IEC which was:

1) That the IS supporters (the party minority) should have a majority of the PB [Political Bureau] to prepare for the PCI congress and 3 months after that congress.

2) Free and democratic discussion, etc., was guaranteed. The IS, etc., would take no organisational measures against the actual party majority.

The majority (in my opinion stupidly) accepted this under the threat of expulsion from the FI.

Naturally, every guarantee was broken, and two or more months before the PCI congress, which was held last week, the actual party minority (led by P. Frank, J. Privas, R. Mestre and Corvin) was preparing to split and to steal the party's equipment. On June 27th they actually broke into the party offices, using keys they had made at the beginning of May, and stole one electrically powered duplicator, two hand operated duplicators, some typewriters, etc. The PCI has written a series of statements addressed to the whole international branding Frank *et al* as the thieves and Pablo as the architect.

The minority were instructed to return the party's equipment, but refused to do so. They were then suspended.

Fifteen days before the PCI congress the minority announced that it would take no part, that it refused to recognise the decisions and elected leadership. Thus on the eve of the congress they split from the party.

Pablo is now arranging (probably has arranged) the expulsion of the French section. The French Healyites will be "officially appointed", etc.

I haven't been able to read the political resolutions carefully, but the central question appears to be that Pablo's faction has proposed, on the basis of a completely neo-Stalinist characterisation of the CPF [Communist Party of France] and the role of Stalinism, the entry of the PCI into the CPF. On this and a whole series of revisionist arguments they were defeated by the PCI members. Only a minority of petty bourgeois elements actually supported Pablo and his gang. Eventually the "faction Pabliste" proposed a "solution"—the carrying out of both tactics; that they should keep the independent party but in their TU work, factories, etc. submit themselves not to a bloc on practical issues, but literally submit themselves to the Stalinist forces.

This is the background to the struggle.

The PCI characterises Pablo's faction as neo-Stalinist liquidators, whilst they do not mention the British experience it is clear they have it in mind.

Fortunately, they are in a better mood and condition to resist Pablo and to rebuild. All the worker elements are with them, and they have some capable comrades in the lead (Lambert). However, I'm afraid that isolated and with the IS on its doorstep it will be very hard for them to survive. Had we some forces we could help [with the] distribution of documents to English speaking countries, etc. Clearly, we must officially contact them, discuss points and see how we can work together.

Gerard Bloch (who is with the majority) is impressed with our journal. He says he will write.

Have you anyone in London who can make first class translations? Mine are not first class (not even tenth!) and in any case it would take a great time to make them. But we must see to it that the declarations are printed in English and distributed. I'll do it under my name to prevent any reflections on the PCI—just in case.

This development is important and in my opinion good. It shows that one can still hope, they are not all lost, and our evaluation of Pablo, Frank, Healy, Cannon, *et al*, has been absolutely correct. These bastards have wrecked the FI [Fourth International]. Sooner or later this truth will penetrate even the thick skulls of [illegible], the Indians and the Americans. (...)

In 1952, there were two congresses of the PCI. The majority had about a hundred members and the minority about thirty. Others dropped out in disgust. Prominent in Bleibtreu's faction was a young worker called Pierre Lambert, a trade unionist and head of the CPI's Labour Commission. Bleibtreu later was expelled by Lambert over disagreements on the Algerian question, and Lambert assumed the leadership of his faction.

Those who followed Pablo's line and entered the French Communist Party, were soon absorbed into the Stalinist milieu or else expelled. In Brest, where the Trotskyists had played a leading role in an important strike in 1950, they disappeared altogether. The destructive effects of Zinovievist methods continued to wreak havoc in the already weakened ranks of the movement. Defeat had turned to rout.

Chapter Five

The Times That Try Men's Souls

These are the times that try men's souls. The summer soldier and the sunshine patriot will, in this crisis, shrink from the service of their country; but he that stands it now, deserves the love and thanks of man and woman. Tyranny, like hell, is not easily conquered; yet we have this consolation with us, that the harder the conflict, the more glorious the triumph. What we obtain too cheap, we esteem too lightly: it is dearness only that gives everything its value. (Thomas Paine, *The American Crisis*)

A voice in the wilderness
By the end of 1950, the wrecking actions of Healy had destroyed the Party. What followed was the most difficult period in Ted's life. It was a grim period, both personally and politically. It brings to mind the words of the Bible: "I am the voice of one crying in the wilderness" (*John*, 1:23). He found himself isolated; the movement itself was struggling to survive. In crossing a desert, every step requires a tremendous effort. A man trying to climb a dune composed of loose sand finds that for every painful step forward, he slips back again, exhausted. This happens again and again. In the desert nobody can hear your voice. And there is no end in sight.

Ted once told me of a conversation he had with Jock Haston in the late 1940s. Haston was already pretty demoralized and was at the point of abandoning the movement. His thinking was clear from this exchange. He said: "What if Shachtman is right and there is a new ruling class that is developing the means of production. Shouldn't we join them?" Ted's reply was absolutely characteristic. "In that case, we would join the slaves, like Spartacus." In this one line you have the essence of Ted Grant.

During the long capitalist upswing that followed the Second World War, the small forces of genuine revolutionary Marxism were reduced to a tiny handful, isolated from the masses. To add to the political problems, Ted was in severe financial straits. After being forced to give up full-time political work, Ted took a job for a while as a door-to-door salesman, selling brushes.

In the late 1940s, Ted had been living in the offices of the RCP, in 256 Harrow Road. The dissolution of the Party therefore made him homeless. Thrown out of the Party headquarters, Ted went to live in Hackney in an old caravan on a derelict bomb-site. It was not very comfortable, but at least it was rent-free. Until, one day, he was served with an eviction notice by the council after a complaint by a woman who must have been unnerved by her unconventional neighbour. In the end, Ted got lucky. The council re-housed him in a flat, 64 Oakley Road, Islington, a road he remained in for the rest of his active life.

In Ted's archives there is a touching letter he received from his younger sister Zena, who had participated in the movement throughout the 1930s. She joined Lee's South African WIL after the war. According to Ted, she became a Shachtmanite, but she dropped out of activity after the break-up of the movement. She remained in South Africa and ended up as a renowned grower of exotic plants and shrubs, which were featured in various magazines. In the latter part of her life, she and her husband were subject to a violent attack at their home, which resulted in them giving up their beloved farm and plants for fear of future attacks. She died of liver cancer in the mid-1980s.

"I never attacked her for these Shachtmanite views", Ted said. But this letter indicates that there had been some pretty sharp disagreements, so much so that she asks him for forgiveness for the harsh things she had said. This letter offers us a fascinating and all-too-rare glimpse into Ted's personal circumstances and relations with his family.

PO Box 2852, Johannesburg

15th December 1955

My dear Ted,

Many thanks for your long and enjoyable letter. It's grand reading what you write but difficult to do so. Be a love and don't write on both sides of the paper!

I was delighted to hear that you had such a wonderful trip to Paris. Actually I was luckier than you having spent in all three and a half months there. Next to Paris—London is the most wonderful City! However don't let's argue about the merits or demerits of either. I'd give a great deal now to be in one or another of them. I'm afraid finances just don't permit any changes or holidays at the moment but one just goes on hoping and planning for the possibility in 1957. As you are no doubt aware SA [South Africa] politically is a cesspool—a demoralising country to live in. Yet one has one's ties and roots and the earning of a living to consider.

Anyway one day I hope to see you again in 1957. I'm sorry to hear that you are in financial difficulties and am glad that Ray and Rae did a little to help. Believe me if ever I am able I shall gladly do what I can. At the moment we are still not entirely on our feet. Raymond has this large family to support and although the Nursery is improving steadily what I draw from it and Teddy's earnings just keep us reasonably paying our way. Our prospects are quite bright as we have improved our facilities and are almost out of debt apart from bonds and the like.

However don't hesitate to let me know if things are really tough. Isy was most impressed by the fact that you never mentioned your circumstances to him. A few hours before he received your letter he had one from Rae asking him to do what he could to assist you. It is at least gratifying to know that you are well and leading an active political life—a life of your own choosing. I was most interested in your attempt to gather the shattered forces of the Movement together and I wish you and your comrades' success in doing all that you want. You have a rare courage and persistence and I admire this notwithstanding [from] where or how it derives, in your unshakeable beliefs and convictions or if you suck it out of your thumb. I do only hope that you get your full measure of satisfaction doing what you want. I doubt if I'd ever be politically active again. I *was* edified and proud of my dear brother, that his work in the RCP has stood the test of time and appears to be so accurate. I suppose being a *true* revolutionary enables one to care so little for one's own "brief spam" and to work for a future so remote and so impersonal.

I'm very glad though that despite the work you had to do in Paris, you found time to play a little and drink the good grape and enjoy the inexhaustible beauty of Paris. I suppose English beer and food is a little stodgy—especially after the fare one has in Paris. I think the most civilized people I know are interested in good food.

Incidentally your little sister Zena is considered an excellent cook—she thinks so too. Perhaps when I come to London next and money and buying possibilities are better than last time I'll be able to spoil you and cook some good meals for you. I always have a tiny ache and regret that perhaps I wasn't as nice to you as I might have been. I did argue and hurt you at times—if so I hope you have at least forgiven me, if not forgotten it. (...)

I want you to get this for Christmas so must get it off in a hurry. I wish you so much happiness and success in all you do. Much love and blessings for Xmas and New Year.

Zena

It takes a particular kind of courage to keep going in a period of general backsliding and apostasy, such as the 1950s. But Ted took all these difficulties philosophically. I mean that in the literal sense of the words. His attitude to adversity brings to mind that of the Stoics, or even more, of the Cynics of ancient Greece. By one of those strange quirks of history and language, the word "cynic" nowadays means precisely the opposite of what it meant then.

History has dealt unkindly with the Cynic philosophers. The term "Cynic" comes from the Greek word κυνικός, *kynikos*, "dog-like", and from κύων, *kyôn*, "dog." It may have been intended as an insult by their enemies, but they seem to have embraced it cheerfully, pointing out that dogs behave more naturally than "civilized" people. The Cynics lived a simple life and tried to reduce their needs to a minimum in order to win freedom. They were also rebels who rejected all the accepted norms of "civilized" behaviour. The founder of this philosophy, Diogenes of Sinope, is famously said to have lived in a barrel. The story goes that when Alexander the Great offered to give him anything he wished, he replied: "Stand aside, you are blocking the sun".

It is this total indifference to material things and social conventions that Ted Grant shared with them. In some ways he resembled the popular image of an absent-minded professor, the kind of man whose shirt buttons are done up the wrong way, who has egg stains on his tie and odd socks on his feet. Of such people it is often said that they have their "head in the clouds". This is meant as a mild rebuke, but in fact it is a compliment. The minds of most people are filled with everyday mundane considerations. Such "practical" thought is useful for basic survival but extremely limited. But a man or woman whose head is "in the clouds" lives on a different level. Their thought has reached a higher level—the level where real human thinking can begin, the level of philosophical thought.

It is only by maintaining one's eyes firmly fixed on the highest principles and broadest historical generalizations that it is possible to rise above objective difficulties. As Trotsky wrote about his own position in the dark days of the 1930s: "Life is not an easy matter... You cannot live through it without falling into prostration and cynicism unless you have before you a great idea which raises you above personal misery, above weaknesses, above all kinds of perfidy and baseness." (Trotsky, *Diary in Exile*, p. 68).

Ted Grant was able to survive this difficult period precisely because he was able to transcend the existing conditions through the power of thought, to see beyond the particulars and rise to the level of the general. That is why he always insisted on the importance of perspectives, which set out from the given, but seeks to uncover the hidden processes that lie beneath the "facts", and allow us to peer into the future. That was the secret of his indomitable sense of optimism. It reminds one of the words with which the young Trotsky greeted the birth of the 20th century:

> Death to Utopia! Death to faith! Death to love! Death to hope! thunders the twentieth century in salvos of fire and in the rumbling of guns.
>
> —Surrender, you pathetic dreamer. Here I am, your long awaited twentieth century, your "future."
>
> —No, replies the unhumbled optimist: You, you are only the present. (*The Age of the Permanent Revolution, A Trotsky Anthology*, p. 41)

Against the stream

In the space of just a few years, Ted had lost almost all his old friends and comrades. The great exception was that redoubtable family from Liverpool, the Deane family: Jimmy, Arthur and Brian. Despite all the difficulties, they managed to keep the Tendency alive. The group had a base in Liverpool around the Deanes, and in the Labour League of Youth, where they published a small duplicated paper called *Rally*. They attempted to regroup and salvage as much as possible from the wreckage of the RCP. Without any full timers or apparatus, the comrades struggled to hold things together.

They faced formidable obstacles. The older generation was largely destroyed, exhausted and burnt out, dragged down by the pressures of family life, their consciousness blunted by the prolonged upswing in capitalism. Their old hopes of revolutionary change seemed now to be hopeless dreams. Some remained loyal to the ideas but became separated from the Tendency, only to return after a delay of many years. But for every one of these, there were many more who lost hope altogether, either dropping out of politics or even drifting to the Right.

The main reason for their isolation was to be found mainly in the objective conditions: the prolonged economic upswing in the United States, Western Europe and Japan. Ted used to say: "Even if Marx, Engels, Lenin and Trotsky had been present it would not have made a fundamental difference. It would still have been a question of winning the ones and twos."

The financial difficulties still persisted. As late as 1958, his relatives in South Africa were still worried about him, as we can see from the following letter from his brother Isy in Johannesburg, dated July 31:

> Dear Ted,
>
> Just a few lines to let you know we are now all well. Sadie has had a rather serious internal operation and Adele an emergency appendix operation but they are now both almost back to normal.
>
> Business in this country has slumped badly, and there is almost a depression taking place. This may be an after effect of the American recession, because there is not much unemployment but money is very scarce. We are in no danger, but many smaller firms have closed down and the owners have lost all they had.
>
> How are things with you? Do you need any clothes? If you do, don't hesitate to tell me the truth, and I will send you some. We hear that England is having quite a wave of prosperity, but I do not usually believe what the newspapers say.
>
> Hoping to hear from you soon, and that this finds you in the best of health,
>
> With love from all,
>
> As ever
>
> Isy

Ted's brother, who was a partner in a wholesale business back in Johannesburg, was not wrong about the economic situation in Britain. Business was booming and there was full employment. Living standards were rising, and people could buy more of the kind of things that seemed to be commonplace in the United States if you could believe the things you saw in the films. For the first time, washing machines and refrigerators appeared in some homes. There were televisions and even cars—second hand of course. Compared to the misery of the 1930s, things did not seem too bad.

The Conservatives won the general election in 1951, although the Labour Party polled almost a quarter of a million total votes more than the Tories and their National Liberal allies combined. In fact, Labour won the highest number of votes of any political party in any

Isy's letter to Ted

election in British history. The economic upswing that followed allowed the Tories to remain in power for the next thirteen years. Their new-found confidence was summed up by the Conservative leader Harold MacMillan in his celebrated phrase: "You have never had it so good!"

In May 1951, the first national conference of the group took place in London. It was reported that there were twenty members in London and eleven in Liverpool, with a scattering of contacts around the country. In the circumstances, the group had no alternative but to work in the Labour Party. The conference decided to launch a theoretical magazine, the *International Socialist*. The programmatic basis of the group was Ted Grant's *Statement to the British Section of the Fourth International*, circulated after his expulsion in the autumn of 1950.

Jimmy Deane, his brothers Arthur and Brian, and others helped to gather funds to launch the new publication. The first issue of the new magazine, with Ted as its editor, appeared in February 1952. It was supposed to come out every two months. However, the lack of resources and a paucity of funds meant that the magazine appeared only spasmodically between February 1952 and April 1954. In Liverpool, a base was established in the Walton constituency. By 1952, Jimmy Deane was chair of the party, and he worked very effectively with the secretary, Laura Kirton. But progress was slow and difficult.

Only a few of the old RCP comrades such as George Macartney and Arthur Cowderoy were left, together with Brian Deane and his wife Beryl, who did excellent work among the youth. They had a trade union base in the Liverpool Central branch of the ETU. There was a trickle of young recruits, but most dropped out. A major boost was the recruitment of a youngster called Pat Wall from Garston. Together with Jimmy, he became a regular delegate to Labour Party conference.

Ted was put forward as the prospective Labour candidate for Walton, but the vote was lost narrowly. In retrospect this was probably not a bad thing. I personally cannot see Ted Grant as a member of the Parliamentary Labour Party, giving lectures on perspectives to the back benches. And while it may be theoretically possible to build a Marxist tendency from such a position, there are always serious risks involved. In such a small group, to have the leading comrade drawn into the morass of parliamentary life would have almost surely had negative consequences.

Although he had very important qualities, Jimmy had a tendency to look for shortcuts. He had put a lot of effort into getting Ted elected, and he took the result very badly. To make matters worse, he was involved in a bad accident and had a series of personal problems. Towards the end of 1954, he suffered a personal crisis. Ted began to have serious worries about Jimmy's morale. The idea that he could lose his most trusted comrade, having already lost so many, must have cost him many sleepless nights. But on January 4, 1955, Jimmy wrote to reassure him that the worst was over:

> Dear Ted,
>
> May I first offer you the warmest greetings for the coming year. I sincerely hope that 1955 will bring some successes in the way of a functioning national group.
>
> I want to say how sorry I was to have been compelled to leave the discussion on Monday. I was in a difficult position, and didn't feel that my action would have been interpreted as it seems to have been.
>
> You need have no anxiety at all about my political future. In this sense your analogy of MS [Max Shachtman] and the Old Man was entirely misplaced. Frankly, the rumoured [sic] attitude of the comrades makes one a little (!) indignant.

Anyway, I've no intention of becoming deeply involved in LP committee work, I'll do what I can from the floor. In the next few months I shall try to get a caucus organised in the Walton area, and an ETU caucus on the TCLP [Trades Council and Labour Party] as well perhaps as get the comrades taking up the real work—for the most part they've missed everything.

One thing which will have to be done is to find a bridge to the industrial elements with Healy in Birkenhead. Pennington is a very good type, so too are many of the others.

My intention quite definitely is to come to London in the summer to work with you in building a functioning centre, developing regular, living, contact with the various elements around us in the provinces, via regular correspondence, model resolutions, directives, and if possible a regular monthly journal.

This, incidentally, would be the greatest help for the comrades in Liverpool and would enable us to win the best elements in the LPRG [Labour Party Marxist Group, led by Healy], possibly training one or two for professional work.

Better than anyone else I know the opportunities in Liverpool (indeed much of it is outside the work of the group, not, of course, deliberately so), but in the end, *as a tendency*, it is a question of building an active functioning centre in London, with a journal and a professional.

Please keep in touch.

With warmest greetings to you and the comrades,

Jim

As subsequent experience showed, Jimmy made a bad error of judgment when he described Bob Pennington, who was one of Healy's main henchmen on Merseyside, as "a very good type". However, this letter shows that he had recovered from his depression and had swung back into activity. Ted wrote back to express his immense relief:

It was a heavy blow to me politically and personally to think you might be drifting away (…) You and I are the last of the Old Guard and I would like to see you playing the rôle which you are fitted for (…) I always thought that both on Merseyside and nationally you had a vital role to play in the building of the Tendency. From this point of view your letter came to me like a hot cup of tea after a cold and exhausting day. (*Ted Grant to Jimmy Deane*, January 12, 1955)

"Will There Be a Slump?"

This barren decade seemed never-ending. It was a frustrating time, a time of small meetings, of long and frequently fruitless journeys to visit just one contact. With his habitual dogged determination Ted trudged from one poorly attended meeting and one draughty hall to another, always carrying his battered old briefcase bulging with speakers' notes (the age of the supermarket plastic bag had not yet dawned). In the *Lewisham Journal*, February 20, 1953 there is a small notice under the heading: *N. Lewisham Labour League of Youth*, which reads as follows:

North Lewisham Labour Party League of Youth were addressed on February 12 by Mr T. Grant on "Russia Today." Those present found this a most interesting talk, giving an entirely new light on an important subject.

Mr Grant said that the plans laid down by Lenin for the Workers' Democracy had been completely disregarded and Russia was now an official bureaucracy.

It was inevitable that a political revolution would overthrow Stalinism and this would probably be largely influenced by a successful Socialist policy in any of the Western countries.

This lecture was the third in a series provided by the National Council of Labour Colleges.

North Lewisham Labour League of Youth meets every Thursday at 61, Lee High Road. All people between the ages of 16 and 26 are very welcome. There are many varied interests, including political education on many problems, theatre visits and ice skating expeditions.

No information is given on how many people attended this most interesting talk, but it was probably just a handful.

Even the youth were affected by the prevailing conditions. They were encouraged to be non-political, to dedicate themselves to buying clothes, shoes and records, to listen to American music, to idolize Bill Haley and Elvis Presley, to drink Coca-Cola and dance Rock-and-Roll. But nothing can ever completely eradicate the innate rebelliousness of young people. Ted used to tell us: you can win over any youngster under 25 years of age, except for careerists and oddballs. I believe that is true. Gradually they began to attract a new layer of youth. But that was later, and it took a long time and many disappointments to get there.

There are certain parallels between this period and the long upswing in capitalism before the First World War. Similar conditions tend to produce similar results. Reformism was reinforced in a period where unemployment seemed to be a thing of the past. In the general upswing, the recessions were so fleeting and shallow that they were hardly noticed. Under such conditions, the capitalists were able to make big concessions.

All the ideological representatives of the bourgeoisie were convinced that capitalism had solved its problems and that slumps were a thing of the past. Keynesianism was embraced by the reformist leaders of the Labour Party in Britain and by the European Social Democracy. The Stalinists soon followed the same path. And so-called Trotskyists like Ernest Mandel and Tony Cliff echoed the same ideas in different ways.

Ted Grant took a firm stand against this trend. In his short but masterly essay called *Will There Be a Slump?* written in 1960, Ted answered the arguments of the Keynesians from the standpoint of classical Marxist economics, and concluded that the boom-slump cycle had not been abolished. He pointed out that Keynesian deficit financing was intrinsically inflationary and that it would inevitably reach its limits and turn into its opposite:

> Undoubtedly the economy, since the Second World War, has developed on somewhat different lines to those following the First World War. But every decade of capitalist development has tended to be different to every other decade. The basic laws underlying the development of capitalist economy have, however, remained intact.
>
> The fundamental cause of crisis in capitalist society, a *phenomenon peculiar to capitalist society alone*, lies in the *inevitable over-production* of both consumer and capital goods for the purposes of capitalist production. There can be all sorts of secondary causes of crisis, particularly in a period of capitalist development—partial over-production in only some industries; financial juggling on the stock exchange; inflationary swindles; disproportions in production; and a whole host of others—but the fundamental cause of crisis lies in *over-production*. This in turn, is caused by the *market economy*, and the division of society into mutually conflicting classes.
>
> None of this has been changed by the developments of the period since the Second World War (...)

Ted concluded:

> Whatever the exact date, it is absolutely certain that the unprecedented post-war boom must be followed by a period of catastrophic downswing, which cannot but have a profound effect on the political thinking of the enormously strengthened ranks of the labour movement.

At the time, the bourgeois believed they had resolved all the contradictions of their system, and the possibility of a serious crisis was ruled out. It took some time, but Ted's perspectives for Britain were brilliantly confirmed by the recession of 1974-75 and the huge swing to the left in the 1970s. Britain saw a massive strike wave and huge demonstrations against the anti-trade union laws of the Heath government, and a sharp turn to the left in the Labour Party and the unions. Those ultra-left sects who had written off the Labour Party were left with their mouths agape. They had understood nothing and foreseen nothing. In a few years, the Marxist Tendency in the British Labour Party, led by Ted Grant, was transformed from a small group into the biggest and most successful Trotskyist tendency in the world.

This shows the vital connection between theory and practice. A correct theory will permit serious progress, as long as it is accompanied by correct tactics, methods and the will to succeed. Ted possessed all these qualities and a marvellous ability to transmit them to others, especially the youth.

The death of Stalin

On March 5, 1953, Stalin died. Ted was convinced that Stalin was murdered. He pointed to the so-called Doctor's Plot as proof that Stalin was planning a new purge that would have wiped out all the other leaders. In January 1953, *Pravda* began to whip up a campaign against threats of "counter-revolution". It was the prelude of another mass purge, as in 1937. These moves sent a shudder through the ruling circle.

Ted said that by this time, Stalin was almost certainly insane: "If you have a regime of absolute power, in which all criticism is prohibited, it eventually drives you insane", Ted argued. "Just look at all the mad tsars and Roman emperors. And Hitler in the end, he was completely mad. His last order from the bunker was that the Germans deserved to die because they had not been able to defeat the Slavs, who would now be the Master Race."

Ted was right. Towards the end, Stalin's mind was clearly unhinged. In the absence of any check or control, he believed himself to be omnipotent. Stalin was completely paranoid. He lived like a recluse in his dacha. He saw enemies everywhere. In his paranoid state, he no longer trusted anyone. Lifelong Stalinists were rounded up and imprisoned. Generals were arrested, tortured to extract false confessions and shot.

Then Stalin turned his attention to the ruling clique itself. In 1952, he accused his faithful puppets Voroshilov and Molotov of being British spies, and banned them from attending meetings of the leadership. Mikoyan was denounced as a Turkish spy, and even Beria was banished from Stalin's presence. He even arrested members of his own family, including both his sisters-in-law, and had them sent to camps.

A new purge would not only mean their liquidation; it would endanger the whole position of the bureaucracy and undermine all the gains of the planned economy and the Soviet Union itself. There were warning signs that the discontent of the masses was reaching its limit. A new purge could be the spark that lit the powder keg.

The story that has emerged since, is that after one of the usual late-night drinking bouts in his dacha, Stalin suffered a stroke. When the guards reported that Stalin was ill, the members of the Politburo told them to "leave him on the couch". When the doctors finally arrived, the Boss was already dead, and they all breathed a sigh of relief.

Was Ted right about Stalin being murdered? He was old and may have died naturally, but at the very least, this was what might now called an assisted death. It is highly probable that this nest of vipers played an even more active role in sending the beloved Leader and Teacher to a better world. They had the motive, the means and the opportunity. If so, the cause of his death was probably not a stroke, but poison. Beria had access to a very wide range of poisons that would be difficult to detect. The fact that no mention of such an act was ever found in the NKVD archives is not surprising. Beria would not have wanted to leave any evidence.

After Stalin's death, things moved quickly. Beria, who was angling to take power, was arrested and shot. After a brief interregnum, in which first Malenkov, and then Bulganin and Khrushchev ruled, power passed into the hands of Nikita Khrushchev. At the 20th Congress of the CPSU in 1956, Khrushchev shocked the world by denouncing the crimes of Stalin. His speech fell like a bombshell on the international Communist movement.

The French connection

Among the not-very-numerous letters by Ted that can be found in his archives, there is a very interesting one that proves that, although Ted and his comrades were formally outside the International, they were following its internal life very closely. Ted and his comrades never lost sight of their international mission, and tried to maintain contact with people in France and other countries. I refer to the highly illuminating correspondence between Ted and Jimmy Deane with their old friend Raoul, which sheds light on these connections.

On December 4, 1955 Raoul wrote a letter addressed to Ted, Jimmy and Arthur Deane:

Dear comrades.

I have not written since your trip because we had lot of things to settle here.

I write you two words about something which is in the line of what we discussed here: Last CC (three weeks ago) representatives of the PCI [Parti Communiste Internationale] in the International Committee (Cannon, Healy, Bloch and some others) told us an international conference was under preparation for the end of spring or beginning of summer. One never knows if those guys will realise what they seem to intend to, but the fact is that this decision is taken.

Texts will be published: International situation—USSR, China and so on—situation in Europe—Problems of the Fourth.

This conference will be organised by and with the "official" sections of the IC. By the way, for the Sinhaleses [Sri Lankan], they say: we are fed up waiting for a clear standing from them, so now, we go on our way and will see what they will do then.

This means, mainly being given the actual situation, that you will not, perhaps, be invited. Obviously, if you do not move, you will not be. It would be obviously meaningless to say suddenly: "We have heard of an international conference—why shall we not be invited to participate under one form or another." But what would not be stupid would be to accelerate the writing of texts on those problems (international situation, etc.), send them to the PCI—and to us—so that, utilising the fact of your contribution, we at least could raise the point of an invitation towards yourself.

There is a CC today here to discuss about the participation of the party to the electoral campaign. I don't know the results for the moment, and will write you when it will have taken some shape.

Apart from that, all is, for the moment, going well.

Will we have the pleasure, some of these days, of a letter from you, explaining, for example, which kind of conclusions your group has drawn from the trip here?

I think we will have soon, no?

Raoul.

NB December 6th. For the first time in its history the PCI decided not to participate in the electoral campaign.

We reproduce Ted's letter of reply in full. It is dated January 8, 1956:

Dear comrade Raoul,

I am sorry that we have not written before, but just the same as you, we had, and still have, a lot of things to sort out, and few comrades to do it.

Now, the first thing we would like to say in relation to the trip to France is that it has been of great value and benefit to the British comrades, as we hope it has been to you. It has taught us (especially me personally) the need for international collaboration and discussion. This is particularly important for the leading comrades in Britain and France where the possibilities of such collaboration are present.

So far as the position in the French PCI is concerned I must say that the experience of discussion both between the majority and minority have given us an understanding of the reasons why your particular faction adopts the attitude that it does, although as yet you do not have a clearly worked out political position. An observation with which I think you will agree.

After discussions with Bloch particularly, and other leaders of the PCI it seems to us that the official leadership of the PCI has largely the position of Pablo and the IS of 1950-51 on the questions [of] China, Russia, Yugoslavia, etc. It is obvious that in the next few years it will be impossible for them to maintain this, and we hope that if you have a firm political position together with material supplied by ourselves, they may be influenced to move in the more correct political position. I hope, of course it is difficult to say over the short and unsatisfactory discussions that we had, that we may be able to move them. That will depend on many things including satisfactory work by ourselves, and partly by the work of your faction, on a firm political basis.

Of one thing we are convinced, and that is the need for firm collaboration between your faction and ourselves. Personal contact, where that is possible, but perhaps even more important close contact in exchange of document, letters, etc.

At the same time we think that it is vitally important for your faction to integrate itself in the PCI. We believe that if you do this on a correct political platform nationally and internationally you will either convince or win the majority in the party. But, unless the faction has clear ideas on national and international questions, then, we think the work of the faction will be entirely barren.

It is true and this I must say for myself personally, if I do not speak for anyone else, as I told you myself, I can understand the feeling of frustration and irritation at the policies of the leadership which affect your faction, but, a programme cannot be based on that, although that is very important.

At the same time I must say that many of the ideas you have on organisation are obviously correct; though, as I told you, you will find most of them in the material of the Movement in the past. Nevertheless, even so, we learned quite a bit on the question of organisation in the discussions that we had with your tendency. As a matter of interest we include a clipping taken from the *Daily Herald* on the organisation of the British CP and the way in which it finances itself. There is no need to make any comment, because it speaks for itself.

We agree with you on the vital importance of participating in the international discussions. Work has been commenced on the production of international documents and all the important questions, and we will send you the rough drafts when they are completed for suggestions and amendments. One way in which you can help us, and this is of vital importance, is to find a way of sending the texts in English of the documents which we will use, especially those of the SWP. (You can take it for granted that the

Healyites, who are theoretically bankrupt, will produce nothing on these questions, but will faithfully tag behind the SWP, whatever they write.) The SWP will undoubtedly also translate the French material as they have resources and are very efficient in this respect (and material in other languages too). Please find a way of getting these texts to us as well.

This is particularly important as we wish, not only to produce our own documents but to write criticisms of the other material. Otherwise as usual with the SWP they will adopt and incorporate some ideas in a distorted and deformed way in order to avoid criticism, and this can be very harmful for a clear discussion and education of all comrades concerned. That is one of the ways apart from lies and distortions in which the discussion after the war was ruined and crushed with the terrible consequences for the whole International that we see. So I reiterate again, the importance of getting these documents to us immediately.

Incidentally, in passing, events have already annihilated the document produced by the SWP on the Soviet Union, even before it has been translated into French! But this of course, you already know and there is no need for me to deal with it.

One point I would like to make is that when the discussions have been put on paper between Chaulieu and myself and Raoul and myself I hope you will send us a copy for amplification, clarification and exchange of ideas. Incidentally, *entre nous*, after reflection I must say that we believe the Chaulieu tendency is even more barren than that of Shachtman, Cliff, Johnson or any of the other revisionists on the question of the Russian state. Really, the whole sum and substance of his position is based on a misconception on the question "relations of production".

Of course all the revisionists take this as their standpoint, but at least recognise that the state owns the means of production, and that the relations of production, are thus, as they put it, between the state and the working class. For Chaulieu the conception is even more muddle. He finds the relations of production in a mystical fashion in the direct relations within the workshop itself between managers and workers or foremen and workers. This is more the conception of Burnham and syndicalism, that has nothing in common with Marxism.

If I were to give an analogy in a society based on slavery he would find the relations of production in the relations between the overseer with the whip and the slave, rather than between the owner of the means of production, the slave-owner and the slave. In fact, as we know in many large numbers of instances the overseer was himself a slave, no matter how brutally he treated the slaves, he himself was a tool of the real owners of the Means of Production. Similarly, foremen are wage slaves, on a slightly higher level than the workers, and even managers are employees of the owners of the means of production. The relations of the means of production in modern capitalist society are the relations between the owners of the means of production, machinery, factories, etc. and the working class. I quote the section of the document against Cliff on this question.

Of course, this is just an aside, and I hope we will have correspondence on this question. Jimmy is translating some of Chaulieu's most important material from the French, and we will write a criticism of it for the French comrades, (much as it goes against the grain). The British comrades have exhaustively discussed this question and come to a conclusion on it.

I would like to say that personally we were very impressed with the devotion of the comrades of the Raoul Faction. You have the makings of a really good group, if they penetrate the working class and find a correct political platform. I would reiterate again, that the leading British comrades have been lax in not participating more actively in the International discussions and in the life of the movement, even though there have been tremendous difficulties in the way. We hope that a collaboration between ourselves can mend this and assist both the British and the French comrades.

A rough draft of a text on British Perspectives has been completed. As soon as it has been duplicated we will send you a copy for suggestions and discussions if you would like to add anything to it.

We would end by thanking again the French comrades for the wonderful political and comradely hospitality, hoping to hear from you again soon.

Yours fraternally,

Ted

In a lengthy postscript, Ted deals with electoral tactics and our attitude to the traditional workers' parties (in this case, the French Communist Party and Socialist Party):

PS: We are writing to you after the election results in France. First, we would like to say that it is difficult for us to make a criticism on the basis of our lack of knowledge of French. But, nevertheless if we are correct in our understanding of the material which appeared in *La Vérité* in the last six weeks we were greatly shocked. We may be wrong of course, because of the question of language, but if we are correct we would have to say that in our opinion it showed complete sectarianism and isolation from the problems facing the working class.

In the first place, it is a pity, as you correctly say, that they did not have a candidate of their own in at least one constituency, though of that we are not competent to judge because we do not know the material circumstances of the party. But, in the middle of an election campaign, merely to put forward the slogan of general strike and of struggle between the classes, is, in our opinion, irresponsible. To call for general strike constantly is to make a mockery of the idea, and not to be taken seriously by the working class.

The material in *La Vérité* in our opinion is on a similar level to that of the ILP, which impartially condemns both the Conservatives and the Labour Party equally and thus alienates the Labour and Trade Union workers. In our opinion, the campaign in France during the election should have been conducted on the basis of a government of the CP-SFIO—with of course, our programme and ideas. Of course, there was much in these articles that was correct in its criticism of the antics of the CP and the anti-revolutionary propaganda, and a treacherous policy of the reformists. This, while necessary, is not enough for agitation among the masses.

We think, and this applies also to the comrades of the Raoul faction, and of course we are speaking frankly here, as between comrades, that they have not a correct orientation in relation to the problem of Stalinism in France. It may be true as both the comrades of the majority and minority argue that many advanced workers up and down the country have seen through the treachery and crimes of the CP in the last ten years.

It may even be true that a large part, perhaps even the majority of these who vote for the CP, are sceptical of the CP and only support it for lack of an alternative. But, and this is a big but, it would be entirely wrong to think that the working class views the problem in the same way as the Marxist Tendency does. So far as the working class are concerned, the tendency after frustrations and defeats where there is not a strong Marxist party to explain the lesson, is to a certain extent to blame the working class for the defeats.

The apathy and indifference to the adventurist and irresponsible action of Stalinism notwithstanding, even though large sections may recognise this in an unclear fashion, does not lead to a clear understanding of the role of the leadership. In some ways it is a similar problem to the mass party of the working class which we face in Britain. Despite 50 years of reformism, the workers are not yet disillusioned with the Labour Party. It will require great events and great struggles before even the right wing of the Labour Party is discredited completely, and only then, if a Marxist wing and a revolutionary wing is built up will it be fruitful.

Similarly, it required great events and 50 years of experience to discredit the SFIO. The Stalinists are far cleverer betrayers, and much more difficult to expose than the reformists. We believe that the election propaganda of our party in France should have been based on a patient appeal to the rank and file militants in the Trade Unions, the CP and the SFIO contrasting the policy of the official leadership to what the policy should have been.

We believe that the problem of the CP remains the key question for our comrades in France, and unless they adopt a correct tactical orientation towards it they will hopelessly isolate themselves from the masses. On the one hand of course, it is necessary to reject decisively the capitulationists of the Frank and Pablo school. On the other hand it is necessary to guard against sectarianism and to study clearly the process that has taken place among the masses. For example, though for us the popular front experience of 1936 and 1945-47 has decisively shown the criminal betrayal of Stalinism to the bourgeoisie, that lesson is not so clear to the masses.

Even if there are many hundreds and thousands of militant workers who are not organised at the present time, and have seen through the betrayal of the CP this does not apply to the millions who vote for the Communist Party; it cannot apply to the mass of the working class. As we told you, when we were in France, a popular front is a virtual certainty, depending upon the foreign policy of the Kremlin.

We believe that the election and its results with the inevitable instability of the social conditions and relations between classes in France mean that the propaganda of the CP can now have a tremendous effect on the working class. At this stage of course, the bourgeoisie is doing everything in its power to avoid such an experience, among other reasons of course because of the foreign policy of the French bourgeoisie that we should orientate towards Washington and not Moscow. But the moment that the mass movement of the working class begins to thrust itself forward, and get beyond the balance of the "normal" relations, they will inevitably turn "to the strike-breaking conspiracy of the popular front", in order to save themselves.

As far as we are concerned we understand that in 1936 it was the struggle of the masses that gained the concession of 40-hour week, holidays with pay, etc., and that these were subsequently taken away behind the shield of the popular front. But the masses do not see it this way and the propaganda of the CP will have a great effect in the present situation in France.

Because of our weakness, and that is an important factor in this situation, there is no force which can explain to the mass of the workers through agitation exactly what a popular front will mean. But even if there were a strong Marxist party, in the given situation, with the mass support for Stalinism even if the comrades are correct, and it is of a lukewarm variety, it is likely that a popular front stage could not be avoided.

The comrades must not think that what is axiomatic for them is axiomatic for the class. The apathy, indifference, despair, weariness and frustration of the masses, the cynicism towards the CP can rapidly change in an initial upsurge once again into enthusiastic support. Of course, this support will be of a watchful character rather than the uncritical acceptance of the CP in the past. But, our comrades will break the neck of the Tendency if they do not prepare themselves and the working class for these events.

It is necessary to conduct a sustained propaganda, as the comrades are undoubtedly doing for independent class action but linked with a skilful criticism of the policies of the CP in order to try and separate the advanced elements from the leadership. We see that already the CP is setting popular front committees in the localities. We do not know what character these are, but we suggest that the comrades should demand that class committees linking all the workers in the factories and the neighbourhood together should be formed, and that all bourgeois elements should be expelled from the popular front committees, as was suggested by Trotsky in the past. If the comrades adopt a correct policy instead of a sectarian one we believe that in the next period it should be possible to make big gains from the CP, even the SFIO and in the Unions and among the factory militants.

Of course, in these few scattered notes and comments I am not dealing with the situation in France as a whole, because, of course, the comrades are thoroughly familiar, and know better than we do the crisis of the regime, the meaning of *poujadism*[9] in relation to the instability of the petit bourgeoisie, and the details of the political problem in France. Nevertheless, the rise of reaction on the right merely reinforces the conclusion which we have drawn here.

We think, however, that the problem is to link the day to day work with the problem of an independent class orientation both of the CP and the SFIO, pointing out as the comrades are already doing that only a class policy directed against big business can win over the vacillating petit bourgeoisie, and solve the problems of the nation as a whole.

If a popular front should be formed under the impact of events, if we prepare the militants in advance, it should be a period when we will make swift gains, after the disillusionment following the first raptures. But the history of revolution in all the main countries seems to indicate that some such stage, given our weakness is inevitable as was the Kerenskyiade in Russia, the coalition government in Germany, a new Labour government in Britain, etc., etc.

This is not a worked out thesis but a few hurried notes, on which we would like your observations. If you disagree with us perhaps we can discuss the matter in correspondence.

The correspondence shows that Ted and Jimmy initially had some hopes for Lambert's faction, while Raoul, for his part, was always keen on getting together with Ted's group. However, it was not to be. By then, Lambert had already entered into an alliance with Cannon and Healy against Pablo.

It is clear from this exchange that Raoul was keen for Ted and the others to be present at an international conference. But things turned out differently. Cannon's manoeuvres had resulted in the PCI joining a second "Fourth International"—the International Committee of the Fourth International (ICFI), of which Gerry Healy was the British representative. Naturally, there could be no question of fusing with Healy.

Nevertheless, Ted always maintained friendly relations with Raoul and some of the other leaders of the Lambertists. The Brazilian Trotskyist Serge Goulart, who was a prominent member of the Lambertists for many years before joining the International Marxist Tendency, recently said: "It is a pity that we did not join with Ted Grant instead of Healy. Who knows what that might have meant?" Alas, the answer to that question will never be known.

Suez and Hungary 1956

The sleepy atmosphere of British politics was rudely shattered by dramatic events on a world scale. On July 26, 1956, Colonel Nasser announced the nationalization of the Suez Canal. The same day, Egypt closed the canal to Israeli shipping. The British press intensified its vicious campaign against Nasser, while the Conservative government of Sir Anthony Eden prepared to launch a military operation, together with the French and Israelis, to seize the Canal and occupy Egypt.

The strategists in Paris and London cooked up a cynical plan, whereby the Israeli army would attack Egypt and then Britain and France would send in troops under the pretext of "keeping the peace" and keeping the Suez Canal open. This was a lie. The British and French imperialists were only interested in defending their own interests. Both Paris and London wanted to

---

[9] Poujadism was a reactionary movement founded by Pierre Poujade in the 1950s. Demagogically attacking the state and government using the tax issue, it appealed mainly to the "small man", the petty-bourgeois, shopkeepers etc. After De Gaulle came to power in 1958, it largely faded away.

overthrow Nasser and reverse his policies of nationalization. Israel, as usual, was pursuing its own expansionist agenda.

In general the mood of the public was against. The young conscripts, who were being sent to fight a war that they neither understood nor wanted, were even more against. The British author David Pryce-Jones recalled that as a young officer, after the ultimatum was submitted to Egypt, he had to explain to his troops why war with Egypt was necessary—without believing a word that he was saying.

Protests against the war erupted as soon as the invasion began. Labour Party leader Hugh Gaitskell and the Labour right wing were quite prepared to back the government, but the overwhelming majority of Labour Party members were opposed to the invasion of Egypt. There were stormy scenes in the House of Commons on November 1, 1956, when a violent debate in which Labour MPs compared Eden to Hitler, almost degenerated into fist-fights.

The Labour Party and the Trade Union Congress organized nationwide anti-war protests, starting on November 1. On November 4, an anti-war rally in Trafalgar Square was attended by 30,000 people—the biggest rally in London since 1945. Addressing the Trafalgar Square rally, the Left Labour MP Aneurin Bevan thundered:

> They have besmirched the name of Britain. They have made us ashamed of the things of which formerly we were proud. They have offended against every principle of decency and there is only one way in which they can even begin to restore their tarnished reputation, and that is to get out! Get out! Get out! (Aneurin Bevan, *Speech in Trafalgar Square*, November 4, 1956)

The crowd at Trafalgar Square then marched on 10 Downing Street, chanting "Eden Must Go!", and attempted to storm the Prime Minister's residence. The violent clashes between the police and the demonstrators were captured by television cameras. This movement shook the government and was a powerful factor leading to Eden's resignation. In the end, it was pressure from the Americans that forced Eden to pull the troops out of Egypt. Conservative voters were deserting the government in droves and Eden was totally demoralised.

However, while the attention of the world was focussed on Egypt, even more dramatic events were being prepared in Eastern Europe. The speech of Nikita Khrushchev at the 20th Congress of the Communist Party of the Soviet Union, in which he denounced the crimes of Stalin, sparked off a chain reaction that spread rapidly through Eastern Europe. There was a revolutionary ferment in Poland, which culminated in the Poznan uprising of June 1956.

A hundred thousand workers and their families poured onto the streets. They occupied a police station and smashed up the city's Communist Party headquarters. Workers released political prisoners and armed themselves. Workers' councils were elected in the factories. There were clashes between workers and the Polish army. Poznan was paralysed by a general strike. Finally, the uprising was put down by military force. But it led to the victory of the "reformist" wing of the Polish bureaucracy, led by Wladyslaw Gomulka, who successfully diverted the movement along nationalist lines.

The Polish events sparked off a revolutionary movement in Hungary that went much further and shook the world. On October 23, my 12th birthday, I was listening to the radio, when reports were broadcast of a mass demonstration in the Hungarian capital Budapest. The Hungarian Revolution had begun. As usual, the revolution started with the students, who marched in their thousands through central Budapest to the Parliament building.

A student delegation entering the radio building to try to broadcast the students' demands was detained. When the delegation's release was demanded by the demonstrators outside, they were fired upon by the hated State Security Police (AVO) from within the building. This was the spark that ignited the fuse. Hungary exploded in revolution. Thousands of workers were organized into militias, which fought desperate gun battles with the AVO. Soviet troops stationed in Hungary fraternised with the workers and turned their guns against the AVO.

The government collapsed. An attempt was made to form a new government along the lines of Gomulka in Poland, but in reality, the Hungarian "reformer" Imre Nagy was suspended in mid air. The real power was in the hands of the workers' councils that sprang up all over the country. The most important was the Budapest Workers' Council, which was a soviet in all but name. By the end of October, the fighting had almost stopped, and a sense of normality began to return.

The Soviet bureaucracy was terrified by the events in Hungary. They could accept, albeit reluctantly, a deal with Gomulka in Poland. But they could never accept the rule of the working class that was beginning to take shape in Hungary. They withdrew the Soviet troops that had been stationed there and had proved unreliable. This move was met by huge relief in Hungary, but it was premature. The Politburo had decided to crush the Hungarian Revolution in blood.

On November 4, a large Soviet force, mainly drawn from backward troops from Central Asia, crossed the Hungarian border. They had been told that they were being sent to put down a fascist uprising in Germany. The Hungarians put up a heroic and desperate resistance that continued until November 10. Young children attacked Soviet tanks with Molotov cocktails. Over 2,500 Hungarians and 700 Soviet troops were killed in the conflict, and 200,000 Hungarians fled as refugees. Mass arrests and denunciations continued for months. Imre Nagy was executed in 1958.

These bloody events caused shock waves. The general reaction was one of revulsion. It caused a serious crisis in the ranks of the Communist Parties everywhere. In Britain, one third of the members left the Party, including thousands of leading trade unionists and intellectuals. I had personal experience of this, since my mother and grandfather were both members of the Communist Party. They were shocked at what they could see on the television screens, but still remained loyal to the CP. My mother, who had stopped going regularly to Party meetings, went to a meeting in Swansea where the Hungarian events were being discussed. She was shocked by what she saw and heard.

The leading light of the Communist Party in Swansea was a man called Harry Stratton. By coincidence, his wife (I forgot her name) was Hungarian, and they often went to Hungary for holidays. I remember that on one occasion (before 1956), he had brought back a badge, which he proudly showed me: "This is the badge of an AVO officer", he told me in hushed tones, like a priest showing off a holy relic. There was a violent scene at the meeting that discussed the uprising, as my mother later told me. Harry Stratton's wife was hysterically sobbing, saying repeatedly: "They are killing my people." Her husband shouted at her: "Shut up, woman." My mother was deeply shocked at this incident. She was a very humane person and could not understand how a man could treat any distressed woman in this way, let alone his own wife. Scenes like that must have occurred in many Party meetings up and down the country.

The Revolutionary Socialist League

These dramatic events found the Fourth International in a lamentable situation. Having been Pablo's stooge in Britain for years, Healy now discovered the Original Sin of "Pabloism", about which he never ceased to rant and rave, conveniently forgetting that he himself had been the original Pabloite. Certain unforeseen consequences flowed from this.

After Healy went over to the Americans (the US SWP), Pablo was left empty-handed in Britain. The British section of the "International" was for a short time represented by a group around John Lawrence. However, under the influence of Pablo's revisionist ideas, Lawrence developed pro-Stalinist tendencies. As a result, most of his group joined the CP and were very soon dissolved into it.

When, in October 1956, the Hungarian uprising caused a massive split in the British CP, Pablo was reduced to putting an advert in *Tribune,* appealing for anybody who wished to re-establish the section. Together with Sam Bornstein, John Fairhead, and a number of individual Trotskyists in sympathy with Pablo, they agreed to set up a section of the International under the name of the Revolutionary Socialist League. Ted's group also joined.

When I asked Ted how was it possible to collaborate with people with whom we had such profound differences, he just shrugged his shoulders: "They helped us at the time. They gave us some money to publish an *Open Letter to the Communist Party*. And anyway, we did not have much of an alternative". He added:

> We had no illusions about Pablo and the others, but as there was nothing to lose, we went along anyway. As a result we found ourselves once more inside the Fourth International. Lacking any viable alternative, Pablo was compelled to recognise us as the basis of a new British section.

There were two full timers for the new organisation, Ted and John Fairhead. Fairhead, however, did not last long. After leaving the group he travelled far to the right and ended up in the right-wing Tory Monday Club. Soon the group was recognised as the British section and they began to publish a modest printed monthly four-page paper called *Socialist Fight.* They also produced a small pamphlet called *Hungary and the Crisis in the Communist Party,* aimed, as the name suggests, at the rank and file of the CPGB.

Pablo seems to have had the idea of uniting all the Trotskyist groups in Britain—including Healy. If that was the case, then he was sadly mistaken. On August 16, 1956, Ted wrote to "Gabriel" (Pablo) on the first steps of the new group and Healy's predictably hostile attitude to it:

> Dear comrade Gabriel,
>
> Please excuse the delay in replying to your letters. As you have probably heard from comrade Bornstein

the work is proceeding as satisfactory [sic] as can be expected. Group meetings are being held regularly and a better spirit pervades among the members. Regular contact is being maintained with our members in the Healy group. Bornstein has informed you of Healy's recent manoeuvres. Personally I agree completely with your approach to the question and we will inform you of any developments.

Last Sunday, Fairhead, myself and Levy attended an open meeting of the friends of *Tribune* where we received a very favourable reception from the members of the Healy group (mostly young and fresh). After the meeting Healy turned up, and disturbed the atmosphere, immediately started to insult and jeer at us, with his usual lies and slanders. We will see what comes of this at next meeting. He will probably try and prevent us from getting any time to speak, but this will only serve to expose him.

But inside the group there were some serious doubts about the whole business. On February 4, 1957, Jimmy Deane wrote a letter to Ted:

Dear Ted,

I was very pleased indeed to see you and to be able to discuss one or two items—the future will give us an opportunity to discuss the various problems more fully. I must say that I am very pleased with the fact that you are now full-time, which I am sure will mean a great deal to our movement and will produce excellent results.

There can be no doubt—and I was one of the sceptics—that the collaboration with Pablo was a wise step. I see no reason why it should not be possible to enjoy a long and fruitful period of collaboration with these comrades, who, judging by the material I have read in the QI [*Quatrième Internationale*], have learned from the past and have, undoubtedly, a lot of talent to bring to the movement.

It is true that they have still the "imminence of war" outlook, but that is by no means a fundamental thing. In any case, the movement has entered a new stage. It is not a matter of being faced with a period of retreats and splits, when it was necessary to fight every innovation tooth and nail; on the contrary, whilst such a healthy attitude is, and always will be necessary, our task today is one of being able to patiently work (and win) with those who may not entirely agree with us, but who, thanks to events themselves, are *travelling in the direction* of understanding and grasping a truly revolutionary Marxist programme.

It seems to me that our own comrades have got to grasp the fundamental change in the situation, and recognise the flexibility of tactics. In this sense it is not so much that SL [Sam Levy] is wrong in exaggerating the LP work, etc., but rather that he resists the employment of tactics dictated by the new situation with regard to the Stalinists.

Incidentally, I've been reading through the 1945 document on perspectives and it is amazing how correct this document is. Even with regard to the crisis of Stalinism and the possibility of gains from the CP this document was absolutely correct. Also, rereading through our statement at the time of the entry of the RCP we have absolutely nothing to correct in it.

This letter is interesting, not so much for what it explains about the relationship with Pablo and the other leaders of the IS, but rather for what it says about Jimmy's infinite capacity for making an excellent case for a bad argument. Revolutionary optimism is one thing, but Jimmy's repeated delusions that these people would somehow learn from their steady stream of mistakes is another. He himself admits he was "one of the sceptics" about the wisdom of collaborating with Pablo and co. How could he not be? He knew better than anybody the appalling track record of these people, having lived for almost two years in Paris as RCP representative in the IS.

The "imminence of war" question was not a secondary issue. Nor was it an isolated case. There were many other differences of a serious character, such as the attitude to the Soviet bureaucracy (Pablo thought that Khrushchev was going to de-bureaucratise the bureaucracy), the attitude to the Algerian Revolution (Pablo gave uncritical support for Ben Bella's "socialism") and so on. Jimmy was not the only one who had been sceptical. Sam Levy, who he refers to in the letter, was so sceptical that he left the group altogether. From what Jimmy writes, it is clear he objected to the turn to the CP. He began to publish a small duplicated publication called *The Socialist Current*, or, as Ted called it, the "Current Bun". It led nowhere, of course.

Under the circumstances, it was correct to appeal to the CP rank and file, which was in a state of ferment. But the RSL was unable to compete with the Healyites, who had a bigger apparatus and a paper. This placed us at a big disadvantage. Ted later confessed to me his surprise when he and Jimmy Deane went to speak to dissident members of the CP: "The old Stalinists knew something about Marxism and Leninism. The first thing they would ask you is: what is your programme? But these people only wanted to know: how many members have you got and what kind of an apparatus do you possess?"

There is in the Ted Grant archive a long list of names on a typed sheet, headed "Contacts, EG." There is no date on it, but it is clearly a list of names of people Ted was supposed to be following up. Many of them were members of the Communist Party who expressed differences with the Party Line on Hungary, such as Peter Fryer, who was the *Daily Worker* correspondent in Budapest at the time of the 1956 uprising.

It is reasonable to suppose that this was in the period 1957-58. Number eight on this list is one "Eric Hobsbawm (CP)". I do not know whether Ted ever spoke to the Professor, who at the time was a lecturer in history at Birkbeck, and, if he did, what kind of answer he got. I suspect that it would not have been a positive one. Like several other CP dissidents, in breaking from Stalinism, Professor Hobsbawm was not moving to the Left, but very, very far to the Right.

Most of the 10,000 or so who left the CPGB over Hungary dropped out of politics altogether. But some were attracted to Healy's organization because it had more resources than we did. These former Stalinists included people like Cliff Slaughter, Tom Kemp, Brian Behan (the brother of the writer Brendan Behan), Ken Coates, Pat Jordan and, last but by no means least, Peter Fryer. That gave a considerable boost to Healy, but it also changed his political trajectory.

The new recruits brought with them a heavy baggage of ideas from the camp of Stalinism. In reacting against the revisionism of the CPGB, they reverted back to the ultra-leftism of the Third Period. Overnight, Healy's line changed from that of the most abject opportunism to the most strident ultra-leftism. Ted expressed his astonishment that instead of Healy giving the Line to these people, they gave the Line to him.

Pablo and the IS

Ted and Jimmy Deane used to attend the meetings of the International Executive Committee in the late 1950s. This did nothing to change Ted's mind about the political calibre of the International leadership. Pablo, the main leader, made one blunder after another. Pablo and the others were always looking for shortcuts. Trotsky warned against this long before, when he criticized the opportunist tactics of Stalin and Bukharin in the 1920s, in relation to Britain:

> If anyone tried to leap over actual and necessary and inevitable stages, it was Stalin and Bukharin. It seemed to them that they would be able through cunning manoeuvres and combinations to promote the British working class to the highest class without the Communist Party, or rather with some co-operation from it. This was also the initial error of Comrade Tomsky. Again, however, there is nothing original in this mistake. That is how opportunism always begins. The development of the class appears

to it to be much too slow and it seeks to reap what it has not sown, or what has not ripened as yet. Such, for example, was the source of the opportunistic mistakes of Ferdinand Lassalle. (Trotsky, *What we gave and what we got,* September 23, 1927; first published in *The New International,* October 1935)

When Khrushchev delivered his famous speech at the 20th Congress of the CPSU, Pablo concluded that the Soviet bureaucracy was going to "de-bureaucratise" itself. This was an attempt to find a short cut to building the Fourth International, which led in practice to the International tail-ending the Moscow bureaucracy. Then came the Hungarian Revolution, which the "reformer" Khrushchev drowned in blood.

The same mistake was made in relation to Algeria. One of the most important developments at the time was the Algerian War of Independence. The International gave a lot of support to the FLN, including material support, which Ted said was obviously correct. He always praised the tremendous courage and spirit of sacrifice of the Algerian people, who were fighting for their national liberation against French imperialism. Whenever he was making a financial appeal and wanted to provide an example of self-sacrifice, he would point to the millions of Algerian workers living in France who gave most of their pitifully low wages to finance the war of liberation.

In 1957, Jimmy Deane actually went to help the Algerian FLN in its fight against the French occupation forces. At Pablo's request, he travelled to Morocco together with another comrade. The idea was to use his skills as an electrical engineer to knock out electrified fences. But according to the story that I was told, they were sent to work in a factory in Morocco, where their hosts were so impressed that they did not allow them to leave. They were kept virtually as prisoners and finally had to escape over the rooftops. Jimmy's only comment to me was: "They were on a very low political level."

As always with the leaders of the Fourth, they carried it to an extreme and veered sharply in the direction of opportunism. Pablo had illusions in the "socialism" of Ben Bella, who was then the leader of the FLN. Pablo carried this to the point of becoming a minister in Ben Bella's government after the victory of the national liberation movement! The whole episode ended in tears when Ben Bella was overthrown in a coup in 1965. By that time, Pablo himself had been ousted from the leadership of the International by the clique led by Mandel, in alliance with the American SWP. But we will deal with that later.

It is quite true that Pablo was responsible for many of the mistakes the International made after the war, but he was not alone. Mandel, Maitan, Cannon, Hansen, Healy, Frank and Lambert, all had essentially the same line. The subsequent attempt to blame everything on "Pabloism" was simply an unscrupulous manoeuvre to divert attention away from the mistakes and crimes committed by all the others.

As a matter of fact, Pablo was by no means the worst of them. Jimmy Deane used to say that, of all the members of the IS at that time, Pablo was the only one who could have learned something. Towards the end of his life, Pablo told some of our Greek comrades: "Ted Grant was the only honest man in the International Executive Committee".

Nevertheless, Pablo made some really hair-raising mistakes that disoriented the International. He thought that a Third World War was inevitable and indeed imminent. He expressed this idea in a pamphlet called *"La guerre qui vient"* (The Forthcoming War), which was published by the International in 1953. Ted and Jimmy completely rejected this view. In January 1957, a young comrade from Liverpool by the name of Pat Wall, who was still in the army, went to

Paris, where he saw Pablo and Pierre Frank and attended the 12th congress of the French section as a fraternal delegate. He wrote to Ted on January 2, 1957:

> Dear Ted,
>
> (...) The Congress was very interesting, almost fifty people attended including several Indo-Chinese and fraternal delegates from Germany and Greece. On the first day's discussion I had a word for word translation on the whole of the contributions on the international situation. Personally I must express my complete disagreement with their line on the war question and I hope that you and the other comrades will not make any concessions on this issue. The position that Pablo himself put I will summarise as follows:
>
> 1) Rise of the revolutionary wave increases the danger of war.
>
> 2) If it was only a question of French and British Imperialism there would be no danger as they are too feeble.
>
> 3) On three occasions the world has been on the brink of war—Korea, Indo-china and Formosa and on one unspecified occasion the General Staffs of both sides mobilised in complete readiness for war.
>
> 4) Owing to the *social* construction of US society (political backwardness of the working class?)—the US can launch war whenever she chooses.
>
> 5) War is considered the last resort of US Imperialism.
>
> 6) Middle East remains a source of world war danger.
>
> 7) All the events since 1945 can be seen as small parts of the International Civil War.
>
> You will remember they once said that Korea marked the beginning of World War Three and as far as I know they still hold that position. To me the whole prognosis based on the theory that US imperialism, if she sees no other way out, will plunge into World War Three to defeat the Revolution in Europe, Asia and Africa is false. Just as false as the policy adopted between 1945-47 that World War Two had not ended. Not only that, but in the last analysis the position of Pablo, etc., can only be one of left-Stalinism.
>
> The French section itself seemed quite a good crowd, serious and quite capable and I have had a very friendly reception from everybody.
>
> Now for the second issue of the *WIR* [*Workers' International Review*] in my opinion it was not as good as the first issue and I have several points to raise.
>
> 1) While there is a primary need for a theoretical paper and one dealing with international problems, I feel that the business of "Documents of the International" is overdone. Far too much space is being devoted to wholesale salutes to all and sundry. While in the main what is said is correct, the wording is somewhat abstract and it is not the best way of presenting our views on Russia, Hungary or Cyprus.
>
> 2) The articles on the Suez, conscription, United Front and most of all the reprint of the excellent *Open Letter* were all very good.
>
> 3) More space should be devoted to dealing with the situation in the Labour Party and Trade Unions and also the economic situation.
>
> 4) The wording of the section on Hungary is very bad and there seems a definite hesitation to come right out and belt the Stalinists. Mind you at the Congress Pablo did correct the position and state that at *no* time was there any danger of reactionary elements playing an important role. It is a pity that you could not have dealt with Deutscher in the issue as both the SWP in America and the Shachtmanites had articles on his views.
>
> Well Ted it is easy to be critical from afar and especially as one who in actual fact is making no

> Paris
> 2nd Jan 1957
>
> Dear Ted,
>
> I would like to raise a few points with you about the paper and also general political policies.
>
> I will be leaving Paris tomorrow, so you should write to the old address and I should be back in England on the 26th of January. While I have been in Paris I have seen Pablo, Frank and in fact I attended the 12th Congress of the French Section, as believe it or not the fraternal delegate from the British Section. This was crazy I had no previous warning I was expected to speak and anyhow I represented nobody, so I spoke for only five minutes and said nothing. Probably they think I am stupid, but it is far better they think that, than had I in all innocence provoked some form of disagreement at this stage.
>
> The Congress was very interesting, about fifty people attended including several Indo-Chinese and fraternal delegates from Germany and Greece. On the first days discussion I had a word for word translation on the whole of the conculation on the International situation. Personally I must express my complete disagreement with their

Pat Wall's letter from Paris to Ted in 1957

contribution to the tremendous volume of work you must have. I raise the points as friendly criticism and no doubt on many of them you can put me right.

Raoul, DeMaseu and all their friends have been wonderful and have gone out of their way to make my stay a happy one. I feel I shall be indebted to them all my life and after ten months in the army it makes me realise what the word comrade really means… and the food!!!

Well Ted I hope your trip up North was a big success. I will send a letter for the WIR on conscription which you can use if you like—it will be unsigned as there is no point at this stage of taking risks.

See you very soon.

All the best for the New Year.

Paddy

PS. Send copies of all our material to a German comrade: Bertold Schaller...

Pat's request for Ted to write something on Isaac Deutscher refers to the first part of his three-volume biography of Trotsky: *The Prophet Armed* that came out in 1954. It was followed by the second volume, *The Prophet Unarmed* (1959), and *The Prophet Outcast* (1963). These books made a big splash. But Ted was very critical of Deutscher and his treatment of Trotsky and his ideas. As far as I know, Ted never did put his views on Deutscher in writing, although he expressed them verbally often enough.

The book was highly influential among the British New Left, and that was enough to put me off it to start with. I took the trouble to read it, however, and found it quite interesting in parts. It was certainly very well written, but as Trotsky always said, content must come before style. There is a Russian proverb that Lenin liked to quote: "a spoonful of tar spoils a barrelful of honey". And here there was not one spoonful but rather whole bucketfuls of the stuff. The last volume was particularly pernicious. Ted said that Deutscher was very resentful because we had won over his supporters, but I have no further information about this.

As for making political concessions to Pablo and co., Pat need not have worried. There was no danger that Ted would compromise on this or on anything else. He pointed out that the imperialists do not wage war for fun but to conquer foreign markets, raw materials and spheres of influence. In a nuclear war, everything would be destroyed. The existence of a nuclear balance of terror meant that a war would signify the complete annihilation of both the Soviet Union and the USA. The Americans had a word for this: MAD (Mutually Assured Destruction).

On the other hand, Ted tried to explain that the international class balance of forces ruled out a world war. The Second World War was only possible after a series of defeats of the proletariat in Italy, Germany, and Spain, etc. But at the present time, the forces of the European working class were stronger than ever. That was a major obstacle in the way of war.

Ted told me one amusing incident arising from this nonsense about an imminent nuclear war. At the end of one meeting of the IS (he did not mention the date but it may have been around the Cuban missile crisis in 1962, when there was a lot of war hysteria in the air), a French female comrade came up to Ted with tears in her eyes. She said: "Goodbye, comrade, this may be the last time we will meet."

Ted replied with his habitual good humour: "Don't worry comrade. Go home and sleep soundly in your bed. There will be no war and I will see you at the next meeting." I do not know whether these words of comfort helped restore her sleep pattern, but they were true enough.

Another consequence of Pablo's theses on war was the lunacy of the Argentinean Trotskyist Posadas, who believed that a nuclear war between the USA and Russia was inevitable and desirable, and would create the conditions for socialism. His main difference with Pablo is that he supported the Chinese bureaucracy in its struggle against the Moscow bureaucracy (this was also the line of Mandel, Maitan, Hansen and all the others).

In the *Programme of the International*, Ted wrote:

> Thus, to work with a perspective of world war in reality meant not only a lack of understanding of all the multiple social and military forces involved, but was a programme of the profoundest pessimism. To imagine war would solve the problems of the Socialist Revolution, was to be as light-minded as the Stalinists in Germany, who imagined the coming to power of the fascists in Germany would prepare

the way for Socialism. In reality, the outbreak of world war would signify a decisive defeat for the working class. A nuclear holocaust would in more likelihood mean the mutual annihilation of countries and classes. At best, handfuls of survivors might succeed in creating some form of slave state and begin again the necessary development of the material productive forces, that with the working class, are the absolutely necessary pre-requisites of Socialism. The Posadists have merely drawn to an extreme the ideas of Pablo, Hansen, Mandel, Healy and co.

On the IEC, Ted was surprised by the strange behaviour of the Argentinean Trotskyists grouped around Posadas. They were ultra-Pabloite loyalists. Every time Pablo proposed something they immediately raised their hands in favour. Observing this conduct, after one session Ted went up to Pablo. "If I were you I would be very careful with those people," he said. "Today they are voting 100 percent with you. Tomorrow they will be voting 100 percent against you." Pablo probably paid no attention, but that was exactly what happened.

In Moscow, in August 1963, the United States, the Soviet Union, and the United Kingdom signed a treaty that banned all tests of nuclear weapons except those conducted underground. The Chinese bureaucracy was opposed to it because Mao wanted to get his own H-bomb. Posadas was even more implacably opposed to it for reasons already explained. The "workers' states" would "win" and we could then start to build a communist society!

In Britain there was a small group of Posadists who produced a paper called *Red Flag*. I remember one issue, which was really a model of sectarian language. It began:

> The phoney words of the peace-mongers [yes, not war-mongers but peace-mongers] may fool bone-headed reformists [members of the Labour Party] and Khrushchevite revisionists [members of the Communist party], but the Chinese comrades [sic] have rightly denounced the Test Ban Treaty as a sell-out of the world's masses to imperialism."

The fact that a nuclear war would kill many millions of people, and devastate the industrial and technological apparatus which is the only possible material base for socialism, appears to have escaped his attention. "In that kind of scenario," Ted joked, "we would have a transitional slogan: Forward to barbarism!"

"Outside the Labour Movement there is nothing"

Ted always used to say: "Outside the Labour Movement there is nothing". The truth of these words has been shown a thousand times. All history shows that the masses, when they enter into struggle, always tend to look for the road of least resistance. The masses do not understand small organizations; they will always first express themselves through the big, well-known organisations: the unions and the traditional parties. They will try, time and again, to transform these parties. Only on the basis of colossal historical events will the working class, having repeatedly tried to change these organisations, begin to look for an alternative.

In March 1959, Ted wrote one of his most important and influential works, *Problems of Entrism*, in which we read the following:

> To the sectarian splinter groups on the edge of, or to the left of the Fourth International (The Workers' League, the Socialist Workers' Federation and other tiny grouplets), the problem is posed in the simplest of terms: the Social Democracy and Stalinism have betrayed the working class; therefore the independent party of the working class must immediately be built. They claim the independence of the revolutionary party as a principle, whether the party consists of two or two million.
>
> They do not take into account the historical development of the movement of the working class, which

conditions the tactics, while maintaining the principles of the Marxists. Without flexible tactics it is impossible to win or train the forces which must be won before a revolutionary party can be built.

Unfortunately, the movement of the working class does not proceed in a straight line. Otherwise, all that would be necessary would be to proclaim from the street corners the need for a revolutionary party—as the SPGB has proclaimed for 50 years the superiority of Socialism over capitalism—but with completely barren results.

We have to start with an understanding of the working class and the Labour Movement as it emerges historically, with the consciousness determined by objective conditions on the one hand, and the betrayal of Stalinism and Social Democracy, which for us are objective factors, on the other hand; and the weakness of the revolutionary forces, which also becomes an important factor of the historical process. How to overcome the weakness and isolation of the revolutionary movement, whilst maintaining its principles intact, is the basic task of this epoch.

Alas! The movement of the working class rarely moves in a straight line. Otherwise capitalism would have been overthrown decades ago. The betrayal of the Revolution by Social Democracy in 1914–20 led to the formation of the Communist International, which was intended as an organ of World Revolution. The degeneration of the Revolution and the subsequent betrayal of Stalinism had its consequence that the world proletariat was disorientated.

However, it is one thing for the cadres of the revolutionary movement to understand the role of Stalinism and Reformism; it is a different matter for the masses, and even for the active advanced guard, who in general only learn by experience.

Things do not happen in a straight line. As Ted observed, if this was really all that was required, then every petty sectarian in history would be as great as Marx, Engels, Lenin and Trotsky put together. In fact, the relation between the class, the party and the leadership is far more complex. Over a long historical period, the working class has built mass organisations. It does not abandon these easily. Before they do this they will first attempt many times to transform the traditional organisations. Only in the last analysis will this process lead to the formation of new mass parties, which normally arise out of splits in the old mass organisations.

This fact will immediately become evident to anyone who takes the trouble to study the way in which the mass parties of the Communist International were formed out of splits in the old Social Democratic parties after 1917. Again, as Ted pointed out:

> The working class does not come to revolutionary conclusions easily. Habits of thought, traditions, the exceptional difficulties created by the transformation of the Socialist and Communist traditional organisations into obstacles on the road of the revolution; all these have put formidable obstacles in the way of creating a Marxist mass movement.
>
> All history demonstrates that, at the first stages of revolutionary upsurge, the masses turn to the mass organisations to try and find a solution for their problems, especially the young generation, entering politics for the first time. The experience of many countries demonstrates this. In Germany, despite the fact that the Spartacists represented tens of thousands of revolutionary workers steeled in the struggle against the First World War, and despite the fact that the Social Democratic leadership betrayed the workers in supporting the war and opposing the revolution of 1918, it was to the latter that the workers first turned after the outbreak of the revolution. It required years of revolutionary and counter-revolutionary struggles (apart from the mistakes of the leadership) before the CP was transformed from a small party to a mass movement.
>
> This experience of every revolutionary awakening in the last 50 years in Europe demonstrates the truth of this theory. With the tiny forces we are able to mobilise at the moment, it would be laughable to suppose that the development of the revolution in Britain will follow any other course. Even as an

independent force—if we had the forces and resources—it would be necessary to take this process into account. How much more so when, in relation to the problems posed by history, as yet we are a tiny handful. The task is to convert this handful into an integrated group with roots in the mass movement and then, from a cadre organisation, into a wider grouping, leading to the development of a mass organisation. How this is to be done is the main tactical consideration which dominates the work of the organisation at this stage. (Ted Grant, *Problems of Entrism*)

He used to say: "If we had the forces we would work in the Boy Scouts and the Girl Guides." This showed his great flexibility. Unfortunately, for some elements, this wisdom is a book sealed with seven seals. Many mistakes have been made by people calling themselves Trotskyists because they think that in order to build the revolutionary party, it is sufficient to proclaim it.

The sectarian groups on the fringes of the Labour movement make a lot of noise, but have not the slightest conception of how to reach the working class or build a mass revolutionary party. This requires patient and systematic work in the mass organisations of the working class, as Lenin explained very well in *Left Wing Communism: An Infantile Disorder*, and as Trotsky repeated a thousand times in his writings of the 1930s.

The battle over Clause Four

Ted explained that the embryo of the new society exists within the old in the form of the organizations of the Labour Movement: the trade unions, the shop stewards committees, the co-ops and the Labour Party. He pointed out that in the rule book of every major British trade union there is a clause that says the union stands for the socialist transformation of society, for the nationalization of that particular branch of industry, workers' control, etc.

Even in something as apparently dry and bureaucratic as a union rule book, one can find fascinating insights into the history of the working class and the class struggle. Dudley Edwards, who was a marvellous old proletarian militant, pointed out that in the rule book of his own engineering union, the AEU, there was a post called "tyler" or the doorkeeper. This was the lowliest position in the union hierarchy, the first step that every budding bureaucrat must take before rising to the heights of the apparatus. Yet, Dudley explained that the post of doorkeeper originated in the days of the Combination Acts, when unions were illegal. In those days, the doorkeeper kept watch at the door with a loaded pistol in case of uninvited guests.

In order to prevent socialist revolution, the bourgeoisie tries by every means to undermine or destroy these embryos of a new society, the basis of working class power. In extreme situations, it attempts to destroy them physically. That is precisely the function of fascism: to destroy the child in the womb to prevent it from being born. Hitler closed down every workers' organization, no matter how innocuous, not just the Social Democracy, the Communist Party and the trade unions, but even the workers' chess clubs.

Normally, however, the capitalists are obliged to live with the Labour Movement. Indeed, they have found it convenient to do so. The reformist leaders of the trade unions and the Social Democracy have acted as a kind of safety valve that has saved capitalism on many occasions. The right-wing leaders are the trusted agents of the bourgeoisie within the Labour Movement. They can be relied upon to do the dirty work, to take upon their shoulders all the odium of unpopular measures to save capitalism in times of crisis, thus preparing the way for the return of the normal political rulers: the Conservatives and Liberals. A period of right-wing Labour government, moreover, has the advantage that it teaches the workers and the middle class a lesson: socialism is bad for you.

Ted used to compare the British parliamentary system to a cricket match. The ruling class has its First Eleven, its chosen team, which is the Conservative Party. But even the best team, as we know, can occasionally get into difficulties, or, as they say in cricket, be on a "sticky wicket". At this point, the Second Eleven can safely be called in to do a spot of batting until it is eventually caught out. Then the First Eleven comes back again, and so on and so forth.

Hugh Gaitskell, the leader of the Labour party in the 1950s, was a perfectly splendid captain for the Second Eleven, from the bourgeois point of view. A respectable middle class gent, he presented no danger to their class interest. But there was a problem, or more correctly, two problems. In the first place, with the economy booming, there was no real need to call in the Second Eleven. Under the very competent leadership of Harold MacMillan (Ted considered him an intelligent bourgeois politician), the Conservatives were doing just fine.

There was, however, a second reason, and a very weighty one. The bourgeois understood that the Labour Party was not just Hugh Gaitskell. Behind him there stood an army of millions of workers and trade unionists. A Labour government, no matter how right-wing, would always be under their pressure, and therefore could never really be trusted. Moreover, Labour had never completely rid itself of its socialist tendencies.

Clause IV, part four, of the Labour Party Constitution, adopted in 1918 under the influence of the Russian Revolution, was the clause that defined the Labour Party as a socialist party, pledged to the abolition of capitalism. Universally known just as Clause Four, it read as follows:

> To secure for the workers by hand or by brain the full fruits of their industry and the most equitable distribution thereof that may be possible upon the basis of the common ownership of the means of production, distribution and exchange, and the best obtainable system of popular administration and control of each industry or service.

After losing the 1959 general election, Labour Party leader Hugh Gaitskell announced that he proposed to get rid of Clause IV, part four. For Gaitskell it represented an obstacle in his road to Number Ten Downing Street. In the words of Macbeth:

> *That is a step. On which I must fall down, or else o'erleap,*
> *For in my way it lies.* (Shakespeare, *Macbeth*, Act 1, Scene iv)

Gaitskell was the true lineal ancestor of Tony Blair. His programme was indistinguishable from that of Macmillan. He stood firmly in defence of Britain's "nuclear deterrent", against the Labour Left which advocated unilateral disarmament. But when he tried to get rid of Clause Four, he bit off more than he could chew. He underestimated the determination of the workers to defend the idea that the Labour Party must stand for a fundamental change in society. His efforts to make the Party respectable in the eyes of the middle class provoked the ridicule of the satirists, who were then becoming fashionable. They wrote a parody of Labour's anthem, the *Red Flag*, which ended:

> *Then raise the umbrella high,*
> *The bowler hat and Eton tie,*
> *And just to prove we're still sincere,*
> *We'll sing the Red Flag once a year.*

Gaitskell declared war on Clause Four with all the passion of a crusader. He was confident of victory. Surely the Party would now see sense and support his bid to modernise it by throwing overboard all that ancient, cumbersome and outmoded ballast? He though it would be easy. But he was wrong. Although the right-wing Labour leaders had effectively turned Clause Four into a dead letter, the working class rank and file were fiercely attached to it. He was immediately faced with a ferocious battle.

In the end, Gaitskell was defeated by the resistance of the rank and file of the Party and the unions. In fact, it was then agreed to include Clause IV, part four, on Labour Party membership cards. For Ted, this was clear evidence that beneath the thick layer of bureaucracy, the proletarian roots of Labour still remained intact, a fertile ground on which the ideas of Marxism could grow in the future, when circumstances changed.

In 1994, Blair eventually succeeded in removing Clause Four as part of his attempted "counter-revolution" in the Labour Party, despite big opposition from the rank-and-file of the trade unions. While this was a setback, Blair was unable to break the organic link between Labour and the trade unions, which reflects the real class character of the Party.

Gulliver and the Lilliputians

In Jonathan Swift's celebrated satire, *Gulliver's Travels*, the hero Gulliver finds himself tied up by a host of diminutive beings known as Lilliputians. The Lilliputians were little men six inches in height, although in their pretensions and self-importance they imagined themselves to be giants. They were mean, nasty, vicious, morally corrupt, hypocritical and deceitful, jealous and envious, filled with greed and ingratitude—just like some real people I have known. Swift's book nowadays is thought of primarily as a book for children, but in fact it was a razor sharp satire on the politics and politicians of the day.

When I think of what Ted had to put up with as the awful decade of the 1950s staggered to a close, I think of him as Gulliver surrounded by the Lilliputians that are continually dancing rings around the movement. Incapable of achieving anything themselves, they are always ready to criticise others who are trying to do something positive.

We have an example of this in the factional activity of a small group led by a man by the name of Pat Jordan, seconded by his sidekick Ken Coates. Jordan and Coates had left the Communist Party over Hungary in 1956. They first associated with the Cliff group. Then Coates joined the Healyite Socialist Labour League (SLL), as his organisation was known by then. Finally, he and Jordan went over to Pablo and Mandel, and thus joined the group led by Ted in Britain.

I met these two men in the early 1960s and formed a very negative impression of both of them. Jordan ran a small bookshop in Nottingham where left-wing literature was offered for sale, along with second-hand comics, and the kind of magazines that are sold under the intriguing heading "for men". His *alter ego* Coates was a self-opinionated and loud-mouthed individual who had that unpleasant pushy manner that is usually associated with a purveyor of second-hand cars. I do not believe that he could have remained long in any group. His outsized ego would never allow it.

There was tension from the moment they joined. Although they were a petty-bourgeois group that represented nothing, they had big ideas. Jordan wanted to do us the honour of accepting the post of National Secretary of the united organization. The men in Paris would have been delighted to have these gentlemen leading the official section of the Fourth in Britain. But there was just one snag. The International already had a British section, and that was led by Ted

Grant. The International leadership got round this inconvenience by manoeuvring with Jordan and Coates to undermine Ted's position.

Since they were not capable of entering into a serious political debate with Ted, they all kept harping on the organizational deficiencies, of which, admittedly, there were many. From January 1958 to June 1963, the Tendency published a small paper called *Socialist Fight*, edited by Ted Grant, which our enemies called the *Socialist Flight* ("here today and gone tomorrow"). It was unkind but there was an element of truth in it. It was poorly produced and full of spelling mistakes. Its publication was irregular to say the least, and its layout was very drab. It usually had only four pages and was black and white. There were very few photographs. I remember whenever there was an article on Russia they would always use the same image—a picture of the Kremlin from a postcard somebody had picked up while on holiday in Moscow. The last few issues did not even have that: they were duplicated sheets stapled together. In the end it ceased publication altogether.

Coates and Jordan immediately organised what amounted to an undeclared Pabloite faction in the group, which was constantly sniping at the leadership. They took advantage of every shortcoming to make a fuss. Given the extremely difficult situation through which the group was passing, such disloyal activity was indistinguishable from sabotage. There are two ways of raising a criticism. One is that of an honest person who wishes to identify faults in order to correct them and improve the workings of the organization. Another, entirely different matter, is when people constantly look for problems, and exaggerate them in order to discredit and undermine the organization. The destructive criticism of Jordan and Coates and their hangers-on was definitely of the latter sort.

Ted was effectively subjected to a state of siege, a kind of slow torture, which he had to face on his own. Every meeting was turned into a wrangle over petty points and every conversation turned into a row. He repeatedly complained to Jimmy Deane, who at first attempted to play the role of conciliator. Blinded by his fervent desire for unity, Jimmy either would not or could not see what was going on. He wrote a letter to Ted dated July 10, 1959 in which he gave expression to his deep-seated frustration:

> The state of the organisation is bad indeed, though the possibilities are very good. In my opinion the whole house has got to be put in order—organisationally (...)
>
> Thanks to you we do have a political line which is correct and has been correct for many years. That is the first and most important thing, but it is not enough. Lenin and Trotsky were not only brilliant thinkers but also brilliant organisers. Indeed it was the latter as much as the former, that permitted them to make the contribution they did to history.
>
> Now I know that you are bogged down with nearly all of the work, and that one cannot do everything. But you could, in every meeting you have with the comrades, drive home this attitude; make them, by decision of the meeting, face up to the practical consequences and tasks.
>
> One must realise that much of the criticism is the result of a certain disregard for organisational efficiency by the leading comrades. It probably is true that they, the critics, are not bright organisers themselves—it usually works out that way. But again, one must recognise, that they are looking for a lead, and that in this sense their criticisms are quite valid.

In fact, Ted made repeated attempts to reach agreement. With almost superhuman forbearance, he endured the constant pin-pricks and sniping. But there are limits for all things. By this time, Jordan had taken over as general secretary. On the eve of a national conference, without any

SOCIALIST FIGHT

LABOUR'S MARXIST PAPER

VOL. 4. No. 9   October, 1962   PRICE 4d

On other pages:
- TUC – No move forward — page 3
- Socialist Foreign Policy?
- South Africa – Sabotage Bill — page 2
- Thalidomide — page 4
- Towards an Irish October — page 3

WHY? Mr Gaitskell WHY?

Three years ago the leadership of the Labour Party, backed up by a majority of the Parliamentary Party, precipitated the Movement into a bitter and debilitating controversy over the very raison d'etre of the Labour Party. They were wrong, treacherously, criminally wrong, and we said so at the time. But they did show guts.

GUTS

It took guts for members of the Parliamentary Party to deny the objects of their own lifetime's work. It took guts for them to spit in the face of the rank and file. It took a very great deal of courage to attempt such a sell-out.

But where is that courage to-day?

WARNING SOUNDED

The leadership is well aware that the conditions it has laid down for accepting Britain's entry into the Common Market will not be met. The leadership is well aware that the overwhelming bulk of the rank-and-file, in both the Unions and the Constituency Parties, is strongly opposed to membership. It has joined the Labour leaders of the Commonwealth in sounding a strong warning against the terms being negotiated. And yet it has not called on the Movement to stop the Government's surrender to the big firms, the monopolies, the suppliers of the Tory Party funds. Why?

CHAUVINISTIC ILLUSIONS

There are many reasons for opposing the Common Market. We, of "Socialist Fight," do not accept the chauvinistic illusions of the

tinue as suppliers of raw materials and buyers of manufactures. We recognize that Britain alone is not big enough nor varied enough to satisfy the demands of these countries for capital goods.

MONOPOLIST'S CHARTER

At the same time we recognise the Treaty of Rome as the monopolist's charter. The provisions for "free competition" are permission

---

warning, and without having raised the question on the EC of which he was a member, Jordan issued an all-out attack on the leadership, centring on the question of the paper. This provocation was too much. Ted wrote an angry letter to Pablo denouncing what was an intolerable situation:

July 20, 1959

Dear comrade Pablo,

I had thought that this letter would not be necessary, as I had hoped the crisis in the leadership would be solved, and we could proceed amicably, with the real task of building the section. But things are taking a more and more serious turn.

It is not a question of political differences, though no doubt if things proceed on the present lines of development, political differences will be manufactured.

The serious thing about this crisis is that it is a crisis of confidence. The issue is not the nature of the paper. Many criticisms of the paper, its weaknesses and shortcomings could be accepted. But the problem then would be how best to improve the quality of the paper, its organisation, circulation and work. It is elementary you would agree, that questions of that sort should be discussed on the National Committee, Executive Committee, etc. before *without any preparation or warning* it is thrown by leading members to the organisation as a whole.

It is impossible to establish a collective leadership, if the members are working against each other.

Surely seldom in the history of the Movement, can there be a situation such as developed in the last few weeks in our Group in Britain. Without raising the question for discussion in the National Committee, or the EC, 2 members of the National Committee, in collusion with the General Secretary, produce a Resolution two weeks before the Conference in the Nottingham branch condemning the paper root and branch and demanding it be scrapped, etc., etc. At the same time issuing an ultimatum to the EC that they have already duplicated the Resolution and will circulate it themselves unless the EC circulates it immediately. When Pat [Jordan] showed me the letter from Tarbuk on these lines, I warned him of the results of activities such as these. The EC naturally were extremely indignant and explained to Pat the elementary rules of democratic centralism on this question.

It is impossible to build a leadership based on trust when a member of the EC, the General Secretary, goes behind the back of the EC and the other professional, *especially on a secondary question of this character*. It is even worse when one considers that for the last four months Pat has been jointly responsible for the Paper and never once raised the question for discussion on the EC or NC. (…)

Naturally the comrades throughout the organisation were indignant at this procedure. The Conference was badly organised. The first day's discussion on the political questions was very good. But the second day because of the way that the agenda had been prepared (we must all take our share of responsibility on the EC for this) there was no real organisational report like that of Fairhead at the last conference, and the discussion on the Tarbuk document, precisely because there had been no preparation was not very good. Despite the fact that he had not presented any document Pat intervened in the discussion on the question in support of the Tarbuk position. I attacked him for this pointing out however that the question would be discussed at the incoming NC.

Tarbuk then proceeded to demand "Tendency Rights" on a secondary organisational question like that! Naturally the comrades were indignant at such an irresponsible attitude.

In my opinion, as I told Pat, he and Tarbuk had deliberately provoked an unnecessary crisis when there were no real differences, in order to provoke the intervention of the IS.

At the NC immediately after the Conference, Brian Deane moved Pat [Jordan] as the General Secretary. Sam Bornstein objected and pointed out that the General Secretary has to have the confidence of the majority of the members. In view of the irresponsible conduct of Pat and Ken Tarbuck of which I had warned Pat of the consequences, I seconded the motion of Sam. (I had explained the position to Pat when the issue had arisen in the form of the "bombshell" of him and Tarbuk). Pat then made a conciliatory statement and I suggested to Sam that under these circumstances the motion should be withdrawn. To the general relief of all the comrades, especially the Liverpool comrades, it seemed as if the question had been resolved amicably.

For the next week I went out of my way to try and smooth things out with Pat and convince him of the need to work together with the EC as a team. We had even agreed jointly to present a document on the paper to the coming Extended NC. This despite the fact that Pat had at first threatened to take the matter to the IS at which I had shrugged my shoulders.

However, he had threatened to split the organisation over the question of the control of the bookshop, saying he would take Glasgow, Nottingham and the colonial comrades with him, in the private discussions he had with me. (He is wrong on this question in any case...)

In spite of this I adopted a conciliatory attitude, hoping that common work and the results of the Conference would convince him. I think I had succeeded in once again establishing friendly relations with him. But all the work of the preceding week was destroyed at the EC. (…)

I can assure you that it is not fear of a discussion which has provoked this crisis but the method by which it was launched. (In fact only a handful of the comrades supported Pat in the organisation nationally.)

So far as my own attitude to the International is concerned it is the same as that of Jimmy Deane.

Perhaps you could visit Britain and discuss the problem with the comrades. There are many other factors which cannot be mentioned in a letter but can only be explained in discussion. I have had some sleepless nights worrying about a sterile and barren crisis, just at the time when important if modest gains can be made. Pulling together as a team and the organisation could possibly double within the next 12 months.

My personal attitude towards you remains as it was. I have always warned you against 100% supporters as they are always dangerous, and can reverse their position at a moment's notice. This is a personal letter written in the hope that the crisis can be resolved.

What eventually precipitated the crisis? The finances of the group were in crisis, so the EC had proposed that Pat Jordan find a temporary job for a few weeks over the summer in order to make ends meet. Jordan was not prepared to accept that. By this time, Jimmy Deane had understood the nature of the problem and had radically altered his views. On July 29, 1959, following a long telephone conversation with Ted, Jimmy wrote from South Wales where he was working:

Dear Ted,

Sorry we were cut off, they didn't even give us the chance to reverse the charges.

(...) You must stand firm on the question of the bookshop. This must come under the control of the EC. Of this there can be no question at all. Anyone who refuses to place his work, etc., under the control of the supreme bodies has no right in the organisation at all—let alone a responsible post.

It must be made absolutely clear that the divergence here has nothing to do with political positions, for which there is all the room for airing and developing. This is a simple matter of elementary loyalties. This has got to be the issue. We will do everything possible to keep all comrades, even where they may feel they have fundamental differences.

The organisation will give them the opportunity to defend their ideas in the way normal to Marxism, in the way indeed normal in political life. That is one thing. That the activities of all the members must come under the control of the leading bodies and appointed comrades goes without saying, particularly the activities of a bookshop which was financed by the monies of the IS and ourselves.

Only the most disloyal and light-minded could behave in the way Pat and Brian B [Biggins] are behaving. It seems to me that they are not at all concerned with building a movement, but only with their own childish fantasies. Between them they will not be able to build anything; only in complete unity and with correct ideas can anything be built.

To split the movement in this way at this stage is a most terrible thing, a severe blow to us and a gift to all of our enemies. It is a crime.

What was wrong with suggesting that Pat should go to work for a few weeks? I don't think that there was any mistake in this at all. For what he is doing for the organisation, I am not speaking about his own *clique*, he may just have well gone to work long ago. These people don't seem to know even the most elementary methods usually adopted in the movement, nor the meaning of responsibility and loyalties.

Again, a comparatively untested and inexperienced comrade has been given an important post. Again we have a mess. Only experienced and tested comrades should be given posts of this nature (including that of sales manager, etc.). It only disillusions those who are not tough enough to withstand the difficulties of a small organisation coping with an enormous task.

On August 11, 1959 Jimmy wrote again:

Dear Ted,

Just received copy of 29/07/1959 EC minutes from GS. Please convey my thanks to GS and do persuade him to do all possible to attend the NC in Liverpool.

The minutes reveal an impossible position. It is quite impossible for PJ [Pat Jordan] to function in any responsible position with such a disloyal and unhealthy attitude. Indeed it is remarkable that he would continue, attempt to continue work, with such an outlook.

If he holds the attitude that the EC is not a trustworthy and responsible body, that it has an anti International attitude, that it has political and organisational misconceptions, surely all of this was not discovered only at the time of the Conference or a few days before it took place. In any case it is clear that his attitude is entirely light-minded and disloyal from the point of view of the IS. He is completely untrustworthy.

We must do everything to integrate him and others into the organisation but none of them can be given any responsible post. (...)

Pat's evasion of the questions in relation to the RSL is dishonest, and, more important, reveal a complete lack of belief in the programme and policy. His characterisation of the EC of which he is a member and an attempt to place *his* conditions on the NC are entirely inexcusable. Who created the factional atmosphere—even to the point of demanding factional rights?

Personally, even if Pat were to agree to hand over the bookshop, etc., I do not feel that he can continue in any responsible post with his present attitude of mistrust and disloyalty.

The letter concludes with a request to Ted to find accommodation for Jimmy in London: "One thing, you must try help me find a suitable place to live in London. Even if at work I could devote my evenings at doing the Secretariat work—and quite a lot of other work too". Finally, in discussing Ted's trip to Liverpool for the NC, he makes an interesting suggestion: "If Arthur can come down with you by motorcycle you will find that it will be cheaper than by train".

Jimmy's idea that these elements could somehow be integrated in the group was a forlorn hope. You cannot unite oil and water; nor can you unite a proletarian tendency with unprincipled petty-bourgeois elements. The crisis was only resolved when Jordan and Coates broke from the group, although that was not the last we heard of the Lilliputians.

Jimmy Deane

Soon after this, Jimmy Deane moved to London and became the General Secretary of the Tendency. When I joined in 1960, I regarded Jimmy as a giant, which he undoubtedly was. A Liverpool proletarian with a thick "Scouse" accent, he was not very big in stature, but was tough and wiry and gave every impression of being a hard man. Jimmy was the leading figure in a true Trotskyist dynasty on Merseyside.

Jimmy was born on January 31, 1921, the eldest son of Gus Deane, a blacksmith from an Irish Protestant family. His mother, the redoubtable Gertie Deane, had trained as a nurse. As a young woman she met many of the leading figures of pre-1914 Marxism, including Henry Hyndman and James Larkin. She was a well-known figure in the Merseyside labour movement, and was to be seen on picket lines well into her seventies. It was Jim and his brothers Arthur and Brian who recruited Gertie to the Trotskyist movement, although she was already from a sound socialist tradition.

Her father, who had been a member of the old Social Democratic Federation, was one of the first Labour councillors in Liverpool. But by all accounts, her dedication to political activism was not accompanied by a great interest in the mundane tasks of housework. The boys apparently would come home from work and find the house in a somewhat anarchic state, with unwashed dishes piled in the sink and their mother reading Trotsky's *History of the Russian Revolution*.

During the early years of the war, Deane served his apprenticeship as an electrical engineer in Cammel Laird's shipyard in Birkenhead. In the absence of a father in the house, it was Jimmy who had to play the leading role in the Deane household. Someone once told me that he used to maintain firm order in the house and administered chastisement to his younger brothers, occasionally of the physical kind! The younger Deane brothers, Arthur and Brian, were also active in the movement. But it was always Jimmy who played a leading role in the Trotskyist movement. All three brothers were active in the Revolutionary Communist Party in the 1940s, which is very well dealt with in Ted Grant's *History of British Trotskyism*.

Arthur and Jimmy Deane with Ted in the mid-1950s

In 1944, Jimmy was sent to work in the mines but was taken ill and invalided out. He spent most of 1945 working as a professional at the RCP centre at 256 Harrow Road, London. He was a member of the party's Central Committee and the on editorial board of *Socialist Appeal*, and was the London Industrial Organiser. He was active in the East London branch, and was particularly involved with work with dockers in the build-up to and aftermath of the great strike in June 1948. It was throughout this period that his lifelong friendship with Ted Grant, which had begun in the early 1940s, was firmly cemented, and lasted until his death.

After the dissolution of the RCP in 1949, Jimmy and his brothers Arthur and Brian played a key role in regrouping the small forces that remained loyal to the genuine ideas of Trotskyism.

Like any other mortal, Jimmy had his weaknesses. He was fond of a drink and could never resist a pretty face. His lack of punctuality was proverbial: he always turned up late to branch meetings. Frank Ward told me of one such incident, which, however, had an ironic twist:

> I'll never forget the time when he kept on being bloody late at the branch, and finally he turned up at some ungodly hour, late. He had all the minutes so we couldn't start without him. He always had a story. This story was that his tram had caught fire, and we bloody censored him. And lo and behold, the following morning, we had seen there was a fire on his tram. The only time he told the truth we passed a motion of censure.

After the split with Healy and the demise of the RCP, Jimmy had played a key role in holding together the comrades in Liverpool, who later played a big role in reviving the Tendency. Gradually, a number of younger comrades joined the Liverpool group, the most outstanding of whom was Pat Wall, who later became one of the three Militant MPs but who died tragically before his time.

After Ted Grant, Jimmy was the outstanding figure in the leadership. He made a profound impression on me. He and Ted were very close both personally and politically. And Jimmy was one of the few people I knew who could call Ted to order. In fact, he used to enjoy teasing Ted in all kinds of ways. We would go to the pub after an NC meeting and there you would see

Jimmy, pint in hand, provoking Ted into a discussion on *Anti-Dühring* or state capitalism or some other theoretical subject. Ted would get quite hot under the collar and Jimmy would have a great time contradicting him, just for the fun of it.

There is no denying the important role played by Jimmy Deane and his brothers in these difficult years. But this was not Jimmy's best moment. He had a lot of family and financial problems, and drank a lot. I remember that he would chair meetings of the NC and be anxiously looking at his watch (the pubs closed at 2pm if I remember rightly). He would quickly close the meeting and literally sprint to the pub. By the time the rest of us arrived he would already be downing a pint.

The fact is that Jimmy was quite demoralised by this time. The responsibility for this must be placed at the door of the so-called leaders of the Fourth International. Yet despite all their crimes, Jimmy still held out hope that the International could be regenerated. This was the triumph of hope over experience! He supported the moves to "reunite the Trotskyist movement", which was a false position. He allowed his naive optimism to get the better of his common sense and political judgement.

Golden advice

As an amusing footnote to this otherwise grim period, I came across a series of letters Ted wrote to his brother Isy, who had a small business in Johannesburg, in which he uses his knowledge of Marxist economics to advise him on investments. He strongly advised him to buy gold shares, which was very good advice, at a time when most bourgeois economists were inclined to write off gold altogether. Here is an excerpt from a letter written on April 16, 1960:

> (...) There is talk in the press here of a possible coalition in South Africa! Gold and all industrial shares will immediately rise if this comes about.
>
> By the way it occurs to me you may have discussed my suggestion to buy gold shares with other businessmen or so-called finance "experts". If you did, take no notice of their advice. They can *only follow the market*. They do not understand the processes that make it tick. They are purely empirics without the necessary all-rounded approach that is necessary to a Marxist like myself.
>
> Anyway this letter is written in a tearing hurry, in the hope that you will seriously consider my advice. It will not be long—perhaps a matter of days or a week or two—when the state of emergency will be ended—and this too will have an almost instant effect on South African shares, industrial and *especially gold-mining shares*. As

Ted's brother Isy and his family

the bourgeois express it *"Confidence will be restored"*—till the next explosion—which will come in the not too distant future.

The South African police think they are safe in their Saracen Armoured vehicles. It is only a matter of time if the Africans take to violence for them to learn the use of Molotov cocktails... to use bottles of petrol to set the tracks on fire and render them useless. In fighting in the workers' quarters in India, in the last decade of British rule, the Indian workers used the same methods effectively against tanks and against the army.

He wrote on the same subject to Rae and Raymond (Friedheim) on July 20, 1960:

> Re the question you ask re shares. My friend bought Oppenheimer shares in mines in the Free state as I advised. He bought Merievale shares. They are paying a dividend of 10% so he is already showing a profit.
>
> Whatever you do, don't make a further mistake and sell your shares. Owing to the outbreak in the Congo there may be a further delay in the rise in these shares. But once conditions return to "normal" in South Africa, and especially when the "emergency" regulations are entirely repealed, and that should be before the end of the year, there should be a rise in the shares. The dividends you receive on your shares should recompense you for the fall in their value. They have reached rock bottom now and unless there are further outbreaks of the Africans in the Union they will not fall any further. Now they can only rise. It is just a question of time. All the mining firms are showing bigger profits than they made last year. They need new capital from abroad. They and the manufacturing interests are exerting pressure on the government for a more "liberal" policy towards the Natives, and over a period are bound to succeed. As usual in South African politics they will probably engineer a split in the Nationalists if they do not make any gestures in the direction they wish. In any case your money is quite safe.
>
> I am looking out for a safe investment which will show a quick rise. If I find one I will of course let you know, and the reasons why, the rest will be up to you.
>
> Have you heard from Isy, Nita and Zena? I haven't heard a word. I am afraid that Nita may be offended because I did not answer her letter right away. Isy owes me a letter as I have wrote three without a reply.
>
> I am now in the pink of condition.

This correspondence raises the fascinating possibility that if Ted Grant had not been a revolutionary, he would have made an excellent hedge fund manager! His deep interest in the science of Marxist economics together with what may well have been an inherited gambler's streak would have equipped him quite well for such a role. But whatever advice he gave to his family, Ted himself was certainly in no position to buy gold shares or anything else.

Chapter Six

THE TIDE BEGINS TO TURN

The sack

A few months after writing to Rae and Raymond, Ted's personal circumstances took a serious turn for the worse. The financial crisis of the group did not allow for them to sustain a professional any more, so Ted had to leave full-time political work. He worked for a time as a door-to-door salesman for a firm called Kleen-e-ze Brush. From what I know, he must have been quite a competent salesman. Anyway, he said: "They were very good brushes." But a letter from his employers shows that Ted had been spending so much time on political work that he was seriously neglecting his duties. On January 12, 1961, Ted received a letter of dismissal from Kleen-e-ze Brush Co. Ltd. It reads as follows:

> Dear Mr Grant,
>
> I wrote to you before Xmas to ring me regarding going out with you on the Thursday after the Xmas holiday but when you did not ring I called about a week after Xmas at your house and was told you were away and that you were in the habit of spending long periods away from your address, although I left a note for you to ring me which you evidently ignored.
>
> It is apparent you are no longer working for this Company and as you have not ordered for 4 weeks and when you do order they are so small it is evident you are only using the Company for the purpose of stamping your cards.
>
> I have, therefore, been instructed by Head Office to withdraw your Outfit forthwith and it will be necessary for you to ring me this weekend on Saturday evening or noon Sunday so that the necessary arrangements can be made for me to collect your outfit. Also the goods I loaned you or their value will have to be taken out before the case is returned to Bristol.
>
> Also I have checked up on the customers I asked you to contact and not one of them has seen you and this is evidence enough for me and I wholeheartedly agree with HO decision.
>
> Awaiting your phone call,
>
> Yours sincerely, [Signature illegible]

To make matters worse, on February 16, 1961 Ted received a postcard from the Ministry of Labour rejecting his claim for unemployment benefit. He was now without employment and without any income. But by the autumn of the following year he got a job with British Telecom as a telephone operator. This was for the international service, so he was obliged to brush up on his French. He was still on a probationary course on September 12, 1962, when he wrote to his sister Rae and her husband:

(...) For the last fortnight I have been on trial on the "Board" of the telephone exchange, taking French calls only, with an instructor listening in. I have passed the test and now require only an oral test, which the other pupils who have passed state is only a "formality". If I do not "muck-up" the final test I will then be, officially at least, a fully fledged "linguist". Anyway I think I will then be able to learn French. Mind you I can now understand both the wireless and when people speak to me in French. The difficulty is to speak French correctly and grammatically. My teacher says that will come with practice. At any rate I hope so.

My health is as usual. My ideas the same! Events I think over a period perhaps the next decade or so, will demonstrate their correctness. (...)

This job was a stroke of good luck. Since Ted was on permanent night shift, he could virtually work as a full-timer during most of the day. This was important because, after a period of extreme difficulty, the situation in Britain was slowly beginning to change. In the same letter he writes:

Last weekend I was in South Wales, in Cardiff, where I was supposed to have a debate with the Labour Shadow Chancellor James Callaghan. At the last moment he squeezed out of it. He failed to turn up in the morning and only arrived for the afternoon session of a Youth School that had been organised for the South Wales area. He refused to debate, saying that he knew nothing of the arrangements, after he and I had answered only one question! It did not matter as I answered question for two hours after he had gone and the contrast between our line and that of the Right Wing in the Labour Party was clear to everyone. Everybody there understood that he had "funked" the discussion. So we came out of it quite well.

I was at that school, although I confess I cannot remember much about it, except that I was impressed by the depth of Ted's knowledge and eloquence. I had first met Ted sometime before, in 1960, when he came to speak to the Swansea Young Socialists, of which I was a member. By a stroke of good luck, I joined the Swansea YS in 1960, which was one of the few in Britain that the Tendency controlled, and I was soon won over, although when I joined I was a convinced Stalinist (my family had strong CP connections). I was sixteen years old and was bowled over by Ted's grasp of Marxism, the clear way he had of expressing even the most complicated ideas in simple language.

The Swansea group had some very fine comrades, all of them working class and first-rate Marxist cadres. Outstanding among them was Muriel Browning, a shop steward at the British Leyland car factory in Llanelli, and Phil Lloyd, a post office engineer who later became the secretary of the Swansea branch of the POEU. But the leader of the group was undoubtedly Dave Matthews, a close collaborator of Ted Grant, and a man with a very high political level. It was Dave who won me over to Trotskyism and encouraged me to study Marxism, which I did with tremendous enthusiasm.

The *Young Guard* episode

The Labour Party relaunched the Young Socialists in 1960, after being closed for years, following Stalinist infiltration. It was quite a promising time for youth work, and the Young Socialists got off to a flying start, aided by a mass movement of youth in the Campaign for Nuclear Disarmament, and two national apprentices' strikes in 1960 and 1964, in which our comrades in Merseyside played a significant role.

Our main field of work was still the Young Socialists. The context was very different from today. The Tory Party had been in power for 13 years, and was completely discredited, mired

Ted Grant relaxing at Rhossili beach in 1960 after a Young Socialist camp with Dave Matthews, Muriel Browning, Phil Lloyd and Adrian Jones

in a swamp of scandal around the Profumo affair. The old right-wing Labour leader Hugh Gaitskell had died. The new leader Harold Wilson had a fairly "left" image and the YS were quite a big force.

At the beginning, the YS attracted a large number of young people, but unfortunately, this promising start was negatively affected by the ultra-left activities of the Healyite Socialist Labour League. Although Healy had denied the possibility of work in the YS, he opportunistically made a turn to the new youth movement and, thanks to his strong apparatus and youth paper *Keep Left*, succeeded in taking control of the YS nationally by various dubious means. The Healyites used their majority on the YS national committee to engineer a break with the Labour Party. It was a criminal policy just when the Labour Party was about to win its first election for 13 years.

The Healyites were on an ultra-left binge, trying to provoke a split in order to establish the mass "Workers' Revolutionary Party". Healy's Socialist Labour League (SLL) was hell-bent on breaking the YS from the Labour Party. To this end they deliberately provoked expulsions. They used hooligan tactics, including physical violence against political rivals. These were methods copied directly from Third Period Stalinism.

I should point out that all the left groups (except for the CPGB and the SPGB) were in the Labour Party at that time. The Cliff group, known then as the International Socialists or IS (now the SWP), had a paper called *Labour Worker*. The Cliff group was based almost entirely on students and was overwhelmingly petty-bourgeois in composition. That was clearly reflected in their political line. They were mainly active in the Campaign for Nuclear Disarmament (CND), the pacifist movement, and at that time they did not even regard themselves as Trotskyists (I imagine Tony Cliff himself would have been an exception to the rule but I cannot be sure). Their material was heavily biased towards a confused anarco-syndicalism. But then, this tendency has never distinguished itself by its theoretical clarity or consistency.

As we have seen, at that time, we were extremely weak organizationally. We had no money, no office, no real newspaper, and no full timers. Ted was working as a telephone operator. In order to combat the Healyites who had a weekly paper and a big apparatus, the comrades decided to collaborate with the Cliff group in setting up a new youth paper called *Young Guard,* with an agreed editorial line and signed articles. This was a big mistake.

The mistake was to look for shortcuts where none existed. I believe Jimmy Deane was largely responsible for the mistake. He was overly optimistic. In my opinion, this was a reflection of frustration and impatience, particularly on his part. Probably there was an element of demoralisation as a result of years in the wilderness with very few results. But as Trotsky said, the search for shortcuts inevitably leads to mistakes either of an ultra-left or opportunist character.

Ted after a dip in Rhossili, near Swansea

I remember being present in a discussion about the *Young Guard*. To the objections of some of the young comrades in London, Jimmy argued that the Cliff people were nothing, they had no level, and we could easily defeat them through the superiority of our arguments. The problem was that the Cliffites did not fight with arguments, but by manoeuvres and intrigues. The superiority of our arguments did not count for much in that milieu.

There was supposed to be a joint unsigned editorial, and then signed articles. Keith Dickinson from Liverpool, in whose name *Rally* had been published, was supposed to be Business Manager. But in practice, the Cliff group, who were stronger in London, packed the meetings and took it over. Immediately, disputes arose over defending Cuba in the 1962 missile crisis, the attitude to the USSR, etc. As a result the whole thing broke down. We made a serious mistake entering the *Young Guard*. After the *Young Guard* episode we faced a very serious situation. We were worse off than before. *Rally* was a dead duck and we were effectively without a paper. This underlines the point: *there are no shortcuts in revolutionary politics.*

Provocations

The SLL would recruit declassed youth off the street on a non-political basis (inviting them to a social, dance, etc.). Then they would incite them to attack YS branches and break up meetings by force. The Party officials would then call the police and the SLL would take photos which appeared in their paper with titles such as "Pabloites and bureaucrats use police against working class youth".

In some areas, the YS organized self-defence against these hooligan tactics, as in Glasgow, where the SLL provocateurs were "introduced to the pavement". In Brighton, we decided that we would do the same and appealed to the students to go to the YS branch to defend it in case of trouble. We would not call the police, but would defend ourselves with all the necessary means. Fortunately, in our case, this was not necessary. I remember one discussion in a pub, when comrades from the Clapham YS were asking Jimmy Deane how they should react to such provocations. He replied: "Naturally, if you are attacked you have to defend yourselves."

There was a particularly bad provocation in Wandsworth YS, where a comrade of ours, a Ceylonese (Sri Lankan) called Mani, was in the chair. A group of "Rockers" entered the meeting with milk bottles in their pockets. The kids were terrified, but Mani kept his nerve and asked them what they wanted. They replied that they had been told "there was a black man here who hates the Rockers". Mani managed to get them to leave, but there were scuffles provoked by the SLLers in which a filing cabinet was broken.

This provocation gave an excuse for the Labour Party bureaucracy to intervene and demand expulsions. At the meeting of the GMC that followed, Mani counter-proposed the expulsion of those who were personally involved in violence. As a consequence, the Healyites persecuted Mani viciously. They raised a big scandal about our alleged collaboration with the bureaucracy in "expelling working class youth".

Typically, these slanders were taken as good coin by the leaders of the United Secretariat of the Fourth International (USFI) led by Mandel. They were prepared to use any stick to beat us, even when it was provided by the enemies of the movement. Ted replied indignantly: "violence is not a political question!" Of course! There is not a single decent trade union branch that would tolerate such hooligan behaviour. Anybody who deliberately and systematically uses violence against members of the labour movement must be driven out.

The sectarian madness of the SLL actually led them to act as strike-breakers during the 1964 apprentices' strike. As usual, their slogan was "rule or ruin". Our tendency played an important role in the strike, together with the YCL (Young Communist League). This was unacceptable to the Healyites who denounced the official apprentices' committee because it was led by "Pabloites" and "Stalinists".

They deliberately split the apprentices' committee, in order set up one under their control. They attempted to sabotage the strike in November, setting another date for their own apprentices' strike three or four months later. During the November strike they distributed leaflets telling apprentices not to strike and to wait for the "real" strike. The resulting confusion naturally had a damaging effect on the strike, which ended in failure. Needless to say the "real" strike called by the SLL never materialised.

The Healyites organized a "YS Conference" at Morecambe in 1965, which represented a de facto rupture with the Labour Party. Anybody who went to this conference would be open to expulsion. The SLL therefore pulled out all the stops to get as many YS members as possible to go to Morecambe. We exerted every effort to prevent it. In Sussex, the Healyites called a conference to vote on a report back from their Morecambe Conference. This was a deliberate provocation. Since that Conference was illegal under the Labour Party Rules, anybody who attended it was liable to be expelled.

We mobilised all the YS branches in Sussex under our influence and went along to the meeting. Right at the start, we moved a vote of no confidence in the chair. This threw the Healyites into disarray. They did not know whether to vote against the motion or to refuse to recognise it. In the end, they decided to ignore it and commenced the report back from the Conference. We then called for a vote, which took place in the midst of uproar. Having passed the vote, we elected a new committee, the members of which stood, one by one, in front of the table while the speaker, by now completely invisible, continued to read a report that nobody was listening to. The vote having been concluded, we declared the meeting closed and walked out, leaving them with the rump. In this way we scotched the provocation and saved the YS, at least in Sussex. In other parts of the country, the YS was completely wrecked.

We had a number of unpleasant experiences with provocative elements who joined the organization at this point, mostly ex-SLLers who played a disruptive role. But by this time we were rallying our forces, and they realised that their provocations could not succeed in wrecking the organization. Gradually, painfully, we were beginning the process of ascent. It was still tough, and our progress was slower than what we would have liked, but we were definitely on the way up. However, there was still one more obstacle to overcome.

Ted Grant in Swansea in the early 1960s

The "International Group"

I have the impression that Jimmy had already decided to throw in the towel, and as a last act of desperation, he threw all his weight behind what he hoped would be a successful unification with the International Group (IG). This was in line with the general position "for the unity of all Trotskyists" of the so-called Fourth International (of which our group was still the official British section). In 1963, the majorities of the two factions that had split the Fourth in 1953 came together and established the United Secretariat of the Fourth International. Ernest Mandel, Pierre Frank, Livio Maitan and Joseph Hansen were part of the new international leadership. With all his experience, Jimmy could not have had any illusions in the so-called leaders of the Fourth, but he deluded himself into adopting a kind of false optimism. It was Mr. Micawber all over again. Against all previous experience, he was confidently expecting that something would turn up. Naturally, all these illusions were in vain. It unravelled almost immediately.

The IG—led by our old friends Pat Jordan and Ken Coates—were a minuscule outfit based mainly in Nottingham. They called themselves the International Group. However, they were really not much of a group, and they were only international in the sense that they said amen to anything that came from Paris. Under the pressure of the United Secretariat we were once again dragged into a shotgun marriage with these hopeless people.

In the summer of 1964, a decision was taken to launch a new publication, and after much debate, the name of *Militant* was chosen. With the support of the leaders of the supposedly united Fourth International, however, once again we had the usual manoeuvres and intrigues. A unity conference was held in Sevenoaks in Kent on September 19–20, 1964. I was invited to attend, but was unable to make it.

With the excuse of helping the new section, the men in Paris sent us a full timer. This was the Canadian Alan Harris, a yes-man of Hansen and the American SWP (he was later known as Ernie Tate, which I guess was his real name).

He was so colourless that he was virtually invisible. I believe he had missed his vocation. He would have made a wholly admirable filing clerk in an accountants' office. However, Harris had one outstanding virtue: he was loyal, that is, he was loyal to his bosses in Paris, and to nobody else. He installed himself in what was supposed to be the organization's bookshop in a tiny room in Bow Lane in the City, near to St. Paul's Cathedral and the Bank of England. This location was no doubt highly convenient for any Bishop desirous of acquiring a copy of Marx *On Religion*, or for a passing banker wishing to refresh his memory as to the contents of *Capital*, but quite useless from the standpoint of building in the labour movement. It was also extremely expensive.

From the beginning, he began intriguing behind the backs of the leadership to build the Jordan-Coates group as "loyal Internationalists" and undermine the position of Ted and Jimmy. Their tactic was to approach the students to strengthen the petty-bourgeois tendency. So when they heard that there was a young student comrade in Sussex University, they immediately invited me to a discussion in London. They did not inform Ted, but he found out about it and turned up anyway. However, Harris miscalculated badly. He tried to play the "studentist" card, following the revisionist line of the American SWP. But I was implacably opposed to this and petty-bourgeois politics in general. They made an even bigger mistake by praising the New Left and Ralph Milliband, all of whom I detested. I told them so in no uncertain terms and Ted was mightily pleased. He told me later: "I was going to intervene but I didn't have to say anything."

Alan Harris asked me what I thought of the Healyites and *Keep Left*. I replied that they were ultra-left adventurists and hooligans and we could have nothing to do with them. His opinion was that *Keep Left* was not a bad paper, "although it had a certain sectarian streak running through it." Not long afterwards he had completely changed his tune. "The SLL is a sick organization", he declared. Obviously he had received new orders from his bosses in Paris. He had absolutely no ideas of his own.

As a postscript, in a recent trip to Canada I was informed that Alan Harris/Ernie Tate was still around, and that he "hated Ted Grant with a passion". I was very sorry to hear this because, as far as I remember, Ted never hated anybody, and least of all the man we knew as Alan Harris. What we have here, then, is a very sad case of *unrequited hate*, which must be considerably more painful than *unrequited love*. Poor Harris could never have given rise to any passion as powerful as hate. At the very most he might arouse a feeling of utter boredom.

The brief fusion with the IG soon broke down. In reality there was no political basis for the fusion. The rupture took place at a stormy meeting of the National Committee in London,

> # MILITANT
> ### FOR YOUTH AND LABOUR
> NUMBER TWO   NOVEMBER 1964   SIXPENCE
>
> **A GREAT START- BUT HELP IS NEEDED**
> By S. MANI, Business Manager
>
> ## Hogg slanders Young Socialists
>
> ## NO RETREAT

which was attended by Pierre Frank and Joe Hansen from the International Secretariat. Pierre Frank created a very disagreeable impression. Of short stature, he had angry eyes, as if he was at war with the rest of the world. He called to mind one of Arthur Rackham's cartoons of the dwarfish inhabitants of Niebelheim. He spoke stridently with a thick French accent.

By contrast, Joe Hansen was taller, with horn-rimmed glasses and a permanently benign expression on his face. He spoke quietly in measured tones and could have passed for a retired headmaster from an old-fashioned school for boys. They were working secretly together with Alan Harris, who organized a clandestine factional meeting before the NC. We found out about this and the matter was raised before the meeting proper had opened.

Jimmy Deane was in the chair, and Hansen and Frank were sitting opposite him on the other side of the table. The room, which as usual was upstairs in a London pub, was very small and there was not much space, so the IS representatives almost had their bellies against the edge of the table.

Jimmy immediately addressed his remarks to them, speaking with his thick Liverpool accent: "Before we start this meeting I demand an explanation from the representatives of the IS for their participation in a factional meeting before this NC." Pierre Frank started to bluster something about how the minority was behaving in a "factional manner" in his barely incomprehensible English: "We consider that ze comrades of ze majority 'ave also treated ze minority in a factional mannaire..."

Before he could finish the sentence, Jimmy sprang to his feet and slammed the table with his fist. The table seemed to jump several inches with the blow and so did Hansen and Frank. Seething with indignation, Jimmy bellowed out: "Factional! Factional! You dare to lecture us about factionalism! You were only in the movement for two minutes and you formed a faction against Trotsky!"

This caused quite a stir in the meeting, with Frank blustering incoherently, the IGers jumping up and down demanding "respect" for the leaders of the International, and Joe Hansen pleading for calm. It was quite a scene. When finally some semblance of order was restored, Ken Coates, in what was clearly a carefully prepared move, insisted on reading a "statement" from the IG. I cannot remember much about what it said, but it consisted of a long list of grouses about the organization. Their main complaint was that we had allegedly "supported the expulsion of left-wingers" from the Labour Party. This was a scandalous reference to the Wandsworth episode that I have already mentioned.

Immediately after reading it, and without giving us a chance to answer, they all walked out. Jimmy demanded that the representatives of the IS clarify their position on "this monstrous behaviour". Naturally, they refused to condemn what was a very clear provocation. Thereafter, things moved rapidly.

The split-off group began to publish a duplicated 12-page "news service for socialists" with the exciting title *The Week* (we used to call them the "Weak People"). The editors were Ken Coates and the New Leftist Robin Blackburn, and it published a long list of MPs and other "celebrities" as its sponsors. In fact, it was not difficult for anybody to sponsor this publication, which was entirely devoid of anything resembling a revolutionary position. It was a carbon-copy repetition of Healy's "Club" all over again.

To describe its line as reformism would be to do it a considerable disservice. I mean, it did not even reach the level of the palest of pink left-reformism. They refused to call for nationalisation, instead talking in general terms about workers' control. They even set up an "Institute for Workers' Control" run by Ken Coates—as if workers' control was something one required to get a diploma in, instead of conquering it through the class struggle! Coates ended up as a Labour MEP, and no doubt got a very nice pension. We were well rid of him.

The IG continued with this opportunist line until the end of the 1960s. Then all of a sudden, they made an about-face and charged off in an ultra-left direction. I suspect that the events of May 1968 in France had gone to their heads. They became extreme studentists. They changed their name to the IMG (International Marxist Group) and walked out of the Labour Party. In the general election of 1970, they not only called on workers to abstain, but even recommended that they go along to Labour Party election meetings and break them up! Needless to say, they never tried to put this brilliant plan into action themselves.

Their most prominent figure was a student called Tariq Ali, who gained a certain (completely undeserved) notoriety as a "revolutionary". As one could safely predict, he has ended up, like so many of the "generation of '68" with a very comfortable job in the media, where he very occasionally reminisces about his "revolutionary days", while drawing a very fat salary for his services.

Expelled from the International

Up to 1965, we were still formally the British section of the "Fourth International" of Mandel and co., which was in the process (allegedly) of unifying all the Trotskyist tendencies in the world into the "United Secretariat". Ted was always sceptical about the so-called unification of the Fourth. Pablo and Mandel had split with Cannon, Hansen and the American SWP in 1953 on an unprincipled basis, and the so-called re-unification ten years later was also completely unprincipled. Ted predicted that they would succeed in uniting two groups into ten. This judgement proved to be quite correct.

The discussions in the International were largely a waste of time, except for one thing. We were able to "cut our teeth" on the debates on questions like the class nature of the USSR, China, Cuba, Eastern Europe, etc. In addition, we had to answer the arguments of the Cliff Group, who defended the theory of state capitalism.

Even before the re-unification congress there were splits: Posadas led a split of the Latin American Bureau, while the British Healyites and the French Lambertists refused to have anything to do with the whole thing. They had their own "International Committee". On the other hand, Pablo, who had been the leader in the past, clashed with Mandel and Hansen on the question of Russia and was promptly kicked out by his old friends. Both sides had an incorrect position. Pablo in effect had a position of supporting the Russian bureaucracy on the grounds that Khrushchev was de-bureaucratising the bureaucracy. On the other hand, Mandel, Hansen, Maitan and co. had the position of uncritical support for Mao (an "unconscious Trotskyist") and the Chinese bureaucracy.

In typically opportunist fashion, Mandel and co. capitulated to Maoism. This capitulation assumed extreme, almost farcical proportions at times. In Italy it led to a disaster. In the early sixties, the Maoists were an insignificant force in Italy. But the USFI soon changed all that. Since there was no Chinese embassy in Italy at that time, Livio Maitan, the main leader of the Italian Mandelites, went to Switzerland to obtain large quantities of Maoist literature from the embassy there, which his followers distributed massively in Italy. The result was the creation of a sizeable Maoist organization in Italy. The USFI gained nothing whatsoever from this. In fact, they lost many of their members to the Maoists. That was only natural. If Mao was an "unconscious Trotskyist", and there was really no difference between Maoism and Trotskyism, what reason was there for the Fourth International to exist?

There was a small Irish group at the time led by a man called Gerry Lawless (he died recently). I met him at the time and found him a personally likeable character but also an adventurer—what we call "a bit of a chancer". He was a great talker and had a strong Dublin accent. The first time we met he informed me that "the trouble with the Irish is that they are obsessed with debt". At least I thought that was what he said. Later I realised that the problem was his accent. What he meant was "the Irish are obsessed with death". Nowadays, though, I think the first variant might be more correct.

In their revisionist stupidity, the International pushed the Irish group into a hasty unification with the Irish Communist Organization, a Maoist outfit led by Brendan Clifford. Gerry must have thought this was a good idea. So they agreed to unite on the basis that neither side would talk about Trotsky or Stalin, an agreement that was loyally kept by the "Trotskyists" but immediately broken by Clifford, who launched an all-out attack on Trotskyism and all its works. Since the leaders of the Irish group had no idea how to answer these attacks they asked Ted Grant to do it for them. The result was an excellent document entitled *The Reply to Clifford*. It was a devastating and comprehensive refutation of Stalinism. The Irish comrades presented it in their own name, but it was entirely Ted's work. Needless to say this unification ended in tears, just like all the others.

The conflict with the International came to a head at the 1965 World Congress. Ted wrote a long document called *The Sino-Soviet Dispute and the Colonial Revolution*, in which he comprehensively answered the arguments of the International leadership. Above all, as Ted explained,

> Trotsky once warned of the possibility of the disappearance of the Fourth International if it did not find a road to the masses. This can be reinforced with a further warning. Unless the basic ideas of Trotskyism, enriched and developed but in fundamentals the same, are not emphasised and drummed into the consciousness of the cadres, the International can degenerate impressionistically and tail behind the left reformists, Chinese Stalinists or Russian Stalinists. There must be no empirical bowing down to events, the basic issues must be brought forward again and again, especially in the theoretical works and journals of the International.
>
> The problem has to be posed sharply: either the colonial revolutions have taken the particular form they have because of the delay in the revolution in the advanced countries... or there is no role for the Fourth International except as self-appointed and benevolent advisors to Castro, Mao and Ben Bella.
>
> Here it should be made clear that from a Marxist point of view the arguments of Plekhanov and the theoreticians of Menshevism—that Russia was not ripe for socialism in 1917 are and were perfectly correct... *if* Russia is taken in isolation from the world and the internationalist perspectives of Bolshevism. All other tendencies, cliques and groupings in the labour movement are doomed to sterility and collapse for lack of the internationalist perspective as the basis for their work. The colonial revolutions mark a gigantic step forward for all mankind. But their very success poses new contradictions and convulsions for all of them. The solution of the problem can only be found in the international arena and in the victory of the working class in the advanced countries.
>
> The conditions in which the revolution has taken place, and is developing in these countries, dooms them to new political revolutions, for the purpose of creating workers' democracy. The task of Marxism consists in arming at least the vanguard in understanding these developments and the problems they pose.
>
> Above all, the advanced elements in the CP can be won on a firm basis, only if they understand this basic approach. An eclectic approach that the Chinese are right in this argument or the Russians right on that, will convince hardly anybody. It can only confuse the cadres of Trotskyism themselves by hair-splitting and scholasticism.
>
> The real reason for the conflict between Russia and China must be brought out sharply. For Marxists this can only be the Great Power National Interests of both Bureaucracies, i.e. the power, privileges, income and prestige of the ruling stratum in both countries. This is not incidental to the argument but must be the central theme. It is impossible to explain this phenomenon, like that of the policy of the Labour Bureaucracy, in any other way and still claim to stand on the principles of Marxism. It is not merely the ideological ghosts and rationalisations that we must be concerned with, but the real and corporeal interests of the bureaucracy.
>
> Today, as always, Marxism remains the science of perspectives. Without a clear perspective, the international movement will be doomed to degeneration and collapse.

Although we had very few resources, the comrades decided to print the whole document and send it to the IS because they did not trust them to distribute our ideas. However, when the comrades arrived they found that the document had not been sent out. Ted remarked indignantly: "Lenin said the Second International was not an International but a post office. These people are not even a post office."

Although the document of the British section was the only opposition text before the Congress, Ted told me he was given just fifteen minutes (including translation) to present it. I do not know if these times were correct, but they must have been very limited, since the leadership was in a hurry to get the business in Britain over and done with.

In theory, the British section was not expelled but only reduced to sympathiser status, on the same level as the International Group. They did not want us as the official section but at the same time they were not too sure that the IG would be viable. Typically, the International leadership wanted to keep their options open. They would continue to intrigue and manoeuvre, playing one group against another.

This was a dishonest expulsion, and Ted was having none of it. He told the Congress: "You have expelled us three times. If you expel us now, we will not be back for a very long time. We have been part of this International for thirty years, and that is enough to draw some conclusions. Anyone can make a mistake. But if you make the same mistake repeatedly and fail to recognize it or draw the conclusions, it is no longer a mistake but a tendency."

This outcome was not really a surprise. We were always in opposition in the Pablo-Mandel International. Pablo and Mandel held openly revisionist positions on everything. They had illusions in China, Yugoslavia, North Vietnam and later Cuba, where they described Castro as yet another unconscious Trotskyist. Summing up his verdict on the leaders of the Fourth, Ted said: "Between them, Pablo, Frank, Mandel, Cannon, Hansen, Lambert, Healy, and Maitan succeeded in completely disorienting the movement, leading it from one crisis to another. In the end, they destroyed it".

"Of course, anyone can make a mistake," he added. "But if you make a mistake you must be honest about it: admit you have made a mistake and learn from it. That was always the method of Lenin and Trotsky. But these people made one mistake after another and were never prepared to admit it. That is why they hated the RCP leadership—because they knew we had been right and they could not accept it. It hurt their prestige, which they put before the interests of the movement. What we have here is a petty-bourgeois tendency, if we are to call things by their right name."

After this, we were isolated internationally, with no supporters outside the UK. We did not even have anyone in Ireland. Despite this, at every meeting of the National Committee (as the leading body was then called), the first session was always on International Perspectives, and only then British Perspectives. We considered ourselves first and foremost as internationalists. It was Ted who insisted on this.

However, he was equally adamant that we must break once and for all with the so-called Fourth International: "We must turn our backs on the sects and face to the mass organizations of the working class," he insisted. Whenever we would receive a letter from one or another of the sects asking for a "united front" on this or that, Ted always said: "Put it straight in the waste paper basket." The only united front he was interested in was the united front with the working class. That was quite correct, and it paid off in the end.

Proletarian Bonapartism

One of the main mistakes of all the tendencies that claimed to be Trotskyist was their complete failure to understand the complex processes of the colonial revolution after 1945. Their whole approach to the question was characterised by formalism and a lack of dialectical thinking. They saw the permanent revolution as an abstract norm that was to be applied mechanically to every situation in a clinically pure form, without taking into consideration the concrete conditions of each case. But the truth, as Hegel pointed out, is always concrete.

Lenin said: "Whoever expects a 'pure' social revolution will *never* live to see it. Such a person pays lip-service to revolution without understanding what revolution is." (*The Discussion on Self-Determination Summed Up*, LCW, vol. 22, pp. 320-360). The mistake of every other tendency was to expect it to conform to the classical model of the Russian Revolution. Whenever the concrete facts diverged from the norm, they refused to accept them.

Such a method has nothing in common with Marxism. This formalistic thinking has more in common with idealism than with dialectical materialism. It is the reason why some so-called Trotskyists fell into the trap of "state capitalism" and "bureaucratic collectivism". It is no accident that Trotsky in *In Defence of Marxism*, accused Burnham and Shachtman of abandoning dialectics. As with the revolutions in Eastern Europe and also with the Chinese and Cuban Revolutions, they tried to mechanically apply an abstract norm of revolution to processes that were substantially different.

Ted's development of Trotsky's theory of proletarian Bonapartism proved invaluable. The permanent revolution was being carried out, but in a distorted way that Trotsky could never have foreseen. In his remarkable document, *The Marxist Theory of the State (Reply to Cliff)*, he comprehensively demolished the revisionist theory of "state capitalism" and showed how Trotsky's analysis of the USSR as a bureaucratically deformed workers' state was correct. The subsequent developments in Eastern Europe, China, and also the peculiar forms assumed by the colonial revolution, given the delay of the socialist revolution in the West, were explained by Ted in his analysis of the phenomenon of proletarian Bonapartism.

The first stage of the colonial revolution was the conquest of national liberation. But the mere conquest of national sovereignty, under modern conditions, solved nothing. The ex-colonial countries found themselves enslaved once more. The only difference was that instead of being enslaved by one colonial master, they were exploited jointly by the imperialist countries. In place of direct military-bureaucratic rule from London or Paris, they were oppressed and robbed through the mechanism of the world market and international trade.

Formal independence solved none of the fundamental problems. As the theory of the permanent revolution explains, there was no way out on the basis of capitalism. Therefore, the national liberation struggle tended to go beyond the limits of capitalist private property. In Cuba, a guerrilla war led to the expropriation of landlordism and capitalism. Having used the guerrilla army to smash the old state, Fidel Castro leaned on the support of the working class to expropriate the imperialists and their local agents, the landlords and capitalists. This was an enormous step forward, which Ted welcomed with enthusiasm.

The comrades regarded it as an international duty to defend the Cuban Revolution. This is an appeal circular from *Socialist Fight*, signed by Ted on November 20, 1960:

Fidel Castro in 1959

The American government, aided by other imperialist powers, is actively seeking a pretext to launch a war against the peoples of Cuba and Central America, who have carried through measures to emancipate themselves from poverty, misery and imperialist bondage. Already the American imperialists have attempted to force the Cuban people to retreat by boycotting her goods and closing the normal outlets for her products.

This organisation calls upon the TUC and the NEC of the Labour Party to declare its opposition to any measures against the peoples of Cuba and its determination to support by all means the heroic struggle of these peoples against imperialism.

However, there was another side to the question. The Cuban Revolution did not take the classical form of a proletarian revolution, and the working class never held power as they did through soviets, as in Russia in 1917. New contradictions flowed inevitably from this fact.

The peculiar forms taken by the colonial revolution since 1945 can only be explained by the delay of the proletarian revolution in the West, and the absence of genuine Leninist parties. The masses in Africa, Asia and Latin America could not afford to wait until the working class came to power in Europe and the USA. Their problems were too pressing. In the absence of the working class and its party, the leadership of the colonial revolution fell into other hands.

The rotten colonial bourgeoisie, as Trotsky had predicted, was organically incapable of fighting imperialism. The leadership of the revolution therefore fell to petty-bourgeois elements, who put themselves at the head of the peasant masses to effect a revolutionary transformation. However, socialism must be based on the democratic rule of the working class. In the absence of a Leninist Party, and with the existence of powerful deformed workers' states in Russia and China, it was inevitable that the Cuban Revolution would suffer a process of bureaucratic deformation from the start.

Syria

An even more peculiar variant of the permanent revolution occurred in Syria, where a section of the military officer caste carried out a coup and proceeded to nationalise more and more sections of the economy, eventually setting up a system modelled on that of the Soviet Union.

After the Second World War, the French were pushed out of Syria, but the country remained under the domination of imperialism. The local bourgeoisie was weak and unable to create a truly modern, independent bourgeois state. It was a corrupt comprador bourgeoisie at the service of imperialism.

In these conditions, Syria could not emerge from its historical backwardness. The peasants could play no independent role, and therefore, the task of modernising the country, which could only be achieved through the socialist transformation of the country, fell to the working class. Unfortunately, the workers were led by parties such as the Syrian Communist Party, which had no perspective of overthrowing the bourgeoisie through socialist revolution. On the contrary, its leaders were constantly seeking alliances with the so-called "progressive" bourgeoisie, which did not exist.

The inability of the Syrian bourgeoisie to develop the country, and the failure of the working class to take power as a result of the treacherous policies of the Stalinists, created a situation of crisis and instability in which the army constantly intervened in politics. However, we must bear in mind that the Syrian army, as in many other Middle Eastern and ex-colonial countries, is not the same as the armies of most developed capitalist nations.

Whereas the officer castes of Europe and the USA are the product of a long historical selection, and more directly represent the interests of the ruling class from which they are drawn, the situation here is more complicated. Whereas the upper echelons of the Syrian army were drawn from the feudal strata, the middle and lower ranks were drawn from the petty-bourgeoisie and reflected the pressures of the latter. Ted wrote on this in 1978:

> In bourgeois countries in the past, where the bourgeoisie has a role to play and looks forward confidently to the future—i.e. when it is genuinely progressive in developing the productive forces—it has decades and generations to perfect the state as an instrument of its own class rule. The army, police, civil service, middle layers and especially all key positions at the top; heads of civil service, heads of departments, police chiefs, the officer corps and especially the colonels and generals are carefully selected to serve the needs and interests of the ruling class. With a developing economy and a mission and a role they eagerly serve the "national interest" i.e. the interest of the possessing class—the ruling class.

In Syria, as in all the ex-colonial countries, the imperialists, in this case the French, partly under the pressure of their rivals, especially American imperialism, were compelled to relinquish their *direct* military domination. The state which emerged is not fixed and static. The weakness and incapacity of the bourgeoisie gave a certain independence to the military caste. Hence the perpetual coups and counter-coups of the military. But in the last analysis they reflect the class interests of the ruling class. They cannot play an independent role.

The struggle between the cliques in the army reflects the instability and contradictions in the given society. The personal aims of the generals reflect the differing interests of social classes or fractions of classes of society, the petit-bourgeois in its various fractions, the bourgeoisie, or even under certain conditions the proletariat in so far as they are successful in gaining power. The officer caste must reflect *the interest of some class or grouping* in society. They do not represent themselves though of course they can plunder the society and elevate their own ruling caste. Nevertheless they must have a class basis in a given society.

Bonapartist regimes do not rest on air but balance between the classes. In the final analysis they represent whichever is the dominant class in society. The economy of that class determines its class character. Some of these countries, as in Latin America, a semi-colonial continent which was under the domination of British then especially American imperialism for the last century, nevertheless, have been nominally independent for more than a century. In consequence, despite a period of turbulence the ruling class of landowners and capitalists has had sufficient period to perfect their state. Sometimes the armed forces of different fractions or factions of armed forces, can reflect different fractions of the ruling class and even the pressures of imperialism, primarily American imperialism.

But, up to now, they have always reflected the interest of the ruling class in the defence of private ownership (...)

Marxism finds in the development of the productive forces the key to the development of society. *On a capitalist basis there is no longer a way forward, particularly for backward countries.* That is why army officers, intellectuals and others, affected by the decay of their societies can *under certain conditions* switch their allegiance. A change to proletarian Bonapartism actually enlarges their power, prestige, privileges and income. They become the sole commanding and directing stratum of the society, raising themselves even higher over the masses than in the past. Instead of being subservient to the weak, craven and ineffectual bourgeoisie they become the masters of society.

The tendency towards *statification* of the productive forces, which have grown beyond the limits of private ownership, is manifest in the most highly developed economies and even in the most reactionary colonial countries.

There is no possibility of a consistent, uninterrupted and continuous increase in productive forces in the countries of the so-called third world on a capitalist basis. Production stagnates or falls. In the world recessions, particularly in the smaller countries, living standards fall. There is no way out on the basis of the capitalist system. That explains the terror regimes of bourgeois Bonapartism like that of Pakistan, Indonesia, Argentina, Chile and Zaire. But with bayonets and bullets, on the basis of an out-dated and antiquated system, only very temporary respite is given. Discontent multiplies and is reflected in the officer caste of the armed forces and throughout the society. This in turn leads to conspiracies of individuals and groups of officers.

The army is a mirror of society and reflects its contradictions. That and not the mere whims of the officers concerned, is the cause of the upheavals as in Syria. It is an indication of the agonised crisis of society, which cannot be solved in the old way. These strata of society can espouse "socialism" of the Stalinist variety—proletarian Bonapartism—all the more enthusiastically because of their contempt for the masses of workers and peasants.

The horrible caricature of workers' rule in Russia, China, and the other countries of deformed workers' states attracts them precisely because of the position of the "intellectual" educated cadres of that society. What is repulsive to Marxism is what attracts the Stalinists.

All that these states have in common with healthy workers' states or with the Russia of 1917-23 is state ownership of the means of production. On that basis they can plan and develop the productive resources with forced marches at a pace absolutely impossible on their former landlord-capitalist basis. This is possible of course for only a *limited period* of time. At some point the Stalinist regimes become an absolute hindrance and a fetter to production. Russia and Eastern Europe are reaching these limits. In common with a healthy workers' state on the accepted Marxist norm is the fact that they are transitional economies between capitalism and socialism. (Ted Grant, *The Colonial Revolution and the Deformed Workers' States*, July 1978)

In the case of Syria, there were a series of coups that reflected the impasse of society under capitalism. But the 1963 coup, however, was very different from the ones that had preceded it. This time, the regime that was created by the coup proceeded to carry out measures of land redistribution and the nationalisation of the private banks, going much further than even Nasser had done in Egypt. This was later followed by the nationalisation of the oil companies and other the major industries.

This provoked the reaction of the mullahs, the small shopkeepers and the "business community", that is, the bourgeoisie, leading to civil war on the streets. For the left-wing army officers it was now a life and death issue. Power was seized by radical young officers who leaned on the masses to carry out a complete social transformation. To carry out the struggle successfully, the Ba'ath government had to appeal to the workers and peasants of Syria for support. Thousands of peasants flocked into Damascus to demonstrate their fervent support for these measures.

The Ba'athist officers set up a militia and a peasant army to smash the reaction and break the power of the old rotten, pro-imperialist, semi-feudal, semi-capitalist regime. In the process, a new state machine was created, with almost the whole of industry in state hands, and a large part of the land as well. To break the possible resistance of the capitalists,

Senior Ba'ath party officials, including General Salah Jadid, 1969

special courts were organised, with powers up to the death penalty for anyone trying to obstruct these new measures.

By 1966, the bulk of the economy was in the hands of the state, which now controlled the development of natural resources, electricity generation, water supplies, most industrial plants, banking, insurance, sections of the transport system, most of foreign trade and the domestic wholesale trade. The government also controlled most of the investments, credit and pricing of many commodities.

Ted Grant greeted this development with enthusiasm, just as he had welcomed the Chinese and Cuban Revolutions. The abolition of landlordism and capitalism represented a huge step forward. However, the revolution had been carried out in a Bonapartist manner, which distorted it from the outset.

We supported the nationalisations. At the same time we had no illusions about the nature of the regime. Although nationalisations and other measures were progressive, the lack of workers' democracy, of workers' control and management of industry, meant that what had come into being in Syria was a system like that in the Soviet Union, that is, a totalitarian one-party dictatorship, with power concentrated in the hands of a privileged bureaucracy. This was not "socialism". As in the USSR, for such a system to move towards genuine socialism would have required a second, political, revolution.

Initially, the nationalization of the productive forces gave good results, providing Syria with a privileged position in comparison to other Arab nations. But subsequent history has shown the limitations and contradictions of proletarian Bonapartism. Even before the fall of the USSR, there was a tendency to swing back in the direction of capitalism. In the case of Syria, capitalist restoration has had the most catastrophic effects. The regime is now in a complete impasse, which has dragged the country into a bloody civil war that threatens to reduce it to barbarism.

Afghanistan

The same process was seen later in Ethiopia and Somalia. But the clearest example was in Afghanistan, where the Saur Revolution of 1978–79 followed a similar process to that in Syria. On this I can speak to some extent from personal experience.

About fifteen years ago I met some of the leaders of the Afghan Revolution, who were at that time in exile in Pakistan. One of them was a tank commander who had led an assault on the Kabul prison where the leaders of the Communist Party were awaiting execution. They blasted a hole in the prison walls and released the prisoners. The other was an air force general who, at the same time as the attack on the prison, led a squadron of MiG fighters that bombed the presidential palace, killing the entire government.

This was no ordinary military coup. It placed power in the hands of the most radical faction of the Afghan Communist Party. Yet Moscow knew nothing about it, and would have opposed it if they had. Since 1947, Afghanistan had been under the influence of the Russian government and received large amounts of aid, economic assistance, military equipment, training and military hardware from the Soviet Union. The Moscow bureaucracy had excellent relations with the Daoud government and monarchy and had no wish to see them overthrown. In addition, a revolution in Afghanistan would upset the delicate balance of forces in the region, and the Soviets' agreement with US imperialism over "spheres of influence".

I had a long discussion with them in Russian, which they all spoke fluently, since they had received their military instruction in the Soviet Union. It is one thing to understand a phenomenon theoretically, in the abstract. It is quite another to see it in concrete terms. Speaking to these men, I could see clearly their psychology and understand the whole process concretely. Given the extreme backwardness of Afghanistan, it was easy to see how they would have been impressed by what they saw just a few hundred miles over the border in Soviet Uzbekistan.

In 1970, while studying in Moscow, I visited Soviet Central Asia and was struck by Tashkent, the capital of Uzbekistan, which was a modern city comparable to any in Europe. Everywhere there were clean streets, blocks of apartments, hospitals, schools and universities. Just imagine the impression this would have made on young Afghan army officers who would have compared these marvels with the dirt, ignorance and poverty of their native land.

The Saur Revolution carried out a whole series of progressive measures. The government passed decrees abolishing the selling of brides and giving equality to women. It announced a land reform and the cancellation of farmers' debts. These measures met with the ferocious opposition of the powerful land owners and moneylenders, whose interests were hit by the abolition of usury. The mullahs joined forces with the moneylenders, although usury is supposed to be prohibited by Islam.

In 1978, Ted wrote a brilliant article about the events in Afghanistan. I showed them a copy that had been translated into Urdu, which they could read. They were astonished by what they read. "That is exactly how it was!" they exclaimed. They found it hard to believe that such an article could have been written by somebody who was not an Afghan and lived thousands of miles away in London.

The position that Ted took in relation to Afghanistan was a very good example of the Marxist dialectical method. By contrast, all the other tendencies on the Left adopted positions that ranged from the incorrect to the criminal. The Stalinists naturally supported the Soviet invasion of Afghanistan uncritically. But the majority of the Afghan Communists, including the men I spoke to, were opposed to it.

They had a point. With their crude bureaucratic mentality, the men in Moscow imagined they could solve everything with guns and tanks. They did not take into account the complex realities of Afghan society and the traditions and psychology of the Afghan people. The Afghans do not like foreign intruders. This truth was made clear to every foreign invader from Alexander the Great onwards.

By blundering onto the scene, murdering the leader of the Afghan Communist Party, and imposing a puppet, the Russians provided invaluable ammunition to the forces of reaction both inside and outside Afghanistan. The result in the end was a disastrous defeat, not only for the Afghan Revolution but for the USSR itself.

The Stalinists to this day argue that the Soviet army did not invade Afghanistan but was "invited in by the Afghan government".

Even worse was the position taken by so-called Marxists like the British SWP, who openly sided with the forces of reaction in Afghanistan. Following their false theory of state capitalism to its logical conclusion, they branded the Soviet invasion as "imperialist" and backed the counter-revolutionary *mujahedeen*, who they described as "freedom fighters"—the same language that was used by Washington and the prostitute media in the West.

That was a blatant lie. There was absolutely nothing progressive about this gang of reactionary cut-throats. They were mainly composed of bandits, drug dealers, and other criminal elements that fused with religious fanatics to form the shock troops of the counter-revolution. They represented the interests of the landlords, the mullahs and the moneylenders, not the Afghan people.

The so-called freedom fighters were supported, financed and armed by US imperialism. On July 3, 1979, US President Jimmy Carter signed the first directive for covert financial aid to the opponents of the pro-Soviet regime in Kabul.

Those groups on the Left that supported these monsters committed a crime. Ted said: "If one could take Afghanistan in isolation, it would be correct to support the Soviet invasion. But it is not possible to take Afghanistan in isolation. One has to take into account the effects of this internationally, on consciousness, and this will be entirely reactionary." That is why we opposed it.

As on every other question, our attitude to Afghanistan was determined by the effects on the consciousness of the working class internationally. The truth is that the Moscow bureaucracy was never in favour of a socialist revolution in Afghanistan. The Saur Revolution was carried out without their knowledge and against their wishes. What they wanted was a relatively stable and friendly buffer state on their south-eastern border. Lacking a revolutionary policy, the masters of the Kremlin based themselves on brute force and an overwhelming display of military might. But this did not work in the concrete conditions of Afghanistan. In fact, it was counterproductive.

The Soviet intervention provided the excuse for US imperialism ("the most counter-revolutionary force on the planet", to quote Ted's words) to intervene, using its Pakistani ally Zia ul-Haq. It enabled the reactionary opposition, which was initially little more than a bunch of bandits, to mobilize the mass of backward Afghan peasants and tribesmen against the foreign invaders. Resentment against foreigners was mixed with religious fanaticism in an explosive cocktail.

Worse still were the negative international repercussions. The American imperialists, together with their Saudi and Pakistani stooges, took advantage of the situation to launch a so-called *jihad* against the "foreigners and infidels", which ultimately led to the creation of reactionary movements like al Qaeda and the Taliban. And it provided US imperialism a propaganda gift, which prepared the way for the aggressive Bush doctrine later on.

I know from my personal discussions with these prominent figures in the Afghan Revolution that many, if not most, Afghan communists were opposed to the entry of the Russian army into Afghanistan, or at any rate had serious doubts about it. At the time, I think not many even of our own comrades understood just how unerring Ted's grasp of the situation was. But how true his words come across today!

The Russian invasion did not save the Afghan Revolution, but fatally undermined it. It created the conditions for Islamic fundamentalist reaction in Pakistan and all over the Muslim world. It spawned monsters like the Taliban, al-Qaeda and Bin Laden. It prepared the way for the events of 9/11 and the US invasion of Iraq and Afghanistan. And we are living with the consequences to this very today.

CHAPTER SEVEN

THE TIDE TURNS

Even the darkest night will end and the sun will rise. (Victor Hugo, *Les Misérables*)

Modest beginnings

At the time of our expulsion in 1965, the organization was going through a very difficult patch. We were very small: not more than about 50 in the whole country. We had no money, no full timer (Ted was still working as a telephone operator), no centre and virtually no paper. Nobody would have given much for our chances. But we had something that none of the other groups had: the ideas of Marxism, correct perspectives, and correct methods and orientation. However, we did make some mistakes and paid a price for them.

The most important turning-point was when we launched the *Militant* in October 1964. But we got off to quite a difficult start. As I recall, Ted was initially not in favour of the name. He favoured *Forward*, which he argued had a tradition in the British Labour Movement. The first issue was a well-produced eight-page paper. The name of the editor was stated as Roger Protz. This caused a major row. Protz had been a prominent Healyite, but his innate egotism led to a split with Healy. He had only recently joined us (I think Jimmy Deane recruited him). Unfortunately, he brought his ego with him.

Jimmy Deane once asked me: do you know what the difference between a petty-bourgeois and a worker is? He said: "When a worker joins an organization—whether it is a trade union or the Labour Party or our tendency—he says: here is a great organization that has been built by the sacrifices of many people over the years. Where can I find my niche where I can serve the movement? But when a petty-bourgeois joins the organization he says: Here am I. What have you got for me?"

Roger Protz was just such an element. I have seen many more like him over the years and they always cause serious problems. As we had no journalists in our ranks, his professional skills were obviously welcome. But his role in the paper was supposed to be purely technical. Nobody would have dreamed of giving him an editorial position.

Naturally, Protz had other ideas. He wanted to be the editor and nothing less. This was unacceptable. A clash was inevitable and Protz left soon after. He joined the SWP and became editor of *Socialist Worker* before moving on yet again. Such politically unstable petty-bourgeois elements cannot remain long in any one place. I believe he ended up in a leading position in CAMRA, the Campaign for Real Ale, a most worthy cause where his talents were no doubt put to far better use.

I can say we breathed a sigh of relief when he left us. The cosmetic appearance of the paper lost out, but the political line was now free of the kind of confused mishmash that was present in some pages of the first issue. On Ted's insistence, the masthead was changed from "For Youth and Labour" to "For Labour and Youth". This small detail was no accident.

We held our first Militant meeting in Brighton in a small room in a pub. As I recall, there were maybe thirty people present. At the time, I doubt if many people even noticed. But within fifteen years, the Militant Tendency was an important element in British politics and was a household name. But to begin with, our apparatus was modest in the extreme.

We managed to rent three small rooms in an office in 397 King's Cross Road, belonging to the ILP, which shared it with us. Opposite the office was a little Italian café called the A1, where Ted was always to be found at lunchtime, ordering a steak (which he liked to be cremated). Here he also held discussions with comrades and contacts over a cup of tea.

About this time (in 1964), Jimmy Deane gave up being National Secretary and went to work in India to pay off his debts (he was a qualified electrician). After that, in effect, he dropped out of the movement, although Ted always kept in contact. This was yet another blow.

The National Committee, which met every two or three months, elected the Secretariat. The NC meetings normally took place in the upstairs room of the Lucas Arms in King's Cross. As explained earlier, the first session was almost always world perspectives, followed by British perspectives. Even though we had no International (we did not even have a group in Scotland, let alone Ireland) we were imbued with the spirit of internationalism.

In Tyneside, we had a small group of loyal old comrades who had been in the RCP during the war. I remember there was Jack and Daisy Rawlings who had a small transport café. They were marvellous old stalwarts. But the most remarkable of them all was old Herbie Bell, a man well-known in the local Labour Movement. Herbie was tireless. He would get up early on Sunday morning and go to the surrounding pit villages to sell the *Militant* door to door. And nobody ever refused to buy a paper from Herbie Bell!

Breakthrough in Sussex

We were gradually developing a base in the YS, not just in Liverpool (where we had had a base for many years), but in London, Tyneside, Swansea and then, in an important development, in Brighton. I went to Sussex University in September 1963. At that time I was the only comrade in the whole of the South of England. I was 18 years old and had no experience of building among students or of building at all on my own. However, thanks to the work of the group in Swansea, and the many political discussions with Dave Matthews, I had a very good grounding in Marxist theory, which was an important, not to say key, element in our remarkable success.

Ted attached a lot of importance to our work in Sussex and came down to speak to us many times. At first I was completely on my own, but that was not for long. I joined the Socialist Society, went to meetings and put the Marxist case very forcefully. At the first meeting I contacted two other first-year students (Bob Edwards and Roger Silverman) who, like me, were in the YS. We began to collaborate on a more or less formal basis.

After some time, they both joined, so then there were three of us. It was a visit from Ted that convinced Roger to join the Tendency. We worked in the Labour Party (mainly the YS), and encouraged the students to do the same. We took a very hard line against the petty-bourgeois pacifist and liberal tendencies. Probably we were too hard. But it paid off in the end. It is necessary to stand out, to stand against the stream, and we did just that. This was quite important at that time, as a means of combating petty-bourgeois prejudices and getting students out of the narrow circle of university politics.

We were very strict on finance. The first day of term every comrade was asked for ten percent of his or her grant. And that was just the start. All comrades were expected to contribute to regular financial appeals from the national centre. This was very important. For some years, the Militant was dependent on the financial contribution from the Sussex comrades. We also got the national centre its first colour duplicator (a donation form a wealthy sympathizer in the CP). We paid the wages of Peter Taaffe, who had recently come from Liverpool to take over the running of the national centre after Jimmy Deane had left to work abroad.

It is no exaggeration to say that our successful work among students in Sussex played a great part in turning the situation around. It was an important breakthrough. The work in Sussex University is important because it was the first time our tendency had carried out systematic student work. It also played a crucial role in building the forces of Militant.

The fight against revisionism

Ted was the only one who originally predicted the post-war economic upswing, although he never thought it would last as long as it did. But he also explained that sooner or later, the laws of capitalism elucidated by Marx would reassert themselves in a crisis of overproduction. In the 1960s, Ted's arguments were rejected by almost everybody, from the bourgeois economists, passing through the Right and Left reformists, to the revisionist sects, who ridiculed his position as "primitive slumpism".

The supporters of Tony Cliff in Britain (now the SWP) completely capitulated to bourgeois economic theory in the form of Keynesianism. They argued that Britain and the USA had established a "permanent arms economy" in which military expenditure had eliminated slumps, and that the working class would revolt against capitalism, not because of economic crises, but because of alienation (!). This implicit acceptance of the arguments of the bourgeoisie and reformism led to a questioning of the central role of the proletariat in the class struggle.

It is a central tenet of Marxism that only the working class can carry through the socialist revolution. This position was later confirmed by the events in France in May 1968. But to the so-called leaders of the Fourth, this was a book sealed with seven seals. The long period of economic upswing in the advanced capitalist countries seemed to give the lie to the idea of the revolutionary role of the proletariat. In many countries, the class struggle was blunted, though not abolished. In conditions of boom, where big profits could be made, the mere threat of a strike was often sufficient to win wage increases. The capitalists could afford to make concessions and did not want to lose money through interruptions in production. Reformism was in the ascendant and the Marxists were isolated.

The Cliffites were not the only ones to abandon the Marxist standpoint. Under these circumstances, almost all the sects in practice abandoned the working class and the labour movement in favour of "other forces"—the students, the peasants, the lumpenproletariat etc. They effectively wrote off the proletariat of the advanced capitalist countries. Ideas such as those of Herbert Marcuse, who wrote off the working class as a revolutionary agent, became fashionable in university circles and the "New Left". Our tendency conducted a pitiless struggle against these poisonous ideas, but the leaders of the USFI completely capitulated to them.

They were politically disoriented and had lost all faith in the working class. Instead, they were looking for saviours *outside* the working class. Following the line of petty-bourgeois intellectuals of the Marcuse type, they looked to the students, the peasantry, the lumpenproletariat, the guerrillas, anything and anybody except the working class. This at bottom was an expression of profound pessimism and scepticism in the future of socialism and the Fourth International. It had the most harmful results in Latin America where an entire generation of revolutionary youth was sacrificed uselessly in terrorist adventures, thinly disguised as "urban guerrilla war" or "armed struggle".

As Ted wrote in *The Programme of the International* (1970) in criticising the USFI:

> It is in this whole milieu and with the even greater discrediting of the Communist Party and the Reformists in Latin America, that the programme of guerrilla war in the countryside and even worse, of "urban guerrillas" has been developed. Young, weak forces of Trotskyism, disorientated by the zigzags of the past 25 years, have been flung into this mess. In Latin America they should be teaching all the advanced elements among the intellectuals, students and above all, the working class, the fundamental and elementary ideas of Marxism. The movement for national and social liberation in Latin America, in Brazil, Argentina, Uruguay, Chile, Guatemala and the other countries in Latin America can only come from a mass movement of the working class and peasants. Desperate duels and kidnappings, bank raids etc., will only result in the extermination of young brave and sincere forces without avail.

A representative of the American SWP was in London and asked to meet us. I cannot remember the exact date but it was in the late sixties. The comrades agreed and we went to a meeting in the usual venue—upstairs in a pub, to hear what he had to say. I had my notebook and pen ready to take notes, but after a while I let my pen drop and just sat there aghast. He was a student and was supposed to be one of their "cadres". But all he talked about was Black Nationalism, Women's Lib, Gay Lib, Vietnam and Cuba. I thought to myself: all that is missing is Flower Power and the joys of marijuana and the picture would be complete. Once again, not a single word about the working class or the class struggle.

This was a sorry epitaph on the party that had shown so much promise in the 1930s, the party of people like Farrell Dobbs who helped lead an exemplary struggle during the Minneapolis strikes in 1934 and wrote marvellous books such as *Teamster Rebellion*. And J.P. Cannon, for all his faults, had a good feel for the workers' movement. Now this party had effectively disappeared. In its place was a monstrous petty-bourgeois sect that ended up expelling the Trotskyists from its ranks.

Yet this was not altogether unforeseen. Trotsky already detected certain indications of petty-bourgeois degeneration even before the war. He warned the SWP that there were too many middle class girls and boys in its ranks. His position on this was quite clear when he advised the SWP to be very careful when recruiting non-proletarian elements. He advised them to put them through a number of tests on all the questions of programme, "wet them under the rain, dry them in the sun, and then after a new careful examination accept one or two". In effect, they had to break from the petty-bourgeois background and put themselves on the standpoint of the working class.

The American SWP was by no means an isolated case. The long period of boom in the post war period meant that the pressure of alien ideas—bourgeois and petty-bourgeois ideas—on the revolutionary movement was intensified. Early in 1968 (before May), Ernest Mandel, the chief theoretician of the USFI spoke at a meeting in London. Our comrades went along to see what he had to say.

He spoke at length about all kinds of things: Vietnam, Cuba, Che Guevara, but without saying a single word about the French working class. When one of our people pointed this out, Mandel replied: "The working class is bourgeoisiefied. It is Americanised, and you can forget about the French working class for the next twenty years."

May 1968

The revolutionary events in France in May 1968 were completely unexpected by these ladies and gentlemen. They had written off the French working class and concentrated all their attentions on the students. Less than four million workers were organised in the unions in France, yet 10 million workers occupied the factories in a magnificent movement. In reality power was in the hands of the working class.

May 68 in Paris

President de Gaulle understood this very well. He told the US ambassador: "It's all up; everything is lost. In a few days the Communists will be in power." This was perfectly possible, but the leaders of the French Communist Party had no interest in taking power. They refused to take power and the opportunity was lost. But the French events demonstrated the utter falsity of the arguments of the sects.

I was sent to Paris to establish contacts with the French Trotskyists of the JCR, for which we had prepared a leaflet stating our position. Basically we were calling for the linking up of the action committees on a local, regional and national basis, to provide an alternative workers' government. There was something electric in the air, something intoxicating. It was the spirit of revolution. I was staying in an apartment in the Latin Quarter, with a Mexican comrade, an intellectual who sympathised with the Mandelites, but was not a member.

He showed me round the streets and on every corner there were signs of a great social upheaval. Trotsky explains in *The History of the Russian Revolution* that the essence of a revolution is the direct intervention of the masses in politics. This was a laboratory example. In every street the walls of houses, metro stations and offices were plastered with posters. But more interesting was the fact that large numbers of people crowded round these wall newspapers, struggling to get a look, reading every line, almost *drinking in* the information. Animated discussions would take place in the street, at the bus stops, in the markets and bars. This is what a revolution is! Some years later I saw exactly the same things in the streets of Lisbon and Oporto after the Portuguese Revolution of April 25, 1974.

The first thing I did on arriving in Paris was to contact Ted Grant, who was already there, staying with his sister. We had been expelled from the so-called United Secretariat of the Fourth International a few years before, when we opposed the capitulationist line of Mandel, Frank, Hansen and the other so-called leaders of the Fourth. But we still had some hope that we might find an echo in the ranks of the French Trotskyists, and as mentioned above, even produced a leaflet in solidarity with their youth organization, the JCR (Revolutionary Communist Youth).

However, our attempts to locate the leaders of the USFI had proved fruitless. We had the address of their office and we went together to see if we could find somebody to speak with.

But the office was closed and there was no sign of anybody. They seemed to have gone underground. With his usual sense of humour, Ted joked: "The only people in Paris who know where Pierre Frank is are the police." The next day we read that he had been arrested.

We soon discovered that it was practically impossible to establish direct contact with the workers. The occupied factories were securely locked and bolted, theoretically against the police and agents provocateurs. That was partly true, but it was also a useful device of the union leaders to keep the workers away from the "harmful" influences of "left-wing agitators". One could sometimes approach the factories and speak to the pickets through the railings, but it was extremely difficult.

In the absence of any other lead, I decided to go to the Sorbonne to try to make contact with the students, although this time Ted was not with me. The university was occupied by the students. In the great central courtyard surrounded with ancient buildings, I saw an incongruous scene. Columns that were dedicated to Cardinal Richelieu were draped with red flags and portraits of Mao, Trotsky, Castro and Che Guevara overlooked the square. However, at that moment there was hardly anybody there. Probably they were on some demonstration (they took place all the time).

On all sides of the courtyard there were a lot of stalls on which one could see the papers of all the left groups. They were all monthlies at that time, and had not had time to publish a new edition after the strike had begun. They all dedicated the front page to Vietnam, Bolivia, Cuba, Che Guevara, Mao Zedong—*in fact, everything and anything except the French working class!* The only exception was the *Voix Ouvrière* (now *Lutte Ouvrière*), which had a semi-syndicalist line.

With these facts before one, it is impossible to come to any other conclusion than that May 1968 was indeed a "*bolt from the blue*", to every other tendency. The other trends did not expect it. How could they, when they had, in effect, written off the working class in the advanced capitalist countries as "corrupt", "bourgeoisified" and "Americanised"? In other words, they had abandoned the ideas of Trotsky in favour of those of Marcuse.

May 1968 was a complete vindication of the idea that Ted Grant had always defended: that when the workers begin to move, they always express themselves first of all through the existing mass organizations of the class. That was certainly the case in France. Millions of unorganised workers were getting organized. But they did not set up new unions or look for new political parties, much less anarchist movements or tiny sects. They immediately looked to the existing mass organizations.

The unions grew with lightning speed. Whole factories that had been non-union became organized overnight. The huge Citroen factory, whose workforce consisted overwhelmingly of immigrants from Spain, Portugal, North Africa and Yugoslavia, was specialised in producing luxury cars like the Citroen DS. It had a regime of terror in which unions were banned and the workers were constantly harassed by security guards, spot checks, identification cards, etc. But once the movement began, it became organised practically overnight as the workers occupied the plant.

But it was not only the unions that were experiencing an explosive growth. I remember reading a copy of the CP daily paper *L'Humanité*, in which there was a small article stating that the CPF had set up over 80 new branches in the Paris region alone. Such was the influx of new members that the Party had run out of membership cards. However, with no sizeable Trotskyist current present within the CPF and the unions to combat the reformist leadership, thousands of these newly awakened communists sank into demoralisation and out of politics altogether after the movement was sold out by the so-called Communist leaders themselves.

Our first theoretical collaboration

Ted was not the easiest man to work with. His profound grasp of Marxism, and his insistence on 100 percent correctness, made him a hard taskmaster, especially where writing was concerned. He would go over a manuscript a dozen times, pen in hand (for some reason he always used a green pen), crossing out, underlining and scribbling indecipherable comments in the margin, while the unfortunate author looked on aghast.

I remember one comrade who was subjected to this experience. When Ted had finished he sat in silence, with a pained expression on his face. "What is wrong?" the comrade asked, to which Ted replied: "It's just... It's just... everything!" This direct manner of speaking upset some sensitive souls, but personally I regarded it as a useful training. After all, the important thing is the ideas, and not the personal ego of aspiring authors. Those who put the ideas first learned a lot.

My first experience of working with Ted in the theoretical plane was in 1969. Monty Johnstone of the CPGB had produced a lengthy document attacking Trotskyism for the benefit of the Young Communist League. However, unlike the old stuff about "Trotsky fascism" this was an attempt to answer with political arguments. This was a very good opportunity for us and we seized it with both hands.

We had had some very good results winning over YCLers in Sussex, so I took the initiative to start writing. Very soon I was asked to go to London and speak to Ted about it. He looked at my draft and then the hard work began. Ted dictated and dictated. I went away and added much more material, and what had begun in my mind as a pamphlet turned into a book.

Ted was a very hard man to please. He was a perfectionist, at least in matters of theory. This was both good and bad. It was very good because it kept us on our toes and was a safeguard against sloppiness. But taken to extremes (and sometimes Ted did this) it can lead to paralysis. I believe that partly explains why Ted had never written a book. In fact, *Lenin and Trotsky—what they really stand for* was the first book he ever wrote.

Despite his toughness, I enjoyed working with him immensely. I did not mind his rigorous approach because I knew that I was learning all the time. I had proposed what I thought was a good title: "In Defence of Bolshevism". But Ted didn't like it. He proposed *In Defence of Lenin and Trotsky* but I didn't like that. Finally we settled on *Lenin and Trotsky, what they really stood for*. The book was a great success and still sells well today.

This was the beginning of a long political collaboration, which lasted as long as Ted lived. He felt at ease working with me and gave me *carte blanche* to change or rewrite his articles and documents. He even said on one occasion: "We can sign each other's articles and books, as Marx and Engels used to do." That is how close our working relationship became.

Internal democracy

One of the things that most attracted me to our tendency was its clean and democratic internal regime. It goes without saying that Ted Grant stood for democratic centralism. But what does that mean? Neither Lenin nor Trotsky ever wrote a book about democratic centralism, although there are many references scattered through their writings. This is no accident. It is not that they underestimated the role of organization. Rather, it is that their conception of organization was dynamic, not static, and the basic principles of democratic centralism had to be adapted to changing conditions.

The same Lenin who insisted on a very firm line in defining the status of a member against Martov's "soft" line in 1903, said in 1912 that any worker who bought and gave money to *Pravda* ought to be considered a Party member. Had Lenin changed his mind? Not at all. But the changed situation (a mass party as opposed to a small group of cadres) demanded a change in the Party's methods.

Ted Grant was firmly in the Leninist line. As we have seen, when Mandel and Co. tried to wave the big stick to get the British comrades to fall into line, he warned them that the only authority they could have over us was a political and a moral authority. That was the only authority that Lenin and Trotsky ever asked for in the Communist International, which was a mass International leading millions.

Throughout the entire history of the Bolshevik Party, internal debates were carried on in a scrupulously fair and democratic manner. It is true that the tone became heated at times, as was natural among men and women who cared passionately about ideas.

Even in polite scientific circles, people who are deeply attached to a particular idea will sometimes express themselves in rather extreme language about ideas held by their critics. However, the final result of such scientific debates will never be determined by the sharpness of the tone but always by the content of the ideas.

The one criticism I remember Ted had of the Bolsheviks was precisely that their tone was too sharp. "The Bolshevik Party was the school of hard knocks," he used to say. But those hard knocks were never delivered below the belt. They were never intended to destroy somebody's reputation or to undermine his political ideas. Such methods have nothing in common with Marxism.

In his famous polemic with Dühring, Engels did not spare the feelings of his opponent but made use of the art of irony. But in the first place, Dühring was not a Party member and Engels rightly saw him as a political enemy. Moreover, Engels never at any time tried to distort Dühring's ideas. On the contrary, he went out of his way to allow Dühring to speak for himself, quoting at length from his writings. If they come across as incoherent, confused and ridiculous, that is not the fault of Engels, but of Dühring himself.

It is immoral to deliberately distort the ideas of an opponent, not for any abstract reasons or sentimentality, but because it is impossible to learn anything from such a "debate". And in the Bolshevik Party, the most important function of a debate was not to crush the enemy or "score points", but to use it to raise the collective political level of the organization.

When Lenin accused Stalin of being rude and disloyal he was accusing him of breaking Party morality. That was a cardinal sin in the Bolshevik Party, which, contrary to the vicious caricature of Bolshevism that has been cultivated by its enemies, was based on very strict principles of honesty and revolutionary morality.

In the early days of the Communist International there were many debates. The majority of the Communist Parties were of recent origin, mostly arising out of splits in the old Social Democratic parties in Europe. The leaders were young and inexperienced and mostly inclined towards ultra-leftism.

Lenin and Trotsky had a lot of problems with the British, Dutch and Italian comrades in particular. But it never occurred to them to resort to manoeuvres or intrigues against their opponents. That was introduced later by Zinoviev and perfected by Stalin. Lenin and Trotsky confined themselves to political argument because they wished to educate people, not destroy them.

Without Marxist theory, democratic centralism is merely the lifeless bones of a skeleton, as Hegel accurately defined formal logic. What in the hands of a Lenin was a perfectly rational and democratic method, becomes transformed into a desiccated husk from which all nourishment has been removed, a senseless formula and a cover for bureaucratic crimes. Formalism is the hallmark of bureaucratic thinking. It is quite alien to Marxism, and above all to the creative dialectics of Leninism. It is the reformist bureaucrat who, instead of dealing with things dialectically and concretely, constantly appeals to the Rule Book—not the revolutionary Bolshevik.

Lenin was always implacable on questions of theory and principle, but he was extremely flexible in organizational and tactical matters. That was his supreme wisdom and a big part of the success of the Bolshevik Party. It was Zinoviev who began to use organizational methods against political opponents in the Communist International, removing leaders who did not blindly accept the "Line". That was not the method of Lenin and Trotsky, who always tried to convince by argument and to correct political mistakes with patience and tact.

The most disastrous consequences of this policy were to be seen in Germany. It is true that the German leaders made many serious mistakes in the early days, but it never occurred to Lenin or Trotsky to solve this by removing them and installing others. Zinoviev did this, however. He replaced Paul Levi, Rosa Luxemburg's successor, with the ultra-lefts Fischer and Maslow.

This was to jump from the frying pan into the fire. Lenin was against this. He said of Paul Levi: "he lost his head, but he had a head to lose." The implication was that the German "Lefts" did not even have that. This was shown by the disastrous March Events, when they launched a premature uprising, which led to many deaths and threw the Communist Party right back.

The Coxhead affair

The extremely democratic nature of the Tendency at that time was clearly demonstrated by the Ted Coxhead affair in 1973. We found out that a small group of comrades had formed a faction without informing anybody and had produced a very long document (more than one hundred pages!) that attacked every one of the most basic positions of the Tendency.

It was very clear from a reading of this document that they were putting forward a Mandelite line, and we were in no doubt that they were conducting factional work on behalf of the Mandelites to foment a split in the organization. They actually had a member who was on our Central Committee, Ted Coxhead, who was effectively the leader of this undeclared faction.

This was a pre-congress period and to add insult to injury, Coxhead had never put forward a single amendment to the congress documents submitted by the EC, nor had he expressed the slightest difference in the debates. Yet when the voting took place he voted against. This was contrary to all the norms of internal democracy and comrades were scandalised. It indicated a cynical and frivolous attitude, which is precisely what we had come to expect from the Mandelites.

Ted with Pat Wall (front) at the bar after the 1973 conference

Ted debating with Coxhead at the 1973 conference

When Coxhead was challenged about the secret document, he had nothing to say. This irresponsible conduct placed us in a difficult position. There was only a little time before the congress. The EC had no time to produce a written reply to a hundred page document. What should be done? From a formal point of view we would have been justified in refusing to distribute the document until we had written a reply.

Instead, we took the opposition document, printed it (that was a big job and cost a lot of money and resources when we had very little of either), and we distributed it, without a reply, to all comrades. We changed the congress timetable to allow a whole session for the debate, and the opposition was given exactly the same time as the EC to speak, despite representing only a fraction of the membership.

At the congress, the Coxhead faction was politically defeated and their arguments comprehensively demolished. It was a sharp debate, but there were no personal attacks or attempts to blacken characters. We had plenty of information that we could have used, including proof that one of the main members of this group had scabbed on a strike. But none of this was ever used. The reason was that we wanted to bring out the political differences and not muddy the waters.

That was always Ted's method—the Bolshevik method of Lenin and Trotsky. The purpose of an internal debate is not to smash one's opponents (the method of Stalin and Zinoviev) but to raise the political level of the cadres. And that was what we achieved. The opposition got no support, and even the few comrades they had succeeded in influencing were won over in the course of the debate.

However, the matter did not end there. After the debate had ended, Ted Grant took the floor. He pointed out that the opposition had broken every rule and had "driven a coach and horses through democratic centralism". He insisted that this method was completely wrong and must never be repeated. Now he issued a challenge. The EC would produce a detailed written reply to the opposition document and we would open a twelve month period of discussion, branch by branch, in which the opposition would be given the same speaking time as the EC. The two documents would then be put to the next congress, which would finally close the debate.

There was a problem at the end of the congress when the slate for the new Central Committee was read out. Coxhead's name was on it, proposed by the EC and CC. This was too much for some of the delegates who protested and tried to get his name removed. Again Ted intervened to defend the proposal. We wanted Coxhead to be present on the CC to defend his ideas.

In the end Coxhead got re-elected, but to no purpose. Once they saw that they stood no chance of winning anybody over to their Mandelite ideas, they resigned from the organization immediately after the congress. By this action they completely revealed their cowardly petty-bourgeois character and lost all credibility. As a result, only a handful left and the level of the whole organization was raised, as was the moral and political authority of the leadership.

A change in the situation

At that time the Labour government was passing from reforms to counter-reforms. The culmination was when Barbara Castle attempted to push anti-trade union laws with her notorious document *In Place of Strife,* in 1969. The bitterness of the workers boiled over. For the first time, miners' lodges were discussing disaffiliation from the Labour Party.

The Young Socialists had suffered grievously from the Healyite split. The LPYS (as the labour youth organization had been renamed after the Healyites had set up their own Young Socialists) was not closed down, as had happened so often in the past, but it had been completely neutered. We were not allowed to elect the leadership, which was appointed by the Labour bureaucracy. They also controlled the LPYS paper, *Left*.

At the annual conference, the bureaucracy would not allow any political discussion or any discussion on international issues. All that was allowed were questions specifically related to youth or organizational matters. This sometimes led to farcical situations. At one conference one wit moved a resolution: "that this Conference expresses solidarity with all members of the Vietcong under 25 years of age." It was ruled out of order, of course.

The situation in the Labour Party itself was even worse. The internal life of the LP was at a very low ebb. One by one, the Left groups abandoned the LP. Only we were left. They all had a good laugh at our expense, of course. A joke was doing the rounds that in the Labour Party wards—as the branches were then known—there were only two kinds of person: old ladies knitting, and young men selling the *Militant*. It was an exaggeration, of course, but there was a grain of truth in it.

Nevertheless, our tactics were correct. They were based on an accurate assessment of how the class would move in the next period. In the end we were in the right place at the right time. Those who laughed at us were left with their mouths open. The 1970s were a political watershed nationally and internationally. The defeat of the Wilson government and the coming to power of Heath ushered in a period of heightened radicalisation in the working class. The fact that the Tendency had won a majority on the national leadership of the Labour Party Young Socialists in 1970 allowed us to start a campaign to build up the youth organisation. Our decision to remain in the LP had been vindicated.

The objective conditions in Britain began to change rapidly after 1970. The Heath government immediately attempted to introduce draconian anti-trade union laws. This provoked a furious reaction and a massive mobilisation of the working class. A decisive turning point was the arrest of the five dockers in July 1972. The decision of the TUC to call a one-day general strike led to their release in a matter of days.

By early 1974, there was a second national miners' strike which succeeded in bringing down the Heath government. It was the first time in British history that an elected government was brought down by industrial action. A Labour government was elected, which imposed an incomes policy known as the "Social Contract", which had the full backing of the left Trade Union leaders, including Jones and Scanlon. Both later admitted that they had looked into the abyss during the massive class battles of the early 1970s and recoiled from what they saw.

The Labour government went from reforms to counter-reforms and ended up rushing to the IMF for a loan in 1976. This led to disappointment and opposition, starting in the trade unions. The dam broke in 1977, with the national fire fighters dispute, which quickly followed the next year by a bitter strike at the Ford Motor company. This was the prelude to a mass movement of low-paid workers known as the "winter of discontent", and contributed to the fall of the Labour government.

The defeat of the Callaghan government in 1979 resulted in a sharp radicalisation in the mass organisations. The shift to the left was a reflection of the disgust with Labour's pro-capitalist policies, and took the form of the rise of Bennism within the Labour Party. Up until the mass radicalisation of the 1970s, the trade unions had been totally dominated by the extreme right wing. A roll-call of the general secretaries of the main unions reads like a real rogues' gallery of the Labour lieutenants of Capital: Lord Carron of the AEU (engineering workers), Lord Cooper of the GMWU (local government manual workers etc.), Sir Sidney Green of the NUR (railway workers) and so on.

Year after year at the Labour Party Conference, the local Parties (CLPs) would vote for left-wing resolutions such as unilateral nuclear disarmament. Then up would get the right-wing union bosses with their block votes of millions and the left resolutions would be defeated. This led many on the Left to demand the abolition of the trade union block vote. Ted was adamantly opposed to this demand. He explained that in future the unions would swing to the Left, and that is just what occurred. In the early seventies, the unions experienced a transformation—something we had confidently predicted for years. One by one, the old right-wing general secretaries were replaced by new, more left-wing people like Laurence Daly of the mineworkers, Hugh Scanlon of the AUEW and Jack Jones of the T&GWU.

Ted speaking at the 1979 South Wales Summer Camp

South Wales Summer Camp 1979

The sects had been calling at every opportunity for workers to leave the right-wing unions and set up new ones. In the 1950s, the Healyites supported the splitting of the Transport and General Workers' Union (today's UNITE union), and the setting up of the National Amalgamated Stevedores and Dockers (the "blue union"). The result was that the unions were split, and for the first time in history, there were non-union workers on the docks of Liverpool. Moreover, contrary to the perspectives of the ultra-lefts, the Transport and General Workers' Union became radicalised and ended up to the left of the "blue union", which later disappeared.

Later on, in the early 1970s, the Cliff group supported the splitting of the GMWU at Pilkington, and the establishment of the glass workers' union; another disaster. Then there was the fiasco in splitting the electricians' union in the same period, with the same result. All the sects wrote off the perspective that the unions would be changed on the basis of events, just as they ruled out any change in the Labour Party. Events proved otherwise.

The general mood of radicalisation in the unions spread to the Labour Party, which swung to the Left in opposition. Under the leadership of the Lefts (Tony Benn and Eric Heffer), the Party was wide open to socialist ideas. By the early 1980s, the right wing had split away from Labour to form the SDP, which further reinforced the leftward shift within the party. The hold of the bureaucracy was weakened.

The list of proscribed organisations had been scrapped. The Constituency Labour Parties gained new life, reflecting the upturn of the class struggle. We were now in the right place at the right time. Thanks to the work of the Militant, the ideas of Marxism gained widespread support in the Labour Party and the unions. This was a concrete expression of the correctness of the ideas, tactics and methods worked out by Ted Grant.

From fewer than 80 comrades in 1966, the Tendency grew to more than 600 by 1975. We had acquired our own printing press and the *Militant* newspaper had gone weekly in January 1972. The Tendency gradually built up its position in the Labour movement. This was only possible because we did not succumb to the pressure of ultra-leftism, but remained within the Labour Party while others left. This was one of the secrets of the later success of the Marxist Tendency in Britain—a breakthrough with no parallel elsewhere.

At the 1973 YS conference in Skegness, Ted Grant had a brief conversation with Tony Benn. Benn recalls in his *Diary* that Ted asserted that "there is no one else in the world who follows Trotsky correctly". Ted struck Benn as being "really a theological leader, a teacher by instinct." These lines betray an honest perplexity. It was probably the same incomprehension with which Cromwell had viewed Gerrard Winstanley and the True Levellers, who became known as the Diggers. Undoubtedly the best and most intelligent of the Lefts, Tony Benn was limited by his left-reformist ideology. He could not understand Ted or his ideas. Nonetheless, he had a sincere regard and respect for Ted, who he correctly saw as an honest man and a fighter.

Tony Benn, leader of the Labour Party left, in 1975

CHAPTER EIGHT
THE MILITANT TENDENCY

Ted's international work: Spain

In 1974, with a tiny handful of comrades in other countries, we set up the Committee for a Workers' International (CWI), which quickly began to grow and spread to other countries. Ted was always very keen on the international work. He wrote all the main documents of the CWI and later the International Marxist Tendency (IMT). His world perspectives were the political foundation upon which all our international work was built.

We paid special attention to the situation in Spain, which we understood to be a key country in the development of the class struggle, as the Franco regime was entering its death agony. Our approach was correct and within a couple of years, starting with a tiny group of just six comrades, the Spanish organisation of the CWI grew to 350, and became the second-biggest section within the International.

Throughout this period, Ted consistently stressed the perspective of socialist revolution and the leading role of the working class. He polemicised against the bourgeois and reformist critics of Marx and the revisionist ideas of people like Mandel and Cliff. His predictions were brilliantly confirmed by the recession of 1974-75, the revolutionary general strike in Spain, and the revolutionary movements in Portugal, Spain, Greece and Italy in the 1970s. Ted was extremely interested in Spain. In 1938, together with Ralph Lee, he wrote an introduction to Trotsky's *Lessons of Spain*, which the comrades published as a pamphlet on their own press. Trotsky wrote a letter congratulating the comrades on this initiative, though sadly that letter has gone missing. In 1973, he wrote a pamphlet which we recently reprinted as the introduction to Felix Morrow's classic, *Revolution and Counter-revolution in Spain*.

The Spanish working class took decades to recover from the terrible defeat of the revolution in the 1930s. However, by the 1960s, there were signs that the proletariat was stirring. Ted greeted with elation the first strikes of the Asturian miners in 1962-63. Between 1964 and 1966, there were 171,000 working days lost due to industrial action. Between 1967 and 1969 the figure rose to 846,000, and from 1973 to 1975, there were 1,548,000. Ted correctly saw in this ascending graph symptoms of a growing revolutionary crisis in Spain. We carried several articles in the paper with the title: "Franco tottering". But he seemed to go on tottering for quite a long time! Nevertheless, Ted had accurately diagnosed the situation.

As a result of a correct perspective, we were able to orientate our small forces to Spain in advance. In the early 1970s, we set up the Spanish Young Socialists Defence Campaign through

Ted Grant (middle) and Alan Woods (top right) with the leadership of the Spanish group in 1978

the British Labour Party Young Socialists. This was an extremely effective campaign, which served to link our international work with our work in the trade union and labour movement in Britain. As a result, we succeeded in winning over a number of trade unionists, including two British Leyland shop stewards.

Through the IUSY (International Union of Socialist Youth) we got contacts with the Spanish Young Socialists, who were working underground. In 1972, I was part of a delegation from the British Labour Party and Young Socialists at the Congress of Toulouse of the Spanish Socialist Party (PSOE). This marked the culmination of a process that would lead to a split between the old right-wing exile leadership of Llopis and the Party in the interior which was far more to the left.

The emerging leader of the PSOE in the interior was a young lawyer from Seville called Felipe Gonzalez. At that time he was a "left", at least in words. But already at that congress I noticed the presence of a smartly dressed German, Hans Matthöfer by name. He was later a minister in the West German government and was there to represent the SPD. The Second International, the German Social Democracy and the CIA were all very interested in Spain and the PSOE.

The strategists of Capital had drawn the same conclusions as us. Spain was on the eve of a revolutionary situation, and something had to be done about it. I made several trips to Spain to try to establish a group, but it was extremely difficult. Not only did we have the problems of underground work, but in those days there was no Internet, Facebook or mobile phones. Letters were slow and you had to be careful what you wrote. Even telephones were not that common.

When Franco finally died on November 20, 1975, Spain was indeed in the grip of a revolutionary situation. We held an emergency meeting in London and it was decided that the only solution was for me to move to Spain. This was a big step to take. My then-wife, Pam, made a big sacrifice in accepting this idea and she did so without hesitation. We had two young children (Stephanie was five and Liza was only two). We lost our house and a lot else besides. But we both considered it necessary for the sake of the Spanish Revolution. We moved to Madrid in January 1976. Pam played an active role in building the tendency in Spain under difficult conditions, and remains active in the movement to the present day.

This is not the place to give a detailed account of how the Spanish section was built. Suffice it to say that in difficult underground conditions we went from just six comrades to 350 in the space of 18 months, and soon became the second biggest and most influential section of the International. That was no accident. We based ourselves on the ideas and methods worked out by Ted, which I have always followed and have always got good results. I might add that more or less at the same time, Lynn Walsh was sent to Portugal in a revolutionary situation and achieved nothing whatsoever.

Ireland

Ted was always an enthusiastic admirer of the Irish Marxist, James Connolly. "It is really extraordinary how Connolly developed the Marxist position on the national question independently of Lenin", he said. He lamented the fact that Connolly had been killed in 1916. Certainly, things would have been very different if he had lived. The petty-bourgeois nationalists would not have found it so easy to hijack the Irish national liberation struggle.

When the Troubles began in Ireland in 1968-69, the movement started with the students, and was undoubtedly a reflection of the events in France. We did not have a base in Ireland at the time, except for one comrade, Paul Jones, in Derry. The Derry Young Socialists played an outstanding role in fighting the Paysleyite reaction. They built barricades and produced a bulletin called *The Bogside Bulletin*. Unfortunately, this revolutionary potential was brutally cut across by the intervention of the British Army and the bombing campaign of the Provisional IRA.

Thanks to Ted's clear thinking, ours was the only tendency on the British Left that maintained a firm class position on the Irish question. We were the only ones who opposed the sending of British troops to Northern Ireland in 1969. All the other groups, including the CPGB, the Labour Left and the SWP supported the sending of troops "to defend the Catholics". We moved a resolution at the Labour Party Conference in the autumn of that year, in which we pointed out that the British Army would be sent to Ireland, not to defend the Catholics but only to defend the interests of British imperialism.

Later, the SWP and the others who had supported sending British troops to Ireland did an about-face and began shouting: "troops out!" They became uncritical cheerleaders for the Provos. That was as much of a betrayal as the previous support for imperialism. Ted was quite merciless in his condemnation of the so-called armed struggle, which he correctly defined as individual terror, a method long ago condemned by Marx, Engels, Lenin and Trotsky.

Ted was implacably opposed to the methods of the Provisional IRA, which was originally a right-wing split from the Official IRA. After the failure of its bombing campaign in the 1950s, the IRA had gone to the left under the influence of the Stalinists, but they also pushed it in a reformist direction. Their biggest mistake was to get rid of the arms. So when the Paisleyite Protestant bigots attacked the Civil Rights demonstrations in 1969, the people were left defenceless. This left the door open to the Provos who were able to offer the youth guns, generously provided by right-wing politicians in the South.

I should add that we were never pacifists and were not opposed to armed struggle in principle. What we were against was any attempt to substitute the conscious movement of the working class for small groups of terrorists. We were in favour of an armed workers' defence force to defend workers from sectarian attacks. But the tactics of the Provos were entirely reactionary and counter-productive.

Ted pointed out that guerrilla tactics were suitable to a peasant country, where, to quote Mao Zedong, the guerrillas would merge with the population "as a fish swims in water". The problem here was that the guerrillas were in a minority, since the majority of the population were Protestants who were implacably opposed to the unification of Ireland. Under such conditions, the IRA's bombing campaign was bound to end in disaster, and it did.

Under difficult conditions we built a group in Ireland that attempted to stand for a class policy. Paul Jones seems to have disappeared and I don't know what became of him. As I recall, the first comrade in the South of Ireland was Finn Geany in Dublin. John Throne came a bit later. The other leading comrade in the North was Peter Hadden, who I had recruited in 1968 when he was a student in Sussex. Tragically, he died of cancer three years ago. We had parted company politically at the time of the split in Militant, but I always had a high opinion of him and maintained fond memories of our time together in Sussex.

My good friend Peter Black, who joined the IRA in 1966, and fought for many years in the ranks of the socialist Republicans, has told me many times that in that same year, on the anniversary of the Easter Rising of 1916, the Republican leader Seamus Costello quoted approvingly from an article that Ted had written about Connolly and the events of 1916. It seems our ideas were beginning to have an effect, although we knew nothing about it until many years later, by which time Costello had been murdered, along with so many Irish Republican socialists.

Shortly before Ted died, I took Peter Black to see him. Peter, a great admirer of Ted, was a bit overawed and seemed at a loss for words. "Shall I ask him a question?" he whispered. "Of course," I said. He said: "Ted, what do you think of the armed struggle?" Ted did not hesitate: "Arms are very good," he said laconically, "but you have to know when to use them." Peter's face lit up. "That is the reply I wanted to hear," he exclaimed. "The reformists always say no to arms, and the militarists only know about arms. But what Ted said is what I agree with."

Ted was implacable in his criticisms of the leaders of the Provisional IRA. At the 1994 Labour Party Conference, he went to a fringe meeting on Ireland which was addressed by a couple of MPs, and also by Mitchell McLoughlin, the Sinn Fein Chairman, who was accompanied by a couple of heavies. There was quite a big audience. After the speeches there were questions from the floor. Ted put his hand up to speak and then proceeded to demolish the Sinn Fein position. He pointed out that 30 years of "armed struggle" had achieved nothing. The Protestant and Catholic workers were divided as never before, and the prospect of Irish reunification had never been so far off as today. "In forty years not a blade of grass has been liberated", he said.

He pointed out that the methods of individual terrorism didn't work and had in fact made the situation worse. The bombing campaign had only strengthened the state apparatus and made it easier for the state to use the same repressive measures against the working class in Britain. It had resulted in the deaths of many of the most self-sacrificing and politically advanced layers of the Republican youth. He then explained that in fact, there was "only one majority in the North of Ireland: the working class".

As one can imagine, this didn't go down very well with many of the Lefts who had been giving fairly uncritical support to Sinn Fein for years. But to everyone's surprise, when McLoughlin replied to the discussion, he spent the whole of his time answering Ted's points. He actually conceded that many of the points that Ted made were true.

After 30 years, what used to be called "armed struggle" ended ignominiously with the sell-out called the Good Friday Agreement. With over 3,000 deaths, and without having secured a single one of their objectives, Adams and McGuiness, the leaders of the Provos, exchanged their bombs and Armalite rifles for smart suits and ministerial portfolios, and entered a coalition government with Ian Paisley and the reactionary UDP.

In the end, life itself dealt a harsh verdict on the tactics of the Provisional IRA, and an even harsher one on those irresponsible elements on the Left in Britain and internationally, who, from the safety of their offices and university seminar rooms, applauded every action of the IRA. What have these ladies and gentlemen got to say now about the actions of their former heroes? They have nothing to say. They remain silent, which is the best service they can render to the Irish people and to humankind in general.

It is ironical that these sectarian numbskulls try to attack our Tendency on the Irish question. Yet left-wing Irish Republicans are showing great interest in what we have to say, and we also are listening respectfully to their views. We come from different traditions, but we are finding a common language because life itself has shown the futility of trying to find a short-cut through the bomb and the gun. A fruitful dialogue has begun between British Marxists and Irish Republicans. It was long overdue.

The Sri Lankan debacle

For a long time, Ted had emphasized the role of objective factors in the defeat of the Trotskyist movement following World War Two. The prolonged economic upswing created the conditions for the strengthening of reformism in the advanced capitalist countries. On the other hand, the victory of the USSR in the war, followed by the overthrow of capitalism in Eastern Europe and China (albeit in a deformed, Bonapartist manner) served to strengthen Stalinism for a whole period. The road to the masses was therefore blocked to Trotskyism.

But as time went on, Ted hardened his attitude in relation to the criminal policies of the so-called leaders of the Fourth. He recalled that the Trotskyists had important forces in countries like Bolivia and Sri Lanka. But it was all thrown away through the blunders of the leadership. In Sri Lanka, there were big possibilities, but the "Trotskyist" Lanka Sama Samaja Party (LSSP) joined a popular front government in 1964. As a result, they were decimated. This was a consequence of the policies of Mandel and co. They thought the permanent revolution was merely abstract. But it is very concrete.

NM Pereira, the main leader of the LSSP, had always had opportunist tendencies. Ted knew the LSSP leaders very well and always referred to them by their first names (or rather their initials). So NM Pereira was "NM" and Goonawardene, was "Leslie". Ted told me that "NM was never a Trotskyist"—a judgement that was all too true.

Ted recalled that in the 1950s, NM Pereira and the other LSSP leaders had a complete contempt for Pablo, Mandel and co. They knew that they had made every mistake possible and a few besides. "We have built a mass organization", they thought. "What have you people built?" The problem was that the leadership of the International did not possess the slightest authority in their eyes.

Ted compared this situation with the colossal authority that Trotsky had held before the war, although he was only one man. The difference was that Trotsky had demonstrated time after time the superiority of his ideas, while the "leaders" of the Fourth made one blunder after another.

This led to an unprincipled situation, where Pablo and Mandel were silent about the LSSP leaders' opportunism, for fear of causing offence. They could then still claim that they had a "mass organization" in Sri Lanka, while NM Pereira and the others could do just as they pleased. The result was a foregone conclusion. The rightward slide of the latter towards the swamp of opportunism continued unchecked, with disastrous consequences.

For years, Mandel and co. had turned a blind eye to the opportunism of the LSSP leaders, and this ended predictably with their capitulation to popular frontism. In 1964, the LSSP joined the coalition government of Sirimavo Bandaranaike. Three of its MPs became ministers: NM Pereira became Minister of Finance, and two other LSSP leaders also accepted ministerial posts.

Then the leaders of the so-called United Secretariat of the Fourth International did a 180 degree turn and expelled the whole party. Instead of launching a political campaign to win over the rank and file of the LSSP, they resorted to a purely administrative measure that excluded, not just the leaders, but the entire party. This was absolutely typical of the methods of that tendency.

The leader of the Mandelite faction was Edmund Samarakody. He came to London at the time, and I met him. He struck me as a sincere man, but he was completely ultra-left and impatient. We advised him to stay and work inside the LSSP, but he could not accept this, and went into the political wilderness. A few years later, when we had already parted company with the Mandelite USFI, we found out about the existence of a left opposition inside the LSSP.

We contacted them and established close connections, and managed to win them over. Ted went to Sri Lanka and played a big role in winning them. He also persuaded them to stay and fight for a majority within the LSSP. After several years of work within the LSSP, our comrades managed to win a de facto majority. This led to a sharp conflict with the old leadership, who, however, refused to convene a party congress, where they knew they would lose control. The comrades, using the party statutes, raised enough support within the ranks to convene a congress anyway.

The old leadership refused to recognise that congress and thus it led to a split with a large group (probably the majority) constituting themselves as the Nava Sama Samaja Party (NSSP) with around 700 members. This very successful work was unfortunately destroyed by the antics of one of its leaders, Bahu (Vickramabahu Karunaratne), who wrecked the whole thing.

In one of his trips to Sri Lanka, Ted delivered a speech at the congress of the party, during which he made a sharp attack on the right-wing President of the island, J.R. Jawardene. Since Sri Lanka is not a very big place, and the name of Ted Grant was quite well known, the news soon reached the President's ears. He was furious and issued an order for Ted's arrest.

For some days, Ted was on the run, going from one comrade's house to another. Finally, he was arrested and taken straight to the airport for immediate deportation. Some years later, Vasu (Vasudeva Nanayakkara, another leader of the NSSP at the time, and an outstanding veteran of the Sri Lankan Trotskyist movement), described to me how Ted was virtually carried by the Criminal Investigation Department to the exit as he continued to shout his protests to the last. "He was the most courageous man I ever knew", said Vasu.

Vasudeva Nanayakkara (Vasu)

However, back in London, we were not so pleased, since Ted's actions, heroic or not, meant that he would henceforth be prevented from re-entering Sri Lanka.

The two main leaders of the NSSP were Vasu and Bahu. In every respect, Vasu was superior to Bahu. He was personally honest and very talented, but he was always very modest. Unlike Bahu, he was a genuine mass leader and a strikingly effective orator. He was well known in Sri Lanka. Yet, for reasons I could never understand, he accepted Bahu as the main leader and "theoretician".

Bahu played a very bad role. I believe he had once been the President of the Oxford University Union and he really had a swollen head as a result. He always insisted on signing his articles and documents as Doctor *Vickremebahu* Karunaratne, although to the best of my knowledge the founder of scientific socialism never signed his books as Doctor Karl Marx.

This pretentiousness was symptomatic of his whole outlook. Puffed up with his own importance, he made one political blunder after another. He had a completely wrong position on the national question, which we endeavoured to correct. But he was completely arrogant and incapable of recognizing mistakes.

We had a whole series of debates with the Sri Lankan leaders. These were a model of democracy in line with the Leninist traditions of the Bolshevik Party. The Sri Lankan comrades were in a small minority in our International. In fact, they did not succeed in convincing anybody in any other section. But they were always treated with the greatest respect and answered in a friendly and comradely manner. That was always the method of the tendency of Ted Grant.

These debates were characterised by the most scrupulous democracy, tolerance and good manners. Despite his intolerable attitude, Ted was always personally friendly to Bahu, or "Wicky" as he called him. But on the political questions, he was, as always, implacable. Many comrades to this day look back with nostalgia to those debates, which were the finest example of the Ted Grant School of internal democracy.

Bahu's criminal policy in the end led to him to actually defend the military intervention of India in Sri Lanka. This, he justified by developing a hair-brained theory that the Indian bourgeoisie was somehow a progressive "industrial" bourgeoisie, whereas the Sri Lankan bourgeoisie was compradore! In the end, we did not succeed in getting the Sri Lankans to correct their mistakes, which ultimately led to the destruction of the section. But those debates served to educate and steel the cadres and raise the level of the whole International. And that, in a genuine Leninist organization, is what counts.

Pakistan and the role of Lal Khan

A big breakthrough for our international work occurred in 1980, although this was not immediately apparent. A young man who had been forced to flee from the military dictatorship in Pakistan came to London to seek out Ted Grant. The man who is now known as Lal Khan was destined to play a major role in Pakistan and in the International.

The son of a Punjabi army officer, Lal Khan decided not to enter the army and instead became a medical student. This was a time of violent class struggle in Pakistan. The magnificent revolution of 1968—9 had been derailed by the reformist leaders of the PPP. This had tilted the whole centre of gravity to the right, leading to the breakaway of Bangladesh, war with India and the rise of Bonapartist tendencies in the army.

Lal Khan was elected general secretary of the students union of Nishtar Medical College, Multan, in 1978, defeating the Islamic fundamentalists, armed and supported by the vicious Zia-ul-Haq dictatorship. There were bloody clashes on the streets and on the campuses between revolutionary students and reactionary Muslim gangs backed by the army. Lal Khan was involved in these shootouts, which nearly led to his death.

He was ordered to be shot on sight by the military command council on May 10, 1980, on the direct orders of the dictator. For twenty days, the military and the police were hunting for him throughout the country. He was arrested, and sentenced to flogging and imprisonment. In the end, he managed to escape to Amsterdam, where he established a small group of revolutionary exiles and published a paper called *The Struggle*.

Lal Khan was told about the Ted Grant group by a left-wing friend in Karachi. He immediately came to look for us in London, where he established very close relations with Ted, who came to regard him almost as a son. Shortly afterwards, I met him at an international meeting, and thus began a close political and personal bond that has united us ever since.

I always had a high regard for Lal Khan, who clearly stood for our ideas and showed great promise. But, apart from Ted, I detected a certain coldness towards him on the part of the other people who were involved in

Ted Grant and Lal Khan, just before he returned to Pakistan

international work in London. I could never understand this at the time. Only later did it occur to me that the reason was that he was not a yes-man.

Lal Khan could see the huge difference between Ted and the others, and they had very little authority with him. This irritated them considerably. Even at this early stage it is clear that an unhealthy tendency was beginning to develop in Britain. This was characterised by constant attempts to play down Ted's role. The layer of pushy youngsters who fancied themselves as future leaders of the world proletariat imagined that they could boost their prestige by running Ted down behind the scenes. For these small minds, Lal Khan's closeness to Ted Grant was therefore not a plus, but a colossal minus.

A surreptitious campaign against Lal Khan went on for years, despite the fact that he was doing very good work in the painful and arduous conditions of exile. In the end, I got so tired of it that I took responsibility for Pakistan, although to tell the truth, I did not have much time with all my other responsibilities. I did it mainly to keep the others off Lal Khan's back. That is how bad things had gotten in the late 1980s. But we will come to that later.

Ted had many discussions with Lal Khan, in which he came to the conclusion that the Pakistani Marxists should work in the Pakistan People's Party (PPP), despite the profound contradictions and peculiarities of that party. Those who questioned our orientation to the PPP were immediately proved wrong when millions of Pakistani workers and peasants came onto the streets to welcome Benazir Bhutto on her homecoming in April 1986. She described the scene in her 1988 memoir *Daughter of the East*:

"The eight-mile drive from the airport to the Minar-i-Pakistan in Iqbal Park usually takes 15 minutes. On the unbelievable day of April 10, 1986, it took us ten hours," Benazir Bhutto recalls. "The figure of one million people at the airport grew to two million then three million by the time we reached the Minar-i-Pakistan. (...) The black, green and red colours of the PPP seemed the only colours in Lahore that day. PPP flags and banners billowed in the dry, hot breeze until they formed an almost continuous canopy. People were wearing red, green and black jackets, dupattas, shalwar khameez, hats. Donkeys and water buffalo had PPP ribbons braided into their manes and tails."

This mass support was a remarkable confirmation of the perspective worked out by Ted for the PPP. It convinced Lal Khan of the urgent need to return to his homeland. As he explained to me:

> After more than seven years of difficult and frustrating exile in Amsterdam, I decided that the time had come to go back. But before leaving I was determined to see Ted again. I travelled to London on October 29, 1987. At first, Ted was doubtful about the wisdom of this step. He questioned me closely about security: "Isn't it too dangerous still? We can't afford to lose you" and so on. But once he saw that I had already taken the decision, he accepted it.
>
> After a long discussion, Ted gave me some very sound advice. He said: "Remember, the country you are going back to is not the same country you left seven years ago. You might not recognize many aspects of social life. Be prepared for a cultural and social shock". He then continued:
>
> "Don't work with the people you worked with in the past. They will have changed so much, adapting to the dictatorship and being out of struggle, that they will have compromised themselves. Hence you must look for a fresh start and build with the youth. The new generation have not been scarred and demoralised by past defeats. They will have fresh minds that will readily understand and accept our ideas".

The very next day I was on a plane to Pakistan. I have never forgotten that conversation and those precious words of advice, which enabled me to reorient myself in what was indeed a very different world to the one I had left behind seven years earlier.

Returning to Pakistan, Lal Khan built an impressive revolutionary Marxist organization under the most difficult and dangerous conditions imaginable. Presently, he is the editor of the *Asian Marxist Review* and the International secretary of the Pakistan Trade Union Defence Campaign. He is the author of 28 books in different languages on various subjects. And the organization that began with just two people now numbers thousands. Actions speak louder than words. Lal Khan has proved his worth not by words but by deeds.

Those who spent years attempting to belittle his work must now hang their heads in shame. The comrades wanted Ted to go to Pakistan but we thought it was too dangerous for his health. Nevertheless, it was his ideas and example that provided the inspiration for that great work, and nobody else, as every comrade in Pakistan knows. It is his portrait that presides over every congress of the Pakistan section of the IMT in Lahore, where over 2,500 workers, peasants and youth gather every year to pledge themselves anew to the cause of proletarian internationalism and the socialist revolution.

Pat Wall

Under the political guidance of Ted, we had created the strongest Trotskyist tendency since the days of the Russian Left Opposition. By the late 1970s, Militant had not only consolidated its huge majority within the Labour Party Young Socialists, but also had a solid base in the Labour Party. We ran the LPYS youth paper, *Left*. We had a comrade from the LPYS on Labour's National Executive Committee. We even succeeded in getting Andy Bevan appointed to the post of Labour Party national youth officer.

From counting the pennies, we now had a turnover of over a million pounds a year, a large premises, a big web printing press, capable of printing a daily paper, and, incredibly, around 200 full time workers—which was more than the Labour Party itself. We had roots in many trade unions and Labour Parties, including about 50 councillors and three Marxist MPs.

I should say a few words about them. All three MPs were admirable comrades in their own way. Dave Nellist took to parliament like a duck to water and became a polished orator, although, needless to say, we always attached more importance to the work outside parliament. Terry Fields, a Liverpool fire fighter, was a very pleasant and sincere man, dedicated to the cause of his class.

Last but not least, there was Pat Wall, who was the ablest and most experienced of the three. A charming, intelligent, quietly spoken man, Pat made a deep and lasting impression on me. He had the same gift that Ted possessed of being able to express the most complex ideas in the simplest language. And just like Ted he was able to speak to anybody about Marxism. I think that after Ted and Jimmy Deane, he was the most outstanding figure in our Tendency, and after them, the greatest influence on me personally.

Pat joined the Tendency at a very young age and played a crucial role in Merseyside in a very difficult period. An avid reader, he had an excellent grasp of Marxist theory. He had very broad cultural interests and had read widely. An ardent supporter of Everton football team, he was a lover of jazz, particularly Charlie Parker. His wife Pauline had become politically active through the Labour Party's youth section. She helped out with the production of *Rally* (the youth paper of the Tendency in Liverpool) and soon joined the work of the Tendency. Pauline recalls how much hard work was put in duplicating the paper, helped by Laura Kirton, secretary of the Walton Labour Party. "It was typed on stencils, duplicated, collated and then bound down the spine with red tape", explained Pauline. They used the Trades Council duplicator to get it out.

Pat's work attracted many others, including Terry Harrison, who was the leader of the apprentices' strike on Merseyside in 1960. In 1958, Terry was thinking of joining the YCL, but picked up a copy of *Rally* at a ward meeting and wrote off to find out more. It wasn't long before he was participating in the work of the Tendency, part of a new generation of young comrades like Ted Mooney, Terry Harrison, Tony Mulhearn and Peter Taaffe.

I would have liked to have had more contact with Pat over the years, but as he worked as a mail-order company buyer, his work took him to many countries: Hong Kong, Taiwan, Sri Lanka, South Korea and even the United States. He told me that, from a personal point of view, his favourite country was Taiwan. But Pat was no ordinary "tourist". He always did his best to establish political contacts on his foreign travels.

Sometime in 1975, I had a very revealing conversation with Pat about Spain. Pat told me about a visit he had made recently to a factory in Vitoria in the Basque Country. With his friendly, easy-going manner, normally he would be able to connect easily with the workers in any workplace. But walking around this factory in the company of management, he could sense a bristling hostility on all sides. "I have never in my life experienced such a mood of burning class hatred", he recalled.

Pat's instincts proved to be very sound. One year later, in March 1976, this mood burst to the surface in a semi-insurrectionary general strike. At the time, I was living in Spain, and we were attempting to establish a group in Vitoria. This was the town where we later built our strongest base. I was in Vitoria during the general strike and was present at a mass meeting in the church of San Francisco, which resembled a meeting of the St. Petersburg Soviet in 1905.

The next day the whole city was in turmoil, with the striking workers playing a game of cat and mouse with the police. On the evening of March 3, 1976, armed police surrounded the church and fired tear gas and smoke bombs through the windows. The church was packed with men, women, and children, and panic ensued. As they came out of the church, the police opened fire with automatic weapons. It was a massacre and a turning point in the struggle against the Franco dictatorship.

In 1987, Pat was elected MP for Bradford North. His remarkable powers of communication enabled him to build strong links with the Asian community in his Bradford North constituency, with the aid of Lal Khan, who was one of the main organisers of Pat's election campaign. Pat won a resounding victory that gave a big boost to the Militant. He had the honour of being attacked as a Marxist in the Conservative election broadcast of May 27, 1987. He was quoted as saying: "A Marxist Labour government would mean the abolition of the monarchy, the House of Lords, the sacking of the generals, the admirals, the air marshals, the senior civil servants, the police chiefs and in particular the judges".

On the day of the election *The Sun* also featured a photograph calling for Pat Wall to be defeated. Pat's campaign cut across this by holding public meetings and also workplace meetings. He won the seat, recording a 9.9% swing from the Social Democratic Party. It was a great victory. His maiden speech in Parliament was typical of the man. Speaking in the House of Commons, January 10, 1990, he told the assembled MPs:

I am the grandson of a dock worker and was brought up politically on the Mersey docks, where I learned to debate and to fight politically among dockers and the dock industry.

This remarkable speech was a great inspiration not just for the workers in Britain but the youth and workers in the South Asian subcontinent. There were plans to invite him to speak in Pakistan, in Kashmir and Lahore on the fiftieth anniversary of Trotsky's death. But his own death prevented it.

Unfortunately, this outstanding cadre of our Tendency never received the recognition that was due to him. Whenever our MPs were mentioned, it was always Terry Fields and Dave Nellist who were singled out for praise. This was no accident. Pat Wall was far too independent for some people's liking. At the offices of the Militant I heard doubts expressed about him, on more than one occasion, and unfavourable comparisons made between Pat and "the other two".

Cut off from direct participation in the activity of the working class, he felt out of place, like a beached whale or a caged tiger. He did not enjoy the life of a parliamentarian, and in the end even questioned whether it was worthwhile. My wife Ana and I invited him for dinner at our house and it was very clear that Pat felt desperately lonely. That was the last time I saw him.

Pat died in August 1990, of a very rare and disfiguring disease that attacked his immune system, causing a collapse of all the cartilage in his body. His tragic death occurred before the faction fight had broken out, but I have not the slightest doubt that Pat would have been on our side. He was, like Jimmy Deane, always a faithful comrade of Ted's, which was why he was virtually sidelined. His untimely death was a terrible loss to the Marxist cause.

Pat Wall, Marxist MP for Bradford North 1987-1990

Chapter Nine

How Militant Was Destroyed

The rise of the parvenus

The revolutionary years of the 1970s ended in defeat. It was not a dramatic defeat like that in Italy, Germany and Spain in the inter-war period. The workers' organizations were everywhere intact. The dictatorships had fallen in Greece, Portugal and Spain. Nevertheless, it was a defeat in the sense that the great expectations of the working class had been frustrated by the leadership, which had once again had saved capitalism.

In 1975, *The Times* published an editorial with the title: "Capitalism is Dead in Portugal". It ought to have been true, and it could have been true, but it was not true. Not by the actions of the fascists, but as a result of the policies of the Socialist and Communist leaders, the marvellous Portuguese Revolution had been defeated. The same was true of Spain, Greece and Italy, where power was within the grasp of the working class.

There is no more dispiriting experience for an army than to be defeated without a fight. In many countries, the advanced workers felt that they were very close to power, and yet it just slipped out of their hands. The resulting demoralization had to be seen to be believed. I had personal experience of this in Spain, where I have never seen such disappointment. This was, once again, a case of counter-revolution in a democratic form.

As was the case following World War Two, the betrayals of the Stalinists and Social Democrats prepared the way for a recovery of capitalism. The bourgeoisie, which had been in a state of panic, recovered its nerve. The governments went onto the offensive. The pendulum began to swing to the right. These were the years of Reagan and Thatcher, of monetarism and attacks on the working class.

In 1979, following a period of sharp class struggle, the Conservative Party came to power under Margaret Thatcher. This marked a fundamental change in British politics and the Conservative Party. The Conservative Party was run by a narrow circle of unelected Tory grandees, all aristocrats. The bourgeois provided the money and the conservative middle class the foot soldiers. For a long time this arrangement worked very well. But by the 1960s, the bourgeois and especially the petty-bourgeois were becoming restive.

Disaster struck when they decided to elect the leader. The election of Margaret Thatcher, a shopkeeper's daughter, as Party Leader marked a sudden shift. In her person were united all the prejudices, ignorance, lunacy and fanaticism of the Conservative middle class rank and file. The Conservative Party rank and file consists of stockbrokers, lawyers, shopkeepers, estate agents and similar riffraff. They are of limited intelligence, mostly fanatical chauvinists, racists, anti-European, pro-hanging and flogging, and extremely right wing.

As long as there was no democracy in the Conservative Party, everything was fine. The aristocratic Party grandees selected the leaders from their own ranks, keeping the middle class rabble at arm's length. Harold Macmillan was probably the last of the old-fashioned Tory grandees. Ted regarded him as an intelligent representative of the ruling class. Macmillan did not conceal his dislike of Thatcher and her policies. He described her policies of privatisation as "selling the family silver", which was not a bad way of putting it. But the age of the Tory grandees had past. The hour of the parvenus had struck.

However much the Tory aristocracy despised this middle-class parvenu, they needed somebody like her to wage all-out war on the working class and the Labour Movement. Brash, ignorant and narrow as she was, she also showed a single-minded determination to get things done. Macmillan had warned that there are three things that no sensible government should ever attack: the Brigade of Guards, the Roman Catholic Church and the National Union of Mineworkers. Thatcher declared war on the miners and decimated the British coal industry. Later, the powerful print unions were smashed. After that, the union leaders were easily cowed.

Not long ago they produced a film about Margaret Thatcher. Even by Hollywood's standards it is a very bad film. Thatcher is portrayed as a truly remarkable woman—somebody to be admired. Her rise in the Tory Party is depicted as the triumph of a brave and talented woman who "succeeded against all the odds." This misses the point entirely. The miners were savagely beaten (the extent of police brutality is only now coming to light), literally beaten into the ground. They were mercilessly smeared by our "free press", arrested and sent to prison on trumped-up charges, their pits were closed, their jobs taken away, their communities destroyed. Is all this to be justified because a shopkeeper's daughter succeeded in "getting on" in the Tory Party?

A man or woman can be brave in a very reactionary cause. Adolph Hitler showed a lot of guts in the early years when he was struggling for power. Does that entitle us to praise him? Nor does the fact that Thatcher was a woman provide any excuse for praising her. She and her government used all the combined force of the state to crush the miners in what resembled a civil war. The true Iron Ladies were the miners' wives who fought with admirable courage and tenacity to defend their communities. Yet none of the Hollywood "feminists" ever thought about making a film about them.

In 1980, after the resignation of Callaghan, Michael Foot was elected leader of the Labour Party. A former Left, he had gone to the Right, although nobody really noticed this metamorphosis. Formerly considered to be a fine orator (in the narrow British parliamentary sense), he was by now so inarticulate that even his own mother could not have made head or tail of what he was saying half the time. He was very successful at losing elections, and needed some excuse for his failure. The gentlemen of the press were happy to provide it: the reason for all of Labour's woes was the Militant Tendency. "The Militant Tendency", he proclaimed, was "a pestilential nuisance". This at last gave the green light for the witch-hunt which the press had been incessantly baying for.

By all the laws of politics, Labour should have won the 1983 general election. The economy was in free-fall; there was mass unemployment; poverty and inequality were increasing, and Margaret Thatcher was deeply unpopular. But events suddenly took a different turn when the Argentine Junta invaded the Falkland Islands (known as the Malvinas in Argentina).

The Falklands War changed everything. The British Marxists did our internationalist duty by opposing our own bourgeoisie. Ted systematically denounced the reactionary war aims of the Thatcher government, which before this had had excellent relations with the brutal Argentine Junta. Only after Galtieri's military adventure did they discover that the regime in Argentina was "fascist". In fact, the Conservative Foreign Minister, Lord Carrington, had been secretly negotiating with the Junta for the handing over of the Falkland Islands at a later date.

However, the Junta was in a hurry. There were mass demonstrations and protests in Argentina, and Galtieri decided to cut across the revolutionary movement by staging a military adventure. He calculated that London would not resist an invasion of the Malvinas. This was a serious miscalculation. Thatcher could never accept the humiliation of the seizure of the islands by the Argentine military.

Ted regarded the war as reactionary on both sides. The Argentine masses have deep anti-imperialist instincts which are progressive. However, there was not an atom of progressive content in the actions of the Junta, which were purely aimed at diverting the attention of the mass protest movement. It was a complete travesty to present this as an anti-imperialist struggle in any shape or form. Unfortunately, large sections of the Argentine left, including so-called Trotskyists, allowed themselves to be carried away by the patriotic wave, in some cases even offering their services to the Junta. All the so-called Trotskyist sects worldwide scandalously supported Galtieri's reactionary adventure, falsely alleging that it was an anti-imperialist struggle.

On the other hand, the arguments of Thatcher about defending the rights of the Falkland islanders were false and hypocritical. Her war aims were dictated purely by the global interests of British imperialism. We carried out consistent anti-war propaganda, but found ourselves isolated. Although at first there was no enthusiasm in Britain for this war, the military victory gave Thatcher the excuse to play the patriotic card in the next election. The end of the conflict produced a general sense of relief, and insured the victory of Thatcher in the next general election.

The rise of Neil Kinnock

For all his faults, Michael Foot was not Tony Blair. He did not like the Militant and would have been glad to get rid of the Marxists, but he was not a witch-hunter at heart and he pursued the matter half-heartedly. The bourgeois were not impressed. Poor old Michael! I suppose his heart was in the right place, although his head was somewhere else altogether. The ruling class needed someone quite different to bring the Labour Party to heel. It needed someone with guts; it needed someone with brass balls; it needed a schoolyard bully. In short, it needed a Neil Kinnock.

Foot was replaced by Neil Kinnock, another ex-Left who had gone far to the Right. He represented a new breed of Labour leader, a very adequate expression of the generalised right-ward shift in society. I am ashamed to say that Neil Kinnock is a Welshman. I too am a Welshman and proud of my people. Above all, I am proud of the Welsh working class, which ever since the days of the Chartists and the Newport uprising has always been in the front line of the class struggle. In particular, I am proud of the Welsh miners, those fine class-conscious proletarians whom I have been privileged to fight alongside.

But there is another side to the Welsh nation, which like all other nations is sharply divided on class lines. There is no snob in the world like a Welsh snob. There is no social climber in the world like a Welsh social climber. And there is no class traitor in the world like a Welsh class traitor. I met quite a few of that breed when I was at university. I can therefore say with absolute confidence: no primitive amphibian lurking in the Cambrian swamp ever slithered out of the primeval slime with such eagerness as these creatures struggle to climb out of the class they have come from. Their sole aim is to "get on", preferably to get on in the Parliamentary Labour Party. I hasten to add that any resemblance between these remarks and any person, alive or dead, is purely coincidental.

The ruling class had had a nasty shock when the Marxists succeeded in winning a sizeable influence in the Labour Party in the 1970s. They organized a split-away of the right wing and the formation of the Social Democratic Party (SDP), in order to undermine Labour, and at the same time orchestrated a vast witch-hunt against the Militant Tendency and the Labour Left. Their chief agent in the campaign to defeat the Labour Left and push the Labour Party to the right was Neil Kinnock.

No sooner had the erstwhile "Left" Kinnock grabbed the Labour leadership from the faltering hands of his ageing predecessor, than he declared all-out war on the Labour Left, headed by Tony Benn, up to whose knees he did not reach, politically, intellectually, morally or in any other respect. But before annihilating the Bennite Left, he first had to deal with the Militant Tendency.

Kinnock knew that it was the Marxists of Militant who gave backbone to the Lefts. Obediently taking his cue from the establishment and the media, he took up the struggle against Militant with the zeal of a crusader. He stepped up the witch-hunt against the Marxists in the Labour Party under the full glare of the media, which was constantly urging him on. In his deluded brain he imagined that this would get him more votes. Instead, it caused a damaging split in Labour, demoralised its activists and lost support. As a result, despite the unpopularity of the Thatcher government, "Boyo" succeeded in leading the Labour Party into resounding defeats in two general elections with no trouble at all.

Labour was fatally weakened in the face of the Thatcherite onslaught. Thatcher and her crew rained blows on the working class, crushing the miners with the tacit or even open complicity of Kinnock. The only serious resistance to Thatcher, apart from the miners and printers, was the Militant Tendency in Liverpool and in the anti-Poll Tax struggle, which finally brought Thatcher down.

In reward for these inestimable services to the Conservative Party, Neil Kinnock is now Lord Kinnock and is drawing a handsome salary from the EU. In addition, he holds the unenviable record of the longest-serving Leader of the Opposition in British political history to date, and the longest never to have become Prime Minister. His actions served to fatally undermine the Party, preparing the way for an openly bourgeois Labour leader in the person of Anthony Charles Lynton Blair, a man who thought the Labour Party ought never to have been created. Incidentally, Kinnock was actively supported by the late Professor Eric Hobsbawm, one of the architects of "New Labour".

Return to London: the *Militant International Review*

I came back to Britain in the autumn of 1983 together with my partner and comrade Ana Muñoz. My return was due to a potentially serious health problem. But that was nothing compared to the problems that were being prepared. Ever since Ana and I had returned to London, we felt that something was wrong. I say "felt" because neither of us could put our finger on it.

Ana told me later:

> I came to Britain with great expectations. This was the centre of our International. It was supposed to be our model. But I saw that things were not the same as in Spain and felt there was something not quite right. There was not the same atmosphere of comradeship.

Peter Taaffe proposed to put me on the British EC and offered me a position. I said that I would accept any post he considered useful. He suggested political education or the theoretical journal, the *Militant International Review* (MIR). I discussed it with Ted, and decided to choose the editorship of the MIR. This had been under Lynn Walsh but it was practically defunct. I took it over and revived it.

The feeling that all was not well was strengthened by my experience on the EC. Of course, Ted did most of the political leadoffs, which were to his usual high standards. But the contribution of most of the EC members was not on a very high level. Looking around the table I could not help thinking: all these years and all these successes, but where are the cadres?

It was a worrying thought, but I immediately found a hundred reasons—or rather excuses—for the low political level of the organization, including its leadership. The comrades were all very busy. The organization had changed since I was last in Britain. There was the pressure of mass work, etc., etc. Still, something had to be done, or else we would be building on sand.

So, with Ted's enthusiastic collaboration, I set to work on the theoretical magazine. It was not easy because I had many other things to do. My main responsibility was in the International. I was away for half the year on international trips. And I had nobody to help me with the MIR. I was the only one working on it and all the time I was the editor it was starved of resources.

Nevertheless, the MIR came out every quarter, as regular as a clock. I always discussed the editorials with Ted, and he often dictated them. By this time he had difficulty in writing and he and I regularly collaborated on articles and documents. The journal was a fantastic success. There was a real thirst for theory among the members and especially among the full timers. At every congress there were always a number of resolutions congratulating us on the MIR and asking for a more regular theoretical journal.

This was out of the question as long as I was working on my own. I repeatedly asked Peter Taaffe for another full timer, but he always gave evasive answers: "we don't have anybody to spare" was the standard reply. But this was not the real reason. Finally, he grudgingly allowed Clive Heemskirk to help with the MIR, but it was still a low priority. Despite the fact that there was a big demand for the MIR, for all the years I was the editor it was never discussed once on the EC. That was no accident.

Part of the problem was that the group around Taaffe had a contemptuous attitude towards theory and "theoreticians". But more importantly, they disapproved of my close relation with Ted Grant, against whom they were already beginning to intrigue. Eventually, Taaffe decided that my running the MIR was too much. Arguing that I had "too much on my plate", he pressed me to give the editorship back to Lynn Walsh. By that time I was too worn out to argue. Reluctantly, I handed the journal back to Lynn Walsh.

Liverpool and the witch-hunt

The rise of Trotskyism within the Labour Party alarmed the ruling class. The right wing and its capitalist backers were beside themselves. They could afford to laugh at the antics of the sectarian groups on the fringes of the Labour Movement, but this was different. Here was a strong Marxist tendency firmly entrenched in the mass organizations of the working class. It was potentially dangerous and not to be tolerated. The full weight of the capitalist media was mobilized to launch a new witch-hunt against the Tendency, demanding our expulsion from the Party.

Our success in Liverpool was the result of decades of consistent and patient work in the Party, which eventually enabled us to win control of Merseyside District Labour Party. As a result, from May 1983 onwards we had effective political control of Liverpool City Council. By this time, the Militant Tendency had become a household name and had grown rapidly in numbers and influence. Under the leadership of Militant, Liverpool City Council led a mass struggle against the Thatcher government, which again brought us into the limelight. The events around Liverpool showed that militant struggle forced concessions from the Tories and was successful.

It is often alleged that Marxists do not stand for reforms. This is false. Marxists understand that without the day-to-day struggle for advance under capitalism the socialist revolution is impossible. Our criticism of the reformists is precisely that they do not struggle seriously for reforms, but continually capitulate to the capitalist class. What happened in Liverpool is an object lesson in the difference between Marxism and reformism.

As a result of our policies, thousands of jobs had been created, and thousands of houses built by Liverpool Council, which forced the government to make big concessions. The Liverpool electorate supported the councillors in every election, with increased majorities. You can imagine if the Labour Party nationally had taken such a stand. However, the right wing was to squander this political capital in the years ahead. Far from welcoming this, the right-wing Labour leadership of the ex-"Left" Neil Kinnock regarded it with overt hostility.

Kinnock could not immediately come out against Liverpool Council, which stood on a programme of opposition to cuts in services as well as any rate increases. He hypocritically offered it "trainloads of sympathy", while doing everything possible to isolate and undermine it. The only hope we had of long-term success was if other Labour Councils followed Liverpool's example. But one by one, the "Lefts" ran for cover in the battle over rate-capping, while Kinnock, reflecting the stance of the ruling class, passed openly onto the offensive against Liverpool and Militant. His pathetic advice to Labour councils was to operate a "dented shield", i.e., capitulation to the Tory government. By 1985, Kinnock launched an all-out assault on Liverpool. At the Labour Party Conference he made a speech that was a vicious attack on Liverpool council and Militant.

It must nevertheless be admitted that some mistakes were made, in particular the issuing of redundancy notices to the council workforce. It is true that this was a tactical move, which was not actually going to be implemented, in order to gain some time. There was never any real intention to carry out the sackings, and this was explained to the unions. But it was a very risky tactic, and Ted raised serious objections to it on the EC. He warned there could be serious consequences and he was right. In his speech, Kinnock laid heavy emphasis on the issue of "a Labour council scuttling around the City in taxis to give out redundancy notices." It had been a propaganda gift to our enemies.

To be fair, even if our tactics had been 101 percent correct, the witch-hunt would have taken place anyway. The ruling class was alarmed at our successes and they were determined to get rid of us. The witch-hunt against the Tendency was being urged on by big business, the state and the mass media. The real reason for Liverpool's defeat was the deliberate sabotage of Kinnock

Ted appealing against his expulsion at the 1983 Labour Party conference

and the right-wing union leaders, and the total lack of support from the Left councils such as Ken Livingstone's Greater London Council, and Margaret Hodge in Islington. So-called Lefts like Livingstone made a lot of noise about peripheral and trendy issues, but when it came to a serious fight over questions affecting the working class, he ran for cover, leaving Liverpool in the lurch. Eventually, they resorted to the capitalist courts to carry through surcharges and disqualifications, while the right wing carried through expulsions.

On February 22, 1983, the Labour Party's National Executive Committee expelled from Labour Party membership the five members of *Militant*'s Editorial Board, including Ted Grant, who was the political editor. There were 85 resolutions protesting against the expulsions to the NEC of the Labour Party and not one in favour! Party regional conferences in London, Scotland and the Southwest, all came out against the expulsions.

The *Militant*'s Editorial Board appealed, and the final decision had to be put to Labour Party conference, where the leadership could count on their control of the union block vote to push the expulsions through. In October of that year, the expulsions were ratified by Conference. Two-thirds of constituency delegates voted against expulsions, but the appeal of each member was lost when the unions cast their block votes, 5,160,000 to 1,616,000 in each case except for one. Ted Grant got 175,000 more votes opposing his expulsion. In a defiant speech to the Labour Conference, Ted said: "We'll be back!" He told them that there is no way Marxism can be separated from the Labour Movement. That was undoubtedly the only correct position to take.

It is entirely false, however, to say that the witch-hunt rendered our work in the Labour Party impossible. On the contrary, the publicity greatly assisted us. We set up a special anti-witch-hunt department at the centre, which coordinated our campaign and organised numerous events. We took on a press relations officer as we were in the media every day. Such was the avalanche of publicity that Rob Sewell's office at Hepscott Road was lined with box files filled with press cuttings from 1982 onwards. The Tendency appeared regularly on TV and radio, and often on *News at Ten* during this period.

It was under the impact of the witch-hunt and the massive publicity that accompanied it that the Militant Tendency grew quite rapidly, with 1,000 active members registered in 1980, and 4,500 by the end of 1983. In the YS, some 320 branches supported the Tendency. By contrast, only 20 supported the sects, 35 supported the left reformists, and around 35 were non-aligned.

In 1984, at the beginning of the miners' strike, our industrial Broad Left initiative, Broad Left Organising Committee (BLOC), had become the largest left force in the trade unions. For the first time in history, a Trotskyist, John MacCreadie, was elected to the General Council of the Trade Union Congress, but was manoeuvred out by the right wing. During the year-long miners' strike, given our position in the mining areas, we managed to win over 500 miners to the Tendency. In 1984, we filled the Wembley Conference centre with a Militant Rally of 3,000 supporters. In 1985, the National Rally filled the Royal Albert Hall with 5,000 supporters. In 1988, we filled the Alexandra Palace in London with 7,500 supporters, who were addressed by Ted and other comrades, including Trotsky's grandson Esteban Volkov, who spoke to the gathering by telephone from Mexico City. This was the high point of the Militant Tendency.

Ted always explained, the right wing will never give up without a fight, with no-holds-barred. The witch-hunt was being stepped up all the time. Restrictions were imposed on MPs speaking at our meetings. True, it culminated in a wave of expulsions. But here again we must have a sense of proportion. At most 220 comrades were expelled, but thousands joined our ranks. On Merseyside alone we had, if my memory serves me, over 1,500 members. A number of parties refused to carry out the bans, although some were taken over and reorganised, resulting in suspensions and expulsions. This was, however, inevitable, as the right wing—and behind them the ruling class—were never going to give up their control of the Labour Party without a ferocious struggle.

Tensions in the leadership

Ted was in general patient, loyal and tolerant in his dealings with comrades. But there was always a line that could not be crossed with him. Like Lenin and Trotsky (and also Marx and Engels), Ted was absolutely intransigent on theoretical matters. He was not prepared to tolerate even the slightest deviation on theory, or the slightest slackness. This did not necessarily make him friends.

Rob Sewell told me of one CC meeting where there was a discussion about the work of the YS. A youth comrade from the West Midlands intervened and said the way to build the YS was to engage in stunts and attract publicity. Ted immediately intervened to correct the young comrade. "Stunts are OUT! Stunts are OUT!" he said, raising his voice, which he never used to do. This time, however, he was determined to drive home the point that we must not build with the method of gimmicks and shortcuts.

I can remember another discussion on the CC, when Bryan Beckenham, who then lived in Bristol, although he was from London and was recruited in Sussex University, made a speech (I cannot remember the subject). Bryan was a good comrade but he can be classed as an "aginner"

Ted with Verónica Volkov, Trotsky's great-granddaughter at the Alexandra Palace Rally 1988

Alan Woods sharing a platform with Ted

Ted speaking at the Albert Hall rally 1985

The Alexandra Palace Militant rally 1988. Ted in the centre with a jacket.

(a kind of permanent oppositionist). On this occasion, Ted got a bit impatient and in replying said: "The trouble with the Bristol comrades is that they do not think!"

This comment merely provoked a few laughs from CC members, who were well-used to Ted and his ways. The comrades knew there was no spite or viciousness intended against Bryan or any of the Bristol comrades. Ted was completely transparent. You could see right through him, and what you saw was what you got. He spoke his mind, put everything on the table, and that was that. For that very reason, he was organically incapable of conducting manoeuvres and intrigues.

There was a growing and now permanent undercurrent of tension between Ted and Peter Taaffe, although it rarely surfaced publicly. In private conversations it was a very different matter. On many occasions, Peter complained bitterly to me about Ted, how he was quite impossible to work with, how he was causing a lot of problems, and what a hard time he (Peter) had in dealing with him. He would say "this man is impossible".

It goes without saying that I was horrified by the idea of a split between the leading comrades. On the other hand, it was not at all clear to me what or who was responsible for these conflicts. I knew that Ted could indeed be difficult and stubborn, and Peter's complaints seemed plausible. On more than one occasion, I remonstrated with Ted to be more reasonable, but was met with a sullen response. Ted already had an inkling that they were intriguing against him, but I could not believe that this was possible, and attempted to act as a conciliator. That was my big mistake.

On reflection, I can see how Peter Taaffe took advantage of every mistake made by Ted, every little conflict or difference on the Central Committee. He would not usually contradict Ted openly, but after the meetings he would approach individuals who had had some minor brush with Ted and say: "You see how this man treats you. This man is incapable of treating people as equals." Ted always sought to give the CC a political and educational character. When some people complained that "the CC is not a school", Ted would rebuke them, saying that that was just what it was. Taaffe, in private, would twist this into the idea that, for Ted the CC was *only* a school, with Ted as the headmaster: "He has no respect for people and treats important CC members like little children."

We only discovered years later how successful this tactic had been. Many CC members were influenced by these false arguments and slowly, by degrees, Ted's authority was undermined. This only shows to what degree the political level of the cadres was falling. This was especially the case after 1980, when it was agreed to make the CC a full-time body. As a result, leading industrial cadres like Pat Wall, Jim Brookshaw, Muriel Browning, Tony Mulhearn and Terry Harrison were excluded and their valuable input lost.

Peter Taaffe constantly boasted of the "high level" of the CC members, but this was just a form of flattery. In fact, the process of theoretical backsliding was becoming more and more evident. This was probably the most important element in the degeneration of the Militant.

The anti-Poll Tax campaign

Following the Liverpool struggle, we organized and led the anti-Poll Tax campaign. This was what led to the downfall of Margaret Thatcher. It was a great success, but the campaign also exposed serious weaknesses in the Tendency. As Ted put it, sometimes successes can be more dangerous than defeats. The success of the anti-Poll Tax campaign went to the heads of some of the leaders. They were, to quote an expression of Stalin, "dizzy with success".

When Thatcher introduced the retrogressive Poll Tax it was the Militant that led the battle against the Tory government, involving millions of people in a mass non-payment movement. Ted had addressed the importance of the Poll Tax soon after the 1987 general election. At the CC meeting he called for a mass campaign of non-payment to beat the tax. He predicted that a national movement could develop like the one against Lloyd George's Rent Act in 1915. This call was taken up by the Tendency, starting in Scotland, where the tax was to be introduced first.

This was to be the biggest movement of civil disobedience in British history, and it was led by the All-Britain Anti-Poll Tax Federation, which we had established and led. In March 1990, 250,000 people demonstrated in London, and a further 50,000 took to the streets of Glasgow. This impressive mass movement terrified the strategists of capital. By this time some 14 million people were refusing to pay the tax. This eventually led to the resignation of Thatcher in 1990 and the repeal of the Poll Tax.

Despite these enormous successes, however, there were serious problems in the Tendency. The most serious was that the political level of the cadres was declining, and the leadership was doing nothing to counter this trend. In the end the reason for this became clear. Ted Grant continually stressed in meetings of the Executive Committee the need to thoroughly educate and train the new comrades who entered our ranks. Unfortunately, these calls went largely unheard.

The new wave of recruits included very raw people. It was correct to recruit rapidly, but on condition that serious steps were taken to raise their political level. But very little was done to educate the new recruits in Marxist ideas. The level of the Tendency, already getting very low, was diluted even further. It was a kind of "Lenin Levy", which Stalin used to water down the Bolshevik Party with large numbers of raw, pliable members. This gave a further impetus to the process of political decline. Indeed, it was during the anti-Poll Tax movement that this process reached a decisive tipping point.

When Ted said, "Sometimes success can be more dangerous than failure", he was absolutely right. The leadership was buoyed up by success. It went to their heads. The membership was plunged into a maelstrom of pure activism. There was constant pressure from the centre to get quick results. Ted was naturally pleased by the success of the Anti-Poll Tax campaign, but he also saw the dangers. His repeated warnings were ignored by the EC who reacted in the same way as a drunken man at a party when somebody warns him that he will have a bad head in the morning. In fact, they were intoxicated with a sense of their own importance.

The dangers of the campaign possibly breaking the organisation were raised at a Regional Secretaries' meeting in September 1990. It was made clear then that the Tendency was substituting itself for the movement, that we were completely overstretched and turning ourselves into an anti-Poll Tax union instead of a revolutionary Marxist cadre organization. There was a big danger we could wreck the organisation if we continued with this. The organization was being stretched to breaking point. In many areas, the branches stopped meeting, or had become *de facto* anti-Poll Tax bodies.

The Tendency was being dissolved into the Campaign. Ted criticised the approach of the full-timers in substituting themselves for the class. "We can't do this at the expense of our organisation", he said. But from the centre the pressure was being piled on. There was no doubt that the campaign was destroying the cadres, who were exhausted by the prolonged years of

The anti-poll tax protest in London, 31 March 1990

struggle. If things were to continue like this, the Militant was on the point of self-destructing. The inner tensions in the leadership were building up. Ted began to complain more loudly.

At one Central Committee (this was after the crisis had come out into the open), he likened the way the anti-Poll Tax campaign was going to the Charge of the Light Brigade. During the Crimean War, somebody gave the order for the brigade of light cavalry to advance down a valley towards a battery of Russian heavy artillery—something that should never be done. Obeying orders, the Light Brigade advanced and was cut to ribbons. Observing this act of foolhardy bravery from a nearby mountainside, a French officer was heard to remark: "C'est manifique, mais ca n'est pas la guerre!" ("It is magnificent, but it is not the way to fight wars!")

"Dizzy with success"

I should say a few words about the role of Peter Taaffe, who came down to London from Liverpool in 1965 to assume the role of secretary of the group, since Jimmy Deane had left the country. He was our first full timer and it must be said that he did a very good job. Peter made big personal sacrifices when he came to London. He and his wife Linda, a very loyal and self-sacrificing comrade, lived in a basement flat in Hackney, bringing up a young family in difficult conditions.

Nobody can deny Peter's role in building Militant in the early years. But let us also be very clear on one thing. All the political ideas came from Ted Grant, and most of the organizational ideas came from the same source. Our successes were all the result of Ted's political guidance. He wrote all the perspectives documents and theses on national and international questions.

He led off in the political sessions of the central committees, conferences and congresses. Above all, he was responsible for the clear orientation to the mass organizations of the working class.

These were the ideas and methods that guaranteed our success, and as long as we continued on these lines we were successful. But later on some of the leaders began to get swollen heads. This was particularly true of a layer of the younger full timers who came to the fore in the 1970s. Our generation had come up the hard way. We had to fight for and earn every position. But these people did not have to fight for anything. They were immediately catapulted into leading positions which they had not won by their own efforts, and which frankly, in many cases they did not deserve.

Peter felt frustrated for a long time. I know because he frequently expressed his frustration to me. He wanted to play a bigger political role in the leadership, but was continually overshadowed by Ted. Over a time this developed into a strong personal antipathy, although he was very careful to disguise it. It emerged as little asides but never as a direct and open political clash. The reason for this was that Peter recognised Ted's colossal theoretical stature and political authority. Peter undoubtedly had talent, although his main talent lay in the organizational field. He was very intelligent and a good speaker, but he was never a theoretician. All the ideas came from Ted.

Even in the later stages of Militant's degeneration, I noticed that whenever Ted spoke, the followers of Taaffe would be looking out of the window or doodling, whereas Taaffe would be carefully taking notes of everything Ted said. There was nothing wrong with that, of course, and it showed that Taaffe was well-aware of Ted's superiority in the field of ideas. But there was another side to him, of which I only became aware many years later: he was ambitious. This had disastrous consequences for the Tendency. I do not believe that this was always the case. It developed slowly over a long period. Gradually it took the form, not so much of a theory, but of a different approach to the work, and eventually, to a very different strategy and ideas about party-building.

A fatal role was played by the group around him. These young revolutionary careerists were arrogant and pushy. They were intoxicated with the successes of the Tendency. Most if not all of them were young students straight out of university. But their knowledge of Marxism was superficial at best. Impatient for quick results, they were always looking for shortcuts and magical formulas. They favoured activism over theory, which they privately regarded with contempt. They were greedy for leading positions, which they could only get by currying favour with the general secretary. Peter encouraged them and did nothing to check their arrogance. He leaned on them for support in his clashes with Ted, and they fed his ambitions. There would be conversations in the pub, in which the parvenus would say: "Ted is too old. He is out of touch. He is putting off the youth. Why do we have to bother with him?"

Ted had always spoken at the LPYS conference Militant fringe meetings, which had become mass meetings of 2,000. There was now a deliberate campaign to prevent him from speaking. There were complaints that he spoke for too long and that he failed to explain things. This was entirely false. Ted was very popular with the young comrades. This is the impression Ted made on Greg Oxley, who had only recently joined the LPYS:

> I remember listening to Ted's speech during the 1974 Conference of the LPYS. He was a most remarkable and inspiring speaker. At times I could feel the hairs bristling on the back of my neck. The enthusiasm he could generate in young workers like myself was not because of any affected style, nor

even of any particular oratory technique. It came from the clarity and power of his ideas. Ted had a profound insight into the politics of the day, and used this to illustrate the fundamental processes at work. With every fibre of his being, he communicated an unshakable confidence in the working class and in the socialist future of mankind.

Taaffe encouraged the fairy story that Ted Grant was unable to connect with the youth. He would argue repeatedly in private: "You don't take a horse around the full race course on the first outing." The problem was that the young careerists wanted to speak and shine in the limelight, but could never compete with Ted. That irritated them and bruised their ego. They argued that the youth needed less theory and more agitation. That was quite wrong.

In fact, most of the youth loved to hear Ted speak, especially on Marxist theory. In the evenings of the YS conferences, drinking in the bar, Ted would give an impromptu question and answer session. "Ask any question you like", he would say. The young audience was completely captivated by his speeches on dialectics, science, human origins and the Big Bang. His clear and consistently materialist explanation of these fascinating questions raised their level, made them think and encouraged them to read.

From behind-the-scenes grumbling and gossip about Ted, it was only one step to behind-the-scenes manoeuvres. In this way, a clique was gradually formed that operated outside the structures of the Tendency. It was not the result of a thought-out strategy. It formed organically, spontaneously, just as crystals will form spontaneously, once a suitable medium is present. The constant backstage criticism, backbiting and jokes were intended to isolate Ted. What they did not realise is that they were behaving like a man who is sawing off the branch he is sitting on. As long as Ted's political authority in the leadership was strong, this served to hold things together. In destroying that authority, they were working for the destruction of Militant.

I was in Spain during the second half of the 1970s, when this process took shape, but I was in regular contact with the work in Britain and came back several times a year to report on our progress. Peter Taaffe, who I was on good terms with, would always ask me what I thought of the British section. He wanted to hear words of praise and usually I did not disappoint him. But I was concerned about some things. In the LPYS Conference, which I often attended, we now had a decisive majority. The right wing (who in the LPYS were really left reformist) were a small minority, and there was another, even smaller minority of sectarians. Neither of them posed any threat to us. Yet I noticed that when they moved critical resolutions, instead of answering them politically and using the debate to raise the level, they were being hammered.

I did not like this and considered it unnecessary and counterproductive. I expressed my concerns to Peter. When he asked me the usual question: "What do you think of the British section?" I said that I was concerned about some of the full timers. "Why?" he asked, surprised. "Well, for one thing I can't get a political discussion with any of them. All I get is 'ECs' and 'CCs', and 'DCs' and 'BCs'.[10] And they don't know their asshole from their elbow." I think he was genuinely shocked. But it was the truth.

Of course, Peter Taaffe was far superior to the elements that surrounded him. He understood Ted's role very well. He did not seek to drive Ted out of the organization. He just wanted a bit more of the limelight. Had he not earned it by his tireless work all those years? And was Ted not becoming an obstacle? What he wanted was for Ted to take a back seat, to retire gracefully and hand over the organization to the "Young Guard".

---

[10] Executive, Central, District and Branch committees

He once said to me: "Don't you think a man of Ted's age should be sitting in front of a fire reading the paper with his slippers on?" He said it in his usual joking style, so I just laughed. But Ted did not see the funny side of it. He said: "What they want is to put me in a back room where I can write the documents and give them ideas. I am not a back-room boy and never will be!"

Looking back on it now, one can see the process that was taking place. Of course, the wisdom of hindsight is the cheapest kind. It was not easy to see a process that took shape only gradually, so gradually as to be imperceptible. That was especially true of me, as I was living in Spain at this time. However, there was another, more important reason. If you are not looking for something, you are not likely to see it. After all, we had spent years fighting to win these positions, so it was like a dream come true. The successes of the Tendency were real and palpable. I was therefore not inclined to seriously criticise or to find fault. That was my mistake.

The notion that a leading comrade could put personal prestige before the interests of the working class and the socialist revolution seemed so alien to me that I never seriously took it into account. One could understand how a person could be greedy for office in a big organization, say the Labour Party, a trade union or the Soviet Union. But to be greedy to hold office in what was, after all, a relatively small and poor revolutionary group—that was beyond my comprehension altogether.

When things finally came to a head, the Majority reacted indignantly to the accusation that there was a bureaucratic regime in the organization (though it was quite true). They said: "From a Marxist point of view, a bureaucracy must have a material basis. Where are our privileges? We do not have big salaries." Answering this argument, Ted said: "A bureaucracy does not necessarily have a material base. You can have a bureaucracy in a football club or an old ladies' knitting circle, not a bureaucracy like that of the trade unions or the Soviet Union, but a particularly poisonous bureaucracy based on personal prestige, back stabbing, intrigues and the struggle for positions." How right he was!

Manoeuvres in the International

Peter Taaffe asked me if I wanted help at the International Centre. There were a number of comrades from Britain who could help. I confess I was very pleased to accept, since we were seriously understaffed. They sent me "reinforcements" in the persons of Tony Saunois, Laurence Coates and a couple of others. The last-named was the son of Ken Coates, who we have already mentioned. If I were a genetic determinist, I might have said that he had inherited all the unlovely traits of his progenitor, multiplied by a factor of ten. He was the worst of a bad bunch, but they were all "cadres" of the Taaffe School. The problems began almost immediately.

In Hepscott Road they habitually referred to the International as "the international department". That little detail speaks volumes about their real attitude to the CWI (Committee for a Workers' International). It was seen as a mere adjunct to the British section and its leadership. Any petty little pygmy from Britain imagined him- or herself a giant in comparison to the leaders of other sections. The International ought to know its place! They basked in the achievements of others and gloried in a borrowed authority that they had not earned and did not deserve.

This psychological attitude was given a physical manifestation when, alleging lack of office space, the "international department" was consigned to a portakabin in the parking space

Ted with Ana Muñoz

outside the main building at Hepscott Road. These young careerists now felt supremely confident. Sitting behind their desks in the portakabin, with a direct line to the General Secretary, they felt they had at last "arrived". They had the "power" and could do just what they liked. The only slight problem was that there were some people in the way, namely Ted Grant, Alan Woods and Ana Muñoz. But so what? They would be dealt with sooner or later.

They began to move into different national sections. The other sections were mainly quite small and their leaders young and inexperienced. The authority of the British section was colossal. So it was quite natural that people would assume that any full timer from the International would have the same authority.

The "cadres" began to lord it over the sections, strutting around like peacocks. Although they had no real grasp of Marxism they saw themselves as great theoreticians. Listening to them reminded me of those books: *Idiot's Guide to Philosophy* or *Politics for Dummies*, etc. When they spoke, the noises that came out sounded vaguely as if they were saying something profound. But when you came to analyse it, they had said nothing at all. This could not last. In the well-known phrase of Abraham Lincoln: You can fool some of the people all of the time, and all of the people some of the time, but you cannot fool all of the people all of the time. There was one conflict after another. I was receiving complaints about the conduct of international full timers. But there was not a lot I could do about it on my own.

I complained repeatedly to Peter about the conduct of some of the young full timers he had sent into the International "department", allegedly to help me. In reality, they were doing the opposite. I would tell him my concerns and he would listen intently and take note. He always appeared sympathetic. He would make all the right noises: "Did he really do that? I see. Well, I must have a word with him about that." "Don't worry, I will deal with it", etc. It was all an act, of course. I am sure he did speak to his "boys" afterwards. He would say something like: "You had better be more careful. Alan is asking questions." Things would calm down for a while, then the whole wretched business would start all over again.

Ted told me I was wasting my time: "You are complaining to Satan against Beelzebub", he said. He was quite right, as it happens. Ana and I were being systematically marginalised. Saunois and Coates had a direct line to the Boss's office and decisions were being made behind our backs. The conduct of Coates towards Ana was particularly despicable. Constant petty harassment, pressure, and humiliation were enough to undermine the morale of a comrade who had always showed exemplary devotion and loyalty to the revolutionary cause.

I have no doubt that this was a cowardly way of getting at me—through my wife. In order not to add to the pressures on me, she did not inform me of what was going on. Ana had been through the harsh school of underground revolutionary work under the Franco dictatorship. She was caught by the police after a demonstration and was detained and beaten up. She is no coward and never complains. Yet she told me later that she suffered more from this harassment than she had at the hands of Franco's police. In the end she had a nervous breakdown.

Is that so hard to understand? We are revolutionaries. We expect to be attacked and harmed by the class enemy. But to be betrayed and ill-treated by one's own comrades—that is very hard to bear. In this way, even the hardest revolutionaries find themselves disarmed in the face of the aggressions of people without any moral scruples who usurp positions of responsibility and abuse them for their own ends.

Things got worse. There followed a whole series of "incidents". The leader of the French section, Greg Oxley, was summarily expelled. The female leader of the Danish group had a nervous breakdown, and there was a crisis in Sweden. There was also a crisis in Greece. We discovered that the Irish leadership had resigned. I believe the decisive year was 1989.

Then in 1990, we learned that the majority of the German EC (four out of six) had resigned. In the case of Germany, this was connected with the revolutionary crisis in the East, where the masses were on the streets and the Stalinist regime was crumbling. I believe that the comrades in West Germany made some political mistakes in their approach to these developments. But it was our job to convince them, not to ride roughshod over them. Instead, the German EC was completely ignored and marginalised.

The method of removing leaders of national sections was first practiced by John Throne in the early 1980s in Germany when he sent Hans Gerd Öffinger, a co-founder of the section, out of the national centre to work in the provinces. This was roughly similar to Khrushchev sending Malenkov to work as the manager of a power plant in Kazakhstan. It was a very bad precedent. From 1986 Bob Labi was put in charge of Germany, a task for which he was entirely unfit. As a result, there was a crisis. A new leadership was installed that could be relied upon to follow the Line from London.

The reasons for these crises and resignations were never made clear to Ted or me. By this time, we had been effectively sidelined. It is clear that all the information was being censored by somebody at the centre. The extent to which we were being kept in the dark only emerged later, when the crisis in Militant had erupted. We sent comrade Alistair Wilson to Dublin in the summer of 1991 to make contact with Finn Geany. I believe Finn was our first member in the South of Ireland. But I had had no direct dealings with him and therefore had no telephone number. Alistair found his phone number in a Dublin telephone directory and I rang him up. The conversation went like this:

> Hello, Finn, how are you?
> Very well, thanks, how'se yourself?
> It's been a long time.
> Yes it has [pause] I suppose you know I am no longer a member of the organization?
> Yes, Finn, I did know that. But I don't know why.
> WHAT?! You mean you have not read our letter?
> What letter?

It appears that the comrades who resigned sent a letter to the IS in 1989, explaining the reasons for their action and making a series of criticisms of the way the Irish section was being run. Neither Ted nor I ever saw that letter. If we had done so, at the very least we would have asked questions. But that letter got as far as somebody's desk in Hepscott Road and no further. Naturally, when the comrades got no reply, what were they supposed to think? They would assume that the IS was united in rejecting them. How many other letters went the same way? We may never know.

The Walton adventure

By now the rise of Militant seemed unstoppable. The BBC journalist Michael Crick, who wrote a book about Militant, described it as the fifth political party in Britain. We were not a party, of course, but there is some truth in this assertion. But all that was soon to be thrown away in an irresponsible adventure. In April 1991, the group around Taaffe convinced him to launch a "new turn" in Scotland and create an open organisation. All this was done behind the backs of the organisation and its elected bodies.

Earlier the same year, a National Conference was held in London. A British Perspectives document, written by Ted dated November 12, 1990, was presented, and adopted by a unanimous vote. In this document there was not the slightest hint of any change in our tactics or the work in the Labour Party. Yet, within a few months the whole situation had changed. In June, the Tendency was demagogically stampeded into fighting a by-election in Walton, Liverpool. The Liverpool comrades decided to stand Leslie Mahmoud as a "Real Labour" candidate against the official Labour candidate Peter Kilfoyle. This was backed by Peter Taaffe.

How is it possible to explain the suddenness of the change? Such an important turn, which represented a dramatic break with all our previous traditions and methods of work, ought to have been the result of a thorough and democratic debate at every level of the organization. It was not. The whole thing had been cooked up behind the backs of the organization. For years, some of the people in Liverpool had been inclined to leave the Labour Party, particularly after the witch-hunt that followed the defeat of the struggle around Liverpool Council. At that time they were dissuaded by the EC. Peter Taaffe agreed with Ted that such a move would be disastrous. But by now he had changed his mind.

The leadership decided to prioritise this campaign. Militant poured in comrades from all over Britain and even abroad. No expense was spared, and the comrades were encouraged to believe that we could win the seat even against the Labour Party. It showed how far out of touch with reality the leading circle had become. The result was a shock. Leslie got 2,613 votes, while 21,317 votes were cast for the Labour candidate Kilfoyle. Despite all the work we had done, and despite the superhuman efforts put into the election campaign, we had been decisively rejected. The members were shattered, but instead of reconsidering their position, the majority leadership proclaimed the disastrous result as a "success", which should be followed in other parts of the country! *Militant* published on its front page a banner heading: *2,613 Votes for Socialism*!

Anybody can make a mistake. But if a mistake is not corrected it will lead to bigger and more serious mistakes. Instead of acknowledging their mistake, the Majority approved a resolution on Walton, which hailed the experience as a great success. In it we read: "We have put down a marker for the future" (paragraph 6). It continues: "We took a principled stand in Walton"; as a result "our credibility will be greatly enhanced". It went on: "We reaffirm the correctness of our decision to stand in Walton" (paragraph 7). "Any decision by us not to stand would not have been understood by the best workers in the Liverpool area. It would have been a dereliction of duty to our class and would have led to the demoralisation of the forces of the left in Liverpool." And so on and so forth.

All the time they continued to feed their supporters with wild exaggerations, like the following: "Real Labour has been going three weeks in Walton. (...) Already Walton Real Labour has more members than the official Labour Party. *We will go on; the left will take control of the City Council within the next two years.*" (Article by Leslie Mahmood in *Militant*, July 5, 1991, my emphasis, AW).

Life itself dealt a fatal blow to these illusions. In the May 1992 local elections, the Broad Left candidates were wiped out and Leslie lost her seat. It was downhill from then on. As Ted had warned, this adventurism destroyed all the gains that forty years of patient work had achieved in Liverpool. And things did not stop there. Within a relatively short period of time, following the subsequent expulsion of Ted, myself, and the rest of the Minority, the leadership of the Liverpool organisation was expelled and the Tendency on Merseyside collapsed, resulting in wholesale demoralisation.

What Ted said about Walton

The group around Peter Taaffe, which was an undeclared faction within the leadership, decided to follow the well-trodden path of all the sects and break from the Labour Party. First there was the Walton electoral adventure, followed in rapid succession by the so-called Scottish turn, which Ted rightly described as a threat to forty years' work.

Ted Grant was naturally opposed to the Walton adventure. But the leading group was determined to press on regardless. In order to do this, they first had to destroy Ted's authority and remove him, and those of us who supported him, from the scene. Very quickly it led to a severe internal crisis and a devastating split.

A minority resolution, drafted by Ted and Rob Sewell, was presented to the CC meeting which was held shortly after the by-election defeat. This was in response to the majority resolution that praised the Walton adventure. It is worth quoting in full:

1. If we are to develop the organisation and prepare the ground for the future, we have a duty to seriously weigh up all our actions in the light of experience and learn the lessons of our mistakes. Those who fail to recognise their errors or admit mistakes, stated Trotsky many times, will never be able to construct a viable, healthy organisation.

2. To characterise the Walton result as some type of "Victory" is to completely misread the situation

Ted with Italian comrades in the late 1980s

and miseducate the ranks of the organisation. Our first responsibility is to tell the ranks what it is, and not what we would like it to be. To dress up a setback in this fashion is the worst kind of deception for a Marxist organisation.

3. In making these criticisms, we do not for a moment take away the sterling efforts and sacrifice of the comrades involved in the election campaign who sought against all the odds to secure an electoral victory.

4. The problem lies squarely with the false policy of standing independently.

5. The policy was rushed through the CC after it was given a completely exaggerated, and therefore erroneous, view of the position in Walton. The majority of comrades, unfortunately, allowed themselves to be influenced mainly by subjective considerations, i.e. their hatred of Kilfoyle. It is true that Kilfoyle is a gangster, but this is the case with most of the right-wing candidates nationally.

6. The argument, used by the majority to justify their position, that we must orient our work for the next period "independently" is nothing new. We have to a great extent, both nationally and internationally, been forced to do so by the collapse of Left reformism, the boom, the swing to the right by social democracy and the virtual collapse in many countries of Stalinist parties. But our orientation towards the mass organisations was crucial. To put up a candidate in Walton was to break with the method, perspectives and theory formulated over forty years. As is the suggestion now that, despite the defeat in Walton, candidates may be put up in Scotland and elsewhere.

Our greatest gain over a period of decades was that we became a crucial and component part of the left. Despite the collapse of the left in both the trade unions and the Labour Party, we would have been strategically placed to become an important and even dominant part of the left.

7. A great part of the political capital of the Tendency in Britain and internationally was the fact that we were conceived as a component part of the labour and trade union movement. We were entirely

different to the sects, who try and create phantom "mass" revolutionary parties outside of the time, experience and consciousness of the masses.

8. Apart from a few countries the classical conditions for entrism have not existed for forty years. This was certainly the case in Britain. All our trade union and political work has to be determined by our orientation towards the Labour Party.

9. The classical conditions for entrism will undoubtedly arise during the next epoch—two, three, five or even ten years—as the crisis of world capitalism, and especially British capitalism, unfolds.

10. These conditions are:

i) A revolutionary or semi-revolutionary crisis.

ii) The leadership of social democracy loses complete control of the Party.

iii) The masses move to left reformist or even centrist conclusions—there is a social ferment within the party. The left membership becomes open to revolutionary and Marxist ideas.

iv) The subjective factor is present to take advantage of the situation.

11. But by putting up a candidate or candidates this work is jeopardised. It can lead to a complete miseducation of the new layers, especially the youth, who may move towards us in the next few years. It is a complete miseducation of the cadres, who can draw dangerous conclusions. They can become ultra-left and adventuristic, this in its turn rapidly leading to passivity and substitutionalism.

12. There could be an argument for an independent revolutionary party, though incorrect. But to put forward the idea of an "alternative" or "real" Labour Party would necessarily be still-born. To be neither fish, nor flesh, nor fowl is to get the worst of all worlds. A few years ago we had a good laugh at the expense of the Lambertists in France who tried to create a substitute Socialist Party. Like the Lambertists, the attempt to create a "substitute" Labour Party in Liverpool can only end in tears.

13. The perception of many workers in the trade union—who regard the Labour Party as their party—would be that of regarding us as alien to their political aspirations. The propaganda in the *Militant* over the last four weeks would reinforce this impression.

14. Up to now workers have recognised that we are organised, but as a component part of the Labour Party. But now the setting up of an "organisation" or Party in Scotland will break this view. The illusion that such an organisation or Party could gain affiliation to the Labour Party, like the Independent Labour Party (ILP) or the Co-op, is false and even dangerous.

15. The ILP and the Co-op, despite the former adopting a centrist policy for a time, had an affinity with the Labour bureaucracy. They were not afraid of the ILP, but regarded it as a possible left flank when the workers moved left, preventing them drawing revolutionary conclusions. They would be terrified of a revolutionary Marxist organisation or Party. The bureaucracy changed the constitution to prevent the affiliation of the CP in the immediate post-war period. There is no possibility of even the most leftward Labour Party accepting the affiliation of a Marxist party or organisation.

16. Now, if before or after the general election Kinnock launches a mass purge nationally the results could be disastrous. Formerly, if a mass purge was launched we would have retained the sympathy and support of wide layers in the Labour Party and trade unions. Now they would be indifferent. If you have an independent party or organisation go ahead and organise it. You can paddle your own canoe without being linked to the line of Labour.

17. The argument that when the conditions for entrism arise we can switch policies will not hold water. Youth and industrial workers, miseducated by an "independent" orientation would not be prepared to change. We would have a crisis in the organisation of massive proportions. Moreover it would be very difficult to get back under these conditions. At the same time we would lose many if not most of the new movement.

19. At best this has been jeopardised by the ultra-left binge in Liverpool and now in Scotland. The full effects of the defeats in Liverpool and nationally will be shown in the next few years.

20. As predicted the "Broad Left" did very little apart from our own comrades. Now it will fall apart. The Broad Left in any event comprises around 400 people—100 in Walton, 300 in the rest of Liverpool.

21. The mistake of the majority comrades was not to understand that the "left" in the trade unions and Labour Party was running in advance of the broad mass of workers. Now the entire Liverpool Labour Party and trade unions have been handed over to the right wing for a number of years.

22. The Liverpool organisation will have to maintain two apparatuses—the "real" Labour Party and Militant.

23. The Labour Party nationally has been reduced to a skeleton. But it is not Labour which will "wither on the vine" but the artificial Labour Party which is being created in Liverpool.

24. The "left", having stubbed their toes on the reactionary policies of the reformists on the councils, in the unions and the national bureaucracy, in their "impatience" can draw for a while ultra-left and "radical" conclusions, only later to go back to reformist conclusions because the mass of workers "let them down".

25. On the industrial front we have the example of Pilkingtons in the early 1970s, when the selling out of a strike by the national leadership of the GMBU under Lord Cooper led in desperation to the setting up of an "independent union". This was supported by the SWP, WRP, CP and the *Tribune* lefts. We alone opposed it and pointed out the consequences. The majority of workers did not support it and the employers and union bureaucracy joined together to smash the union.

26. Unfortunately, many of the Liverpool comrades, on the basis of their success in the council elections, thought they could repeat this on the parliamentary plane. Instead of most of the leading comrades of the Tendency firmly opposing this, they capitulated to this mood. This will have grievous consequences for the Tendency in Liverpool and nationally.

27. That is the lesson of the attempts to create independent "left" Labour Parties in the pre-war and post-war period. All such efforts were doomed to failure. This new adventure on the part of the Liverpool comrades will inevitably fail, and will have as a spin-off a bad effect on the Liverpool organisation which right up to the present has to be subsidised by the national Tendency.

28. The new layers in the trade unions, even with a right-wing Labour government will not orient toward us but towards the Labour Party in order to change it. Far from being a "detour", it is a blind alley to which the comrades are being led.

29. The argument that there was no alternative to standing is false from beginning to end. The fact that 500 workers attending Eric Heffer's funeral wanted a candidate to stand showed the lack of objectivity and sense of proportion of the Liverpool and national leadership. Liverpool has a population of 500,000—Walton is a constituency of 70,000.

30. The idea that we had to stand, due to pressure from the working class, was proved to be false given the vote and the lack of participation by the Broad Left. In effect, the organisation substituted itself for the Broad Left.

31. At each stage, the majority comrades had to change their over-exaggerated views and expectations given the response from the workers of Walton. As the campaign progressed, reports varied from "victory" to "neck and neck", then "substantial vote", down to 10,000 votes, 5,000 votes, then lastly to 3,000 votes. Of course this change was not alluded to in our public material and seemed to disorient our comrades and supporters.

32. Big concessions were made to the non-comrades in the Broad Left: not to sell papers openly,

collect FF [Fighting Fund], etc., no Militant leaflets on the official canvass. Recruitment was not seen as the priority despite the majority targets of doubling and trebling the membership on Merseyside. Everything was subordinated to maximising the vote. Even the programme that we stood on was not a revolutionary one. There was no explanation of the capitalist crisis and the need for a socialist planned economy, etc. The programme we offered the workers of Walton was in effect a left-reformist one. Our ideas were sacrificed to preserve the "unity" of the Broad Left—which refused to participate in the campaign in any case. It appears now they are preparing to attack us for undermining the campaign!

33. The argument that if we had refused to stand the rest of the Broad Left would have nominated a candidate is specious. We had a majority of the Broad Lefts and could have exerted pressure against this. In reality we pushed the issue. On the other hand if a splinter "Broad Left" had stood we could have disassociated ourselves from them. We could have supported the official Labour candidate while criticising Kilfoyle and the local and national bureaucracy of the Labour Party and putting forward a socialist and revolutionary policy.

34. There is nothing "new" in this. We have maintained this position in contradistinction to the sects for many years. A campaign of education of our Tendency in Liverpool could have prevented the fiasco of Walton. In the next period we could lose members and supporters in Liverpool as the futility of maintaining a dead "real" Labour Party becomes obvious to all.

35. For the last decades we have been criticised by the sects for alleged "passivity" and "adaptation" to the bureaucracy because we refused to break with the Labour Party. We laughed at this stupidity. Now for want of a better argument the majority have adopted the same spurious criticism of the minority. A continuation of the tried and tested policy of Marxism is hardly passivity.

36. We have been to the fore in advocating that the Tendency takes initiatives and independent work, but always with the proviso that all the work is subject to our general orientation, perspectives, strategy and tactics.

37. The action has undoubtedly played into the hands of Kinnock, Kilfoyle and Rimmer, who were able to portray the result as a victory for them and a rejection of the organisation by the workers of Walton. It will now be used, as was predicted beforehand, as the excuse for a purge in Liverpool and elsewhere.

38. In order that we can avoid disastrous mistakes of this type in the future, it is necessary to recognise the reality of the situation and draw out all the lessons concerning the medium and long-term development of our work.

39. Above all, we must strive to avoid the sickness of ultra-leftism and impatience. The Walton episode can only be seen in this light. That is why the proposed "Scottish turn"—the launching of an independent organisation—would be a grave mistake and result in the abandonment of 40 years of entrist work.

Only two votes were cast for this resolution, but Ted and Rob asked for it to be circulated to the membership. After a long delay, it was circulated, clearly marked "minority". In addition, an addendum was attached giving the CC voting figures, a practise that had never been seen before, even with the Coxhead document. The reason for this was to show that the "minority" was *crushed* by the "majority", and to give a clear message to the rank and file. For the "majority", every means was permissible if it served to secure their victory.

The Scottish turn

Pressurised by our criticisms, the Majority still paid lip service to the importance of the Labour Party. The Majority resolution says that "Under the impact of major industrial and political conflicts, left-reformist and even centrist currents will appear inside the Labour Party" (paragraph 11) and that *"the Labour Party remains the mass party of the British working class and it remains imperative that we orientate towards any developments within it"*. (*Majority resolution on Walton*, July 1991, paragraph 12, my emphasis, AW).

Soon after this, the Majority stated:

> We will not therefore, as the sects in the past have done, put a minus against the Labour Party... Even if the official ink with the unions is broken, this will not mean that the Labour Party will be historically "exhausted".
>
> Inevitably, a movement of the proletariat will find its reflection within that party from the direction of the trade unions. (*Nationalism, Scotland and the Marxist approach*, May 1992, pp. 13-14)

However, within a comparatively short period, this whole perspective was unceremoniously jettisoned. Almost overnight, and with no serious explanation, the Labour Party allegedly became a "bourgeois party", no different from the Tories and Liberal Democrats. Now, instead of "orientating towards any developments within the Labour Party", they are calling on the unions to disaffiliate from Labour.

Peter Taaffe at the Royal Albert Hall rally 1984

During the so-called debate over the "turn", they systematically distorted the ideas of the Minority: "Irrespective of time, place or circumstance the task, said Ted Grant, was for Marxists to merely sit in the Labour Party waiting for support to materialise when 'objective' conditions had sufficiently matured." (Peter Taaffe, *Militant's Real History: In Reply to Ted Grant and Rob Sewell*, October 2002). Where did we ever state this nonsense? There is no reference, as no reference exists. It is merely a repetition of the lies spread by the sects about us in the past!

The Walton adventure was quickly followed by the Scottish turn. In the beginning, this was presented as a purely local, Scottish affair, which they justified in terms of the concrete conditions in Scotland: The Majority document says: "*There exist in Scotland specific conditions which have forced us to reconsider a major tactical shift.*" (*Scotland—Perspectives and Tasks, 1991*, my emphasis, AW)

Thus, the supporters of the Majority argued that the need for a "major tactical shift" was dictated *by purely local conditions in Scotland*, namely the rise of Scottish nationalism and the growing electoral strength of the SNP. Ted pointed out that the real position of the Majority was not peculiar to Scotland. He warned that the Scottish turn would be the British turn tomorrow, and the international turn the day after tomorrow.

The "major tactical shift" was the setting up of an independent party in Scotland, although nowhere was this stated. The Minority document, which was dictated by Ted, answered this argument as follows:

> That the SNP might begin to grow on the basis of the betrayal of reformism is entirely possible. But the argument that we can somehow prevent this from happening by setting up an open organisation in Scotland is false from beginning to end. Only by the struggle to arm the labour movement with a correct policy can a movement towards nationalism be checked. (Ted Grant, *The New Turn—A Threat to Forty Years Work*)

How vehemently did they deny this! They accused the Minority of telling lies, of putting words into their mouths and so on. All the while they were prodding the Tendency in the direction of the sectarian swamp, while loudly proclaiming their innocence. They proceeded cautiously, like a hunter who does not wish to startle his prey before shooting it.

As late as 1993, they were still indignantly denying the accusation that they would break with the Labour Party:

> We are not repeating the ultra-left mistakes of the sects, particularly of the SWP. For them the Labour Party is dead and there is no question of it being brought back to life with an influx of workers in the future. (*EC Reply to ex-Minority*, February 10, 1993)

And once again:

> Nothing that we have said or done can be misconstrued as a "break" with the perspective we have worked out for the Labour Party. Nowhere have we proposed an "open Revolutionary Party". The ex-minority tries to build such a case on the basis of one or two isolated off-the-cuff comments. (*Ibid.*)

The Majority document called *Scotland: Perspectives and Tasks* (1991), states in paragraph 7:

> Of course, it is necessary to avoid the quagmire of ultra-leftism. As a tendency, we have always resisted the temptation to run too far ahead of events, to overestimate our own forces, to rush into rash and reckless decisions which we would later regret. History is littered with the corpses of would-be revolutionary groups who have run aground on the rock of ultra-leftism.

The irony is that this precisely happened to them. And again:

> It is not true that "all the sections of the old international are moving to break away from the mass organisations" (...) There is no International Turn. (*EC Reply to ex-minority*)

These constant denials reminded one of the famous line in Shakespeare's *Hamlet* (Act III, scene II): "The lady doth protest too much, methinks." It was all a lie. Ted comprehensively demolished the dishonest attempts by the Majority to present the turn as a little local "detour" dictated by local conditions:

> The advocates of the Scottish turn allege the existence of specific conditions in Scotland, which do not apply elsewhere. The same argument about specific conditions in Liverpool was used only yesterday to justify the Walton turn and we predict that tomorrow, we will be told about special conditions in Wales, Birmingham, London and elsewhere to justify the same thing. (Ted Grant, *The New Turn—A Threat to Forty Years Work*)

This analysis was one hundred percent correct. While continuing to deny any intention of breaking with Labour, they were slyly inching towards this inevitable conclusion, as we see from this statement:

> While the Scottish turn arose from specific conditions in Scotland, it has now to be recognised that similar conditions (...) exist throughout Britain. (*CC Resolution*, November 1992)

They soon discovered that "similar conditions" existed, not only throughout Britain, but throughout the world. Just as Ted had predicted, the Scottish turn soon became the British turn. In the rest of Britain, they followed suit, adopting the name of Socialist Party of England and Wales, to demonstrate their separate identity from Scotland (though why Wales should be any different to Scotland remains a mystery).

What was supposed to be a little local "detour" dictated exclusively by peculiar conditions to the north of Hadrian's Wall was now a universal principle, applicable to the entire terrestrial globe.

They did not feel confident enough immediately to break all links with Labour. In Walton they had stood as "Real Labour". In Scotland they set up Scottish Militant Labour. But this transitional stage, was neither fish, nor flesh, nor fowl. So they inevitably ended up by creating a separate, politically autonomous Scottish party, ostensibly to speak in the name of the Scottish working class.

This soon became evident when, in 1998, Scottish Militant Labour was transformed into the Scottish Socialist Party and adopted the aim of an "independent socialist Scotland". This initiative in Scotland was an attempt to emulate the earlier split-off from Labour in 1976, when John Sillars and Robertson set up the ill-fated Scottish Labour Party. We condemned this split at the time, but this was conveniently forgotten.

Adapting to nationalism

The Scottish turn was supposed to be a reply to the continued rise of nationalism in Scotland. It consisted in setting up an independent party, under the name of Scottish Militant Labour. This was supposedly meant to undercut the dangers of Scottish nationalism. In effect, although they vehemently denied it, the leaders of the majority group were bending to the pressures of nationalism. Soon after our expulsion, Ted Grant wrote a public document called, *Scotland: Socialism or Nationalism*, where we read:

> The attempt to create a breakaway "independent" movement in the form of the SML is an adventure, doomed to failure, and will not have the desired effect of preventing the growth of nationalist moods among sections of the youth and workers. On the contrary, the type of arguments now being advanced by these comrades, which in effect pander to nationalist prejudices will have the opposite effect. (Ted Grant, *Scotland: Socialism or Nationalism?* March 1992)

The truth was that the leaders of the Majority in Scotland were impressed by the success of the bourgeois SNP and were inclined to adapt to nationalist prejudices. This, however, they hotly denied:

> On no occasion have we adapted our programme to take account of the positions of the SNP or Liberals, and of course, the ex-minority cannot give any details. It is enough for them simply to shout "popular front" and their case is proven. Fortunately, comrades are not so easily duped. (*EC Reply to ex-Minority*)

But facts are stubborn things. Although Taaffe and the leaders of the Militant majority strenuously denied this pandering to nationalism, we can see how things turned out. Alan McCombes and Tommy Sheridan, the main leaders of the SML, leaned ever-more towards nationalism. This became more pronounced and even more disastrous with the transformation of SML into the Scottish Socialist Party (SSP). By the end of 2000, both McCombes and Sheridan broke publicly with Taaffe and the CWI, and took with them the SSP, together with the vast majority of its members. Taaffe was left with a tiny group mainly based in Dundee.

Initially, the SSP did make an impact. Given the growing disillusionment with the Blair government in London, they were able for a while to tap into the mood of a layer to the left of Labour and managed to win six SMPs and two councillors in May 2003.

Ironically, this success pushed them further in the direction of Scottish nationalism. The leaders of the SSP became the greatest champions of independence. Tommy Sheridan and Alan McCombes wrote a book called *Imagine*, which they published shortly after their break with the CWI and reveals to what extent they had already abandoned Marxism:

> Socialists should be prepared to support such a step [independence], even on a non-socialist basis as promoted by the SNP.

Furthermore:

> The material foundations already exist in Scotland for a thriving, blooming socialist democracy (...) We have land, water, fish, timber, oil, gas and electricity in abundance. We have a moderate climate, where floods, droughts and hurricanes are almost [sic!] unknown. (Sheridan and McCombes, *Imagine—A socialist vision for the 21st century*, pp. 183-4 and p. 189)

The trajectory of the SML and the SSP represented the abandonment of everything we had stood for in the past. They were repeating the mistake of John MacLean who put forward the need for a separate Scottish Workers' Republic. MacLean's mistake arose also from frustration and a lack of confidence in the militancy of workers in the rest of Britain, but within a few years, the whole of Britain was rocked by a General Strike in 1926.

The opportunism of the SSP leaders was shown even more when, in 2004, Alan McCombes went so far as to proclaim the benefits of the SNP electing a "left" candidate to lead the SNP.

> A victory or either Roseanna Cunningham or Alex Neil—both of them capable and charismatic figures—would have the effect of regenerating interest in politics generally. It would help to shift the ideological centre of gravity in Scotland further to the left and, at the same time, strengthen support for independence. All of this would create a more politicised climate, favourable to both the SNP and the SSP. (Alan McCombes, *Where now for the SNP*, *Scottish Socialist Voice*, July 2, 2004)

The SSP leaders went on to propose the establishment of an "independence convention", a bloc between the SSP, SNP, and the Greens. They became champions of independence. "The clearest route to independence", stated McCombes, "is the fast, broad highway of the independence convention, involving a *united front of the SNP, the SSP, the Greens and other pro-independence forces*." (*Scottish Socialist Voice*, March 5, 2006, my emphasis—AW)

What is being proposed here is not a united front of workers' organizations, but a popular front on nationalist lines, including the bourgeois SNP. There is not an atom of class content in it. And how the SNP was supposed to accept the idea of an "independent socialist Scotland" is anybody's guess. Clearly, the word "socialist" in the slogan of the SSP was intended purely for decorative purposes.

Ted had already explained:

> One cannot fight nationalism by pandering to the nationalists and separatist prejudices. (...) The launching of SML is an adventure. The comrades lack a sense of proportion and are repeating the experience of sectarian groups on the fringes of the Labour movement. It will end in disaster. (Ted Grant, *Scotland: Socialism or Nationalism*, March 1992)

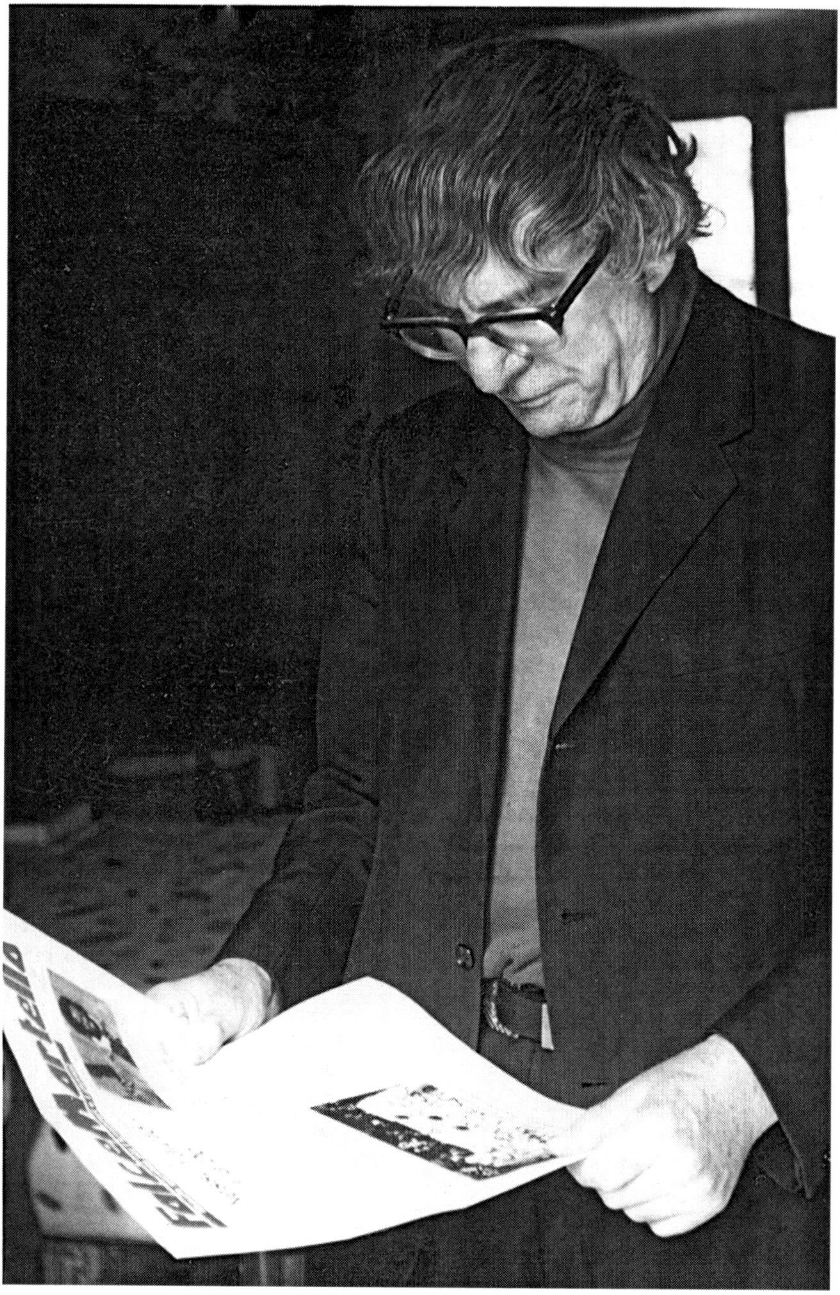

Subsequent events, with the evolution and collapse of the SSP, have shown this to be a hundred percent correct.

The early successes of the SSP gave them big ideas. Its leaders were riding high. They soon concluded that they had no further need for the people in London and split away. The powerful Scottish organization that Militant had built was no more. Taaffe was left with hardly anything in Scotland.

By 2007, however, the initial gains by the SSP, which showed that there was indeed a constituency for the Left in Scotland, were all lost and the party imploded. It gives one no pleasure to say this, but it is time to remind the comrades of the SSP that in the building of the revolutionary party there are no shortcuts.

From the very beginning the venture was fatally flawed. To pander to Scottish nationalism was a complete break with the Marxist approach to the national question, which, while defending the right to national self-determination, emphasizes and fights for the sacred unity of the working class across national and ethnic lines. Even if one were to accept the need for an open party, as Ted did in the specific conditions of the Second World War with the RCP, it would have to stand on a clear revolutionary Marxist and internationalist banner. Otherwise it would have no reason to exist. It would moreover face towards the Labour Movement and offer a united front against the Tories, Liberals and Nationalists on the basis of a socialist programme. But the SSP did no such thing. It stood on a purely reformist programme with a fatal admixture of Scottish nationalism. In other words, it attempted to combat the SNP by stealing its clothes.

The attempt to break the political dominance of the Labour Party, or even establish a sizeable party to its left, ended in ignominious failure. It did not displace the Labour Party; nor did it do anything to combat nationalism. On the contrary, by spreading nationalist illusions in a layer of advanced workers and youth, it merely served to provide an even greater space for the Scottish nationalists.

The crisis breaks

In the history of the Marxist movement it often happens that splits take place that apparently have no political basis. But in fact, there is always a political basis. The classic example was the split between Lenin and Martov in 1903. That split ultimately led to the creation of the two main trends in the Russian labour movement: Bolshevism and Menshevism.

However, if one reads the minutes of the Second Congress of the RSDLP one would look in vain for any political differences. Apparently there were none. The differences were in fact implicit in the clash between the "Hards" and the "Softs". The real political differences only emerged in the months following the split.

The split in Militant definitely had a political basis. The Majority were hell-bent on pushing the Tendency down the ultra left road. Within the leadership, Ted, Rob Sewell and I were firmly opposed to this ultra-left "turn". Hegel pointed out, that necessity expresses itself through accident. A few months before the Walton affair, a violent row broke out within the international leadership. The immediate clash occurred, not immediately over the "turn", but on a seemingly insignificant matter: the speakers' list at an international meeting. That would appear to be an accidental question.

Peter Taaffe was a very cautious individual, and was not anxious to provoke an open rift with Ted and myself, the outcome of which was uncertain. But his protégés, our "Young Turks", were pushing all the time. They were greedy for prestige and reckless about the consequences. Like all petty-bourgeois, they put their personal interests before those of the class and the party.

Taking advantage of my absence (I was in Mexico), they put forward a list of speakers for an international school, all of whom were selected from the Taaffe clique in Britain. Not one of them was an elected member of the IS, or even the IEC. Quite apart from the fact that this was a complete breach of accepted procedure, the proposed speakers had not been chosen for their political abilities (which were at best limited), but purely on their loyalty to the general secretary. It was a blatant attempt to up the ante in an effort by the leading clique in Britain to take control of the International.

Ted objected strenuously but was outmanoeuvred. When I got back to London, I rang Ted straight away to find out what had happened. When I heard his voice I was quite shocked. He sounded exhausted and very low. He said: "Alan, you are making a big mistake. There is a clique in the leadership and Taaffe is at the head of it." I asked him to come and see me, which he did immediately.

He told me about the manoeuvring over the speakers' list and I agreed that this was unacceptable and would take it up at the next IS meeting. This unleashed a chain of events that neither Ted nor I expected. I prepared what I thought was a reasonable and quite unanswerable case to put before the International Secretariat. But before I had chance to say anything, Taaffe launched a savage personal attack on me. There was no intention of having a rational debate. The aim was to intimidate, bully and crush us. Of course, it had the opposite effect. The leading group was quite prepared to go to any lengths because it felt threatened. It had to act quickly, to take defensive action, and as we know, the best form of defence is to attack.

Since the leading group did not possess the necessary political armoury to take on any opposition in a fair fight, they used the weight of the apparatus, the full timers, the weapons of slander, gossip and character assassination, to attempt to wear us down and drive us out. A hysterical witch-hunting atmosphere was created. In total contrast, Ted had never resorted to the use of the apparatus and administrative measures to deal with internal conflicts. He relied on the strength of the ideas. That was the method in which he had educated us. The methods utilised in this conflict were entirely alien to our traditions.

Our first reaction was to raise forcefully the existence of a clique at the head of the organisation, and to denounce the unhealthy internal regime which was being fostered. But there was a problem. Although the existence of the clique was a fact, it was almost impossible to prove. It came to most of the comrades as a shock, a fact which was exploited cynically by Taaffe and co. to create a hysterical atmosphere within the organisation. Taaffe swiftly called a CC in order to rubber stamp their authority and isolate Ted and me. Most of the comrades in the British organisation and in the International could not understand at first what was happening. Only with the emergence of political questions (Walton, etc.), and by experiencing the Majority's behaviour, did the question of the regime become clear.

The oldest trick in the book is to describe an opposition as people who wish to destroy the organization and appeal to the Party to "unite" against an alleged "external threat". They played on the comrades' sense of loyalty. The comrades had been psychologically prepared by years of fighting to defend the organization against the Labour bureaucracy, and the leadership cynically based themselves on this natural desire of the comrades to unite "to defend the organization".

Ted, Rob, Ana and I had dedicated our entire lives to building this organization, yet we were presented not as comrades with arguments to be answered, but as enemies to be crushed. They immediately mobilised the full strength of the apparatus to do just that. The story was put around that Ted and Alan had "gone mad" and were "attacking the organization".

"This is Healyism!"
Immediately after the initial clash, Taaffe summoned an emergency meeting of the Regional Secretaries (a subcommittee of the Central Committee), where Ted and I were going to be "put on trial". The two of us waited to be called in. Eventually, Ray Apps came in grim-faced and we both stood up. "Not you," Ray snapped at me. They wanted to grill Ted—a 78 year old man—on his own. After some time, Ted came back, looking very tired. "How did it go?" I asked. "They have given me the third degree", he said, referring to the methods of police interrogation.

When it was my turn, I told them: "Comrades, I will do my best to convince you of the correctness of my position. But I tell you now that if I do not convince a single one of you, if I am in a minority of one, I will take this to the end." This caused a certain amount of consternation, but, as I foresaw, it did not change any minds. However, when I think of the faces around that table, I see that the majority of them later either dropped out of politics, or were expelled or split from Taaffe. Very few now remain.

The leading clique used every conceivable method to intimidate and demoralise us. When we came to the centre in the morning to work we were greeted with a wall of silence. Nobody said a word to us. Then they decided to make us open our bags and submit to a search before leaving the premises. In other words, the word had gone out: we were to be subjected to a systematic boycott, or as they used to say: "sent to Coventry".

They must have thought this intimidation would break our will. If so, they made a bad mistake. I recall one meeting of the Executive Committee, when Lynn Walsh, one of the chief hatchet men, launched a hysterical attack against Ted. All the years of frustration, bitterness and resentment were distilled in this essence of bile. However, things did not go to plan. When Lynn was in full flow, Ted suddenly stood up and headed for the door. "Where are you going?" the would-be orator demanded to know. "I have to go for a jimmy-riddle. I need to go to the toilet", Ted answered innocently, and the rhetorical balloon was deflated like a slow puncture.

The most vicious campaign was waged against Rob Sewell. Taaffe was particularly angry because Rob was in charge of the Organization Department, which Taaffe regarded as his personal fief. In his work, Rob had played a central role, and Taaffe was anxious to get him on his side. The Organisation Department was originally established in 1982 to fight the witch-hunt, but developed and became responsible for a whole host of things: the campaign against the witch-hunt and expulsions, recruitment, membership, Labour Party work and Conference intervention, Parliamentary work, the full-timers, the national annual rallies, press and publicity.

Rob, as national organiser, had also played an important role in the campaign against the Poll Tax. He was the author of the only two national pamphlets put out by the Tendency against the Poll Tax, *Battle against the Poll Tax* and *We Won't Pay*, arguing the case for mass non-payment, which sold in their thousands. He was responsible for the organisation of the 250,000-strong protest in London in March 1990. Taaffe hoped that Rob would join his camp and was furious when he immediately came down on the side of the Minority.

Rob was going through an extremely difficult patch personally, because of concerns about the health of his recently born son. Despite this, intense pressure was put on him. Every meeting of the CC from then on became a hate session straight out of Orwell's *1984*. In one particular CC, there was an especially vicious session on the conduct of Rob Sewell. But Rob could not attend, as the CC had dragged on to a late hour and he had child-minding difficulties. This did not stop them.

One after another, the loyal CC members got up to stick the knife in. But this time they got more than they bargained for. Ted put his hand up to speak. His speech was brief and its effect devastating: "I have seen all this before!" he roared. "This is Stalinism! This is Zinovievism! This is Healyism!" He told the CC members that with the ideas and methods now being adopted, the big centre, the printing press, the full-time apparatus "would all turn to dust". He sat down to a stunned silence.

Rob Sewell chairing the *Militant* rally at the Royal Albert Hall in October 1984

The coup in Russia

Although they were united in their hatred of Ted (I cannot think of any other word for it), the leaders of the majority faction were painfully conscious of his enormous theoretical superiority. This was revealed in a rather amusing fashion in the late summer of 1991, when a faction of the old Soviet bureaucracy tried to carry out a coup d'état in Moscow. The news fell like a bombshell. A meeting at the centre of the leading comrades, including the International, was hastily convened. The aim was to decide our attitude to the events in Russia and the line to be taken by the paper. In spite of everything they had been saying about Ted, it was from him that they were expecting some ideas. All eyes were on Ted who, very uncharacteristically, sat silently looking out of the window.

After a pregnant silence, John Throne said: "Aren't you going to say anything Ted?" "About what?" "What do you think about the coup in Russia?" Ted waved his hands defensively: "Well, the thing is, comrades, I have not been feeling very well lately, and I am a bit tired this morning. But anyway, what do *you* think about it?" There was a stir in the room, and someone muttered: "Ted's on strike!" Needless to say, the "discussion" that followed was just a heap of empty platitudes, while Ted looked on with evident satisfaction.

Without the firm guiding hand of Ted Grant, the leadership of the Militant immediately lost their bearings. As could be expected, the line of the paper was completely wrong. The front page headline was "People's Power", referring to the Yeltsin crowd. In other words, they merely echoed the line of the bourgeois press. This amounted to *de facto* support to Yeltsin and the forces of capitalist counter-revolution.

The split showed just how hopeless these people were when it came to working out a political line on any question. The events in Russia showed that very clearly. They made a "slight error" in confusing revolution with counter-revolution. We proved this with abundant quotes from *Militant* in a document entitled *The truth about the coup*. In order to cover their backside, they spread the fairy story that Ted and I supported the Stalinist coup. That was a lie. In fact, it was impossible to give support to either side in this struggle. It was a case of snakes against crocodiles.

Even worse was the position they later took on Yugoslavia. The breakup of Yugoslavia was a criminal act, which was not in the interests of any of the peoples of that country. It was actually the result of the machinations of German imperialism, which, following the unification of Germany and the collapse of the USSR, had ambitions to dominate the Balkans and Eastern Europe.

As one might expect, every one of the self-styled Trotskyist sects immediately took sides in the bloody civil war that followed, lining up behind one or other of the reactionary bourgeois nationalist cliques that crystallised around the former Titoist bureaucracies in Croatia, Slovenia, Serbia, Bosnia, Macedonia and Kosovo. That was a crime against Yugoslavia and a complete abandonment of the class point of view.

Lenin defended the right to self-determination but, like Marx, he never considered it to be an absolute right. It was always subordinate to the general interests of the proletariat and the class struggle internationally. Whether we support the right to self-determination in a given case depends on whether it furthers or hampers the struggle for international socialism.

In this concrete case, the breakup of Yugoslavia was entirely reactionary and has set back the cause of socialism, sowing hatred between people who previously lived and worked happily together, all in the interests of different greedy and rapacious ruling cliques. The criminal wars by which this end was achieved revived all the old demons that most people believed to be extinct. Massacres, pogroms, mass rape, racism and fascism turned Yugoslavia into a hell on earth.

All that has happened subsequently is the penetration of German and US imperialism into the Balkans, the enrichment of the ruling cliques and the impoverishment of the masses. And yet there were people who called themselves Lefts and even Trotskyists who thought that all this was worthwhile—on the grounds of "self-determination". What a disgusting farce! The Taaffeites did not waste any time in falling into the same error. They enthusiastically embraced the cause of so-called "self-determination".

During a debate we had in Madrid, with Ted and myself on one side, and Peter Taaffe and Tony Saunois on the other, one supporter of the Majority tried to heckle Ted by yelling: "Where do you stand on self-determination for Croatia?" To this pearl of wisdom Ted replied: "You mean: do we support the Chetniks or the Ushtase?" That is to say: do we support the Serbian fascists or the Croatian fascists? That was a very good answer.

"Fight and fight again!"

Soon after the conflict erupted, a handful of us met in my flat in Bermondsey. With his usual optimism, Ted said: "well, we will fight and fight and fight again, and if it takes two or three years we will win the majority." I said: "Ted, you are mistaken. We haven't got two or three years. We will be expelled by Christmas." "Do you think so?" he said. "I know so", I answered. It was clear from the way they were acting that they were determined to get rid of us. They could not permit a serious political debate, precisely for the reasons Ted had given. My calculations as to the timetable for the expulsions were off by just one month.

The majority faction was anxious to expel us as soon as possible in order to prevent the discussion from penetrating the ranks in Britain and internationally. They rigged the discussion in the International by inventing a rule (which was not written down anywhere) that only IS members could defend the case of the Majority and Minority. Since only Ted and myself supported the Minority on the IS, and Ted was not in the best of health, this was utterly impossible. The Majority got round this little difficulty very easily. The supporters of the Majority would also explain the ideas of the Minority! This absurd pantomime was carried out in several parts in Britain and even in the International. At the same time, the centre disposed of the services of some 200 full timers to "put the case" of the Majority.

The dirty tricks department was working overtime. All kinds of rumours were put in circulation: Everybody was informed that: "Ted Grant is senile." This rumour had been quietly started long before. Lynn Walsh had books on dementia on the shelves of his office. They seem to have been his favourite bedtime reading. As for the author of these lines, they showed truly remarkable inventive skills. I learned that I had been offered a well-paid academic job in a Spanish university and was planning to abandon politics (I am still trying to find out which university that was). Rob Sewell was also said to be planning to abandon the cause, and apparently planned to move to the Highlands of Scotland.

I remember the astonishment Ted showed at Taaffe's manoeuvres' and intrigues. With an expression of utter perplexity, he said: "He's got more tricks than a monkey in a box! I don't understand it. He must spend all his time thinking up intrigues. He must think that this is what revolutionary politics is all about. That shows he is just a provincial politician".

They held a special conference to defeat the opposition by a big majority. They were always obsessed with the idea of "big majorities", as if that decided whether ideas were correct or incorrect. This is a sure indication of a psychology that is alien to Marxism and Leninism. It betrays the cowardly mentality of a bureaucrat who always desires to be on the winning side and seeks to hide his political spinelessness behind the idea that the majority is always right.

Towards the end of his life old Engels wrote: "Marx and I were in a minority all our lives, and we were proud to be in a minority". Here we have the authentic voice of Marxism! When he returned to Russia in 1917 after the February Revolution, Lenin said: "I hear that in Russia there is a trend toward consolidation. Consolidation with the defensists—that is betrayal of socialism. I think it would be better to stand alone like Liebknecht—one against a hundred and ten." (See Trotsky, *History of the Russian Revolution*, Volume One, Chapter 15, "Lenin and the Bolsheviks".)

Let us remind ourselves that until the April 1917 Conference, Lenin was in a minority in the leadership of the Bolshevik Party. His April Theses were published in the Party's daily *Pravda* under his own name. And let us remember that Trotsky had to fight as a minority to defend the genuine traditions of October against the Stalinist bureaucracy. No! It is not the Marxists but the traitors to Marxism who are always anxious to be with the "big majority".

Some months before the final Conference, Ted made a highly perceptive and uncannily accurate prediction of what would happen. He said: "This will have four stages: 1) 'collective leadership', 2) the emergence of the Leader, 3) the expulsion of the opposition and 4) the destruction of the organization." This proved to be correct in every detail.

I noticed that the delegates to the Conference fell into three broad categories. First, there were those we called the "head bangers", mostly full timers who expressed their "loyalty" by their strident denunciations of the opposition. These were hopeless elements. Secondly, there was a layer of raw youngsters, who were completely uneducated in Marxism. It was clear that they did not understand what was going on, and voted in the way the full timers indicated. Most of them soon left the organization and dropped out. The big majority of those who voted to expel us, even at a leadership level, are now out of politics altogether.

Last, and most important, there were a number of older, more experienced comrades, many of them trade unionists with a long experience of the Labour Movement. They were clearly unhappy about the whole proceedings and more than one sympathised with our ideas. But the weight of the apparatus, a misplaced sense of loyalty and fear of a split, compelled them to vote for the Majority.

In the end, of course, Taaffe got his "big majority". The whole thing was a farce. In the rigged October conference in Bridlington, some 93% voted for the Majority, a figure that Stalin would have been proud of. Those who were responsible for this criminal act of folly attempted to disguise this as a little tactical manoeuvre, a "detour", to which Ted, with his customary sense of humour, replied: "Yes, a detour over a cliff". And it most certainly was. The Majority faction argued that once we broke with the Labour Party, "We would grow by leaps and bounds." The opposite was the case.

Expelled from Militant

Relations grew from bad to worse. At the end of November, Rob was forced to go to a CC meeting on his own, as Ted was ill and I was away. The whole thing turned into a bear-baiting operation. At first, the "Central Committee" excluded him on the grounds that it constituted itself as the CC "Majority". Once they had dealt with all the business and made the decisions, they invited Rob into the farce to rubber stamp things. He was then subjected to denunciations and abuse from all and sundry. Taaffe announced that the "boycott of the Minority meant a split". Rob's record of attendance at the office was again raised, his lack of cooperation, his "sabotage", "unacceptable behaviour", "abysmal record", "organisational incompetence", his "scandalous" voting against the recruitment, subs and fighting fund targets, etc.

The meeting then passed a resolution, proposed by Ray Apps: "[This] CC reprimands RS for his failures to carry out his duties and responsibilities and putting factional activities before the interests of the Tendency (...)". He was then pressed to resign, which he refused to do.

Ted was now clear that he would be expelled: "The sects always expel the Leader," he explained. It did not take long for this particular prediction to materialise.

The day of our expulsion from Militant, in January 1992, was a real circus. Ana, Ted, Rob and I drove to the centre at Hepscott Road, where the farce commenced before we even got into the car park. We were kept waiting for a long time before the person on the front desk deigned to open the gates. Perhaps they thought we were carrying a bomb! Finally we were admitted into the tiny vestibule where all who entered the building were vetted. There we waited—and waited—to learn our fate. The only company we had were the potted plants that only Ana occasionally watered. After some time we could see some movement on the stairs that led up inexorably to the Executive Room.

The pantomime continued. Suddenly, through the large glass panel, we could see the Comrades of the Executive Committee marching in step like well-wound automata down the stairs. They marched grim-faced and stared straight ahead. The General Secretary came last. Eventually this Solemn Procession came to a halt at the bottom of the stairs. A dramatic gesture from the General Secretary, and the door that had been firmly shut against us swung open as if by magic. Such power! I was impressed.

But my initial awe was immediately transformed to disbelief. The purpose of opening the door was not, as I had foolishly imagined, to let us in, but to let the Comrades of the Executive Committee *out*. One by one, the Solemn Procession streamed out into the tiny vestibule (or rather, squeezed out, for there was not really room for all of us and the flower pots as well). Without further ado, Lynn Walsh began to read a prepared script on a piece of paper. This was already too much. I interrupted him: "Either you open that door and we have a proper meeting inside the building, or we are leaving right now!" The Comrades of the Executive Committee did not seem to be prepared for this unexpected *contretemps*. There was an embarrassed silence. Someone, I think it was Keith Dickinson, always anxious to be helpful, said: "But why can't we meet here?" Then Ted, with his usual exquisite sense of timing, said in a loud voice: "I need to go to the toilet! I want a jimmy-riddle!"

Yet another sudden and sharp change in the situation! The Comrades of the Executive Committee looked at the General Secretary. He hesitated for a moment, like Napoleon carefully weighing up his next command at the Battle of Waterloo. Then he waved his hand: "Let him in", he muttered. It was not his proudest moment. Once again the door swung open as if by magic, and Ted disappeared in the direction of the nearest available lavatory. There was yet another moment of pregnant silence.

I looked at Peter Taaffe and thought of all those years we had worked together building the organization. He then pointed to Rob and said: "Well, here is the new General Secretary, I see." Probably this remark was intended to cover his embarrassment, or break the atmosphere, which you could have cut with a knife. But the sheer pettiness of this comment aroused in me a deep sense of indignation. So the pathetic ambition of one man, the stupid obsession with an empty title, was sufficient cause to wreck the work of forty years.

I turned to Taaffe and said: "Well, Peter, I always thought you were a big man. But now I see that you are a small man—a *very* small man." Clearly nonplussed, the General Secretary looked the other way and said nothing. The rest of this sorry charade is hardly worth recalling. We were finally admitted to the Executive Room, and after the briefest of brief exchanges, the "charges" were read and we were duly expelled. This meeting was quite irrelevant, since the decision to get rid of us had been taken about twelve months earlier.

We left that sad building, its General Secretary, and the Comrades of the Executive Committee, with no regrets, rather, with a palpable sense of relief, like a man who has woken up after a bad dream. We had turned the page and could now commence a new beginning.

CHAPTER TEN

A NEW BEGINNING

I was ever a fighter, so—one fight more,
The best and the last!
I would hate that death bandaged my eyes, and forebore,
And bade me creep past. (Robert Browning, *Prospice*)

Alien methods

The last days of Militant present an unedifying spectacle from which most people will turn aside with distaste. Is this the way they behave in Trotskyist organizations? The answer to this perfectly reasonable question is an emphatic "no"! These methods were entirely alien to our movement and contradictory to everything Trotsky ever said or wrote.

Sometime in the 1980s, when Ted was in Paris visiting his sister, he had a conversation with Raoul, an old friend of his who was a veteran Trotskyist and a member of the Lambertist organization. He asked Ted if he would meet its political leader, Lambert. Ted was not very keen, but out of friendship he finally agreed. Then he found out that Lambert had recently expelled one of their leaders, Stephane Just. Not only did they expel him, but anyone who defended him was also expelled. When Ted found this out he was indignant. He told Raoul that he would not meet Lambert. He said: "Anyone who behaves in this way will never build a revolutionary party in a thousand years."

The poison of Stalinism has been carried over into the many sects that pretend to stand for Trotskyism, although usually in its milder form, which we know as Zinovievism. This pernicious disease comes from the fact that the leaders of these groups do not possess the political level to answer criticisms, and are therefore obliged to use other methods: insults, distortions, intrigues and administrative measures.

These methods are sometimes interpreted as a sign of Bolshevik "toughness". But in reality, they are proof, not of strength, but of extreme weakness. The appearance of a monolithic unity is merely a screen to disguise a leadership that has no confidence in itself, its ideas or in the membership. Such organizations are inherently unstable and prone to splits and crises.

With such methods it is impossible to build a genuine Bolshevik organization. The history of the Fourth International is clear proof of this. Ted Grant was always implacably opposed to those methods. He was always confident in his ability to answer any criticisms whatsoever. In the last analysis, it was this colossal political and moral authority that guaranteed a healthy internal regime.

Ted Grant always had his eyes firmly fixed on the high ground. Like Trotsky, his actions were dictated, not by petty manoeuvres and intrigues, but on political principles and Marxist perspectives, and these are what are decisive in the long run. Ted lost the vote but won the argument, as the history of the last twenty years has amply demonstrated.

Ted's "mistakes"

> *Now that the old lion is dead every ass thinks he may kick at him.* (James Boswell, *Life of Samuel Johnson*)

The political differences that were present during the factional fight did not emerge as clearly as they should have, in great measure because the Majority deliberately concealed its real objectives, which have since become manifest. The mistakes of the Majority have deepened and become organic. They stumble from one blunder to another and constantly lose members.

In order to conceal their mistakes and hide the genuine causes for the split, the leaders of the Majority faction constantly harp on Ted's alleged "mistakes". This whole approach is completely dishonest. Taaffe later wrote:

> Important political differences occurred over the world financial crisis in 1987. As soon as the 1987 share crash took place, Grant was predicting a world economic slump, "within six months", along the lines of 1929-32. His thinking was unfortunately, reflected in the pages of *Militant*. In its initial comments on these developments it stated: "A major slump in production and trade is assured, perhaps even before the summer of 1988". His co-thinker, Michael Roberts, stated that the October crash "is a barometer predicting the impending storm that will exceed anything experienced by capitalism in the post-war period, possibly matching the great slump of the 1930s".
>
> This approach was vigorously opposed by me and Lynn Walsh in the British Executive and National Committees, and by me, Tony Saunois and Bob Labi in the International Secretariat of the CWI. As usual, Woods slavishly supported Grant. (Peter Taaffe, *Militant's Real History: In Reply to Ted Grant and Rob Sewell*)

This is false from start to finish. If it is true that Peter Taaffe and the others "vigorously opposed" Ted's position in 1987, then this "vigorous opposition" must be available in written form, either in an alternative document, or at the very least in an amendment. Yet our "vigorous opponents" never quote a single line from their documents and amendments, for the simple reason that they do not exist.

Even more astonishing is what he writes about the paper. The EC was supposed to be in charge of the political line of the paper. The majority of the EC were loyal supporters of Peter Taaffe. If the line of the paper was so bad, why did they allow these bad articles to be published? Or if they did not agree with an article in the paper, what was to stop them from publishing a reply? You can be sure that Ted would have been delighted to have a written debate, either in the paper or in the internal bulletin. I do not think that Peter Taaffe or any of the other people mentioned were shrinking violets. So why did they not write a reply?

The truth of the matter is that never, at any time, did they "vigorously oppose" anything. What they did do—and they did this systematically and over a long period—was to make smarmy comments in the corners about Ted and his ideas. If later—as was normally the case—what Ted said turned out to be correct, they kept quiet. But if by chance some things did not turn out *exactly* as he had predicted, then they were jubilant: "You see! I told you so! He is losing his grip! He is out of touch! etc., etc."

Was Ted mistaken in predicting a slump in 1987? Let us see. The stock exchange crash did in fact lead to a recession in 1990, but it was a relatively mild recession, not a deep slump. The main reason for this was the emergence of new markets in China and elsewhere in Asia, which temporarily gave capitalism a breathing space. There was a boom, followed by another recession in the early 2000s, expressed as a decline in economic activity, mainly in developed countries. The recession affected the European Union during 2000 and 2001, and the United States in 2002 and 2003. Britain, Canada and Australia avoided the recession for the most part.

Ted explained that the boom was kept going by a massive expansion of credit, which, as Marx explains, can temporarily take capitalism beyond its limits, before bouncing back like an elastic band stretched almost to breaking-point. A further element in the situation was the colossal increase in the public deficit of the USA and other capitalist countries, which fuelled the boom for a while, but which could not be sustained indefinitely.

Precisely these factors, which served to prolong the boom of the last twenty years, have now turned into their opposite. The reason the Western world is finding it so hard to drag itself out of recession now is because during the boom they used up the mechanisms which capitalism typically uses to try to get out of a slump. The uncontrolled expansion of credit has left the West (and Japan) with a painful hangover in the form of huge consumer and state indebtedness.

What we have now is precisely what Ted predicted over 20 years ago: this is the worst slump in the entire history of capitalism. It has indeed "exceeded anything experienced by capitalism in the post-war period, possibly matching the great slump of the 1930s." So what was Ted's mistake? It was a mistake of fact, but not of method; it was a mistake of timing, but not of theory. That is all. Taaffe and his friends, who were incapable of predicting anything, make a big song and dance over this. Yet Ted Grant was not alone in making such "terrible mistakes".

After the defeat of the revolutions of 1848, Marx and Engels believed that a new revolutionary wave was imminent, and said so on more than one occasion. Yet no such thing occurred. Indeed, Engels later wrote of the "forty years winter sleep" of the English proletariat. The reason for their error was that capitalism was entering into a phase of expansion on a world scale, the extent of which was not immediately clear to them. Once the facts asserted themselves more clearly, they changed their perspectives accordingly.

Let us take another example, which we have mentioned previously. In 1938, Trotsky said that in ten years, not one stone upon another would be left of the old organizations of the Stalinists and Social Democrats. What would comrade Taaffe and his friends have said about that? Would they have "vigorously opposed" Trotsky, Marx and Engels? Sadly, we will never know.

Trotsky's prognosis was falsified by history, just as happened with Marx and Engels after 1848. They were mistaken. But their mistakes were of a factual, not a methodological character. What do we mean by this? Marxism is a science, but it is not an exact science, like mathematics or astronomy. An astronomer can establish the position of a galaxy millions of light years away, often with absolute certainty. But there are sciences and sciences.

Geology is a science. It can tell us precisely in what places on the earth's surface an earthquake is likely to take place. But it cannot tell us exactly when such an event will occur. Predictions in this area are merely educated guesses.

Medicine is also a science, but not an exact one. Basing himself, on the one hand on his knowledge of medical science, and, on the other, on all the available symptoms, a doctor arrives at a diagnosis. There are always various possibilities: for example, a stomach pain may signify an

Ted Grant with John Reimann

ulcer, colic or stomach cancer. But, at the end of the day, the doctor must decide which is the most likely, because he must pass from theory to action, in order to cure the disease.

However, even the best doctor can make a mistaken diagnosis, usually because some of the relevant facts were unknown to him or her. This does not necessarily disqualify the doctor. Nor does it invalidate medicine as a science. It most certainly does not mean that a doctor must never give a diagnosis because it may be mistaken. That would render all of medicine completely useless.

"Conditional perspectives"

It is quite wrong to ask more of a perspective than it is able to give. To do so would be to discredit the very idea of perspectives. Perspectives are not a blueprint for precisely what will happen, but only a working hypothesis, dealing with general processes. They must be constantly revised, fleshed out, and checked against the facts and actual developments. We must modify the perspectives accordingly, or, if necessary, discard them altogether. If the gap between perspectives and reality is too great, then we must change our perspectives, since we cannot change reality.

Those who demand that perspectives must accurately foretell every detail are not looking for Marxist perspectives, but a crystal ball. Unfortunately, such an instrument is not yet available to us, so we must manage as best we can without it. In reality, this demand for infallible perspectives is closely related to a bureaucratic and formalistic mentality. It is closely connected to the idea that the Leaders cannot be wrong.

Paradoxically, this leads to the complete abandonment of perspectives and their replacement by vulgar empiricism. That is what happened to Taaffe and his supporters after the breakup of Militant. Taaffe was so afraid of making a mistake, and thereby revealing himself as a mere mortal, that he developed the idea of "conditional perspectives", which is really a kind of theoretical double book-keeping.

We were already well-accustomed to this phenomenon when we were part of the Mandelite International. Whenever Mandel would write a perspectives document, he would, to use a vulgar expression, write it in a way to cover his backside. When writing about economic perspectives, he would present various scenarios: there could be a slump; on the other hand, there might be a boom; on the other hand, there might be something else altogether. As the man in the fairground would say: *you pays your money and you takes your choice.*

The problem with such a "perspective" is that it is completely useless. The only purpose of such "conditional perspectives" is to demonstrate the Papal Infallibility of the Leader. It tells us nothing, and therefore makes it impossible to arrive at a correct orientation. It would be like a doctor who tells his patient that he might have an ulcer, colic, or stomach cancer and then cheerfully pockets his fee and says goodbye.

Actually, all perspectives are by definition of a conditional character. Of necessity, perspectives have an algebraic, not arithmetic, character. The unknown quantities must be filled in on the basis of actual experience. Perspectives can be added to, modified, or even rejected if they are falsified by events. Mistakes are inevitable in working out perspectives.

For a Marxist, even a mistake can be turned to good account, on condition that it is identified, explained and corrected. In the same way, in the history of science, an experiment can be of great utility even when it does not yield the desired result, since it serves to point the way to a more fruitful avenue of investigation and increases the sum total of our knowledge, albeit in a negative sense.

The problem arises when a leadership is not prepared to admit its mistakes and learn from them. Twenty years ago, comrade Taaffe and his friends confidently predicted that the Labour Party would "wither on the vine", and their organization would "grow by leaps and bounds". In the mid-1990s they even had the perspective that they would soon become a "small, mass party of tens of thousands". These were mistakes that flowed from a fundamentally flawed method. But twenty years later, there is not the slightest attempt at self-criticism. That means that the mistake will be repeated and magnified until what is left of their organization is destroyed altogether.

"He's just a lightweight"

The Majority faction "won" the factional struggle twenty years ago. Does that prove they were right? Does it prove they were cleverer or more far-sighted than the Minority? The image of Militant in the Labour Movement was seriously damaged by these developments.

After Ted's expulsion from Militant, Tony Benn publicly berated the leaders of Militant at a Labour Party Conference fringe meeting in Brighton in 1992 for what they had done. He said they had expelled Ted Grant for forming a "party within a party". With a strong dose of irony, he said that this was exactly the reason the Labour leaders had given for the expulsion of supporters of Militant from the Labour Party. This gave rise to general hilarity, save for the handful of Militant comrades present who sat stony-faced and completely isolated.

When Jimmy Deane found out about the split, he was scandalized by the way Ted and the Minority had been treated. His first comment was: "Taaffe? He's just a lightweight!" The rest of his comments were unprintable. Some might be tempted to reply: But after all, you might say, this lightweight knocked out his heavyweight opponent. That argument is superficial and utterly false. For many years it has become almost a platitude to interpret the struggle between Stalin and Trotsky as a clash between two individuals, in which Stalin defeated Trotsky because he was a more skilful tactical manoeuverer. Such superficial observations are explanations that explain nothing.

Ted pointed out that under the given circumstances, the defeat of the Left Opposition in Russia was virtually a foregone conclusion. He explained that Trotsky knew that he could not win from the beginning. Why then did he continue to fight on? Ted answered:

> Trotsky was fighting to preserve the real traditions of Bolshevism and the October Revolution for the future generations. Zinoviev, Kamenev and the others capitulated to Stalin and thought that they were great realists. But they lost everything. Today nobody looks to them or takes their ideas seriously. Trotsky left us a clean banner.

Yes, the Majority "won". They did not win on the strength of their arguments, but on the basis of manoeuvres, lies and the force of the apparatus. The Majority faction deliberately deceived the membership, not only about the ideas of the Minority, which they systematically distorted, but about their own ideas and intentions, which they concealed from start to finish. They said that Ted and Alan wished to bury themselves deep in the Labour Party and wait passively upon events. They could never find a single sentence that Ted or I ever said or wrote that could be interpreted in this way, for the simple reason that such a thing never existed, except in their fevered factional imagination.

On the other hand, they deceived the members concerning their own position. Ted warned that the Scottish turn was not really a Scottish turn, not a small tactical adjustment, but a radical change in our whole orientation and strategy: "Tomorrow the Scottish turn will be the British turn, and the day after tomorrow the international turn." With what furious indignation did they deny these statements! But that is precisely what happened.

What was the end result? It ended in the complete destruction of the organization we had built through many years of patient work. The former Majority faction thought they had solved their problems by getting rid of the Minority. They were wrong. Ted's prediction that the "turn" was a "shortcut over a cliff" proved to be all too true. It is very difficult to build, but only too easy to destroy.

We urge these "clever" manoeuverers to republish now what they wrote then. The Majority argued that all that was necessary was to break the link with the Labour Party, and the Tendency would "grow by leaps and bounds". Was that what happened? Ted warned that, on the contrary, they would "sink like a stone". And that was exactly what occurred.

Their mistake is to exaggerate their forces, displaying a complete lack of proportion. The idea that a small organisation can compete with the Labour Party is ludicrous in the extreme. In reality, the workers do not even notice these people. All their attempts to construct a "new workers' party" outside the Labour Party have ended in ignominious failure. The facts speak for themselves. At its peak, the Militant had 8,000 members. We had a big headquarters and a printing press capable of producing a daily paper. They lost everything we built. They immediately lost the MPs who stood against official Labour candidates and were annihilated. They had to sell the big centre in Hackney Wick because of debts. They lost the printing press and had to lay off full-timers. Many comrades dropped out of politics altogether, including members of the Executive. Within a relatively short period, they had expelled the leadership of the Merseyside organisation, resulting in the collapse of the Tendency in what had been our stronghold, and the whole of the Scottish organisation split away on an opportunist and nationalist basis. These were the strongest areas of Militant, but were reduced to rubble.

Today, nothing is left of the Militant but a vague memory, and even that is fading fast. Militant had three members of parliament and many local councillors. We were literally a household name. It took the best part of forty years of patient work to conquer this position. But all this was thrown away in an instant in the most light-minded way imaginable. What lessons can be learned from all this? What we did once we can do again. But that will only be possible through a complete rejection of sectarianism and a return to the real traditions of our Tendency, the authentic traditions of Trotskyism—the traditions of Ted Grant.

Regrouping the forces of Marxism

Victor Hugo once wrote: "I represent a party which does not yet exist: the party Revolution-Civilization. This party will make the twentieth century. There will issue from it first the United States of Europe, then the United States of the World". Of course, for the author of *Les Misérables,* this aim necessarily had a purely abstract and utopian character, since he was unable to conceive of human civilization outside the limited horizons of bourgeois society.

For Marxists, however, the building of the revolutionary party and International is not a dream, but an urgent necessity. With the passing of time, that necessity becomes more, not less, urgent. Once one grasps this fact, no setback or defeat can dishearten or make one digress one millimetre from this goal.

At the time of the split in Militant, Ted was already a "young man" of 78. While many comrades were demoralized by the split, he just shrugged his shoulders as if nothing had happened. For him, the building of the revolutionary tendency, to which he dedicated his entire life, could never be interrupted. He was undaunted by all setbacks and absolutely irrepressible.

In a speech to the British CC, in September 1994, Ted said: "We have made very few serious mistakes. But if we make a mistake it must be corrected not only at the IS level but in all the sections and used to raise the level. If this is done correctly, it does no harm and can be useful. But we must maintain a sense of balance and proportion."

Reflecting on the split, Ted drew the following conclusion: "For some years we have been part of a tendency that had a correct Trotskyist political line and a Zinovievist organizational apparatus." That accurately summed up the real situation. But such a position could not be maintained. Either the Trotskyist trend would correct the Zinovievist deviation, or the latter would end up by eliminating the Trotskyists. In the end the latter variant triumphed. But the price they paid for this "victory", as Ted predicted, was the destruction of Militant.

I remember those meetings of a small group of comrades in my flat in Bermondsey. I remember, as if it were yesterday, Ted's remarkable good humour. After we were expelled from the Militant, he joked: "Well, that is the best split I've ever been through!" But in truth, we found ourselves (in Britain at least) facing a lot of difficulties.

At the time of the split, the Taaffe faction had a big apparatus, lots of money and a team of about 200 full timers. We did not even have a typewriter. Not only had we lost a very important organization, but we had to reorganize our forces in an unfavourable objective situation.

The collapse of Stalinism produced an unprecedented ideological counter-offensive against the ideas of Marxism and Communism, and the prolonged boom in capitalism reinforced the right wing of the Labour Movement and further isolated the small forces of Marxism. But neither Ted nor I were worried in the slightest. We had the ideas of Marxism, and that was all that mattered.

In Britain, the Opposition had the support of a significant number, mainly experienced cadres and trade union activists. The situation was far more favourable in the International. In fact, if we exclude Britain, we had the majority of the international Tendency on our side. The IMT was formed by those comrades who remained loyal to the ideas of Ted Grant, and wished to preserve the genuine traditions of our movement.

Ted played a leading role in refounding the International, which we renamed the Committee for a Marxist International, and later, the International Marxist Tendency (IMT). He was active in it until his death in 2006. Despite his age (he always said he was 21), he just carried on as before, travelling to other countries, delivering speeches of an hour or more. He seemed determined to carry on forever. At times it seemed that he had convinced himself that he would do just this. It was a truly formidable performance.

In 1992, we launched the *Socialist Appeal* magazine, which has earned a solid reputation for serious analysis, comment, and militant policies in the Labour Movement in Britain and internationally. Our output of high-quality Marxist theoretical material is second-to-none. In 1995, we began the publication of books, which have made quite a spectacular impact internationally, starting with *Reason in Revolt*, (by Alan Woods and Ted Grant). This was the first attempt since Engels' *Dialectics of Nature* to apply the method of dialectical materialism to the results of modern science.

This was followed by *Russia—From Revolution to Counter-revolution*, *Bolshevism—the Road to Revolution*, and a new expanded edition of *Lenin and Trotsky—What they really stood for*. Our books have been translated into Spanish, Portuguese, Italian, Greek, German, Dutch, Russian, Turkish and Urdu. Our articles and pamphlets have also been translated into these languages, and also into French, Chinese, Vietnamese, Korean, Rumanian, Serbian, Macedonian, Polish, Indonesian, Arabic, Hebrew and many other languages.

We can say without fear of contradiction that the political authority of our Tendency, both nationally and internationally, has never been greater than it is now. In 1997, we launched the extremely successful web site *In Defence of Marxism* (www.marxist.com), which has had far-reaching international appeal, and has been visited by hundreds of thousands of people worldwide.

Some well-meaning people ask why we do not combine with other groups to advance the cause of unity. Such a proposal, despite its apparently reasonable character, would be a recipe for disaster. The attempt to unify tendencies that stand for different ideas, principles and methods is counter-productive. In simple mathematics one plus one equals two. But if there are two people in a boat rowing in opposite directions, one plus one equals zero.

In the *Correspondence* of Marx and Engels, there is a very interesting letter from Engels to Bebel, dated June 20, 1875, in which he answers those followers of Marx who wished to unite with the Lassalleans, who had a bigger following among the German workers.

> (...) Our view, which we have found confirmed by long practice, is that the correct tactic in propaganda is not to draw away a few individuals and members here and there from one's opponent, but to work on the great mass which still remains apathetic. The primitive force of a single individual whom we have ourselves attracted from the crude mass is worth more than ten Lassallean renegades, who always bring the seeds of their false tendencies into the Party with them. And if one could only get the masses without their local leaders it would still be all right. But one always has to take a whole crowd of these leaders into the bargain, and they are bound by their previous public utterances, if not by their previous views, and have above all things to prove that they have not deserted their principles but that on the contrary the Social-Democratic Workers' Party preaches true Lassalleanism. This was the unfortunate thing at Eisenach, not to be avoided at that time, perhaps, but there is no doubt at all that these elements have done harm to the Party, and I am not sure that the Party would not have been at least as strong to-day without that addition. In any case, however, I should regard it as a misfortune if these elements were reinforced. (Marx and Engels, *Collected Works*, vol. 44, pp. 511-12)

The message is quite clear: although there may be some good elements among the followers of Lassalle, it would be a mistake to recruit them because a) they will bring with them all the confusion they have learned in the old organization; and b) they are organically inclined to factionalism and will disorganise the proletarian tendency. In the time that would be required to straighten out one of these elements, it would be possible to win ten or twenty ordinary, fresh German workers whose brains have not been addled by sectarian nonsense. Therefore, the "primitive force of a single individual whom we have ourselves attracted from the crude mass is worth more than ten Lassallean renegades". That is very good advice! But what about "unity"? Engels answers that too:

> One must not allow oneself to be misled by the cry for "unity". Those who have this word most often

on their lips are those who sow the most dissension, just as at present the Jura Bakuninists in Switzerland, who have provoked all the splits, scream for nothing so much as for unity. Those unity fanatics are either the people of limited intelligence who want to stir everything up together into one nondescript brew, which, the moment it is left to settle, throws up the differences again in much more acute opposition because they are now all together in one pot (you have a fine example of this in Germany with the people who preach the reconciliation of the workers and the petty bourgeoisie)—or else they are people who consciously or unconsciously (...) want to adulterate the movement. For this reason the greatest sectarians and the biggest brawlers and rogues are at certain moments the loudest shouters for unity. Nobody in our lifetime has given us more trouble and been more treacherous than the unity shouters. (*Op. Cit.*, p. 513)

And he concludes thus:

> For the rest, old Hegel has already said: a party proves itself a victorious party by the fact that it splits and can stand the split. The movement of the proletariat necessarily passes through different stages of development; at every stage one section of people lags behind and does not join in the further advance; and this alone explains why it is that actually the "solidarity of the proletariat" is everywhere realised in different party groupings which carry on life and death feuds with one another, as the Christian sects in the Roman Empire did amidst the worst persecutions. (*Op. Cit.*, p. 514)

Exactly the same point was made by Lenin many times, starting with *What Is to be Done?*, "Before we can unite, and in order that we may unite, we must first of all draw firm and definite lines of demarcation." (Lenin, *What Is to Be Done?—Dogmatism and Freedom of Criticism*)

In Defence of Marxism

In the last two decades we have witnessed an unprecedented offensive against the ideas of socialism on a world scale. The collapse of the bureaucratically controlled planned economies of the East was held up as the definitive proof of the failure of "communism," and, of course, of the ideas of Marx.

Lenin pointed out that "the role of vanguard fighter can be fulfilled only by a party that is guided by the most advanced theory". Serious workers and youth are seeking the ideas of revolutionary socialism, that is to say, Marxism. They are looking for serious explanations, not empty "agitation". That is why, in addition to the day-to-day struggle for socialism, we pay serious attention to the production of theoretical work.

It is ironic that precisely at this time, when the crisis of capitalism has completely vindicated Marxism, there is a veritable race on the Left to throw Marxist theory overboard, as if it were so much useless ballast. The former Communists no longer even speak of socialism and have consigned the writings of Marx and Engels to the dustbin. Matters are no better with the ultra-left sects who exist on the margins of the Labour Movement. Though they invoke Marx, Lenin and Trotsky in every other sentence, they do not even bother to reprint their works, preferring more "modern" (or "post-modern") ideas that they have taken over uncritically from the bourgeoisie and petty-bourgeoisie.

We deplore the attempts to ditch Marxist theory, to water down ideas and drag the level of the movement down to the lowest common denominator of mindless activism. This represents a fundamental departure from Marxism. The abandonment or neglect of theory, the search for a shortcut to the masses, leads inevitably either to the swamp of opportunism or the dead end of ultra-leftism.

Without the struggle for theory it is impossible to build a revolutionary tendency. Lenin pointed this out long ago. Already in *What Is to Be Done?* he explained: "Without revolutionary theory there can be no revolutionary movement. This idea cannot be insisted upon too strongly at a time when the fashionable preaching of opportunism goes hand in hand with an infatuation for the narrowest forms of practical activity."

That is a fundamental truth that all the great Marxists have insisted on. Lenin's words ring particularly true in the present epoch of the ideological offensive of the bourgeoisie, of scepticism, capitulation and apostasy. The struggle for Marxist theory has played a fundamental role in the building of the IMT, and Ted's role on this vital front was absolutely crucial.

In analysing the debacle of Militant, we concluded that one of the main reasons for the degeneration of the old organization was the low political level and the neglect of theory and cadre-building. Ted said: "Under Taaffe and Saunois, the world congresses became mere 'rah-rah' rallies. The political level was very low. We must educate all our comrades on the basis of Trotsky's writings—which the so-called Trotskyists of the Fourth never did."

After the fall of the Soviet Union, there was a general mood of pessimism on the left. Marxism was under attack from all sides. What was our duty in such circumstances? Our response to this general backsliding was to defend the fundamental ideas of Marxism. As explained above, we produced a series of books, beginning with *Reason in Revolt*, which played a big role in re-arming the cadres and attracting the attention of many people who wished to continue the fight for socialism. The struggle for Marxist theory has always been at the centre of this Tendency and has played the main role in its development.

Ted had a profound grasp of Marxist economics, a subject on which he frequently lectured. His pamphlet *Will There Be a Slump?* is a little masterpiece, while *The Marxist Theory of the State* is one of the very few works of modern Marxism that can be said to have added to and developed the theories of Marx and Engels. He continued to make a substantial contribution to Marxist economic theory almost to the end of his life.

He was very sceptical about the prospects for the euro, at a time when most people—including some Marxists—had big illusions in it. Initially he did not even believe that the European bourgeois would be able to launch a single currency. He pointed out that it was impossible to unify economies that were moving in different directions. Economies as different as Germany and Italy could not have the same rate of interest, without causing serious problems.

The euro was finally introduced, and at first appeared to be a success. Ted explained that they could maintain the single currency as long as the boom lasted but he warned: "Let there be a deep slump and the euro will collapse amidst mutual recriminations." Those were his exact words, ten years before the collapse of 2008. They proved to be uncannily accurate.

The fall of Stalinism

The fall of Stalinism came as no surprise to Ted, who had predicted it in advance, following in the footsteps of Leon Trotsky, who had already analysed the bureaucratic regime in the Soviet Union in the 1930s and, using the Marxist method, explained the inevitability of its collapse. We should point out that Ted Grant actually predicted the collapse of the Stalinist regime in Russia as early as 1972, and explained why it was inevitable. Up until about 1965, the Russian bureaucracy was still able to play a relatively progressive role in developing the productive forces under the nationalised planned economy of the USSR, although at a very high cost in terms of bureaucratic mismanagement, corruption, swindling and chaos.

But bureaucratic totalitarianism is ultimately incompatible with a nationalised planned economy. In the end, the bureaucracy undermined and destroyed the last remaining conquests of the October revolution. In his book *Russia—from Revolution to Counter-revolution* Ted traces the whole process, from 1917 to the fall of the Soviet Union, and explains exactly what happened.

In the 1970s Ted concluded that the bureaucratic regime in the USSR was doomed. He saw that the Soviet economy was not capable of getting the same results as capitalism. The rate of growth, which had reached 20 percent annually in the 1930s, fell to 10 percent after 1945 (still an impressive figure), and to about 6.5 percent under Khrushchev in the mid-1960s. But by the 1970s, under Brezhnev, it was virtually at a standstill.

In 1974, Ted explained that, "The bureaucracy cannot even get the same economic results as the bourgeois in the West. The Soviet Union has more scientists than Britain, the USA, Germany and Japan together, yet they cannot get the same results. On that basis, they are doomed."

However, in one important respect, Ted was mistaken. He thought that the collapse of Stalinism would lead to the workers taking power in Russia. But Stalin had succeeded in wiping out the Bolshevik Party, physically exterminating its cadres in a one-sided war against "Trotskyists". Decades of bureaucratic, totalitarian rule had erased the memory of the real programme and policies of Bolshevism and October.

The so-called Communist Party of the Soviet Union had degenerated so far that it was incapable of fighting capitalist restoration. Its members left in droves, and many of the old "Communist" leaders became capitalists, as Ted put it, "like a man moving from one carriage of a train to another." He was genuinely shocked by this. Even he did not appreciate just how far the degeneration had gone. He thought that something of the old traditions of Lenin and the Bolshevik Party would remain. But there was virtually nothing.

Ted emphasized that Trotsky's original analysis in *The Revolution Betrayed* had been strikingly confirmed—even in detail. By contrast, the so-called theory of "state capitalism" has proved to be false in theory and disastrous in practice. History has shown that Bruno Rizzi, Shachtman and Cliff, with their theories of "bureaucratic collectivism" were wrong, and that Trotsky was right.

What could the supporters of the theory of state capitalism say about capitalist restoration in the USSR? Were we supposed to be for or against? If one accepts that the USSR was state capitalist, then it follows that we ought to be indifferent to capitalist restoration. Unless, that is, state capitalism is progressive in relation to "ordinary" capitalism! But it is frankly monstrous to propose that the working class should accept the privatization of the means of production in Russia.

As explained in an earlier chapter, the theoretical explanation for all this is to be found in Ted's remarkable work *The Marxist Theory of the State—Reply to Tony Cliff*, written in 1949. In fact, Ted's most important contribution to Marxist theory has perhaps been on the question of the state and his writings on Stalinism in Russia, Eastern Europe and China after the Second World War.

Naturally, the bourgeoisie and its apologists were euphoric at the collapse of the USSR. But what was the position after capitalist restoration? It was a catastrophe of unprecedented dimensions. In the first three years of capitalist restoration, there was a decline of industrial production in Russia of about 40-45%. This was a staggering collapse—far worse than the slump of 1929-32 in the West. Investment fell by 45% in 1992, and an additional 12% in 1993, and continued to fall. Inflation topped 20% every month in mid-1993. The rouble collapsed, and the rate of exchange reached 1,250 to the dollar and higher.

Ted observed that this situation could only be compared to the effect of defeat in a devastating war. The effects on the population, which was rapidly reduced to absolute misery, can best be shown in the sudden deterioration of life expectancy. Under the planned economy, the people of the Soviet Union enjoyed a level of life expectancy, healthcare and education on a level with the most developed capitalist countries, or in advance of them.

The Financial Times of February 14, 1994 carried a front-page article with the title *Russia faces population crisis as death rate soars*. The article pointed out that: "In the past year alone, the death rate jumped 20 percent, or 360,000 deaths more than in 1992. Researchers now believe that the average age for male mortality in Russia has sunk to 59—far below the average in the industrialised world and the lowest in Russia since the early 1960s."

These figures merely confirm what is self-evident: That the attempt to impose a "market economy" on the peoples of the former Soviet Union has been a finished recipe for destroying all the gains of seventy years, driving down living standards and plunging society as a whole into an abyss.

The fall of the Soviet Union led to widespread pessimism and disorientation in the workers' movement. But Ted did not draw pessimistic conclusions. His faith in the socialist future remained as firm as ever. He pointed out that capitalism could offer no future to the Russian people, and made the following remarkable prediction: that the fall of Stalinism would only be the first act of a worldwide drama which would be followed by an even more dramatic second act—the global crisis of capitalism.

Only two decades later, that prediction has come true, although Ted did not live to see it. Ted said that we were entering the most turbulent period in the whole of human history. Even some of his own supporters thought that was an exaggeration. But it was not.

The capitalist strategists promised us a world of peace and prosperity, thanks to the wonders of the Free Market Economy. Now all these dreams have become reduced to ashes. Instead of peace there is war after war. The "peace dividend" that was supposed to come with the end of the Cold War never materialised. The USA alone spends over $800 billion a year on arms. Terrorism is spreading like an uncontrollable epidemic. From a Marxist perspective, terrorism is a reflection of insoluble contradictions in society. The strategists of Capital have no solution to the present crisis. They are seized with moods of black despair. In the Middle Ages, the Church had a saying: all roads lead to Rome. Now the capitalists must be thinking: all roads lead to ruin.

Ted with Georgos Skiniotis at the Old Street office of *Socialist Appeal*

Today, when the fall of Stalinism in the USSR has produced widespread perplexity in the workers' movement internationally, Ted's writings on this subject retain their full force and validity. In contrast, one would seek in vain in all the journals and books of the former Communist Parties of the world for any serious Marxist analysis. They prefer to ignore the question altogether, or else confine themselves to empty, mechanical generalisations that explain nothing.

The movement has been thrown back

Here we must state a self-evident contradiction. Lenin was always honest. His slogan was: always say what is. Sometimes the truth is unpalatable, but we need to state the truth always. *The truth is that, for a variety of circumstances, both objective and subjective, the revolutionary movement has been thrown back, and the forces of genuine Marxism reduced to a small minority.* That is the truth, and whoever denies it is merely deceiving himself and deceiving others.

Decades of economic growth in the advanced capitalist countries have given rise to an unprecedented degeneration of the mass organizations of the working class. It has isolated the revolutionary current, which everywhere has been reduced to a small minority. The collapse of the Soviet Union has served to sow confusion and disorientation in the movement, and set the final seal on the degeneration of the former Stalinist leaders, many of whom have passed over to the camp of capitalist reaction.

Many have drawn pessimistic conclusions from this. To those people we say: it is not the first time we have faced difficulties, and we are not in the least frightened by such difficulties. We retain unshakable confidence in the correctness of Marxism, in the revolutionary potential of the working class and in the final victory of socialism. The present crisis exposes the reactionary role of capitalism, and places on the order of the day the revival of international socialism.

There are the beginnings of a regroupment of forces internationally. What is required is to give that regroupment an organized expression and a clear programme, perspective and policy.

Here we come to the central contradiction. If the capitalist system is in the deepest crisis in history, why are the forces of Marxism so weak? The movement has been thrown back, undoubtedly. But this does not apply only to the Trotskyist movement. It applies a thousand times more to the Communist Parties, which only a few decades ago were a mighty force, and have now been reduced to a shadow of their former selves.

The crimes of Stalinism over more than half a century have had to be paid for. The collapse of the USSR caused terrible disorientation and demoralization in the workers' movement internationally, which went far beyond the limits of the Communist Parties. I remember the words of an Argentine worker twenty years ago: "When I heard about the collapse of the Soviet Union, I felt sad. I cannot really explain this because I have been a Peronist all my life. But I felt we had lost something important." This was a very widespread phenomenon.

The collapse of Stalinism gave the bourgeoisie and its agents in the Labour Movement an opportunity not to be missed. They launched an unprecedented ideological offensive against socialism. In this they were assisted by a large number of defectors: ex-communists, ex-Trotskyists, ex-Maoists, ex-intellectuals—the world has never seen such an avalanche of apostasy since the fall of the Roman Empire.

The central contradiction remains the same as Trotsky pointed out in 1938: the conditions for socialist revolution have matured on a world scale, but the leaders of the mass organizations are not reflecting the real situation. They are the product of the past—of a long period of capitalist boom—not the present.

It is a dialectical contradiction that precisely at a time when the capitalist system is sinking, all the leaders—both of the trade unions and the workers' parties—are clinging to it even more determinedly than in the past. This is as true for the former Communist parties as it is for the Social Democracy, and as true for the left reformists as the right reformists. In the words of Trotsky, the crisis of humanity can be reduced to the crisis of leadership of the proletariat.

More and more, the willingness of the workers and youth to struggle is becoming manifest. But this will to fight has not yet found a reflection in the traditional mass organizations, which have become monstrous obstacles in the path of socialist revolution.

This has led among the radicalised youth to the growth of a kind of semi-anarchist tendency to reject all organizations in general. It finds its expression in the Occupy movement and its variants worldwide. But this has its limits. The occupation of squares in and of itself can solve nothing. It turns out to be yet another dead end, although it serves notice on the bourgeoisie that the patience of the youth is being exhausted. While it is not the revolution of which its participants dream, it is a clear symptom of the growth of revolutionary tendencies in the youth and in society at large, with colossal implications for the future.

Failure of the sects

> *Glendower: I can call spirits from the vasty deep.*
> *Hotspur: Why, so can I, or so can any man*
> *But will they come when you do call for them?*
> (*Shakespeare, Henry IV, part 1*, Act 3, Scene 1)

What is striking about the present situation is the failure of the sects to win significant support, despite the crisis of capitalism, and the fact that a large number of young people are alienated from the reformist mass organizations. All the attempts of the sects to construct an alternative to the mass organizations of the workers have ended in ignominious failure everywhere.

The bankruptcy of the leadership of the mass organizations, and the growth of radicalisation outside them that flows from it, has served to further convince the sects that it is possible to build a revolutionary party outside the mass organizations. But this is just as illusory as it was before. It is an ABC proposition for Marxists that the advanced elements must not separate themselves from the class or go too far in front of them. Jimmy Deane once said to me: "If you are in a factory, before you make a step forward you must first look over your shoulder to see if the others are following."

One of the greatest crimes of the sectarians is precisely that they try to separate the vanguard from the rest of the class, instead of finding a road to the masses. In Trotsky's words, every sectarian seeks to build his own "mass movement"—outside the masses. In so doing, all that is achieved is to reduce these workers to sterility, to miseducate them and demoralize them.

The older generation understood very well the need for a sense of proportion, and the need for the small forces of revolutionary Marxism to establish firm links with the working class and to sink roots in the Labour Movement. As Trotsky warned: "You cannot shout louder than the strength of your own throat; if you try to do so, you will only lose your voice." That was just what wrecked the Militant.

In France the New Anti-Capitalist Party made a lot of noise for a while, mainly because it suited Sarkozy to build up its profile to take votes away from the Communist Party. But it is now in crisis, split and declining.

The votes of the Left have been channelled into the Left Front of Mélenchon, of which the main organized force is the Communist Party. The majority of the workers voted for the Socialist Party. We see the process still more clearly in Greece. In a pre-revolutionary situation, the radicalisation of the masses has been reflected in the rise of Syriza, the result of a split in the Communist Party in the past. Not long ago, the party on which it is based struggled to get four percent of the votes. Now it has around 30 percent in the polls and is set to win the next elections. A similar development can be seen in Spain around the United Left.

In Britain, the sects have failed completely to build an alternative to the Labour Party during the past twenty years. Yet in theory, this was the most favourable situation for such a move to succeed. Over the last decade, the Labour Party was in power under a right-wing leadership. Tony Blair was deeply unpopular. The sects first launched the Socialist Alliance. It soon split and fell to pieces. Then some of them set up Respect. Exactly the same thing happened.

The complete failure of the sects is reflected in the constant fall of their votes in local and parliamentary elections. Despite the last 25 years of right-wing domination, and more than 10 years of right-wing Labour government, the sects have not been able to displace Labour. As a national organisation, Respect has collapsed. The Scottish Socialist Party in Scotland has been reduced to complete insignificance.

It is true that at this stage, the Labour Party remains under the control of the right wing, and the most militant layers of the workers and youth are repelled by the policies and conduct of the Labour leaders. But they do not look to the sects or their electoral fronts. This is shown by the results in every local and national election.

TUSC (Trade Unionist and Socialist Coalition, an electoral front including the Socialist Party led by Taaffe), the latest attempt to supplant the Labour Party on the electoral front, has been a complete damp squib. In the 2010 general election, TUSC achieved 12,000 votes in total and the SSP got 3,150 in the whole of Scotland, while the Labour Party got 8,600,000 votes nationally. It was the worst collapse ever for those standing to the left of Labour. This was followed by the Socialist Party's councillor, Dave Nellist, the former Labour MP, losing his council seat in Coventry. The SP, who previously boasted of their three councillors in Coventry, now has nothing.

The same dismal performance was replicated in the by-elections they contested. In the Rotherham by-election, TUSC came in ninth position with 1.22% of the vote. In Manchester Central, TUSC came in tenth, with 220 votes (1.32%), behind even the Pirate Party. In the Eastleigh by-election in February 2013, they did even worse. The TUSC candidate came 13th out of 14 candidates, with 62 votes (0.15%), behind the Beer Party, the Christian Party, the Monster Raving Loony Party, the Peace Party, as well as the Elvis Party!

Despite all the crimes of the leaders of the unions, the working class needs these organizations now, in conditions of crisis, falling living standards and mass unemployment, even more than before. Yet, the leaders of these unions constitute a very conservative force. Instead of mobilizing the workers at the very least for defensive actions, they are constantly striving to reach deals with the bosses. How is this contradiction to be solved?

Some ultra-lefts call for the setting up of new unions. That is a false and reactionary position. The workers cannot do without the unions. And all the attempts to create new unions by splitting the old ones have ended in disaster. In every case, the new unions ended up to the right of the old unions, and the latter, under the pressure of the masses, have tended to become more radical. To advocate splitting the unions is therefore a crime.

At the moment, the movement of the workers is being channelled through the unions. It takes the form of strikes and demonstrations. We have also seen big movements of the students, riots of the unemployed youth and occupations by #Occupy and related movements. And still the government continues with its policy of cuts. Nothing seems able to stop it.

There are moments in history when strikes and demonstrations can force a government to change course. But this is not such a moment, as we can see in the example of Greece, where there have been over 24 general strikes since 2010, but the austerity still continues. The crisis is too deep and the bourgeois see no alternative but to cut living standards and take back all the concessions that were won through struggle over the past half century.

At a certain point, the workers will draw the conclusion: "We must get rid of this government." Defeated on the industrial plane, they will swing back to the political front. And where will they go? Not to the sects, whose existence they are not even aware of, but to the Labour Party, and for one simple reason: there is no alternative.

In the next period, all the old mass organizations will be shaken from top to bottom. The old right-wing leaders will be vomited out. Either they will place themselves at the head of the struggles of the workers, or else they will be removed and replaced with others who are more responsive to the will of the workers. Our task as Marxists is to be in the forefront of the struggle to transform the unions and turn them into fighting organizations of the class.

The complete disorientation of our former comrades, who have been reduced to just another sect, is shown by their demand for the unions to *disaffiliate* from the Labour Party. This has long been a central demand of the British bourgeoisie, which has always protested about the "undue influence" of the trade unions on the Labour Party. It does not even occur to them that the demand to separate the unions from the Labour Party was the main demand of the Labour right under Tony Blair, and was aimed to turn the Labour Party into a bourgeois party like the US Democrats.

Their argument that the Labour Party is now a bourgeois party, indistinguishable from the Conservatives and Liberal Democrats, completely ignores the fact that the main trade unions in Britain are organically linked to the Labour Party. This alone gives it its real class character. They say the Labour Party will never change and shift to the left because the right wing has changed the rules. As if the rulebook stands mystically above the class struggle! At root it shows they have no confidence in the capacity of the working class to change their organisations, let alone to change society. We believe, as history has demonstrated, that as the class moves politically, it will inevitably transform its traditional organisations in the process. The movement of the working class does not take place in a vacuum, but in real existing society, warts and all.

To think that the working class, when it moves, will simply bypass its traditional organisations, is to completely ignore the past, and is contrary to all we ever stood for or explained. Len McCluskey, the leader of the UNITE the union, has called on union members to join the Labour Party and take it over. This position was overwhelmingly endorsed by the UNITE Conference in 2012. That is the correct way to pose the question. That the way forward has to be pointed out by a reformist trade union leader is a measure of the utter disorientation and complete lack of perspectives of the sects.

The ideas of Ted Grant are therefore more relevant and necessary than ever before. He explained what is, or ought to be, obvious: the working class does not understand small organizations, even if their ideas are one hundred percent correct. On the other hand, the mass organizations, despite the crimes of the leadership, exercise an irresistible force of attraction for the masses, akin to the force of gravity between large bodies.

CHAPTER ELEVEN

MEMORIES OF TED

Natura il fece, e poi roppe la stampa
Nature made him, and then broke the mould
(Ludovico Ariosto, *Orlando furioso*, x 84)

What was Ted like?

The readers of *Socialist Appeal* and the *In Defence of Marxism* website know Ted Grant as a Marxist theoretician of stature. But what of Ted Grant the man? He was a very humane person—not at all like the stereotype of a sinister revolutionary of popular imagination. He was always approachable and would converse on all manner of subjects with anybody who happened to be handy—a bit like Socrates in the Agora at Athens, only it was more likely to be the bus stop or the fish and chip shop.

So completely was Ted identified with revolutionary politics that he literally lived in the office of the RCP, and later was more at home in the office of *Militant* and *Socialist Appeal* than in his own house. He would stay at the *Militant* centre in Hepscott Road until very late, reading the papers and drinking endless mugs of tea. Since there was always a night shift of comrades guarding the centre, he was never lonely. He spent a lot of time talking to comrades on the night rota, as Terry McPartlan recalls:

> I worked at the Militant Centre for a couple of years in the mid 1980s during the miners' strike and the Liverpool Council battles. I worked in the print shop, but used also to do the night rota regularly. Ted used to work late at the centre, sometimes till 9 or 10 at night. I used to sit and chat with him. I always had lots of questions. I remember him as being very approachable and friendly. He always had time for us youngsters. I was only 21 or 22 at the time but he was never too busy to spare us a few minutes. I would take him to Brick Lane for a curry, or fetch him one in from the curry shop as he called it. I became friendly with Ted and stayed in touch with him up to the time he died.

He always made a deep impression on people who met him. This was above all the result of his encyclopaedic mind. I remember when I was at university in Sussex we had won over a couple of students from Healy's organization. They were very bright kids and wanted to speak with Ted, so I fixed up a meeting. The conversation went on for a long time, and they were obviously mesmerised. Afterwards I asked them how it went and they said they were amazed at the encyclopaedic scope of his knowledge. At one point one of them asked him if he knew anything about Scandinavia, to which he replied: "Not much" and then commenced an hour-long speech on the politics, history and economic life of Norway, Sweden and Denmark.

He had the knack of immediately connecting with workers and trade unionists, listening intently to their problems and opinions and then making very concrete suggestions on how to act. He knew the trade union and Labour movement like the back of his hand, and this knowledge always enabled him to give sound advice on the practical problems of day-to-day work. But with Ted the overall perspectives were always the main thing. The general aims of the movement had always to be kept firmly in mind.

About his personal life there is little to say. I was told he once had a "crush" on Millie Lee, but if that is the case, nothing ever came of it. Ted never got married and had no children. If he had had a family during the hard years of the 1950s, who can say whether he would have survived politically? The pressures of capitalism find their most painful expression through the family. In reality, Ted saw the movement as his family and in a way looked upon us as his children. About his blood relatives he spoke very little. However, there was one big exception.

He had a special affection for his elder sister Rae, whom he would ring up daily. She was a diminutive little thing, like a doll. She looked so fragile you felt that if you gave her a hug she would break in pieces. But she was a very charming and intelligent lady and had quite a strong character. She lived in a very smart apartment in a prosperous suburb in the outskirts of Paris called Meudon-la-Forêt, which was tastefully adorned with French modern and impressionist paintings.

She spoke with the accent of the cultured British upper classes, and she had the British "stiff upper lip". On one occasion I asked her whether her first husband, who lived in South Africa, was still alive. She answered in her usual measured tones: "No. He died." I enquired about the circumstances of his demise. She replied, as cool as a cucumber: "Some men broke into his farm and tortured him to find out where his money was. And he died." I was taken aback by this: "That is absolutely terrible!" I said. "Yes," she said in exactly the same tone: "Jolly bad show."

This brought to mind a story about the Duke of Wellington. During the Battle of Waterloo, he was sitting on his horse observing the course of the fighting, when an officer alongside him said: "Good Lord, Sir, a cannon ball has just taken off my leg". To which the Iron Duke replied imperturbably: "Good Lord, Sir, so it has."

Rae hero-worshipped her brother and was always asking questions about him. To my astonishment, she once asked me: "Does Ted have a girlfriend?" She must have been ninety and he was in his late eighties at the time. I replied diplomatically: "Not as far as I know".

He would visit her every year. Her husband (his name was Raymond) had been a prosperous jeweller, but had died years before. She said he had been active in the French Resistance, but I never learned any details about that. Anyway, he left her enough money to live comfortably and she would give Ted money to buy clothes. This seems to have been a tradition that went back for many years. There is quite an amusing letter written to Ted by Jimmy Deane from Paris, where he had been in contact with Rae. It is dated June 24, 1947:

Dear Ted,

I called upon your sister as requested. She has quite a lot of useful things for you—with them you *should be* the best dressed man in the party! They are all neatly packed in a big suitcase which is also meant for your use, i.e. you can keep it.

Harry will be over here soon and will return to London long before I will, so I shall get him to take the case.

Your sister is very interested to know how things fare with you. You should reply to her letters. You will look far to find such an excellent supporter… (Incidentally she wants to know why she has not been receiving the *SA* [*Socialist Appeal*]—perhaps you would arrange this Ted).

As you probably know your younger sister is now in New York. Rae, herself, is in very good health, and is much relieved at being able to keep her apartment a little while longer.

She was very kind to me, an excellent meal and an insistence that I should take away a few, but valuable, things like cigs, tea and coffee.

Incidentally, you should really try to come over for a couple of weeks' holiday. It would do you the world of good, relieve you of mental (and physical…) constipation. If you put yourself to it you could have it all fixed up in a few weeks and it would be better that you came before the Congress (August) and not after. Why don't you try? I am sure Rae would assist you—she would be very pleased if you came.

So much for now Ted. Would you pass the enclosed address to Solidaritat. The comrade is doing good work amongst POWs in the south and wants material direct from London.

Be good, and try to get over there for a few weeks.

Very best wishes,

Yours,

Jim

Note the carefully worded sentence: Ted "*should be* the best dressed man in the party!" Between "should be" and "is" there is a vast difference! Jimmy knew very well that Ted had an extraordinary talent for appearing badly dressed, and that all his sister's efforts to endow him with the blessings of *haute couture* were doomed to fail. He was not at all fashion conscious, nor did he usually pay any special attention to his appearance. Even on sunny days he would be dressed in a suit and tie, usually also with a raincoat and invariably with an old cloth cap on his head. He once walked along a beach in Italy in summer dressed in this attire—to the astonishment of the Italians, all of whom were showing off their sun-tanned anatomies in the latest skimpy swimwear.

The exception was when he visited Rae in Paris. Rae, unlike her brother, was extremely fashion conscious. She was always impeccably dressed and used lipstick even when she was in her nineties and she would not be happy unless her brother appeared before her suitably dressed. But Ted always forgot to buy clothes until it was time for the next trip to Paris. Some weeks before leaving to see his sister, the alarm bells would be ringing. Ted would start pestering comrades to help him to buy a new suit.

To this urgent demand he would attach strict conditions. It had to be a blue serge suit, he explained, because that was what Rae liked. He would go from one shop to another, leaving a trail of chaos behind him until finally he obtained what he was looking for. After many years of this performance, somebody asked Rae what she thought of Ted's new suit, to which she answered in exasperated tones: "I wish to goodness somebody would tell him to stop buying those awful blue serge suits!"

He had another sister, Anita, who lived in California and was a talented artist. I met her once. She was the youngest of all of them but she died before Rae. Rae passed away about a year before Ted. We did not tell him, for fear of the negative impact on his health. Strangely enough, he never asked about her. I think in his heart he knew.

The art of public speaking

Ted did not just have a profound grasp of politics. He had a very highly developed political *instinct*, a keen insight into the workings of bourgeois politics and the minds of politicians. Indeed, sometimes he talked about the leading politicians of the day as if he knew them personally. I believe he studied the articles in the press so assiduously that he could think his way into their heads, anticipating their actions and seeking out the hidden meanings behind their words, exposing their calculations.

In other words, he had a profound grasp of psychology, by which I mean *class* psychology. I have found something very similar in the writings of Marx and Engels. They also spoke in familiar terms of the leading bourgeois politicians like Lord "Johnny" Russell and Palmerstone. This is particularly the case in the marvellous correspondence of Marx and Engels, that wonderful Aladdin's cave of ideas.

Ted was a good writer, particularly in his earlier years, but where he really came into his own was public speaking. He would usually speak for an hour—sometimes more—and could always hold people's attention. His speeches showed a thorough grasp of the subject matter, with plenty of facts ("facts, figures and arguments are what is needed", he used to say, when advising on writing or public speaking).

He sometimes turned the volume up for added effect. In the 1970s Ted visited West Rainton, a small village outside Durham where there was a branch of the Militant. The comrades held a meeting in an upstairs flat. It was a red hot day and the windows were open. So people outside could hear Ted in full flow out of the window attacking capitalism and so on. Later, after Ted had gone back to Gateshead, the comrades went to the pub. A group of workers were sitting in the corner talking about something they had heard on the way to the pub. "Did you hear that bloke speaking on the radio? He's right what he was saying", they said. In fact they had been listening to Ted at full volume.

How many people have heard him begin in the time-honoured fashion: "Comrade chairman and comrades..." He never read his speeches. He told me that the purpose of a good set of notes is not to use them. "Read them through once before speaking then put them on the table and forget about them", he said. This last piece of advice could be a serious problem for the person in the chair. The audience would be in place, the chair would be looking at his watch impatiently, but Ted would sit there, oblivious to the world, reading through endless pages of notes with an expression of the utmost concentration on his face. The chairperson's proddings were completely ignored: "I'm just going through my notes", he would say. Nothing, but nothing, could ever make Ted hurry.

In the end, however, the audience's patience, and the chairperson's sufferings, would be amply rewarded. It was always an inspiration to hear Ted Grant speak. It was not just the content of his speeches, but the obvious enthusiasm he always showed. This was contagious, and this was much appreciated. Ted never used speeches to make personal attacks, as the sects so often do. There was none of that kind of negative, mean-spirited, spiteful element in his speeches that so often characterises the ranting of the sects. There would be no personal attacks, but he would often give vent to his sense of humour, especially when speaking of the bourgeois or right-wing leaders.

Sometimes he would even burst out laughing when speaking of the stupidities of these ladies and gentlemen, and this was so infectious that it would have everybody splitting their sides. However, the real reason for his success as a speaker was his extraordinary grasp of Marxist theory. This is what gave his speeches such a wealth of content. Without a firm grasp of theory, no amount of facts and figures will suffice. This is something many people who think it sufficient to stuff their speeches and articles with a pile of undigested statistics and imagine they are great Marxist orators would do well to ponder.

Many people have commented that Ted always used the most extraordinary arm movements during his speeches. This often placed the chairperson in mortal danger, and glasses and bottles of water, and even his own eyeglasses frequently went flying. This was a source of harmless amusement for everybody except the long-suffering chairperson. "That was your fault!" he would say jokingly to the chair. Was this perhaps the reason why Ted always began by addressing himself to the Comrade Chairman, as if to excuse himself in advance? We shall never know.

He was very adept in dealing with hecklers and people who interrupted or attacked him in meetings. Once, while he was speaking in Madrid on the Spanish Civil War, he was furiously attacked by an old Spanish Stalinist. At the end, in his summing up he said: "We have had a free and democratic discussion in the best traditions of our movement—not like the Stalinists who settled their differences with ice-picks." On another occasion in Italy a hardened sectarian made a nuisance of himself speaking at inordinate length and abusing Ted in the usual way. In his reply Ted announced: "We have had a very democratic discussion, in which everybody could express his views—including the Man from Mars."

Ted's newspapers

Ted had a limitless appetite for political work and discussion. But he had his own routine and would not allow himself to be deflected from it. He did not read the daily papers—he devoured every line. "You must read them all, from the first page to the last." He would say: "This is contemporary history". He considered the British press to be the best in the world. By contrast, he regarded the American press as parochial.

Every day he read *The Financial Times* and—for reasons that I could never grasp—*The Daily Express*. He also read the *Morning Star* for Labour movement news and also to see what the Stalinists were saying. In later years, he took a special interest in the numerous obituaries that were carried in it—an indication that it too was a dying organisation. "Another one gone", he would exclaim, with a mischievous smile. As if that were not enough, every evening he also read *The Evening Standard*.

When I first knew him he used to read *The Times*, which was then a very fine paper indeed. Ever since it first appeared in the 18th century its front page was filled with small advertisements—no photos or striking headlines, in fact, nothing to attract the attention whatsoever. This sober and serious appearance expressed the very nature of this great organ of the British ruling class.

Trotsky pointed out that the British ruling class did not think in years but in centuries. Nowadays they are incapable of seeing further than the end of their nose. The decline of British capitalism has been mirrored in the decline in the perspicacity and intelligence of their political representatives. This, in turn, is reflected in the fate of *The Times*. The contents of *The Times* were wide-ranging and comprehensive, and its editorials provided a serious analysis of events. Of course, everything was written from the standpoint of the ruling class, but it was written by the serious representatives of the bourgeoisie, the people Ted used to call the strategists of Capital.

Ted observed that the serious representatives of the bourgeoisie often arrive at similar conclusions to those of the Marxists, although from a different class point of view. It was therefore a great disappointment when *The Times* was taken over by the Canadian press baron Thompson. The change was immediately noticeable. The content was thinner, the analysis more superficial, and everything was geared to the "market". In the 1960s I happened to meet a man who was high up in *The Times,* and I told him I thought *The Times* had never been the same since they took the adverts off the front page. He disagreed, of course, on the basis that one must move with the times (the pun was unintentional). It subsequently ended up in Murdoch's hands and went completely down the drain.

In retrospect, what happened to *The Times* was no accident. Ever since the British aristocracy and the bourgeoisie reached a compromise in the 19th century, with the creation of the modern Conservative Party, the bourgeoisie was content to allow the aristocrats to decide the political line and strategy, especially foreign policy, in return for letting them get on with what they understood best—the gentle art of moneymaking. In reality, they had a division of labour.

The bourgeois in general are incapable of broad generalizations and strategic thinking, being limited to the immediate need for maximum profit. The landowner (assuming he is of the wealthier kind), has no such need, and consequently is able to think in broader terms. But the middle class Tory rank and file are another matter altogether.

Proud of their insular ignorance and total lack of culture, they are prone to sudden attacks of hysteria, as we have seen lately over the issue of Europe. This makes them dangerous to the British public at large, and potentially dangerous to the ruling class itself. For generations, the Conservative grandees kept this rabid dog on a short leash. Its views and prejudices found their

Ted selling the *Socialist Appeal*

expression in the pages of papers like *The Daily Mail*, *The Daily Express*, and to some extent *The Daily Telegraph* (Ted referred to the latter as "a clerk's paper"), but not *The Times*.

The final indignity was when *The Times* was bought by Rupert Murdoch, the Australian billionaire and media mogul. Murdoch dragged the British press down to his own gutter level, starting with *The Sun*, which used to be a Labour paper in the past but is now fit only for use in the gentlemen's lavatory, and then only in dire emergencies. *The Times* did not escape this general decline. Once it had fallen into Murdoch's palsied claws, its fate was sealed. The Old Thunderer was silenced forever. Ted gave up his beloved *Times* and took up *The Financial Times*, which now occupies the same place. He was reading *The Financial Times* the morning he died.

Ted was very good at reading papers but he was also very good at selling them. On demonstrations he would always be there, pacing up and down the lines of marchers, with his *Socialist Appeal* held out boldly in front. He invariably sold more than anybody else. Terry McPartlan also remembered how Ted sold papers:

> I was on the 1992 miners' demonstration in London. The Tories wanted to get rid of the remaining pits. We produced a *Socialist Appeal* four-page broadsheet. It went down very well on the train down to London and I sold about 100. It was raining stair rods and we were all absolutely drenched. I bumped into Ted on the Embankment near one of the bridges. He was soaked to the skin and was carrying some very soggy broadsheets. "How many have you sold Ted?" I asked. "About 120" he said, "but have you got any dry ones?"

Greg Oxley formed the same impression:

> Ted was not just a theoretician. He was a militant in every sense of the term. The delegates making their way into Labour Party, LPYS and trade union conferences would find him standing in their path,

waving the paper around and calling out to them. In this, as in raising money for the movement, his sheer enthusiasm and his bold, direct approach got excellent results. He would say "Have you got your copy of the *Militant*?" with the same forthrightness as one might say "Have you got your entrance ticket?" Ted was a man it was difficult to say "no" to!

Literary tastes

Ted had a very wide range of interests and could speak about football and horse-racing (as we have seen, he enjoyed the occasional bet), as well as literature and culture in general. He had read all of Dickens and Shakespeare. He used to quote the famous lines from Julius Caesar:

There is a tide in the affairs of men,
Which, taken at the flood, leads on to fortune;
Omitted, all the voyage of their life
Is bound in shallows and in miseries.
On such a full sea are we now afloat;
And we must take the current when it serves,
Or lose our ventures.

But his favourite author was the American socialist writer Jack London. He particularly liked Jack London's *The Iron Heel*. He said: "It is really incredible how Jack London could foresee fascism twenty years before Hitler came to power in Germany". He also admired London's short stories, especially *The Scarlet Plague*, which describes the world after a catastrophic epidemic of a disease that has no known cure. The handful of survivors of this catastrophe soon reverts to a primitive level of culture. Even language is affected, since there is no need for complex sentences to express complex ideas. One of the survivors, an old man, was a scientist. But nobody now remembers the great achievements of science and technology, and when he tries to explain these things to his grandchildren, they think he is telling them a fairy story. Ted thought this was a perfect description of what could occur after a nuclear Holocaust.

The reason he liked this story so much is because of its materialist approach. Human culture and civilization has a material base. If industry is destroyed, culture will begin to deteriorate and decay. He contrasted Jack London's materialist method to the lunacy of the Argentinean "Trotskyist" Posadas who considered that a nuclear war was inevitable and that we would build socialism on the radioactive ashes.

A writer he prized most-highly was the English novelist Galsworthy. Of the *Forsyte Saga* he once remarked to me: "he [Galsworthy] showed the bourgeois as they really are, and they never forgave him". What a wonderfully perceptive piece of literary criticism! However, he and I could never see eye to eye on James Joyce, who I regarded as the greatest novelist of the 20th century, while Ted did not approve.

Another author he liked was the American writer John dos Passos. He recommended the second part of his great *USA Trilogy*, called *1919*, as a marvellous description of that revolutionary year. He detested Agatha Christie because her books were so full of the self-satisfied smugness of the English middle class: "Here everything is for the best in the best of all bourgeois worlds", he once said. Of Orwell's famous book *1984*, Ted said: "You can tell this was a book written by a dying man. It is so full of black pessimism". George Orwell was in fact dying of tuberculosis at the time. But I think that the pessimistic tone also had political roots.

A section of the Left intelligentsia had been impressed by the theories of bureaucratic collectivism and state capitalism before the Second World War. After the war, the whole world was divided up between monopoly-capitalist imperialism and Stalinist Russia. The idea gained ground that the corporate-bureaucratic system of monopoly capitalism in the USA and the Stalinist totalitarian system in the Soviet Union were essentially the same, and humanity was condemned to a bleak future as a result.

The terrifying image of a boot stamping on the face of humanity forever is an expression of both the organic pessimism of the petty-bourgeois intellectual and a false political theory. It is noticeable that in *1984*, the working class is presented as ignorant and brutalized "proles", entirely subservient to the ruling elite. This adequately expresses the real opinion of the working class held by so many "Left" intellectuals even today.

Ted liked to quote from the Bible. And why should he not? The King James Authorised edition is, alongside Shakespeare, one of the jewels of the English language, and contains many pearls of wisdom. Among his favourite quotes was "*Behold, there ariseth a little cloud out of the sea, like a man's hand.*" (*Kings*, 18:44). How many times did he refer to a particular phenomenon as "a cloud no bigger than a man's hand" without comrades realising where it came from?

Another favourite was: "*No man can serve two masters: for either he will hate the one, and love the other; or else he will hold to the one, and despise the other. Ye cannot serve God and mammon.*" (Luke, 16:13). Ted used this very striking quotation to explain the contradictory position of reformist Labour leaders who try in vain to "serve two masters", that is, the workers who elect them, and the bankers and capitalists who own the means of production and exchange and make all the important decisions.

His all time favourite was: "*Yet man is borne unto trouble, as the sparks fly upward*". (Job, 5:7). Was he thinking about the trials and tribulations of his own life? I do not think so. It was simply the beauty of the poetry that attracted his attention. But he often referred to another, very different Biblical quote: "*As a dog returns to its vomit, so a fool repeats his folly*". (Proverbs, 26:11) Ted often used this quote when referring to the mistakes of Mandel and the other leaders of the Fourth International. More than once we decided to cut this phrase out of a document for fear it might provoke more than the usual controversy. I don't suppose it would have helped matters if we had pointed out its saintly origins. In a similar vein, he liked to use the words that Oliver Cromwell addressed to the Presbyterians of Scotland: "*I beseech you, in the bowels of Christ, think it possible you may be mistaken*".

To descend from the Kingdom of Heaven to more mundane matters, Ted had a lifelong weakness for cowboy films. This goes back to the 1940s when such films were very popular. It seems that they even played a role in the faction fight with Gerry Healy. After yet another tense battle of nerves, the comrades would relax by going to the movies. The film would naturally be a Western, and they would decide in advance which actor would represent different characters in the faction fight. Of course, the villain would be Healy, and when he eventually got his just deserts, the comrades would roar with laughter, which inclined the rest of the audience to entertain serious doubts concerning their sanity.

There is a story (the truth of which is impossible to establish) that Ted and Jock Haston were supposed to write an editorial for the old *Socialist Appeal*. As usual the article was late. So Jimmy Deane decided to take drastic measures to call the miscreants to order. He ordered the pair into an office and sat them down at a table with lots of paper, pens and ink. He then locked the door. Things went very quiet—too quiet—and after a while they opened the door to discover that Ted and Jock had escaped through the window and gone to the local cinema to see a Western.

When Rob Sewell joined the Tendency, he went to London and was taken by Ted to see a cowboy film. Rob says it was an unforgettable experience. Throughout the film there was a constant stream of banter and laughter from Ted, as well as a running commentary about the political significance of various things, in particular the weakness of the bourgeois state apparatus the further West you travelled in the US, hence the name Wild West! The rest of the audience for some reason were not especially pleased by these commentaries, but Ted certainly enjoyed himself.

His other hobby was betting on the horses, a trait that he may or may not have inherited from his father. On Saturday afternoons in the 1980s, I would walk past his office and overhear snatches of a telephone conversation. What important aspect of world revolution was he talking about? Then occasional sentences became clear: "What! Greased Lightening came last in the 2.30! It is a swindle! We were robbed!"

Optimism

Ted insisted that without enthusiasm one can accomplish nothing. He himself was always brimming with enthusiasm, and his enthusiasm was contagious. He always ended a conversation with an encouraging phrase: "Keep up the good work!" "Bring home the bacon!" or "Keep the Red Flag flying!" In all the years I knew him, with the possible exception of the brief phone conversation we had just before the crisis in Militant, I cannot remember a single moment when he was depressed or pessimistic.

I was once in Dublin and met Matt Merrigan, who was then district secretary of the AT-GWU. He later became president of the Irish Congress of Trade Unions. He had known Ted in the 1940s. He asked me if I knew Ted Grant. I answered in the affirmative. He said with that half ironical, quizzical voice that Dubliners adopt when they are about to pull your leg: "Tell me, is he still optimistic?" I said he was. He said: "Let's face it: Ted Grant would be optimistic if he was falling off a cliff." The comment was meant to be ironical, but I guess it could be true.

In the course of his long and active life, Ted Grant often found himself isolated and in an apparently impossible situation. That was the case when the old RCP was destroyed by Healy in 1949. It was the case in the barren years of the 1950s and beginning of the 1960s. It was the case in 1991 after our expulsion from the Militant Tendency, which also took place in an objectively difficult situation. But Ted and those of us who followed him were not at all worried. We knew that the correct ideas, methods and perspectives would triumph in the end. And that has been proven by the march of events.

Ted was amazingly unconcerned about his personal safety. Sometime in the 1980s, I was walking with Ted in Victoria railway station in London. It was in the middle of an IRA bombing campaign and as a precaution, the authorities had removed the litter bins. Ted wanted to throw some rubbish away and expressed his annoyance at the absence of the appropriate receptacles: "I don't understand all this fuss over a few bombs," he said. "During the war I used to walk around in the Blitz. It never bothered me."

I listened to these words in astonishment. The image of Ted strolling absent-mindedly through the streets of London with bombs falling all around him stayed in my mind ever since.

I do not doubt it for a moment. He was always blissfully unaware of his surroundings, being on another plane altogether. He could read, work or sleep amidst any amount of noise. For example, he was knocked down by a lorry in 1940 when crossing the road and hospitalised. This made him unfit for service, which fortunately allowed him to remain full time for the organisation. It kind of makes sense now. He always was oblivious to dangers of crossing the road.

At parties and socials Ted could be induced to sing songs—if singing is the appropriate word, for he had no singing voice at all. He always sang out of tune and often forgot half the words, but his singing voice nonetheless had a pure, child-like quality, and the comrades enjoyed it immensely. Apart from the South African songs already mentioned, other songs in his repertoire included (to the tune of My Darling Clementine):

> In Siberia, in Siberia, where the Arctic Sun doth shine,
> Sat an Old Bolshevik who they called a dirty swine:
> Party Comrade, Party Comrade, what a sorry fate is thine.
> Comrade Stalin does not love you, cos you left the Party Line.

And (to the tune of Auld Lang Syne):

> And should Old Bolshies be forgot
> And never brought to mind,
> You'll find them in Siberia
> With a ball and chain behind.
> A ball and chain behind, my dear,
> A ball and chain behind.
> And Stalin shot the bloody lot
> For the sake of the party line.

He also used to sing a parody on Brecht's celebrated United Front Song (here the Popular Front Song):

> So zig-zag-zig
> Then zig-zag-zig!
> There's a place, Duchess, for you!
> March on to the Bourgeois United Front,
> For you are a Bourgeois too!

Ted's sense of humour

Many years ago, when I was a young student, Ted once asked me: which are the most important qualities needed by a revolutionary. I thought to myself: maybe courage, or a high political level? Ted smiled and said: *A sense of proportion and a sense of humour*. In this reply we have Ted Grant's character expressed in a few words.

As the years have passed I have understood the real meaning of Ted's words. A revolutionary has to understand what is possible and what is not possible at a given time. One needs to understand how the working class moves and adapt to it, without losing for a moment the general perspectives and principles. It is necessary to learn the rhythm of history and try to keep in step with it. This is an art that cannot be learnt from textbooks. It involves, on the one hand, a profound knowledge of the dialectical method, and on the other hand, the necessary experience that gives one a *feeling* for the workers' movement.

Part of the secret of his eternal optimism was the fact that Ted always had a great sense of humour. He had the capacity to laugh at almost everything. He would roar with laughter at the

Ted singing revolutionary songs at the world event in 2000

stupidity of Bush and Blair, of Reagan and Thatcher, and the foolish antics of the sects, fiddling and fussing on the fringes of the Labour Movement. Ted was always ready to laugh at even the most serious situation. His sense of humour had nothing in common with the unpleasant, cynical jibes of the petty-bourgeois, a type of humour that is not really humorous at all, but contains a poisonous element: a kind of sneer disguised with a forced smile.

His humour was of the good, healthy proletarian kind. He said: "Take any shop steward or convenor in a factory. You will never find one that lacks a sense of humour or is too serious with his workmates. They are always good humoured, ready to have a laugh, drink a pint of beer and talk about the latest football match. If they were not, the workers would never vote for them."

This is very true and accurately reflects the healthy psychology of the working class. It is in direct contrast to the narrow, humourless psychology of the sectarian, who imagines that you cannot be a serious revolutionary unless you look as if you have just consumed half a pint of vinegar. I am never quite sure whether they are born with this strange facial expression, or whether it is the result of years of practising in front of a mirror. Either way, such individuals will never be listened to by the workers, who will regard them as extraterrestrials—an opinion which in some cases I am inclined to share.

Often Ted would cause a riot of laughter quite unintentionally. One of the causes of this was his invariable tendency to mispronounce foreign words and names. Despite his devotion to internationalism, Ted was not very good at foreign languages. He had made a valiant effort in the past to learn French, but he spoke very little and with a barbarous accent—in fact, he made no attempt to master the French pronunciation at all. His lack of linguistic aptitude led to some comical situations.

In the 1970s, after the fall of the Junta, there was a revolutionary situation in Greece. The PASOK was formed by Andreas Papandreou and adopted a very Left stance, bordering at times on centrism. Ted often mentioned this in his speeches, but there was just one snag. He was organically incapable of pronouncing Papandreou's name properly. It always came out as "Pappy Andrew". The comrades attempted to correct him many times but eventually were forced to give up, and so Papandreou remained Pappy Andrew forever after.

I remember an even more comical mistake in the 1980s, when I had returned to Spain after eight years. The radical Basque nationalists had launched a party (or rather an electoral coalition) called Herri Batasuna. One day Ted was reading his *Financial Times* as usual, but with a grimace on his face that indicated a mixture of perplexity and indignation in equal measures. Finally, irritated beyond measure, he exclaimed: "That's a stupid name to give a party!" I asked him what party he was talking about. "You know—that Basque party." "You mean Herri Batasuna?" "Yes, he replied irritably. Whoever heard of calling a party after a man! And who is this *Harry Batasuna*, anyway?" I explained that the name means Popular Unity in the Basque language. But I could see he remained unconvinced.

Ted's humanity

I have been active in the revolutionary movement for many years and have known all sorts of people, many of them admirable, intelligent and dedicated comrades. But I have never met anybody who commanded such deep respect and sincere affection as Ted Grant. Even his enemies respected his integrity. But his closest comrades looked upon Ted with the same warm feelings of affection that are normally reserved for a close relation.

Ted was a very humane person. He loved children, though he never had any of his own—perhaps it was for that very reason. Whenever he passed a child in the street, he would say hello and pat them on the head—sometimes to the consternation of their parents. He revelled in the company of comrades' children and would always spoil them.

He would never pass a beggar or homeless person in the street without rummaging in his pockets for some change. He would always stop and talk to the newspaper seller on the corner near the Old Street office who would slip a free copy of the *Evening Standard* into his plastic bag. When alighting from the bus, he would unfailingly call out to the driver "thanks, driver!" even if it meant infuriating the passengers by holding up the bus.

He always showed the greatest concern for comrades' health and well-being. If a comrade was ill, he would always receive a phone call from Ted enquiring after his health and giving unsolicited and very insistent advice on what should or should not be eaten (or drunk), and a complete guide to exercise. The nature of the advice depended on whatever bits and pieces he had read that day in the papers: sometimes it was hot and cold baths, other times it would be to eat plenty of onions, etc. Above, all you were urged to drink plenty of tea, which Ted drank literally by the bucket.

Ted was generally mild-spoken, rarely raising his voice. But for him Labour's right wingers were always "the Neanderthal Men and Women", which I thought was a bit unfair on our Palaeolithic ancestors. He did not like bad language, however, and never swore. I can think of just two exceptions. He would sometimes refer to Margaret Thatcher as "that bitch".

Nowadays that might be considered slightly politically incorrect (not that Ted was ever bothered about political correctness). But then, this lady was responsible for the wholesale destruction of Britain's mining communities. She habitually displayed to an extreme that cold cruelty that is specific to the British ruling class, so Ted's attitude was understandable. And I imagine she was referred to in far less flattering terms in the public bars in Wakefield and the South Wales Valleys.

The other exception was Tony Blair, the right-wing leader of "New Labour", of whom he always spoke of in terms of utter contempt: "Blair is a bourgeois. He is only a member of the Labour Party by accident. He could equally well have been a Tory". Ted would refer to Blair as "that bastard", or, if he was feeling more charitable, "that odious little carpetbagger". He would only very rarely speak like that, and then only in internal meetings.

However, in the Labour movement Ted always insisted that we should avoid personal attacks and the kind of accusatory strident language of the ultra-lefts always use. He was delighted when we came across a letter written from Marx to Engels, dated November 4, 1864, in which he explains the manner in which he dealt with the English reformist trade union leaders in the International Workingman's Association:

> It was very difficult to frame the thing so that our view should appear in a form that would make it *acceptable* to the present outlook of the workers' movement. In a couple of weeks, the same people will be having *meetings* on the franchise with Bright and Cobden. It will take time before the revival of the movement allows the old boldness of language to be used. We must be *fortiter in re, suaviter in modo* [strong in deed, mild in manner]. You will get the stuff as soon as it is printed. (Marx and Engels, *Collected Works*, Volume 42, p. 11)

Ted always stressed the importance of youth. "He who has the youth has the future," he said, quoting Lenin. As a young student I sometimes thought he was a bit hard on some of the older comrades. It was quite natural that, as a youngster, I looked up to older comrades who I regarded as veterans. But Ted was neither sentimental nor nostalgic.

He lived for the present—and above all, the future. He was impatient with the "old glories" whose main interest in life was talking about the old days. So he would always avoid the company of the old-timers who frankly bored and irritated him with their inane chatter and endless anecdotes about the past. At the end of every national meeting, conference or Marxist School, you would always find Ted sitting with the youth, talking animatedly about politics, theory or the present world situation.

There was one exception, however. He was fiercely loyal to that very small number of older comrades from the RCP days. When some of the younger comrades wanted to remove Arthur Deane from the National Committee, arguing that he was not playing a proper role, Ted sprang to his defence. He insisted that it was necessary to keep comrades like Arthur on the NC. I am sure that Ted had no illusions about the role Arthur was now able to play. But he regarded him as part of our historical capital, of what he called the "Unbroken Thread". Doubtless, he also felt that he owed a debt of gratitude for past loyalty to the Tendency through many difficult times.

When Jimmy Deane was very ill in hospital at the end of his life, Ted would ring him regularly every day. Jimmy had had a stroke, but he continued stubbornly to smoke in bed. As a result, there was a fire, and he was burnt. Of course I could only hear one side of the conversation. Ted persisted to the last in encouraging him: "Jimmy, you must not give in. You must fight, do you hear? You must keep your brain active. You must read. Keep on reading, Jimmy. Keep on reading!" There was something deeply touching about these conversations between

Alan Woods with Brian, Margaret and Arthur Deane at Ted's funeral

two old comrades, each nearing the end of his life, and each fighting a losing battle against an inescapable destiny.

Ted last saw Jimmy in January 1993, when he and Rob Sewell visited him at his care home in Liverpool. Jimmy asked to dictate a letter to *Socialist Appeal*, which was probably the last thing he wrote:

Dear Comrades,

I would like through the pages of the journal to express my best wishes to all the comrades. The ideas you represent today have a very long history. I myself took up those ideas in the mid-1930s and helped to pioneer Trotskyism in the Liverpool area. Given the collapse of Stalinism and the attack on Marxism today, it is necessary to support and defend those ideas as we did in the old days.

The establishment of *Socialist Appeal* is a valuable asset in this work, and I would like to share with you the sense of achievement in what you have accomplished so far. A Marxist tendency must combat any traces of ultra-leftism that arise out of impatience. Patience was one of the great virtues of Trotsky. He suffered terribly, but had the ability to learn from events and arm a new generation of comrades. He had the perspectives, the theory and also the faith in the working class. He educated the youth that there are no shortcuts. Those who go down this path will only cut their own throats. I have seen it many times in the past.

The most important thing is to learn and address the real movement of the working class, using the scientific ideas of Marxism. You have to go back to basics all the time. There are no easy solutions to difficult problems. But there will be big opportunities in the future.

I have known Ted Grant for decades. He has played a vital role as the key theoretician of the Trotskyist movement. He has made, and continues to make, an historic contribution through the development of Marxist theory and the training of Marxist cadres. I wish you every success and am confident that you will go from strength to strength on the basis of correct theory, perspectives and methods.

Jimmy Deane, Liverpool

Diet and exercise!

Ted was always very health-conscious. "Marx and Lenin did not look after themselves", he used to say, with a reproving look, as if he were scolding the founders of scientific socialism for their carelessness. He was also very particular about his diet. He would eat enormous quantities of fruit for breakfast, for example. He did not smoke and only began to take the odd glass of red wine with food in the last few years because he read somewhere that it was good for you.

On the other hand, he had a voracious appetite, and more than one comrade found himself eaten out of house and home after one of Ted's visits. He had a disconcerting habit of describing what was put on the table as "poison", and then eating everything in sight. Ana and I often had Ted round for dinner. Ana asked him if there was anything he could not eat. He answered: "Oh I eat everything." The first course was onion soup, and we noticed that Ted was painstakingly removing all the onions with a fork. This task, however, proved beyond the capabilities of even the most educated Marxist.

Breakfast would consist of bananas, apples, and oranges, all of which he would wash painstakingly and then peel. Lunch would usually be very thick slices of wholemeal bread, thickly spread with butter (which would also be spread liberally on his copy of the *Financial Times*), and filled generously with chunks of Cheddar cheese. His favourite dinner was a curry (mild) in an Indian restaurant in Brick Lane, with copious quantities of rice (he usually wheedled the owner into giving him a free extra portion, and he kept his own jar of chutney in the restaurant's fridge).

He was inordinately fond of sweets—any sorts of sweets—chocolates, and of course, cakes, which he devoured by the plateful, and then looked round for more. And he drank tea in industrial quantities. Well, maybe "tea" is putting it too strongly. What we normally refer to as "tea" Ted dismissed as "beer". He liked weak tea—VERY weak tea, in fact, it was more like a cup of hot water that he waved a tea bag over.

His eating habits tended to attract unwelcome guests in the form of mice. The enormous mounds of newspapers that adorned his desk (as well as the table of his front room) provided them with first class hotel accommodation. When the comrades complained of this, Ted indignantly denied that there were any mice in his office. One day Peter Taaffe entered his office while his face was buried, as

Ted working at his desk in the Old Street office

usual, in the *Financial Times*. A mouse was gambolling quite happily on the desk in front of him. When finally his attention was drawn to the offending rodent, he put down his *Financial Times*, waved his hands and said: "shoo!" The mouse scarpered and Ted looked at it guiltily.

Ted had a theory for everything, so he naturally had a theory for getting rid of mice. He informed me that the only way to get rid of mice is to remove all traces of food and thus starve them out. He confessed in a low voice that he had once killed a mouse by throwing a slipper at it: "I felt like a murderer!" he confided to me, as if fearful he might be overheard and apprehended for a dreadful crime. The man who was portrayed in the bourgeois press as a sinister revolutionary was literally incapable of harming a mouse.

Despite putting away enormous quantities of food, he did not put on weight because of a strenuous programme of exercise carried out religiously for at least an hour every night before going to bed, as he called it, his "daily dozen". Only in the last few years, when he could no longer take exercise, did he begin to acquire a belly. When I say strenuous, I mean strenuous. He would do all kind of stretch exercises, run on the spot and punch the air as if he was engaged in a boxing match. Finally he would look in a mirror and distort his face into all kinds of amazing grimaces.

This exhaustive programme of physical jerks would astonish the people in whose houses he was staying during his frequent speaking trips to the provinces. They included one exercise (taken, it seems, from yoga) during which he would stand bolt upright on his head. He explained that the purpose of this was to allow a free flow of blood to the brain. Whether this worked or not is anybody's guess. But there is no gainsaying the fact that Ted's brain was in perfect working order all his life.

When I was in Sussex University, he came down to address the Socialist Society, and I informed the comrades of Ted's exercise routine, including the head-stand. The comrades were rather sceptical, so, half in jest, I invited Ted to do a practical demonstration for the Fighting Fund. Within seconds, we found ourselves speaking to Ted's shoes, while keys and coins came clattering out of his upturned pockets. They were soon returned to their rightful place, accompanied by several pounds for the Fighting Fund.

There was nothing spiteful about Ted. He was not personally malicious, and was incapable of dishonesty, manoeuvres and intrigue. This probably placed him at a disadvantage in the kind of ugly factional struggle that led to the demise of Militant. He was used to fighting on an altogether different and higher plane: the plane of theory and ideas. On that plane nobody could touch him.

Banquo's ghost

In Shakespeare's Scottish play there is a famous scene when Macbeth is confronted with the ghost of Banquo, who he has murdered. Confronted by the spectre of his murdered victim, he loses all self-control, and before the assembled nobility, breaks out into speeches which must inevitably betray his guilt.

Sometime in the 1990s, Ted was selling the *Socialist Appeal* outside the Labour Party Conference. When right-wing MP Roy Hattersley walked up to the Conference hall, Ted boldly stepped forward to offer him the paper. Hattersley looked at him in astonishment and for a moment was lost for words. Then he finally exclaimed: "Ted Grant! But I thought we had gotten rid of you!" It was a speech worthy of a Shakespearean tragedy, though it is not recorded whether he bought the paper.

On another occasion, Ted was at the Labour Party Conference. As usual, it was being held in very smart surroundings in a Conference Centre. Because of our financial limitations, Ted always stayed at a modest bed and breakfast place. However, in British seaside resorts, even the most modest bed and breakfast places are noted for their English breakfasts, which, unlike the skimpy trifles one gets served on the European Continent, are serious affairs. Here one can confidently expect a feast of bacon, eggs, sausages, black pudding, baked beans, fried bread and similar dainty cholesterol-laden morsels.

But Ted had a problem. He was always late for breakfast. So he was obliged to go directly and breakfast-less to the Conference Centre. While partial to all this traditional English fare, Ted was very particular about his breakfasts. He was especially insistent on having fruit: fruit in abundance, fruit in industrial quantities, fruit without any restriction, let, or hindrance. Moreover, it had to be fruit of a pristine kind, polished and sparkling. He had read all about the evils of pesticides and therefore took the most extraordinary care to wash his fruit before introducing it into his mouth.

All this is perfectly sensible and conforms to the highest known standards of alimentary science and hygiene. It has, however, to be admitted that comrade Grant took these very sound principles to unusual extremes. He would insist in washing not only apples and pears, but also oranges and bananas. He would scrub them thoroughly in the kitchen sink before peeling them, in readiness for consumption.

So far so good, but on this particular morning, Ted had a problem. In the rather splendid building that had opened its doors to the Labour Conference, there was no convenient kitchen sink in sight. He found a convenient table in the foyer, where he spread out all his fruit. But as much as he searched, no such thing as a sink could be discovered. However, being of a nimble and resourceful mind, he soon discovered a highly suitable alternative.

Opening the door that had the word "Gentlemen" written over it, he proceeded to unload his large bag of fruit into one of the porcelain wash basins conveniently provided by the management in the interests of personal hygiene. He was completely wrapped in thought, busily scrubbing a banana, when a New Labour MP in a smart suit and shoes like plate glass mirrors strode through the door, urgently pursuing the call of Nature.

The said gentleman—who was so famous that I have forgotten his name—stood there aghast. The sight of an elderly gent dressed in what appeared to be second-hand clothes, washing a banana in the men's room, with apples and oranges bobbing up and down in the sink as water splashed everywhere, momentarily deprived him of the power of speech. After a few seconds it returned sufficiently for him to pronounce five monosyllables: "Good God! It's Ted Grant!"

The gentleman hurried out without having accomplished his intended mission. In consequence, they attempted to deny Ted Grant access to the Labour Party Conference—even to the humble part of it designated for man's most basic needs. We pointed out, politely but firmly, that Ted was a member of the National Union of Journalists and thus entitled to be admitted as a Gentleman of the Press. Yes, right to the end they could no more rid themselves of Ted Grant, than Macbeth could get rid of Banquo's ghost.

Marxist philosophy and science

Ted Grant's knowledge of Marxism was tremendously wide-ranging, from economics to history, from philosophy to science. His lively and inquisitive mind turned its attention to all kinds of things that go well beyond the immediate sphere of politics. In connection with his passionate interest in Marxist philosophy, he followed all the developments of modern science very closely. He subscribed to *The New Scientist*, which he devoured every week from cover to cover.

He had a very poor opinion of modern bourgeois philosophy. He described the modern philosophers as flea-crackers, using Marx's language. This is a harsh judgement but it was completely accurate. Ever since the death of Hegel, "official philosophy" has added little or nothing to the sum total of human knowledge. The endless quibbling over the meaning of words, the meaningless speculation over "morality in general", the monstrous abstruseness that makes even the most complicated pages of Hegel seem like models of literary clarity—this is what passes for philosophy in the universities today.

One only has to compare this rubbish to the great philosophers of the past to see a very concrete example of the senile decay of bourgeois thought and culture. It brings to mind something Hegel wrote: "By the little which can thus satisfy the needs of the human spirit we can measure the extent of its loss." (*Phenomenology of Mind*, Preface, 1:8).

There was one remark that struck me as particularly profound. Ted said that in the human mind, "matter has finally become conscious of itself". A more beautiful way of expressing philosophical materialism it would be difficult to imagine.

Ted had very firm views on many scientific questions. For instance he strongly disagreed with the view that was common a few years ago, that the neutrino was a particle with no mass. "How can the neutrino have no mass?" he argued. "That is impossible! They will eventually discover that it has some mass, although a very small amount. You will see!" And that was precisely what

Ted at Labour Party Conference with Dave Nellist in the background

they did find. Forty years ago, he would give enthralling lectures on dialectical materialism and science in which he challenged the two rival theories of the universe that were vying with each other at that time: the "Big Bang" and the steady state theory.

Later on, the latter theory was shown to be false. Fred Hoyle, the British scientist who had first advanced the steady state theory, publicly repudiated it. Ted was very impressed by Hoyle's intellectual honesty: "It must have taken a lot of guts to renounce a theory that one has held for years", he remarked. After the collapse of the "steady state" theory, the Big Bang seemed to have won by default. It was generally accepted as "the only show in town", but ever since, doubts have remained and contradictions have piled up.

Ted remained convinced that this theory will also in the end be replaced with another. I think he was right. He was very keen that *Reason in Revolt* should appear as soon as possible for the following reason. The Americans had plans to launch a rocket into space with a powerful telescope that could penetrate deeper into space than ever before. The further one looks into space, the further back in time one can see. So eventually, they should be able to see the Big Bang. But Ted always maintained that the Big Bang theory of cosmology is incorrect. "They will not see the Big Bang", he insisted. "All they will see is galaxies and still more galaxies stretching into infinity". So far, none of the observations have contradicted Ted's prediction.

Ted was convinced that many of the mistakes and mystical trends in modern science were because too many scientists were influenced by science fiction. When you think of ideas like parallel universes where supposedly every life is exactly replicated in different time-scales, it is hard to disagree. At one time he enjoyed reading science fiction novels. But he stopped reading them because he became increasingly irritated by the strain of mysticism and idealism that was creeping into them. One day, he expressed great indignation at a novel that included a cloud that had consciousness. "A cloud cannot think!" he snorted angrily. And that was that.

Necessity and accident

When we were working on *Reason in Revolt*, he gave a very striking example of the dialectical relationship between necessity and accident: "It is an accident that the earth was at a distance from the sun that permitted the development of life. But once life had arisen from natural causes, it developed according to the laws of natural selection—that is to say, it developed according to necessity".

He always had a materialist answer for all kinds of mysticism. For example, when the Spiritualists said that they heard a voice when nobody was present, Ted retorted: "If there is a voice then there must be vocal chords, or else I do not know what a voice is!" He described religion as "spiritual booze", which I thought was very apt.

One time, when he was staying at my house in Brighton (I was still at university), there was a knock at the door. It was a Jehovah's Witness. In my experience, it is best to avoid getting entangled in pointless discussions with them. But Ted didn't mind. He stood on the doorstep for quite some time arguing with the man. At one point the latter said: "You can't prove evolution". That was a big mistake. Ted went into a long speech explaining in great detail why Darwin was correct. In the end, the unfortunate Jehovah's Witness had to beat a hasty retreat.

This knowledge of science was of particular interest to the younger comrades. He outlined Engels' brilliant essay *Labour in the Transition from Ape to Man* is a simple and comprehensive manner. He explained how the opposable thumb and fingers was a necessary precondition for the development of labour and the brain, holding up his hand to illustrate the point. Ted maintained that if other life forms reached the development of a conscious brain, physically, they too would have two hands, two eyes, and would in many ways be similar to us.

He also considered the question of whether life existed on other planets, and if so, what would it look like? To the former question he responded with a resounding yes. Religious people believe that life in general, and humankind in particular, is the unique creation of the Almighty (or, as Ted used to call Him, the "Ju-Ju Man"). But amidst the billions upon billions of galaxies in the universe, the material conditions for life must exist. Recently, scientists have discovered that there are at least 17 billion stars that have planets like the earth circling them. In reality, there are many billions more, and the probability that at least some of them have the conditions for the development of life is overwhelming.

In regard to life on other planets, Ted would say that they would also be subject to the laws of evolution and therefore would be similar (though obviously not identical) to life on earth. This argument of Ted's is not at all as strange as it might seem. Nature furnishes many examples of the way animal morphology develops, and it shows how similar forms can emerge, conditioned by the need to adapt to a given environment. For example, scientists have proven that the organ of the eye has evolved independently on the planet Earth between 50 and 100 times. The notion that alien life forms can assume any shape whatsoever, which is popular with the authors of science fiction novels, is entirely false. Likewise, the wild imaginings of mythology and religion are contradicted by the laws of animal morphology.

For example, the Christian idea of an angel as a humanoid creature with wings is impossible in nature. Given the size and weight of the human body, the wings would have to be extremely large. But such large wings would need to be supported by a huge breast bone (sternum). So instead of the beautiful creatures we see in Renaissance paintings, we would have an ugly monstrosity with a huge bone protruding from its chest—not something the Virgin Mary, or anyone else, would like to be visited by on a dark night.

Animal morphology is not something arbitrary. It must be determined in very specific ways, and similar initial conditions will always tend to produce similar results. Let us take three examples: a dolphin, a shark and a plesiosaur. The first is a mammal, the second a primitive fish and the third a giant reptile. They are completely different species, and they evolved entirely separately, their development being separated by millions of years. But all three have a shape that is very similar.

The reason for this is that the forms of life are determined by the physical environment, the laws of natural selection and, ultimately, the laws of physics, which are the same throughout the universe. The streamlined bodily form of marine animals like dolphins, sharks and plesiosaurs is determined by the need to overcome the density of water in order to swim at fast speeds.

The same forms are constantly repeated because they obey the same rules of physics and what is called convergent evolution. The wing is yet another example of convergent evolution in action. Flying insects, birds, and bats are completely different species but they have all evolved the capacity of flight quite independently. They have "converged" on this useful trait.

We know what conditions are needed to give rise to life in carbon-based organisms, and we also know how natural selection works. It is therefore entirely probable that "alien" life forms will not be that much different from the forms that have evolved on earth. Of course, these forms have displayed a wonderfully rich variety, but they are all determined and limited by definite laws. At the very least we can safely rule out little green men with three heads and clouds that think.

Thirst for theory

Shortly before his death, Ted commented on the lack of Marxist theoreticians in the movement internationally: "Cliff and Mandel were bum theoreticians, but at least they were theoreticians", he said "Who do they have nowadays?" Then, with a look of perplexity he added: "I don't know why Lenin wrote so many books, because nobody reads them anymore, and if they do, they don't understand a single word".

In the field of theory, Ted was head and shoulders above any of his contemporaries. He was thoroughly grounded in Marxist theory and knew the works of Marx, Engels, Lenin and Trotsky like the back of his hand. His admiration for that great revolutionary and martyr, Leon Trotsky, whom he habitually referred to as "the Old Man" was boundless.

From a very early age, he was always a voracious reader. He always stressed the vital role of Marxist theory. He always insisted that young comrades should make a careful study of the works of the great Marxist teachers. Apart from Marx, Engels, Lenin and Trotsky, the writers he most admired were James Connolly, Plekhanov (especially *The Monist View of History*), Rosa Luxemburg, Labriola, and, to a lesser extent, some of Bukharin. Ted's writings cover an enormous variety of subjects, from fascism to the colonial revolution, from the history of the Communist International to the Spanish Revolution.

Whenever he had to write a theoretical work, Ted always first went back to the Marxist classics. He called this "moulting", though I could never understand why. Perhaps it was because when an animal moults it casts off a lot of dead fur or feathers and acquires a fresh outfit. Anyway, you would often find Ted in his room, green pen in hand, completely absorbed in *Anti-Dühring, State and Revolution*, or something of the sort. This was in addition to *The Financial Times*, which was his daily bread.

A careful attitude to theory was the basis of all his work and the secret of his success. It explains how he was able to keep together a small group of loyal comrades in the dark and difficult years of capitalist upswing that followed the Second World War, when the forces of genuine Marxism were isolated for a whole historical period, reduced to a tiny handful of supporters in Liverpool, London and South Wales.

We can learn a lot from Ted in this respect. He did not treat theory as if it were some fossil from a museum, but as a vital element in the equation, a compass that could show the way forward, a searchlight in the dark. He tried to teach us to approach it in the same way. For my part, I took this lesson very much to heart. Unfortunately, not everyone did. I consider it to be the first duty of every serious revolutionary to study theory. If this is not done, it is impossible to build serious cadres. At best, one will have half-trained people who are capable of mindlessly repeating undigested ideas and slogans. Such people can never think for themselves. That is quite dangerous for a Marxist tendency.

I have known many capable people, loyal comrades and sincere revolutionaries. They read the papers and scour the Internet and always have a lot of useful and interesting information about current events, facts and figures, quotations, and so on. Yet they do not have a serious grasp of the subject they are talking about because they do not possess a serious grasp of theory, of the dialectical method. Hegel once wrote:

> It is in fact, the wish for rational insight, not the ambition to amass a mere heap of acquisitions, that should be presupposed in every case as possessing the mind of the learner in the study of science. (Hegel, *Philosophy of History*, III. Philosophic History § 13)

This marvellous sentence sums it all up, that rigorous attitude to theory that was Ted's outstanding characteristic at all times. It was sometimes a bit frustrating for young comrades to submit their articles to his exacting attention, for Ted was a perfectionist and unsparing in his criticisms. But this was the way in which we were trained to fight for Marxist theory and to develop an implacable attitude to principles.

A question that is sometimes asked is why Ted did not write more books. The books that he did write were in the last period of his life and were written in collaboration with myself. There are several reasons for this. Always extremely self-critical, Ted would take a long time before putting pen to paper. He would insist on reading and re-reading the Marxist classics before writing. These delays would cause great frustration among comrades impatient to receive the results of his theoretical labours. But he would not be rushed.

Perfectionism has its good side but can also have very negative consequences, for the simple reason that the world is not a perfect place. By setting a very high theoretical yardstick, on the one hand, Ted made sure that no revisionist ideas crept into the organization, and that was extremely positive. He would insist on going over everything people wrote with a fine-tooth comb. It might be said that this could have the effect of discouraging people from writing. But in answer to this complaint, one could equally say that it also discouraged people from writing nonsense.

Alan Woods with Ted in September 2005, a few months before Ted's death

Because of his uncompromising attitude to theory, not everybody found it easy to collaborate with him. More importantly, Ted was not prepared to entrust the important task of writing to anybody. I began my literary and theoretical collaboration with him in 1969, with *Lenin and Trotsky, what they really stood for*, and over many years we developed a special relationship, based on mutual trust and respect.

In the latter years, his hands began to tremble and his writing, never very brilliant, became almost unreadable, even for him. By this time he could not type, either, and never learned to use a computer (he often threatened to do so but nothing ever came of it). He was therefore physically unable to write. His articles were dictated to a secretary, but this was not a very satisfactory arrangement, since it was never enough merely to type the words. One had to understand the precise meaning of what he was saying.

I spent many hours discussing the content of documents and articles with Ted. Sometimes he would dictate, but it was always necessary to discuss and clarify. In the end, there was a very close bond between us. Only after the split in Militant was it possible to raise the question of writing another book. I proposed writing a book on Marxist philosophy and science, but Ted was unenthusiastic. "We should produce a weekly paper first," he said.

He was still nervous about the idea of a book, but I persevered and commenced work anyway. Eventually, he came round and was very pleased with the result. He collaborated much more readily with the following book on Russia, which was partly dictated and partly compiled from his marvellous earlier writings on the subject. A few years before he died, he reminded me that Marx used to put his name on articles written by Engels and vice versa, and suggested we could do the same. I regarded that as a very moving compliment.

"Mere theoreticians"

During the faction fight that led to the split in Militant, the Majority faction said that Ted Grant and Alan Woods were "mere theoreticians". This winged phrase says all that needs to be said about that tendency. When *Reason in Revolt* came out, our former comrades commented sarcastically: "You see! Ted and Alan have abandoned politics to write books about philosophy!" That philistine attitude towards theory was answered long ago by Karl Marx himself.

The Russian writer, Annenkov, who happened to be in Brussels during the spring of 1846, has left us a very curious report of a meeting at which a furious quarrel occurred between Marx and Weitling, the German utopian communist. At one point, Weitling, who was a worker, complained that the "intellectuals" Marx and Engels wrote about obscure matters of no interest to the workers. He accused Marx of writing "armchair analysis of doctrines far from the world of the suffering and afflicted people". At this point, Marx, who was usually very patient, became indignant. Annenkov writes: "At the last words Marx finally lost control of himself and thumped so hard with his fist on the table that the lamp on it rung and shook. He jumped up saying: '*Ignorance never yet helped anybody*'." (*Reminiscences of Marx and Engels*, p. 272, my emphasis, AW).

As a matter of fact, *Reason in Revolt*, played a key role in establishing the International Marxist Tendency. It has been translated into many languages and has been commended by many workers, socialists, communists, trade unionists, and Bolivarians, including Hugo Chávez himself. My first contacts with Hugo Chávez were made through the book *Reason in Revolt*. Chávez was an avid reader and was enthusiastic about the book, recommending it to everybody.

Hugo Chávez was curious to know about Ted. He asked me: "Who is the other author of *Reason in Revolt*?" I told him it was Ted Grant.

Is he a scientist?

He is a scientific socialist—a Marxist.

Ah! Very good. Please send my warmest greetings to comrade Ted Grant.

I told Ted about this conversation and informed him about the advances of the IMT in Venezuela. He brightened up: "So we are doing well, then?" "Yes, Ted, we are doing very well. And it is all thanks to you". More in order to get him to speak than anything else, I asked him: "If you were to meet with Chávez, what would you say to him?" He answered immediately: "*I would tell him to take power.*"

In effect, for the last ten years, we have been advocating the taking of power by the working class in Venezuela at every opportunity and using every possible forum. In countless speeches and articles, in meetings in steel mills, to oil workers, in mass rallies of peasants, in the newspapers, on the radio, and in television interviews, I have consistently argued that it is impossible to make half a revolution, and that in order to succeed, it is necessary to expropriate the landowners, bankers and capitalists.

As I write these lines, we heard the tragic news of the untimely death of Hugo Chávez following a long battle with cancer. His death places a question mark on the future of the revolution. Despite numerous advances, the main task still remains to be done: the expropriation of the oligarchy. The workers and peasants are striving towards this end. They want to take the power, yet power eludes them. Now, after Chávez's death, the fate of the revolution is in the balance. The question of leadership has never been posed so sharply and urgently as now.

For many years, Ted followed the twists and turns of world relations and gave many speeches on the subject. Thanks to the thorough education we received from him, the International Marxist Tendency has been able to find its way unerringly through the intricate labyrinth of world politics and explain every new turn, from the wars in the Balkans to the war in Afghanistan, and the latest criminal adventure of t imperialism in Iraq.

But Ted's work was not only about world politics and theory in general. He wrote a tremendous amount on the tactics of the working class movement and the building of the revolutionary tendency. His grasp of tactical questions was always second-to-none. Basing himself on the ideas of Lenin and Trotsky, he systematically worked out the way that Marxism could be established as a mass force in the present epoch through work in the mass organisations of the working class.

Theory is not an optional extra like the angel on the Christmas tree. There is a thirst for theory. The advanced workers and youth want to understand what is happening in society. They are not attracted by tendencies that merely tell them what they already know: that capitalism is in crisis, that there is unemployment, that they live in bad houses, earn low wages, and so on. Serious people want to know *why* things are as they are—what happened in Russia, what Marxism is, and other questions of a theoretical character—and more importantly, *what to do about it*.

Ted meets Esteban Volkov in 2003

That is why theory is an essential tool of the revolutionary struggle. The attitude of the so-called practicos to Marxist theory is in the true tradition of Weitling and the Bolshevik Committeemen, but not at all in that of Marx, Engels, Lenin and Trotsky.

Esteban Volkov and Pierre Broué

In 1997, Esteban Volkov, Trotsky's grandson, said that Ted Grant's "deep knowledge of Marxist theory, and particularly the thoughts and works of Leon Trotsky, leap from the written page. Such knowledge is the fruit of a long life tenaciously dedicated to the meticulous study of Marxism both in theory and in everyday practice." I think Esteban and Ted only met on one occasion, when Esteban attended a World Congress of the International Marxist Tendency (it was Ted's last World Congress). But he was well-aware of Ted's history and ideas, and greatly appreciated his writings. They embraced warmly, and in that moment one could sense the meaning of one of Ted's most characteristic utterances: "retying the knot of history."

I first met Esteban Volkov in Mexico 25 years ago. We formed a close personal and political friendship that has lasted till now. This is not the place to relate the details of his life, which has been so full of tragedies. Now a sprightly 86-year-old, Esteban is the survivor of a family that was decimated by Stalin. At fourteen years of age Esteban, was present in the first attempt on Trotsky's life in May 1940, when a Stalinist murder squad led by the Mexican painter Siqueiros assaulted the Trotsky home, spraying the bedrooms with bullets. Miraculously, the family survived, but Esteban was wounded in the foot by a bullet. Not long afterwards, he saw his grandfather when he was mortally wounded by another of Stalin's assassins. For the rest of his life, Esteban Volkov has been tirelessly working to defend the memory and ideas of Trotsky.

Not long ago, Esteban spoke at a meeting organized by the Brazilian section of the International Marxist Tendency in São Paolo, which was attended by over 1,000 people. When he saw the size of the audience and the enthusiasm for Trotsky's ideas he became very enthusiastic. He told the comrades: "I attended an IMT meeting in Pakistan with over 2,000 people present. It was marvellous, but I thought it might have been an exception. But now I see a similar number here in Brazil. Something is definitely changing in the world!"

Esteban had frequently mentioned Pierre *Broué* to me. They were extremely close, but I never had the time or opportunity to meet Pierre until just a couple of years before his death from cancer. It is a matter of deep regret that my friendship with Pierre began late, when he was already suffering from the illness that eventually ended his life. I was, of course, well acquainted with his works and greatly admired his books. For his part, Pierre followed Marxist.com and the work of our Tendency with the keenest interest. We were on the same political wavelength and this political agreement eventually led to his adhering to the International Marxist Tendency.

As a young man, Pierre joined the French Resistance, in the dark days of the Nazi occupation of France. Pierre is internationally renowned for his tireless work as a historian of the international revolutionary movement. His histories of the Bolshevik Party, the Communist International, the German Revolution, the Spanish Revolution, and above all his magnificent *Life of Trotsky* have been widely admired. His book on the Left Opposition was another major contribution by this outstanding Trotskyist writer, who dedicated his life to the fight for international socialism.

The first time Pierre contacted me, in 2000, was to ask for permission to translate my article *The Real Story of Red October,* which I willingly agreed to. Unfortunately, by the time I met

Pierre in person, he was gravely ill. I visited him in Grenoble, together with Greg Oxley, the editor of *La Riposte*. I found him lively and alert, with a sharp and very Gallic sense of humour. His revolutionary spirit shone through in every sentence. He was delighted to see us.

He said: "This is a new beginning for me in many ways". From that time on, we developed a friendship that lasted until Pierre's tragic death. I remained in phone contact with Pierre on a regular basis and he remained optimistic to the end. His collaboration with the IMT undoubtedly gave him a new lease of life. He frequently told me of his plans to work and write when he recovered. He was full of ideas, plans, and suggestions. Unfortunately, his death put an end to these plans. At the hospital in Grenoble I mentioned to him that Ted Grant had just celebrated his ninetieth birthday, and asked him to say a few words to him. I reproduce in full what he said:

> Ted Grant is known to me for many years, of course. As we say in France, he seems to have been around since the days of Clovis! Unfortunately, I do not believe we have ever met, but we had a mutual friend in Raoul, who was a longstanding militant in the Trotskyist movement in France. He often spoke to me of Ted, and held him in very high esteem. However, for some reason, perhaps for fear of being accused of "factionalism" or whatever—that's the way things happen in the organisation to which we both belonged at that time—he never showed me any of Ted's written material.
>
> Regrettably, I didn't make the effort to get in touch with him at the time. Only in the last few years have I been reading his material, which I found very interesting. Anyway, I am now very much looking forward to working together with your tendency. We must discuss politics, and methods of work, of course, and try to arrive at the fullest agreement. I believe this is quite possible.
>
> To Ted himself, I would like to say: Ted, you were always a fighter. You have been struggling for many years. You have always defended revolutionary ideas. This was very important work, and you accomplished a great deal. At ninety years old, you are not a young man any more, but I think I might yet be attending your 100th birthday party!

Sadly, Pierre died soon after and Ted never lived to see his hundredth birthday.

The final chapter

Hegel wrote in his *Lectures on the Philosophy of History*: "Life has a value only when it has something valuable as its object". The one, overriding object of the life of Ted Grant was the noblest object of all: the struggle for the emancipation of the working class, for a better world, for a higher stage in humankind's social development.

In the last few years of his life, Ted was not as active as he would have liked to be, for reasons of health, but his mind was still often clear and alert, and his conviction in the final victory of socialism undimmed. He was a man who only lived for the cause of the working class and the socialist revolution. That was the alpha and omega of his life right to the end.

Ted himself seemed to be convinced that he would never grow old, never mind die. That explains his well-known aversion to birthdays. I believe the first time we were able to celebrate his birthday was when he was ninety. And even then we had to trick him, taking him to a room upstairs in a pub where a large number of comrades, past and present, were waiting to "ambush" him. When Ana and I went to visit him on his 93rd birthday, he was completely indifferent to the decorations that the staff had kindly put on the door of his room. He wanted only to hear of politics, the revolutionary struggle and the work of the International Marxist Tendency.

Ted being filmed while speaking at a meeting in London 2002

The following incident may serve to underline the point. During the period when we were under attack in the Militant organization, Ted, Ana, Rob and I were gathered in my flat, trying to analyse the situation. At one point I said: "You realise what this is all about, Ted?" He looked curious. I went on: "Taaffe calculated that you were going to die, and I could be isolated and he would take over everything". Ted's face expressed utter disbelief. Then he threw his head back and started to laugh. I had never seen him laugh so much! He laughed so uncontrollably that the tears rolled down his face and he almost slipped from the sofa onto the carpet. "What! *Me*? Die?" he roared, helpless with laughing: "I'll *never* die!" And it sounded as though he really believed it.

As time went on, the natural process of ageing began to take its toll, although Ted would never accept it. He regularly took a siesta after meals, but these naps grew longer and longer. During meetings of the IEC he would doze off, then wake up suddenly and make out that he had been listening to every word: "Just resting my eyes," he would say. And if anybody asked him his age he would still reply: "twenty one". But one can only defy Nature up to a point. Finally, Nature presented her bill. Ted was speaking at a meeting in London when he suddenly stopped in his tracks. Rob soon realised he had had a small stroke, and sent him to hospital. Thereafter, his ability to speak was severely impaired.

At first, I was pessimistic about the outcome. However, despite my misgivings, he made a good recovery. He had an iron constitution all right, but the red light was already flashing. Some dedicated comrades helped Ted as much as was possible (in particular Steve Jones and Sue Norris), but his physical condition was clearly deteriorating. This deterioration accelerated after an operation for prostate trouble. I spoke to him after the operation and he seemed exhausted. He never really recovered his powers after that. He was no longer able to carry out work as before, and only rarely spoke at meetings.

He had lived for many years in a small one-bedroom flat in Islington. The flat was cramped and austere, but he was very attached to it, and he would not leave it on any account. But in reality it was a death trap. In order to get to it you had to climb a flight of very steep stairs, which was dangerous in itself. There were still more dangers inside the flat. On one occasion, Ana and I went to see him with a comrade from the International. As usual, he was absorbed in his *Financial Times*. I noticed a smell of gas in the room and immediately opened a window (they were all shut). He had switched the gas fire on but it had failed to ignite. Half an hour later and he would probably have been dead.

On another occasion, Steve Jones knocked on his door in the morning (as he did every morning), but got no reply. It turned out that Ted had had a fall during the night and was unable to get up. He had been lying on the floor all night. In the end, he needed full-time professional care, which we could not provide. Steve and Sue found a very nice residential home in the countryside near Romford, where he would be near to them and also to Rob Sewell. Here he had his books and was visited by comrades who made sure he was well looked after. The staff were very pleasant and Ted was comfortable enough. He was physically strong for his age, still able to walk unaided, and not in any pain, but he was not happy. He longed to get back to work, and often told us so.

In the last period, it seemed as if all Ted's strength was devoted just to keeping going. Normally very talkative, he became increasingly taciturn. It was an effort to make him talk. On sunny days, Ana and I would sit with him on a bench next to the duck pond. I tried to get him to engage him in conversation, and Ted listened and made the occasional comment, but his mind was far away. He longed to be active again. He wanted something no power on earth could give him. He wanted to be young again.

Ted's last speech

In advanced old age, the body shuts down gradually, until all that is left is sufficient strength to stay alive. In the end, that goes also. Although in general, Ted's concentration and memory were deteriorating, he had lucid spells when he was quite capable of participating in political discussions. I took advantage of these days to make some interviews on the history of the movement, which we published on Marxist.com.

This was the situation a few months before we took him to the World Congress of the IMT in Barcelona, in the summer of 2005. It was the last Congress he would ever attend. He had been looking forward to it for months. He now looked very old and frail. His memory was failing, although, as is always the case in old people, his long-term memory remained acute. His old powers of speech had gone, but most of those present at the Congress were unaware of the real state of affairs.

Ted had been around for so long, and he seemed to contradict all the laws of human ageing, that they could not imagine that he would fail to address the Congress. Some of the older comrades began to insist that Ted should speak. This caused us a lot of anguish. What if Ted were unable to complete his speech? What if he became incoherent? The thought that the last memory of Ted Grant in people's minds would be a confused old man was too painful to bear. The comrades who were insisting did so with the best of intentions but they were wrong. Nevertheless, they were persistent and in the end we reluctantly gave in.

At the end of the Congress proceedings, shortly before the closing remarks, Ted advanced slowly to the platform. He stood before the microphone waiting for the applause to die down. Then he began to speak: "Comrade Chairman and Comrades…"

I confess I cannot remember much of what he said. Like other comrades who knew what the real situation was, I was in an agony of suspense. With every faltering sentence, with every pause that seemed like an eternity, I held my breath. Every person present was willing him to succeed, but I guess by now everyone realized that he might fail. But Ted Grant did not fail. This was his last battle, and he triumphed in that battle. The man was clearly struggling with every sentence, but he finished every one. Every word he spoke was like climbing Mount Everest, but he struggled onwards and upwards to the end.

When he spoke his final word, the entire Congress rose to its feet as one amidst thunderous applause. Ted looked on impassively as the applause continued. It was an emotional moment. Some comrades were in tears. What were they applauding? The old man who stood before them with stooping shoulders and a tired face was only a shadow of the Ted Grant who had been our inspiration for so many years. His speech was only the palest of pale reflections of the great oratory of the past.

Partly they were applauding the greatness of the human spirit, the incredible courage and determination of a man who refused to give in even to the powers of nature, which sooner or later must conquer us all. Partly they were paying a well-earned tribute to the past. But there was something much more important than all that.

This diminutive figure that stood before us was the last remaining representative of a generation of giants, the still-living and breathing embodiment of the Unbroken Thread. This applause was for the ideas of Ted Grant, or more correctly, the ideas of Marx, Engels, Lenin and Trotsky, which Ted had defended, preserved, developed and enriched. Life is a marathon. It was as if he was saying: "I have run the race of time and the race is nearing its end. I now pass on to you the baton that I have carried all my life. It is up to you to carry it on to victory". I do not think that anybody who was present will forget that moment.

Ted's heritage

He was a man. Take him for all in all.
I shall not look upon his like again.
(Shakespeare, *Hamlet*, Act 1, Scene 2)

The last time Ana and I visited Ted was on his 93rd birthday. On the day of his birthday, as on every other day of his life, he wanted only to hear of politics, the revolutionary struggle and the work of the International Marxist Tendency. Small talk never interested him in the slightest. He seemed a lot slower than usual and did not talk very much. He was still able to walk us to the front door when the visit ended. But as left, we thought the outlook was not good.

I used to speak to him on the phone almost every day. On the Wednesday before he died, he phoned and asked when I was going to visit him. I answered that I would call in on Friday morning. He said goodbye and that was the last time we spoke. That meeting was destined never to take place. On the morning of Thursday, July 20, 2006, we heard the tragic news of the death of comrade Ted Grant, just a few days after his 93rd birthday.

Despite the fact that we had had plenty of warnings, when it finally came, the news of Ted's death from a heart attack was a great shock to all of us. Despite his age and the obvious deterioration of his condition in the last period, we had grown used to the idea that he would always be there, a permanent fixture amidst all the turbulence and change.

Now Ted is no longer with us. The man who did so much to defend the ideas of Marxism, and who almost single-handedly saved the heritage of Trotskyism from shipwreck, has passed on. For those of us who were educated by Ted, who worked and struggled by his side to build the revolutionary movement, and who have remained loyal to him to the end, this was an irreparable loss.

Ted was the last living representative of a remarkable generation—a generation of revolutionary giants who fought under the banner of Leon Trotsky and who saved the honour of the October Revolution and preserved its heritage to hand it on, intact and immaculate, to the new generation. In the final 15 years of his life, Ted played a leading role in rebuilding our Tendency from scratch.

Ted Grant made his mark on politics in Britain and internationally. When Ted passed away, bourgeois papers wrote respectful obituaries that paid tribute to a man who had been their declared political enemy all his life. Prestigious papers such as *The Times*, *The Guardian*, *The Telegraph*, all carried obituaries that paid tribute to his achievements. Even the *Socialist Worker*, a tendency Ted had fought against ever since his polemics with Tony Cliff, had the honesty and dignity to write a decent and respectful obituary. The only exception was a spiteful article written by Peter Taaffe, which offended even members of his own Socialist Party.

Shortly before his death, I asked Ted what was left of the Fourth International today. He answered without the slightest hesitation:

> There is nothing left—except the ideas, methods, programme and traditions of Trotsky and the Left Opposition. And you can only find these in our Tendency—the tendency that we founded, that used to be the *Militant* and is now *Socialist Appeal* and Marxist.com.
>
> We have kept the banner flying. It has been very hard, but we have kept the ideas of Marx, Engels, Lenin and Trotsky alive and handed them over to the new generation. And we were the only ones to do so. I might add that over the past forty or fifty years, I have made a modest contribution to the ideas, adding to them and extending them on the basis of experience.
>
> The sects have learned nothing. They have absorbed all the nonsense of the petty bourgeois—women's lib, gay lib, black nationalism, guerrillaism—you name it! Not a trace of the old ideas remains. In fact, some of them, like the American SWP, no longer even call themselves Trotskyists. That is history's revenge for the policies and conduct of the leaders of the SWP in the past!
>
> The French Mandelites have abandoned the dictatorship of the proletariat (that is, revolutionary Marxism). They even called on the French workers to vote for Chirac in the Presidential elections, supposedly as "the lesser evil" as opposed to Le Pen. The Old Man must be turning in his grave! And naturally, they are splitting in pieces everywhere. Everywhere you look now on a world scale, the sects are in disarray.
>
> These groups have no future at all because they lack the ideas of Marxism and are completely divorced from the mass organizations of the working class. They are busy building phantom "mass revolutionary parties" in the clouds. We wish them well as we wave them goodbye and get on with the serious work of building the genuine forces of Trotskyism, nationally and internationally.
>
> Unfortunately, I have not been able to be as active as I was in the past. But as you see I am still a young man and I am as fit as ever and optimistic about the future. We have a galaxy of talent with us now, nationally and internationally. The future of the Fourth International is our future!

At the present time, the political and moral authority of the International Marxist Tendency founded by Ted Grant has never been higher. Today, the ideas of Ted Grant are receiving a wider audience than they ever had in his lifetime. Through the work of the IMT and the growth of the "In Defence of Marxism" website (Marxist.com) his works are attracting a growing following. This is no accident. Twenty years after the fall of the USSR, the initial shock has passed, and there is now a growing audience for Marxist ideas and particularly for theory. Books like *Russia: from Revolution to Counter-revolution* have played a major role in explaining and educating the cadres on the basis of the Russian experience, while *Reason in Revolt* has acquired the status of a modern Marxist classic. These books have been widely acclaimed as important and original contributions to Marxist theory.

In the general ferment on the Left that has followed the fall of the USSR, it is possible to discern the outline of a regroupment on an international scale. Doors that were previously closed to us have begun to open slowly. The IMT has made significant progress in opening a dialogue with people who come from different traditions to ours: Venezuelan Bolivarians, Irish Republican socialists, Cuban revolutionaries, and veteran leaders of the Brazilian Communist Party.

I can say without exaggeration that we were the only Marxist tendency internationally to understand the significance of the Bolivarian Revolution. None of the other groups were able to intervene in any meaningful way. They had not the slightest idea of what was happening. It was thanks to Ted's profound understanding of the nature of the colonial revolution and his grasp of flexible tactics that we were able to intervene so effectively.

In fact, one of the aspects of the work of the IMT that most impressed Pierre *Broué* was our work in Venezuela. He praised our work highly and had nothing but contempt for those Trotskyists who had failed to understand the significance of the events unfolding in South America. Our successes in Venezuela attracted a lot of attention in Latin America, and it was largely responsible for winning over an important group in Brazil, which was leading several factory occupations and was impressed by our work in the occupied factories in Venezuela. That is the best testimony to the correctness of Ted's ideas and approach. It is the justification of his life's work, for which we are all eternally indebted.

Our opponents have written many times about the demise of the IMT, confusing desires with reality. To paraphrase the famous words of Mark Twain: "Rumours of our death have been greatly exaggerated". The IMT is in very robust health. It is growing steadily in numbers and influence. The prior condition for the building of a genuine Marxist International is the defence of the basic principles of Marxism.

This implies an implacable struggle against all kinds of revisionist ideas, which in essence reflect the pressures of alien classes on the Marxist movement. We have broken radically with opportunist and sectarian tendencies and individuals, and this, far from weakening the IMT, has enormously strengthened it.

An idea whose time has come

Old Victor Hugo was quite right when he wrote: "There is one thing stronger than all the armies in the world, and that is an idea whose time has come". You cannot murder such an idea. You cannot shoot it or lock it up in a dungeon. You cannot send it to Siberian exile. It cannot be bullied or blackmailed into silence. All the efforts of the bourgeois and their hired apologists in the prostitute media and the universities to wipe out Marxism have failed.

The crisis of the euro, which Ted Grant foresaw over twenty years ago, shows that the bourgeoisie has no idea how to solve the problems of Greece, Spain and Italy, which in turn threaten the future of the European common currency and even the EU itself. This is a potential catalyst for a new economic collapse on a world scale, which will be even deeper than the crisis of 2008.

Yet the present crisis was not supposed to happen. Until recently most of the bourgeois economists believed that the market, if left to itself, was capable of solving any and all problems, magically balancing out supply and demand—the "efficient market hypothesis"—so that there could never be a repetition of the crash of 1929 and the Great Depression.

Marx's prediction of a crisis of overproduction had been consigned to the dustbin of history. Those who still adhered to Marx's view that the capitalist system was riven with insoluble contradictions, and contained within itself the seeds of its own destruction, were looked upon as mere cranks. Had the fall of the Soviet Union not finally demonstrated the failure of communism? Had history not finally ended with the triumph of capitalism as the only possible socio-economic system?

That was then. But in the space of 20 years—not a long period in the annals of human society—the wheel of history has turned 180 degrees. And now the erstwhile critics of Marx and Marxism are singing a very different tune. All of a sudden, the economic theories of Karl Marx are being taken very seriously indeed. *Das Kapital* is now a best seller in Germany. A growing number of economists are poring over its pages, hoping to find an explanation for what has gone wrong.

In July 2009, after the start of the recession, *The Economist* held a seminar in London to discuss the question: What is wrong with Economics? The conclusion of a growing number of economists is that mainstream economic theory has no relevance. Nobel Prize winner, Paul Krugman, actually admitted "that the last 30 years development in macroeconomic theory has, at best, been spectacularly useless or, at worst, directly harmful".

This judgement is a fitting epitaph for the theories of bourgeois economics. Nothing that has happened since then gives us any reason to doubt it. The grinding crisis has served to underline the complete inability of either economists or politicians to offer a solution.

Twenty years ago, Ted Grant predicted that the collapse of Stalinism was only the prelude to an even greater drama—a global crisis of capitalism. We are now witnessing the painful death agonies of a social system that does not deserve to live, but which refuses to die. That is not surprising. All history shows us that no ruling class ever surrenders its power and privileges without a fight. That is the real explanation of the wars, terrorism, violence, and death that are the main features of the epoch in which we live.

But we are also witnessing the birth-pangs of a new society—a new and just society—a world fit for men and women to live in. Out of these bloody events, in one country after another, a new force is being born—the revolutionary force of the workers, peasants, and youth. Millions of people are beginning to react. The Arab Revolution brought millions onto the streets of Tunis, Cairo and beyond. The revolutionary wave that swept through Latin America in the previous decade is now sweeping through Europe. The magnificent movement of the masses in Greece and Spain is the answer to all those who argued that revolution was no longer possible. It is not only possible, it is absolutely necessary, if the world is to be saved from impending disaster.

The movement has so far lacked a far-sighted revolutionary leadership and a coherent programme to change society. That is its great weakness. It is destined to pass through a whole series of stages before the final denouement is reached. That programme must be elaborated, and a working-class leadership worthy of the name must be built.

"A wheel always turns"

After the fall of the Soviet Union, the defenders of the old order were jubilant. They spoke of the end of socialism, and even the end of history. They promised us a new era of peace, prosperity and democracy, thanks to the miracles of the free market economy. Now, only two decades later, these dreams are reduced to a heap of smoking rubble. Today not one stone upon another remains of those illusions.

The crisis of capitalism finds its expression in a crisis of ideas. In place of the earlier optimism, which stated confidently that capitalism had solved all its problems, there is an all-pervading mood of gloom. Not so long ago, Gordon Brown confidently proclaimed "the end of boom and bust". After the crash of 2008, he was forced to eat his words. The bourgeoisie and its strategists have no explanation for the present crisis, much less a solution. It has lately even become fashionable to quote Marx in bourgeois journals. They ask themselves nervously whether old Karl was not right after all. But we could have told them the answer to that question a long time ago.

Ted Grant always said: "events, events, events" are needed to transform the situation. New and turbulent events are being prepared, which will have a profound effect on the consciousness of the working class. Despite what Francis Fukuyama says, history has not ended. In September 1939, when Poland was overrun by Hitler's army, a Polish officer defiantly told his German captors, "A wheel always turns. This one will." That officer showed a correct understanding of historical change.

The same is true of the Labour Movement, which will be shaken from top to bottom by the social and political explosions that impend. It is true, at present the right wing seems to be in complete control of the Labour Movement. But its apparent strength is in reality an optical illusion. It reflects the past, not the present or the future. It is the heavy weight of inertia. *"Le mort saisit le vif"* is a French phrase meaning "the dead seizes the living". The Labour Movement that has emerged from the 1990s and 2000s is dragged down by the dead weight of those years.

To many on the Left the situation seems impossible. That is because they lack the dialectical method and see only the surface of things. We must learn to penetrate beneath the surface, to bring out all the hidden contradictions, and to understand that sooner or later, everything changes into its opposite. It will take time and events to shake off the heavy burden of routine that we have inherited. But the force of history is far stronger than the most powerful bureaucratic, state or media apparatus.

Ted frequently drew an analogy between the working class and the giant Antaeus, the giant of Libya, who wrestled with Hercules. The giant was thrown repeatedly to the ground, but on every occasion he arose again, having drawn new strength from his mother, the Earth. The working class, he said, is like that giant of Greek mythology. After every defeat and setback, it always rises once more, ready and willing to resume the fight.

That the working class and the youth are prepared to fight is shown by the events in one country after another: Venezuela, Greece, Spain, Portugal, Egypt and Tunisia. Ted Grant's great contribution was to preserve the Unbroken Thread of genuine Marxism—of Trotskyism. On this unshakeable foundation we will prepare the cadres, theoretically, politically and organisationally, for the great tasks that lie ahead.

Sooner or later, the class struggle must find its expression inside the mass organizations. All the attempts of the right-wing bureaucracies of the Labour Movement to eradicate Marxism through expulsion and proscribed lists will also fail. Ted always used to say: "There is no way that Marxism can be separated from the Labour Movement, of which it is an integral part".

The cynics and sceptics can only see the backside of history. They have had their day. It is time to push them out of our road and carry the fight forward. The new generation is willing to fight for their emancipation. They are looking for a banner, an idea, and a programme that can inspire them and lead them to victory. That can only be the struggle for socialism on a world scale. The choice before the human race is socialism or barbarism.

The task we are confronted with is by no means easy. It is roughly analogous to that which confronted Marx and Engels at the time of the founding of the First International. Even that organization was not homogeneous, but composed of many different tendencies. However, Marx and Engels were not deterred by this. They joined the general movement for a working class International and worked patiently to provide it with a scientific ideology and programme.

Speaking of the philosopher Anaxagoras, Aristotle likened him to "a sober man among a crowd of drunkards". One could say the same thing about Ted Grant. There was nobody like him when he was alive, and nobody can replace him now he is gone. But in the ranks of the International Marxist Tendency there are many experienced cadres who have absorbed his ideas and methods, and are fully equipped to carry them into practice. His collected writings, which we are publishing, contain a wealth of important ideas.

The Roman poet Horace wrote a famous Ode: *Exegi monumentum aere perennius*. It starts with the words:

> *I have created a monument more lasting than bronze*
> *And loftier than the royal structure of the pyramids,*
> *That which neither devouring rain, nor the unrestrained North Wind*
> *May be able to destroy nor the immeasurable*
> *Succession of years and the flight of time.*

The monument to which the poet referred was his immortal verses. But we are striving to erect a monument on a higher level: not in ink, or in stone or in brass, but an imperishable monument in the form of a proletarian revolutionary organization. In fighting for the ideas of Marxism, we will build a living monument to the memory of comrade Ted Grant, and help to provide the working class with the tools that it needs in order to achieve the final victory.

Index

A

Ali, Tariq 152
Anaxagoras of Clazomenae 279
Annenkov, Pavel Vasilyevich 268
Antaeus 278
Apps, Ray 220, 224
Atkinson, Harold 56, 62
Atlee, Clement 32

B

Baldwin, Stanley 28
Bandaranaike, Sirimavo 182
Banerjee, Kamlesh 91
Basch, Max 21–26, 31
Bebel, August 234
Beckenham, Bryan 196, 199
Behan, Brendan 50, 126
Bella, Ben 126–127, 154
Bell, Herbie 164
Benn, Tony 175–176, 192, 230
Beria, Lavrentiy Pavlovich 45
Bernard, Claude. *See* Raoul
Bevan, Andy 186
Bevan, Nye 66
Bevin, Ernest 65–66
Bhutto, Benazir 185
Blackburn, Robin 152
Black, Peter 180
Blair, Tony 134, 135, 191, 192, 216, 241, 243, 255, 257
Blank, Adelle. *See* Margolis, Adelle
Blank, Isaac 10, 10–25, 130
Blank, Israel 11
Blank, Israel (Isy) 11–12, 15, 108–111, 122, 142–143
Blank, Max 10–15
Blank, Rachael (Rae) 6, 11–20, 30, 91, 108, 143, 144, 245–246
Blank, Rose 12–15
Blank, Zena 12, 15–18, 21, 108–109, 143
Bleibtreu, Marcel. *See* Favre, Pierre
Bloch, Gerard 106, 116–117
Bornstein, Sam 62–64, 124–125, 138
Boswell, James 227
Braddock, Bessie 97–98
Brezhnev, Leonid 237
Bright, John 257
Brockway, Fenner 66, 95, 97
Brookshaw, Jim 199
Broué, Pierre 270, 276
Browning, Muriel 145–146, 199, 226
Budyonny, Semyon 75
Bukharin, Nikolai 38, 63–64, 88, 104, 126, 265

C

Caesar, Julius 251
Callaghan, James 145, 174, 190
Campbell, John Ross 46
Cannon, James P. 17–18, 39–42, 46, 59–61, 77–82, 86, 91–94, 105–106, 116, 121, 127, 152, 155, 166
Cardenas, Lazaro 38
Carron, Lord William 174
Carter, Jimmy 162
Castle, Barbara 173
Castro, Fidel 154–157, 168
Chaulieu, Pierre 118
Chávez, Hugo 268
Chiang Kai-shek 86–87
Christie, Agatha 251
Churchill, Winston 50, 65, 69–70, 74–76, 78
Citrine, Walter 29
Clausewitz, Carl von 58
Clifford, Brendan 153
Cliff, Tony 84–85, 88, 114, 118, 126, 135, 146–147, 153, 156, 165, 175, 177, 237–238, 265, 275
Coates, Ken 126, 135–136, 140, 149–152, 204
Coates, Laurence 204, 206
Cobden, Richard 257
Connolly, James 50, 179–181, 265

Connolly O'Brian, Nora 50
Cooper, Arthur 60, 80
Cooper, Lord John 174, 211
Corvin, Mathias 105
Costello, Seamus 180
Coxhead, Ted 171–173, 212
Crick, Michael 207
Cromwell, Oliver 176, 252
Cunningham, Roseanne 216

D

Daly, Lawrence 174
Davies, Stephen Owen 66
Davy, Bill 66, 68
Deane, Arthur 101, 110, 112, 116, 140, 141, 257, 258
Deane, Beryl 112
Deane, Brian 101, 110, 112, 138, 140, 141
Deane, Gertie 140
Deane, Gus 140
Deane, Jimmy 5, 7, 56, 62, 70, 82, 84–85, 91, 93, 98–105, 110–113, 116, 118, 121, 125–128, 136, 139–142, 147–152, 163–165, 186, 188, 201, 231, 241, 245–246, 252, 257–259
Deutscher, Isaac 128–130
Dewar, Hugo 31
Dickens, Charles 14, 251
Dickinson, Keith 147, 166, 225
Dühring, Eugen Karl 142, 170, 266

E

Eden, Sir Anthony 121–122
Edwards, Bob 164
Edwards, Dudley 133
Engels, Frederick 8–9, 18, 30, 47, 84, 87, 110, 132, 169–170, 179, 196, 223, 228, 234–236, 247, 257, 264–265, 268, 270, 274–275, 279
Etienne. *See* Zborowski, Mark

F

Fairhead, John 124–125, 138
Favre, Pierre 105
Fields, Terry 186, 188

Fischer, Ruth 171
Foot, Michael 190–191
Franco, Francisco 177, 179, 187, 206
Frank, Pierre 26, 55, 77, 82, 83, 86, 98, 105, 128, 149–152, 168
Friedheim, Raymond 143, 245
Frost, Sid. *See* Basch, Max
Fryer, Peter 126

G

Gaitskell, Hugh 122, 134–135, 146
Galsworthy, John 251
Geany, Finn 180, 206
Gelderen, Charlie van 34, 99
Glass, Frank 18
Gluckstein, Yigael. *See* Cliff, Tony
Goethe, Johann Wolfgang von 8
Goldberg, Lauren 10
Goldman, Albert 78
Gomulka, Wladyslaw 122–123
Gonzalez, Felipe 178
Goonawardene, Leslie 182
Gordon, Sam (Stuart) 59–61, 80, 82, 91, 94, 96
Gorky, Maxim 18
Goulart, Serge 121
Gow Purdy, Murray 17–18, 22, 43, 90
Green, Sir Sidney 174
Groves, Reg 31, 66
Guevara, Ernesto "Che" 167–168

H

Hadden, Peter 180
Hansen, Joseph 42, 46, 78–79, 92, 103, 127, 130, 131, 149–155, 167
Hanson, George 99
Harber, Denzil Dean 34, 36, 43
Harris, Alan (Ernie Tate) 150–152
Harrison, Terry 187, 199
Harte, Robert Sheldon 46–47
Haston, Jock 7, 34–36, 42, 49–50, 56, 62, 65–70, 71, 79–80, 82, 83, 92, 94–104, 107, 252
Haston, Millie. *See* Kahn, Millie
Hattersley, Roy 261

Healy, Gerry 33, 34, 42, 46, 49–50, 56, 79–80, 82, 91, 94–106, 113, 116, 121, 124–127, 131, 141, 146, 152, 155, 163, 244, 252, 253
Heemskirk, Clive 193
Heffer, Eric 175, 211
Hegel, Georg Wilhelm Friedrich 8, 63, 156, 171, 218, 235, 262, 266, 271
Heijenoort, Jean van 93–94
Hitler, Adolf 25, 28–29, 31, 36, 38, 46, 49–51, 55–56, 58, 63–66, 70, 74–76, 78, 115, 122, 133, 190, 251, 278
Hobsbawn, Eric 126, 192
Hodge, Margaret 195
Horace (Quintus Horatius Flaccus) 279
Hoyle, Fred 263
Hughes, Olwyn 72
Hugo, Victor 163, 232, 276
Hunter, Ian 22–23
Hyndman, Henry 140

J

James, Cyril Lionel Robert 31, 39–41
James, David 86, 88
Jayewardene, Junius Richard 183
Johnstone, Monty 169
Jones, Jack 174
Jones, Johnny "Crown" 72
Jones, Paul 179–180
Jones, Steve 272–273
Jordan, Pat 126, 135–140, 149

K

Kahn, Millie 6, 19, 20–24, 34, 40, 42, 56, 62, 99–102, 245
Kamenev, Lev 36, 64, 231
Karunaratue, Vickramabahu (Bahu) 182–184
Keen, Ann 65, 66, 68
Kemp, Tom 126
Khrushchev, Nikita 38, 116, 122, 125–127, 153, 237
Kilfoyle, Peter 207–209, 212
Kinnock, Neil 191–194, 210, 212
Kirov, Sergey 38

Kirton, Laura 112, 187
Klennerman, Fanny 18–20
Koston, Paul 24
Krupskaya, Nadezhda 51

L

Labi, Bob 206, 227
Labriola, Antonio 265
Lake, Raymond 21, 108
Lal Khan 184–187
Lambert, Pierre 106, 121, 127, 155, 226
Landles, Bill 8, 66
Larkin, James 140
Lassalle, Ferdinand 127, 234
Lawless, Gerry 153
Lee, Heaton 62, 65, 66–69, 101
Lee, Millie. *See* Kahn, Millie
Lee, Ralph 6–7, 17–24, 32, 34, 36, 39–43, 150, 177
Lenin, Vladimir 8, 10, 18, 24, 27–31, 36–38, 46–47, 51–58, 63–64, 72, 80, 84, 88–90, 104, 110, 113, 130, 132–133, 136, 154–156, 169–172, 179, 196, 200, 218, 222–223, 234–237, 239, 257, 259, 265, 267, 269–270, 274–275
Levi, Paul 80, 171
Levy, Sam 56, 125–126
Liebknecht, Karl 223
Livingstone, Ken 195
Lloyd, Phil 145, 146, 200
London, Jack 18, 251
Lovestone, Jay 64
Luxemburg, Rosa 171, 265

M

MacCreadie, John 196
MacDonald, Ramsay 28, 32
MacLean, John 216
MacMillan, Harold 112, 134
Mahmood, Leslie 208
Maitan, Livio 92, 127, 130, 149, 153, 155
Maitland, Frank 40

Mandel, Ernest 77–78, 79, 81–82, 92, 103–105, 114, 127, 130–131, 135, 148–149, 152–155, 166–167, 170, 177, 181–182, 230, 252, 265
Mani, S 148
Mao Zedong 86–88, 131, 153–154, 168, 180
Margolis, Adelle 11–15
Martin, Jeanne 26
Martov, Julius 170, 218
Marx, Karl 8, 18, 25, 30, 47, 62, 70, 76, 84, 110, 132, 165, 169, 177, 179, 183, 196, 222–223, 228, 234–236, 247, 257, 259, 262, 265, 268, 270, 274–275, 277–279
Maslow, Arkadi 171
Matthews, Dave 145, 146, 164
McCombes, Alan 215–218
McGovern, John 32, 66
McLoughlin, Mitchell 180–181
McPartlan, Terry 244, 250
Mercader, Ramón (Jacson) 45, 47
Merrigan, Matt 253
Mestre, Michael 105
Mikado 36
Milliband, Ralph 150
Millie Lee 40
Milligan, Spike 63
Molinier, Raymond 26–27, 77, 98
Molotov, Vyacheslav 64, 115, 123, 143
Montgomery, Bernard Law 60, 63
Mooney, Ted 187
Morrison, Herbert 32, 65
Morrow, Felix 78–80, 177
Mosley, Oswald 29, 51
Mulhearn, Tony 187, 199
Muñoz, Ana 6, 7, 188, 192, 193, 205–207, 220, 224, 259, 271–274
Murdoch, Rupert 249–250
Mussolini, Benito 28, 31–32, 50

N

Nagy, Imre 123
Nanayakkara, Vasudeva (Vasu) 183
Nasser, Gamal Abdel 121–122, 159
Neil, Alex 216

Nellist, Dave 186, 188, 242, 263
Norris, Sue 272
Noseda, George 99

O

Öffinger, Hans Gerd 206
Orwell, George 221, 251
Oxley, Greg 202, 206, 250, 271

P

Pablo 77–82, 91–97, 103–106, 117, 120, 121, 124–131, 135, 137, 152–155, 182
Paine, Thomas 25, 107
Papandreou, Andreas 256
Parker, Charlie 186
Passos, John dos 251
Paton, Andy (Andrew Scott) 56, 59, 62
Pennington, Bob 113
Pereira, NM 182
Posadas, Juan R. 130–131, 153, 251
Poujade, Pierre 121
Privas, Jacques 105
Protz, Roger 163
Pryce-Jones, David 122
Purdy, Murray Gow 17, 18, 22, 43, 90
Pyatakov, Georgy 38

R

Rackham, Arthur 151
Radek, Karl 38
Rakovsky, Christian 38, 76
Raoul 91, 102, 105, 116–121, 129, 226, 271
Raptis, Michel. *See* Pablo
Rawlings, Daisy 164
Rawlings, Jack 66
Richardson, Al 62, 69
Rimmer, Harry 212
Rizzi, Bruno 237
Roberts, Michael 227
Robles, Gil 28
Roosevelt, Franklin Delano 74–75, 78
Roy, Ajit 33
Rykov, Alexei 38

S

Samarakody, Edmund 182
Saperstein, John 21
Sara, Henry 31, 40
Saunois, Tony 204, 206, 222, 227, 236
Scanlon, Hugh 174
Schapper, Karl 62
Scott, Andrew. *See* Paton, Andy
Sedova, Natalia 38
Sedov, Leon 26–28
Sewell, Rob 6, 20, 22, 55, 72, 196–197, 208, 212–213, 218–225, 227, 253, 258, 272–273
Shachtman, Max 39, 41–43, 83–86, 93, 107, 112, 118, 156, 237
Shakespeare, William 134, 214, 240, 251–252, 261, 274
Shaw, George Bernard 18
Sheridan, Tommy 215–218
Silverman, Julian 38
Silverman, Roger 38, 164
Silverman, Sydney 38, 66
Siqueiros, David Alfaro 45
Slovo, Joe 12
Smirnov, Ivan Nikitich 36
Sokolnikov, Grigory 38
Spartacus 107
Stalin, Joseph 15, 27, 28, 38, 45–47, 49, 64–65, 74–78, 83, 86, 88, 90, 115–116, 122, 126, 153, 170–172, 200, 224, 231, 237, 254, 270
Stratton, Harry 124
Stuart. *See* Gordon, Sam (Stuart)
Sudoplatov, Pavel 45, 47
Suzman, Helen 12
Sverdlov, Yakov 64
Swift, Jonathan 43, 62, 135

T

Taaffe, Peter 165, 187–188, 193, 199, 201–225, 227–231, 233, 236, 242, 259, 272, 275
Tarbuk, Ken 138
Tate, Ernie. *See* Harris, Alan
Tearse, Roy 62, 65, 66, 99, 101
Terence (Publius Terentius Afer) 9

Thatcher, Margaret 189–192, 194, 199, 200, 255, 256
Thomas, Alun 7, 70
Throne, John 180, 221
Tolstoy, Leo 14
Tomsky, Mikhail 64, 126
Trotsky, Leon. *passim*
Tukhachevsky, Mikhail 38, 75

V

Vogt, Karl 62
Volkov, Esteban 45–46, 196, 269, 270
Volkov, Verónica 197
Vyshinsky, Andrey 36

W

Wainwright, William 66
Wall, Pat 5, 112, 127, 130, 141, 172, 186–189, 199
Wall, Pauline 186
Walsh, Lynn 179, 193, 220, 223, 225, 227
Ward, Frank 58, 141
Wells, Herbert George 18
Wicks, Harry 31
Williams, David James 70
Willich, August 62
Winstanley, Gerrard 176
Wolff, Erwin 26
Woods, Pamela 179

Y

Yakir, Iona 38

Z

Zborowski, Mark 27–28
Zeller, Fred 27, 77
Zinoviev, Gregory 36, 38, 64, 94, 171–172, 231

Other titles from Wellred

▸ **In the Cause of Labour - History of British Trade Unionism**
By Rob Sewell
Our Price: £7.00

Pub. Date: 2003
Format: Paperback
No. Pages: 480

History of British Trotskyism ◂
By Ted Grant
Our Price: £ 8.00

Pub. Date: 2002
Format: Paperback
No. Pages: 310

▸ **Lenin and Trotsky - What they really stood for**
By Alan Woods and Ted Grant
Our Price: £6.00

Pub. Date: 2000
Format: Paperback
No. Pages: 221

Bolshevism - The Road to Revolution ◂
By Alan Woods
Our Price: £ 10.00
Pub. Date: 1999
Format: Paperback
No. Pages: 636

Reason In Revolt
By Alan Woods and Ted Grant
Our Price: £10.00

Pub. Date: 2005
Format: Paperback
No. Pages: 346

Writings Volume One
By Ted Grant
Our Price: £ 10.00
Pub. Date: 2010
Format: Paperback
No. Pages: 392

Writings Volume Two
By Ted Grant
Our Price: £11.00
Pub. Date: 2012
Format: Paperback
No. Pages:

Anti-Duhring
By F. Engels
Our Price: £8.00
Pub. Date: 2011
Format: Paperback
No. Pages: 365

▶ 1905
By Leon Trotsky
Our Price: £10.00

Pub. Date:2005
Format: Paperback
No. Pages: 346

Four Marxist Classics ◀

Marx/Engels/Lenin/Trotsky
Our Price: £ 5.00
Pub. Date: 2012
Format: Paperback
No. Pages: 218

▶ Ireland:Republicanism and Revolution
By Alan Woods
Our Price: £6.00
Pub. Date: 2005
Format: Paperback
No. Pages: 221

What Is Marxism? ◀
By Rob Sewell, Alan Woods & Mick Brooks
Our Price: £6.00
Pub. Date: 2007
Format: Paperback
No. Pages: 176

▶ Reformism Or Revolution
By Alan Woods
Our Price: £10.00

Pub. Date: 2008
Format: Paperback
No. Pages: 415

Not Guilty! ◀
The Dewey Commission Report
Our Price: £ 10.00
Pub. Date: 2004
Format: Paperback
No. Pages: 448

▶ Dialectics Of Nature
By F. Engels
Our Price: £10.00

Pub. Date: 2007
Format: Paperback
No. Pages: 407

Order from Wellred Books online at wellredbooks.net or send orders to PO Box 50525, London E14 6WG (add 20% p&p). Cheques payable to Wellred (UK accounts only)

You can also subscribe to **Socialist Appeal**, the Marxist voice for Labour and Youth via the above website or by post for just £18 from us at PO Box 50525, London E14 6WG